Principles of Natural Theology

by

George Hayward Joyce, S.J.

Edited by
Paul A. Böer, Sr.

VERITATIS SPLENDOR PUBLICATIONS
et cognoscetis veritatem et veritas liberabit vos (Jn 8:32)

MMXIII

AD MAJOREM DEI GLORIAM

TABLE OF CONTENTS

Principles of Natural Theology

by George Hayward Joyce, S.J.

Longmans, Green and Co.

New York, Toronto, Bombay, Calcutta, and Madras

1922

INTRODUCTION

It is, perhaps, the most notable feature of the Scholastic system that it covers the whole ground of philosophical investigation, and provides a closely-knit and consistent body of doctrine, dealing with each of the great problems which confront human reason. It applies its principles to the consideration of God, of the world, and of man; and offers us as the result of the enquiry treatises on *Natural Theology*, on *Cosmology*, and on *Rational Psychology*, not as so many independent sciences, but as integral parts of a single synthesis. Nor does it stop here. In *Logic* it deals with the problem of knowledge and with the laws of thought: in *Ethics* with human conduct: alone among philosophies it furnishes a satisfactory theory of extended and discrete quantity as the basis of *Mathematics*. Every department of human thought is gathered up into one vast scheme, the conclusions of each part bearing out the results of all the others. The minds -- and they were many -- which laboured at the work, aimed at and achieved a synthesis universal in its range. These men were not content to leave one region of being, and that the most important, unexplored. They held that, if only the right path were chosen, the peaks might be scaled. It was left for a later generation at once less sure of foot and duller of vision to aver first that the heights were unattainable, and finally that they were a mere mirage to which nothing real corresponded.

It follows from what we have said that in the Scholastic philosophy Natural Theology is no unessential adjunct, no mere afterthought, but a substantive and vital part of the system, without which it would be radically incomplete. It claims to establish from assured first principles the existence of a Supreme Being, distinct from the finite and mutable things of experience. It maintains, further, that though the limitations of the human intellect render all our knowledge of Him inadequate, we are not wholly ignorant of His nature. There are certain attributes which can be affirmed of Him with certainty, though they are His in a manner more perfect than any which we can imagine. Above all, He is intelligent and free, and therefore possessed of personality. In Him it finds the source and origin of all finite beings, and the final cause in view of which such beings exist.

The attitude of much recent philosophy in regard of the subject of which we are speaking, shews us the very antithesis of this. The contrast could hardly be more absolute. The question, it is true, receives ample discussion, as the successive volumes of Gifford lectures bear witness. Moreover, of the thinkers whose philosophical views derive from Kant and Hegel, many, at least, maintain the existence of God. Yet it does not seem too much to say that in no case is a Natural Theology an essential part of their system. Indeed, we feel, as we read, that the system would be more harmonious, more self-consistent, if a personal God were ruled out. The fact is that the conviction of God's existence is, as we shall shew, almost ineradicable from the human mind. Speculative reasons may seem to make against it -- *tamen usque recurret.* Hence room is made for it even at the cost of inconsistency. Sometimes too ethical considerations are operative, as they were with Kant himself: it is felt that there can be no basis of moral obligation unless the existence of a personal God be admitted. Yet the treatise is of the nature of an excrescence to the metaphysics of the system. And the positive conclusions are of so meagre a character that they cannot be said to form a Natural Theology: they are mere salvage from the wreck. We are told that God is not a Creator: that He is not omnipotent: not infinite: not really distinct from the world or from the human soul, and consequently not simple: and that the proofs for His existence are not valid. We are hardly surprised when we are told that He is not personal and not moral: or when a pluralist writer assures us that we ourselves are just as self-existent as is God: that He is merely *primus inter pares.*

We have spoken of Natural Theology as forming an integral part of any complete philosophy. It is, in fact, the most important section of all -- the key-stone of the arch. Apart from it philosophy has failed of its object. "Philosophy," says Aristotle, "is the science which treats of primary causes and principles."[1] This is its distinctive characteristic, by which it differs from the special sciences. They are concerned with the different particular types of reality, viewed under their various aspects. The object of philosophy is nothing less than the universe as a whole. Its goal is the ultimate ground of the manifold of experience -- the primary principles which constitute its explanation. It follows that unless Natural Theology be a pure delusion, it is the supreme treatise -- that for which all others should serve as a preparation. For it claims to find in God that ultimate explanation of which it is in search. It shews that He is the first efficient cause, the source and origin of all that is not Himself: that He is the exemplar cause, of whose perfection all finite perfections -- all types and forms of being, from the highest to the lowest -- are the reflection: that He, too, is the final cause of all, since the same necessity which demands that all things should come from Him, requires no less that He should be the end for whom they exist. Here then, and here alone, is the object which philosophy sets before it. The system which has no room for this treatise has failed of its end.

The vital nature of the issue at stake may be seen from another point of view besides that to which we have just adverted. If there be such a science as Natural Theology, then -- viewing man purely in his natural faculties and apart from revelation -- in that science lies the noblest occupation of the human mind: and to mislead us on this subject, to represent the knowledge it confers as illusory, is to inflict on us an injury of the gravest kind. When Aristotle enquires in what human felicity consists, he replies that it must lie in the exercise of our highest faculty upon the highest of all subjects -- in the exercise of the intelligence upon eternal verities.[2] Without entering upon the question of felicity, which is outside our present scope, it is easy to see that the reason given shews the knowledge of God to be the highest thing of which human nature is capable: that it gives us the true measure of our dignity as men. It follows that to deny our power to attain to this knowledge, to maintain that a science of Natural Theology is non-existent, is to strike a blow at the dignity of human nature, and to place mankind on a lower plane of being.

The method which Scholasticism employs in dealing with this branch of philosophy is well known. It is that of demonstration from axiomatic metaphysical principles. Since the objective validity of these principles has been denied, we have devoted a special chapter (chap. ii.) to this question, and have there shewn that the intellect is not deceived when it unhesitatingly affirms their universal and necessary validity: that in so doing it is acting in its proper sphere, and judging with full competence in regard of its appropriate object. If this be the case, it is plainly idle to object, as is sometimes done, that *a priori* reasoning based on a universal premiss is unconvincing to the mind, inasmuch as the assumed universal is liable to be upset by a single contrary instance. Undoubtedly this would be the case if we had no capacity of apprehending necessary truth. But we affirm that within its due sphere the human mind possesses this power. He would be a bold man who should maintain that the proposition, twice two are four, might be invalidated by an exception. And where the first principles of metaphysical truth are concerned the intellect judges with no less certainty than about the primary verities of mathematics.

Our organon of proof is Aristotelian logic, the ultimate test of each step being the principle of contradiction. It is indeed not to be expected that those who have embraced the Hegelian philosophy should he other than disdainful of such a system. Thus Principal John Caird, who has treated our subject from the standpoint of Hegelianism, writes: "The unity of the spiritual world is a thing which lies beyond the standpoint of formal logic. . . . How can an organ of thought, which tests all things by the law of contradiction, compass, or in the attempt to compass, do anything else than misrepresent, the realities of a world, where analysis is ever revealing contradictions, and whose absolute opposition can only vanish in the light of a higher synthesis."[3] The Scholastic philosophy is fully prepared to take up the challenge. We maintain that the proofs which we advance are conclusive: and that our reasoning, so far from misrepresenting reality, achieves a very>, pp. 199, 200. ample measure of knowledge of indubitable validity regarding the object of our enquiry. Reality, we affirm, contains no contradictions. Those which the Hegelian believes himself to have discovered are mere mare's nests due to his own inaccurate analysis: they have no basis in fact.

To other writers it appears that the right method to adopt in the study of Natural Theology is that of an interpretation of the religious experience of mankind. This is the view maintained by Mr. C. J. Webb in his striking volume, *God and Personality*. He tells us that, in his judgment, "Natural Theology is to be regarded, not as a science consisting of truths reached altogether independently of a historical religion, but rather as the result of reflection on a religious experience, mediated in every case through a historical religion."[4] Such a view supposes, of course, that the intellect cannot arrive at a knowledge of God by direct systematic proof, but only by reflection upon the various modes in which the human spirit has sought to direct itself towards its Divine source. Here, too, the issue is a clear one. We contend that the method of direct reasoning is open to us: and not merely that it lies within our power, but that no just exception can be taken to a very large body of conclusions already reached.

Indeed, if our mind is capable of determining aright the implications of man's religious activities as brought under observation in the history of religions, and of gathering in this way certain trustworthy conclusions regarding God, it is hard to see why a valid metaphysic should not reach Him by a less circuitous route. The science which treats of primary principles and causes must surely be able to tell us something of the source of all being. And if it be held that this is beyond the mind's competence, have we any ground for supposing that it is to be trusted in the conclusions which it draws from the religious experience of the race? Moreover, the method pursued is open to criticism on another count. It assumes gratuitously that religions are all natural in their origin. This, however, must be proved: it cannot be taken for granted. Is there anything unreasonable in the hypothesis that other factors have been operative? that on the one hand God has Himself intervened to communicate to man truths beyond the scope of unaided reason: and, on the other, that maleficent influences have been at work, diverting in many cases the practice of religion to ends wholly opposed to that which belongs to it by right, and rendering it a cult, not of God, but of evil? If this be so, it is impossible to treat the historical faiths as data for determining Natural Religion. In view of the fact that in every religion it is assumed as beyond all question that the teaching is not due to the unaided efforts of the human spirit, but to communication made *ab extra*, the demand for some proof that this is not the case can hardly be considered extravagant.

From what has been said it will be manifest that the object of our enquiry is the validity, not the genesis, of the conclusions regarding God at which we shall arrive. Statements such as "the highest proof of any idea is an account of the process by which it has been reached,"[5] we hold to be entirely false, and utterly opposed to any true view of the aim of speculative thought. There are, of course, certain provinces of knowledge in which the genesis of an idea is a question of the highest moment, inasmuch as in them the validity of a proposition is dependent on its origin. In the sphere of dogmatic theology it is essential to shew that a doctrine which only became explicit at a comparatively late date was legitimately derived from one which was at all times explicitly held. But speculative philosophy does not fall within this category. Doubtless it is of interest to trace the elements of a given system to their various sources -- to see in what the Schoolmen were indebted to Aristotle, in what to the Platonism of Augustine or of the Pseudo-Areopagite, in what to the moral teaching of the Stoics. But the interest here is historical: and the question has little, if any, bearing on the truth of the teaching under consideration. During the past century the enquiry into origins has absorbed an immense amount of attention in regard to many different subjects, as *e.g.*, anthropology, biology, jurisprudence, language, etc., etc., and in some it has borne much valuable fruit: the natural consequence of this being that some minds came to regard it as the one and only road to all truth. That it certainly is not. And where the investigations of speculative philosophy are concerned, it has, we contend, no place. The point at issue is not how an idea arose, but whether it corresponds with the reality of things: Is it true?

In the preface to a work on Scholastic philosophy some reference seems necessary to the prejudice against which that system has to contend. It is, indeed, not many years since outside the Catholic schools it was regarded as undeserving of serious attention. At our universities the volumes in which it was contained lay neglected. And the opinion was commonly entertained that the middle ages had contributed nothing to the progress of human thought: that from the days of the Neoplatonists to the seventeenth century there was a blank in the history of philosophy. A far saner view now prevails. It is recognized that just as in art, in literature, and in architecture, the thirteenth and fourteenth centuries were a period of rapid advance and of brilliant achievement, so the same is true in regard to philosophical speculation. Nevertheless, it is still widely held that, whatever value the system may have had for the period at which it arose, and whatever the intellectual eminence of those who fashioned it, it would be absurd to look to it at the present time for a tenable metaphysic of being. It stands, it is believed, committed to assumptions once generally received, but now recognized to be altogether erroneous. Given these assumptions, it provides a wonderful synthesis of knowledge. But now that they are rejected, it can afford no solution to the great riddles with which philosophy is concerned. No one, we imagine, will dispute the fact that such is the estimate taken of it by very many thinkers, even by those who are far too well informed to be affected by the old-time prejudices to which we have referred. Yet, certainly, those who thus think should find cause for reflection in the fact that on the continent Scholasticism is not a matter of merely historical interest, but is likewise a powerful factor in contemporary thought. The Neoscholastic movement has taken firm root, and is a living thing. The present writer has spoken of this elsewhere, and will not here repeat what he has already said.[6] Besides, the fact must have been brought home to many in this country during the late war. The widest interest was taken in the fate of the university of Louvain, and in the personality of its founder, Cardinal Mercier. And one of the most notable features of that university is that its philosophical school is a stronghold of Neo-scholasticism.

There are, however, two objections which are regarded by many as fatal to the claim of Scholasticism to rank as a living philosophy. Of these notice may suitably be taken here. It is not infrequently asserted that Scholasticism is a dualistic system, and that the human mind has outgrown the stage in which it can accept any form of dualism. The answer to this is easy. The term dualism has more than one sense: and it is here employed sophistically. As ordinarily understood it signifies a system which supposes two first principles of being, independent the one of the other. As a rule these are conceived as being a good and an evil principle, the sources respectively of spirit and of matter. Taken in this sense, it is true enough that the human mind has outgrown the possibility of accepting dualism. Reason is seen imperatively to demand a single first principle, the origin of all that is. But Scholasticism is emphatically not dualistic after this fashion. It teaches the existence of one self-existent Being, God, the first cause of all that is not Himself. This is not the sense in which the reproach of dualism is urged against it. Those who raise the objection are of the school of Hegel: they affirm the unity of all being, and reject as philosophically inadmissible any ultimate distinction between God and the world. For this reason they style themselves monists: and it is because Scholasticism is emphatic in asserting that God and the created world are absolutely distinct that they accuse it of dualism. But who has ever shewn that the human mind has outgrown dualism in this sense of the term? Doubtless there are difficulties in holding the coexistence of the finite and the Infinite. But we contend that these difficulties are capable of solution, whereas the manifold difficulties involved in any system of monism, whether spiritual or material, admit of no satisfactory answer whatever. The contention that Scholasticism is to be rejected because it is dualistic, owes such plausibility as it has, wholly and entirely to the ambiguity of the term. Indeed, it is open to Scholastics to turn the argument back on their opponents -- *retorquere argumentum.* There is, it is admitted, a sense in which a system of dualism is impossible. Reason will not tolerate the supposition of more than one self-existent Being. It seeks for one first principle of things, not for many. Yet the more recent development of Hegelianism has landed us in precisely this impasse, and offers us a philosophy of *Pluralism!*

Still more frequently, perhaps, do we hear the objection that the philosophy of the Scholastic doctors is vitiated by their utterly erroneous notions regarding physical science. They accepted, it is contended, the geocentric hypothesis as indisputable: they never doubted that the sun goes round the earth. And the rest of their ideas about nature were on the same plane. Do they not appeal to principles such as that heavy things tend downwards and light things upwards, and the like? Where the outlook is so radically faulty, the resulting philosophical system cannot, we are told, be other than futile. It is, of course, not to be disputed that in many respects their scientific knowledge was extremely imperfect. The last two centuries have been a time fruitful in physical discovery in many directions -- perhaps the most fruitful period in this respect which the history of man has known. It is not altogether unnatural that the possession of this new knowledge should generate some disdain towards those who lived and died long before this era of discovery dawned, and who were content with a measure of physical knowledge which to us appears so totally inadequate. Yet it would be a grave mistake to argue from their ignorance of the special sciences that their metaphysics must necessarily be at fault. It is possible surely for man to reason aright regarding first principles without a training in the sciences. He may grasp the true significance of notions such as unity, truth, reality, substance, efficient and final causality, etc., etc., without any knowledge of the mysteries of electricity. We do not hear the masters of Greek thought belittled for their imperfect acquaintance with physical science. In their case men seem to understand that the treatment of moral and metaphysical subjects is largely independent of physical knowledge. This, surely, holds good equally of the Schoolmen. Moreover, in Justice to these latter it should be observed that they were quite aware that the Ptolemaic system of astronomy was an hypothesis and not an established certainty. They knew better than to conclude that because it served well as an explanation of the facts, it must needs be true. And here some of our own contemporaries might learn a useful lesson from them. How often have we not been asked to accept unquestioningly as an established truth in philosophy, or it may be in physical science, or in anthropology or in history, some hypothesis which, though it affords an ingenious explanation of a certain number of the facts, is as yet far from being proven.

We have made it our constant aim to express the Scholastic reasoning in a form which shall be intelligible to anyone who cares to follow the argument. The Schoolmen themselves, when establishing a conclusion, frequently appeal for proof to a formula embodying a principle of Aristotelian metaphysics. To those familiar with the significance of the formula, and with its application in the Aristotelian philosophy, no more was needed: the proof was adequate. But to those who read it without the same mental background little or nothing is conveyed. This constitutes a real difficulty at first to the student who wishes to acquaint himself with the system: and doubtless is in some degree responsible for the frequency with which even scholars of reputation fall into the strangest errors regarding Scholasticism. We are in consequence not without hope that this work may be of interest even to some who differ, perhaps widely, from us. In view of the historical importance of the Scholastic philosophy and of its growing influence to-day, there may be not a few who, while disinclined to study it as encumbered by its native technicalities, will be glad to see its Natural Theology in an English dress. If such there are, we venture to direct their attention more especially to the metaphysical proofs offered for the existence of God. It is so often confidently asserted that Kant shewed once and for all the total inadequacy of the traditional arguments, that it is a matter of no small moment to observe that his criticism fails altogether to touch those arguments as they are proposed, *e.g.*, by St. Thomas Aquinas. The first essential in criticism is to know what your adversary maintains.

Yet the chief end of our work is practical. There is, we are convinced, urgent need at the present moment for a reasoned defence of the principles of theism. The prevalent philosophies are all either pantheistic or materialist in tendency, leaving no room for belief in a personal God. Moreover, the controversy is not debated only among the learned. Unbelief has become militant. Rationalism carries on an active propaganda of its own, attacking the very foundations of all belief in God, and seeking to persuade all, educated and uneducated alike, that there is no life but this, and that the, only worthy object of effort is material well-being. Since the challenge is made on grounds of reason, it is on grounds of reason that it must be met. Meanwhile the need is acute. Many a young man finds himself brought face to face with some specious objection urged against the first principles of religion: and though he instinctively feels that the reasoning is fallacious, he is unable to see where the fallacy lies. To him the difficulty is new, and therefore disconcerting. He wonders whether a satisfactory answer can be found. In these cases -- and they are numerous -- a reasoned grasp of the main truths of Natural Theology would afford an adequate protection against a very grave danger. Hence it is incumbent on the defenders of religion to do what in them lies to make this part of philosophy more widely known. The system of thought elaborated by the great Scholastic thinkers is, we are convinced, grounded on such solid arguments, its various parts are so consistent with each other, and the whole so concordant with reality, that it provides us with all that we need to defend ourselves against the more or less plausible objections which are met with to-day. But so long as a knowledge of it is confined to academical circles, its effects can be but small. That it should be rendered accessible to many is the main purpose with which this book has been written.

Among recent works written from the Scholastic standpoint I desire to express my obligations to *Dieu, Son Existence et Sa Nature* by R. Garrigou-Lagrange O.P., and to the treatise -- for it far exceeds the usual limits of an article -- *Création* by H. Pinard, S.J., contained in the third volume of Vacant and Mangenot's *Dictionnaire de Théologie*.

My grateful thanks are due to the Rev. L. W. Geddes and the Rev. M. C. D'Arcy for much valuable help. On many points I have sought counsel from one or other of these friends, and always to my advantage. I am also very greatly indebted to the Rev. J. Brodrick for his kind assistance in the correction of the proofs.

G.H.J.
ST. BEUNO'S COLLEGE,
ST. ASAPH.
Nov. 15, 1922.

NOTES

{1} *Metaph.*, I., c. i.

{2} *Eth. Nic.*, X. c. vii., 1177a 13-21; cf. St. Thomas Aq., *Summa Theol.*, 1a 2ae q. 3, art. 5.

{3} *Introduction to the Philosophy of Religion*

{4} *God and Personality*, p. 32.

{5} J. Caird, *op. cit.*, p. 298.

{6} *Principles of Logic*, pp. i.-xii.

Part I. The Existence of God

Chapter I. The Scope and Importance of Natural Theology.

1. The Scope of Natural Theology.

2. Natural Theology as one of the Sciences.

3. The Importance of Natural Theology.

4. Relation of Natural and Supernatural Theology.

1. *The scope of Natural Theology.* Natural Theology is that branch of philosophy which investigates what human reason unaided by revelation can tell us concerning God. The end at which it aims is to demonstrate the existence of God, to establish the principal divine attributes, to vindicate God's relation to the world as that of the Creator to the creature, and, finally, to throw what light it can on the action of divine providence in regard of man and on the problem of evil. In the discussion of these questions the Natural Theologian bases his conclusions purely and solely on the data afforded by natural reason. He claims that these are sufficient for his purpose: that in this manner the mind may rise from the contemplation of the visible universe to a knowledge of the First Cause from whom it proceeds: from the experience of finite beings to a knowledge of the Infinite Being, whose perfections are faintly shadowed forth by the things of the created world.

Another name given to this science is *Theodicy.* The term seems to have been coined by Leibniz,[1] and its literal meaning is 'the justification of God.' As used by him it implied his own special standpoint, which was that of an exaggerated optimism. He conceived it to be the function of Theodicy to shew that, notwithstanding all the physical and moral evils of the world, we have no valid reason for thinking that the existing order of providence is not the best that even divine omnipotence could have devised. With later writers, however, the word no longer has this

23

significance, but is simply synonymous with Natural Theology. In this sense it is appropriate enough. For Natural Theology has as its professed object to vindicate our belief in God, and to deal with the manifold objections, which from a wide variety of standpoints have been urged either against His existence or against His infinite perfections. The philosophical systems which assert the existence of God fall into three classes, deism, pantheism and theism. Deism teaches that God created the world, but that having created it, He leaves it to the guidance of those laws which He established at its creation, abstaining from further interference. He acts thus, it holds, both in regard to the physical and moral order. There is no such thing as a personal providence: nor does prayer avail to obtain His special assistance. The externality, not to say the remoteness, of God in relation to the world is fundamental in this system. Pantheism goes to the other extreme. It denies that there is any distinction between God and the universe. Nothing exists, it contends, except God. The universe is, in fact, simply the Divine Being evolving itself in various forms. Theism holds a middle position between these. Like deism, it maintains the doctrine of creation, affirming that finite things are fundamentally distinct from their Infinite Maker. But it rejects the teaching which makes God remote from the world. It asserts, on the contrary, that God is, and must be, ever present to every created thing, sustaining it in existence and conferring upon it whatever activity it possesses: that "in Him we live and move and are" : and further, that He exercises a special and detailed providence over the whole course of things, interfering as He sees fit, and guiding all things to their respective ends. The Natural Theology which we defend in this volume -- the Natural Theology of Scholasticism -- is through and through theistic. We contend that the conclusions of theism may be demonstratively established, and that it will appear that no other system is capable of a rational defence.

2. *Natural Theology as one of the Sciences.* Natural Theology is rightly termed a science. A science is an organized body of truth regarding some special object of thought. In these days, it is true, we sometimes find the term employed to denote the physical sciences alone. This is an altogether

misleading use of the word. The characteristics of scientific knowledge as distinguished from the mere experience of particulars are generality, organization and certainty. These characteristics are most fully realized when the system of knowledge consists of principles of admitted certainty and of conclusions derived from these by a rigorous process of deductive proof. Such, for instance, is mathematics. The method and object of Natural Theology are very different from those of mathematics; but it is science for the same reason. Both disciplines offer us a body of securely established truths regarding a specific object, reached by deduction from general principles, and organized into a systematic whole.

In claiming for Natural Theology the character of science, we must not be understood to maintain that it solves all difficulties concerning God and His providence over man. Difficulties remain, even when the human mind has done its utmost, as indeed they remain in the physical sciences. This does not destroy a science's value. Does any one propose to dismiss the whole science of light, because we know nothing certain regarding the medium of propagation which we term the ether, or the science of electricity, because we are wholly tn the dark as to what electricity is? We have far more reason to anticipate obscurity in our knowledge of God than we have to look for it in the physical sciences. The human intellect finds its connatural object in that material world which the senses reveal to it. Only by a laborious process of reasoning does it attain to any knowledge of what is immaterial. Hence it stands to reason that its knowledge of the Infinite Being must be fragmentary and imperfect. Yet where the supreme object of human thought is concerned, even such imperfect knowledge as is within our reach is of far higher worth than the most perfect acquaintance with any aspect of the created order, and its attainment affords an end more deserving of effort than the discovery of any physical law. Moreover, though the idea of God thus gained is fragmentary, it is at least vastly more adequate than the conceptions of Him which arise in the mind apart from scientific reflection. These latter spontaneous notions of God are invariably deeply tinged with anthropomorphism. Only through philosophical analysis do we learn to attribute to God perfections made known to us in creatures, and yet to abstract from them in this reference the manifold limitations which adhere to them as realized in the finite order.

Natural Theology, it is to be noted, is not an independent science in its own right, but a portion of the science of metaphysics. For it to rank as a complete science distinct from others we should have to possess a direct insight into the Divine Nature itself, and be able to derive our conclusions from the principles proper to that nature as such, just as, *e.g.*, we derive our conclusions in plane geometry from the principles proper to spatial extension. This, of course, we cannot do: the Infinite Nature is utterly beyond our ken: in this sense there is no science of God. The point is a very important one, for here we have the ultimate reason for the incomplete and fragmentary character of Natural Theology. Our knowledge of God consists of a series of conclusions concerning Him, viewed simply as the First Cause of Being. Being is the object of metaphysics: and the body of truths which relate to the Supreme Being form a section of that science. The older writers, indeed, do not distinguish between the two, but regarded Natural Theology as an integral portion of metaphysics, and termed metaphysics Theology as being the science which treats of God.[2]

3. *Importance ot Natural Theology.* The problems here brought under discussion are the most important which can be presented to the human mind. We are not concerned with barren academic disputes, but with vital issues which force themselves upon the mind of every rational being, and call imperiously for an answer. If it be demonstrably certain that there is a God, infinite in all perfections, the Creator of all things and exercising a direct and immediate supervision over every action of His creatures, it follows that His will must be the rule of our life: that our primary duty is the observance of His laws: and that only in so far as we employ our freedom to this end, can we hope to obtain the beatitude which is the goal of our endeavour. If, on the other hand. there is, as so many declare, no sufficient ground for affirming the existence of God or of divine providence, we are bound by no such obligation: and human beatitude is not to be sought in the attainment of the Supreme Truth and Supreme Goodness, figments devoid of objective reality, but in such a measure of

temporal felicity as may be within our reach. It is manifest that a man's whole attitude in regard to life and its activities depends on which of these alternatives he adopts. Nor does the choice between theism and materialism affect his individual life alone: its consequences are not less profound in the social and political order. To see this it is only necessary to realize how different are the conceptions of human progress which men will entertain in the two cases. For progress consists in advance towards a worthy end: and no end is worthy of man's pursuit which diverts him from the ultimate goal of his being, and which cannot be brought into relation to that last end. Where no other end of human effort is recognized than temporal well-being, progress will be held to consist in such things as the advance of the arts and sciences, the development of material resources, and the increase of national wealth. But if throughout society there is a firm conviction that man's true end lies in the attainment of God, then, though men will not cease to set a high value on temporal well-being, they will recognize that it may be bought at too dear a rate, and that if obtained by the sacrifice of a higher good, national prosperity may be detrimental, not beneficial, to those who secure it.

The controversy with deism and pantheism is not less decisive as regards our outlook on existence than that with materialism. The philosophy of deism is wholly incompatible with personal religion. According to this system, as we have seen, God is entirely remote from His creatures. He does not intervene in their lives, but leaves the world to the working of natural law. The personal relation between God and the human soul, which is the very presupposition of religion, has no existence. Of pantheism a good deal will be said in the course of the volume. It will be sufficient here to say that the pantheist, if faithful to his principles, can neither admit personality in God nor free will in man. Further, he must deny any ultimate distinction between moral good and moral evil. To him both are moments in the one all-inclusive substance, which is God.

We must not, however, be here understood to imply that the detailed proofs of Natural Theology are requisite to convince men of the existence of God. On the contrary, we maintain that the evidence for that truth is so plain to see and so cogent, that no rational being can long remain in inculpable ignorance regarding it. The mind of man instinctively asks whence came this visible universe which surrounds him, and of which he forms a part: and the answer which forces itself upon him is that it was formed by the will of a Supreme Being, a personal agent as he himself is. Moreover, within him the voice of conscience enforces the authority of the moral law, approving all obedience and sternly condemning any disobedience to its commands. And this sense of obligation conveys to him the assurance that that law is the expression of the will of a Supreme Lawgiver, to whom he is responsible. In these ways -- and others might be mentioned -- reason spontaneously and without any laborious research affirms the existence of God.

Natural Theology gives us the scientific elaboration of these arguments. It shows that, simple as they are, they are philosophically valid: that no lurking fallacy renders them worthless: that they are, if properly estimated, irrefutable. Further, since difficulties and objections are apt to suggest themselves to thoughtful minds, it deals with these, and shews that satisfactory answers can be given to them: that none can be adduced which is such as to shake the certainty of the conclusion. Again, it goes further, and provides other proofs. There are many ways of establishing God's existence: some of them simple, such as those which we have instanced, others of a more recondite character and demanding a trained intellect to appreciate their value.

Yet the idea of God which springs spontaneously to the mind is, as we have already noted, very imperfect. It sets before us a Supreme Being, endowed with intellect and will, to whom man owes the debt of obedience and of worship. But further than this it hardly goes. On the attributes of that Being it throws little light. God's infinite perfections, His omnipotence, His office of Creator of the world, His justice, His mercy -- these are not matters of immediate recognition. For any assurance about them, recourse must be had to the reflective reason if we prescind for the moment from the question of a supernatural revelation. Man needs a true philosophy of God -- in other words, a sound Natural

Natural Theology limits the existence of God to the natural world, operating through the laws of Nature

Theology. And unless he is thus armed, he will go widely astray, and fall into errors fraught with the most fatal consequences.

4. *Relation of Natural and Supernatural theology.* The question naturally suggests itself: What are the relations between Natural Theology and Revelation? How do they differ? How comes it that the one or the other is not superfluous?

It should be observed, first, that, though both treat of God, they are radically distinct as branches of knowledge. Natural Theology, as we have seen, treats of God solely in so far as He is known by the natural reason. The principles from which it derives its conclusions are the intuitions of the mind and the facts of experience. Moreover, the scope of those conclusions is very limited. They relate to God purely and solely in so far as He is the First Cause of Being. A science of God as known in His own essential nature is utterly beyond the range of the unaided intellect. By it alone we know no more of God than we can gather from the philosophy of being. Dogmatic Theology has a very different character. It is based, not on natural knowledge, but on what God has taught us regarding Himself in the Christian revelation. Unlike Natural Theology, it is derived from a direct and immediate intuition of the Divine nature as such: for its ultimate source is God's knowledge of His own essence. Its data, so far as we are concerned, are truths regarding that nature made known to us by God the Son and His chosen apostles, and contained in Scripture or ecclesiastical tradition. Differing thus in the sources whence they draw the premises of their arguments, the two sciences differ likewise very largely in regard of the matter of which they treat. Thus it belongs to Dogmatic Theology to deal with many subjects which are altogether beyond the scope of Natural Theology, such as, *e.g.*, the mysteries of the Trinity and the Incarnation. It does not, indeed, profess so to explain these doctrines as to make them in all respects comprehensible: for the mysteries of the Godhead are of necessity beyond the reach of man's intelligence. But it analyses their precise meaning, establishes their mutual relations, and demonstrates that they do not conflict with the assured conclusions of reason. Thus it would be a grave error to confuse the two sciences. They view God under different aspects: and even when they teach the same truth, *e.g.*, the unity of God, they reach it by totally different paths.

Both of these branches of knowledge are necessary to us. Neither would suffice for man's needs without the other. Were the arduous path of reason our sole means of learning about God, our provision for the practical conduct of life would be indeed inadequate. A knowledge of the fundamental truths of religion is requisite to all, to the unlettered toiler as well as to the philosopher, to the boy and girl no less than to the man of mature years. All alike need to know that God is one and is supreme: that He is hampered in His action neither by blind fate nor by an opponent principle of evil: that whatever befalls us, happens by His permission: that, if we are but faithful, He will turn all things to our good: that He will reward the good and punish the evil. Moreover, they need to know these things as certainties beyond all possibility of question. Conclusions, still matter of speculative doubt, will not serve their turn: for what is dubious lacks force to determine man's action in situations of real difficulty. And they need to have this knowledge, not as the result of long and anxious reasoning, but forthwith. Reason, we allow, can establish these truths. But we are now considering men in the concrete, and not the ideal specimen of the *homo rationalis*. And how few there are who have either the ability or the leisure to engage in these discussions. 'The great majority of men are early forced to a life of labour which precludes them from speculation. Nothing can be more opposed to common sense than the idea so generally entertained that on moral and religious questions every man is bound to test all his beliefs by the cold light of reason, and admit none save those which reason shews to be valid.[3] Men require some shorter, easier way of attaining truth than speculative enquiry -- some way which is within the reach of all. This requirement a well-authenticated revelation can alone supply. Indeed, the learned can no more spare the assurance which revelation gives than can the unlearned. Though reason is capable of proving these truths, yet it is most liable to err: and the science of metaphysics is notoriously full of pit-falls for the unwary. The history of human thought bears witness how even the acutest minds have fallen into the gravest errors on these subjects. Here, then, revelation affords a sure safeguard. It warns the mind from error in many of the matters discussed in Natural Theology, and points out in which direction truth is to be sought.

Nor can it be alleged, on the other hand, that if a revelation be given, Natural Theology must lose its value and become unnecessary. Belief in Christianity demands as its basis a rational certitude of God's existence. The man who is persuaded that the human mind is incompetent even to determine whether there be a God or not, will inevitably turn a deaf ear to those who claim to be His accredited messengers. Only those who are already assured that there is a God, capable, if He should see fit, of manifesting His will to men, are in a position to attend to the proofs of revelation. In her work of preaching the Gospel the Church has to deal with many who either doubt God's existence, or in some way identify Him with the universe which He has made. For such as these only proofs drawn from natural reason can be of service. Moreover, materialism and pantheism are permanent factors in human thought, and in every age they are found in open conflict with the Church as the great bulwark, not merely of revealed religion, but of theism. The Church cannot defeat their disastrous propaganda unless she is able to meet them on their own ground, and establisb by irrefragable arguments the existence and principal attributes of a personal God.

In yet another way also Natural Theology lends support to revelation. God's revealed word is not confined to the mysteries of the Faith, but deals also with matters which fall within the scope of rational investigation. It is plain that truth cannot contradict truth: that a revelation, if it be really such, cannot be at issue with any incontrovertible conclusion of the speculative reason. And it is no small confirmation of the Christian religion that, where its teaching admits of being tested by our natural powers, it can invariably be shewn that no discrepancy exists: that the doctrines of the Faith are in full agreement with what may be learned about God from the data which natural knowledge supplies.

We have enlarged somewhat on the difference between Natural and Revealed Theology and on their reciprocal relations, because during the past half-century a new theory on this subject has obtained currency, according to which all distinction between the two is denied. The author chiefly responsible for the prevalence of this view was Schleiermacher (1768 -- 1834), a rationalizing theologian, whose works have exercised a far-reaching influence. His doctrine of God was a pantheism, founded on the system of Spinoza. Yet he followed Kant in holding the speculative reason to be incompetent to afford us any positive knowledge about Him. Moreover, his rationalism could find no place for the idea of revelation in the sense of an objective divine message. Starting with these presuppositions he sought a new basis for theology in religious experience. It should, he held, be the intellectual expression of our inward experience, and hence develop as that experience develops. It follows that no doctrinal formula is to be regarded as having permanent value, inasmuch as it must in time be superseded by one of fuller meaning. The significance of many dogmas is purely symbolical: they are not to be understood literally. Thus the Christian doctrines of the final judgment and the corporeal resurrection are to be accepted as symbols, not as realities. Here we have the origin of the view to which we have already adverted,[4] according to which Natural Theology is simply the speculative system involved in some particular phase of religious experience. Schleiermacher, however, contended that the modes in which the religious experience finds expression may justly claim to be at one and the same time Natural and Revealed Theology. It is natural as being the work of reason. It is revelation because our experience is God's manifestation of Himself. Indeed, since he found room in his system for a certain number of the doctrinal formulas of Christianity, he was actually regarded as a defender of revealed religion. He has unfortunately been followed by many subsequent writers in the entirely new sense thus given to the familiar terms, Natural Theology and Revelation.[5] Some of these, as, *e.g.*, the Modernists (chap. viii. § 4) start from philosophical premises not unlike his own. The standpoint of others (as of Mr. Webb) is different. But in all cases the identification of the two sciences implies that the idea of revelation as a direct communication of truth from God to man has been abandoned, and that reason is no longer regarded as able to afford certain, even if restricted, knowledge concerning Him. We hope in the following pages to make good the power of the human mind to possess a true Natural Theology -- -a body of conclusions regarding God derived by logical demonstrations from principles of indisputable truth. The possibility of revelation, truly so called, lies outside the scope of our work, but is adequately vindicated in many treatises on Apologetics.

NOTES

{1} *Essias de Théodicéé sur le bonté de Dieu, etc.* (1710).

{2} Cf. Aristotle, *Metaph.* VI., c. i., 1026a28.

{3} Cf. Lord Balfour, *Foundations of Belief,* pt. iii., ch. ii., p. 195. The current theory appears to be something of this kind. Everyone has a right to adopt any opinions he pleases. It is his duty before exercising this right critically to sift the reasons by which such opinions may be supported, and so to adjust the degree of his convictions that they shall accurately correspond with the evidence adduced in their favour. Authority, therefore, has no place among the legitimate causes of belief. If it appears amongst them, it is as an intruder, to he jealously hunted down and mercilessly expelled. Reason, and reason only, can be safely permitted to mould the convictions of mankind utiments like these are among the commonplaces of political and social philosophy. Yet looked at scientifically, they seem to me to be, not merely erroneous, but absurd. Suppose for a moment a community, of which each member should deliberately set himself to the task of throwing off as far as possible all prejudices due to education: where each would consider it his duty critically to examine the grounds whereon rest every positive enactment and every moral precept which he has been accustomed to obey . . . and to weigh out with scrupulous precision the exact degree of assent which in each particular case the results of this process might seem to justify. To say that such a community, if it acted upon the opinions thus arrived at, would stand but a poor chance in the struggle for existence, is to say far too little. It could never even begin to be: and if by a miracle it was created, it would without doubt immediately resolve itself into its component elements."

{4} *Introd.*, p. xii.

{5} The following passage from Mr. C. J. Webb's *God and Personality* may be cited in illustration: "I should hold that a definite type of religious experience, expressed in an historical religion, is presupposed in every system of Natural Theology: while the ultimate goal of all human speculation, which can be so named, must be a system which presupposes all the religious experience of mankind: an experience to which indeed those who regard Religion as genuine experience, and not as mere illusion throughout, cannot surely deny the name of Revelation" (p. 33). It is manifest how far removed is the sense here given to the terms from that which in the history of human thought has ever been regarded as their proper meaning.

Chapter II. The Demonstrability of God's Existence.

1. *The possibility of a demonstration denied: sensationalist standpoint.* Before we proceed to develop the proofs of God's existence it will be well to establish the validity of the reasoning to be employed in them. Our principal arguments -- those which belong strictly to the science of metaphysics -- rest on certain fundamental conceptions of the intellect, such as *substance* and *efficient cause*, etc., and on certain first principles immediately connected with these, such as the principle of causality, that *Whatever comes into being must have a cause.* We thus establish the existence of a necessary substance, the cause of the contingent substances which experience makes known to us. The value of this reasoning is at the present day widely denied. The neo-hegelian, the follower of Kant, the sensationalist, though their respective standpoints are so widely divergent, are at one in declaring that the conceptions and principles in question are destitute of objective validity. Until this preliminary question is settled it is hardly worth while to propose our arguments. Unless we can shew that the notion of substance -- and by this term we understand something which is no mere transient qualification of 'the real,' but which possesses independent subsistence as an integral unit in nature -- is no chimera of the imagination, it is idle to argue that the world is due to the activity of a

Supreme Substance. Unless we can vindicate the worth of the concept of efficient cause -- that which by its action makes a thing what it is -- it is useless to commence a proof of a First Cause, or a Prime Mover. The purpose of this chapter is to establish the worth of our fundamental conceptions and of the axiomatic principles which we shall employ. In doing so we shall take note of the opposing theories, and shall endeavour to make good that they are irreconcilable alike with facts of experience and with reason. We shall deal first with the sensationalist position, reserving our discussion of other schools till the end of the chapter. In connection with the former, we shall touch on the philosophy of M. Bergson: since, though his system is in many respects original, his attitude on the point under consideration is identical with that of the sensationalists.

The sensationalist philosophy admits no other knowledge than that obtained by the experience of the senses. We know, its adherents contend, particulars and particulars only. We have no means of obtaining certainty in our universal judgments except by experience of each several individual embraced in the class of which we are speaking. In every general proposition, which includes in its scope others besides those which have actually fallen under observation, there is involved of necessity a leap in the dark. And even of particulars all that we can know are the perceptions of sense. The so-called 'substance' -- something which persists identically the same, though its qualities, the direct object of sense-perception, are subject to change, and which, amid all their multiplicity, is somehow or other but one -- is, they say, a creature of our imagination. Similarly as regards our own minds. We know nothing, they contend, of the mind save transient states of consciousness. The term 'substance,' as applied to it, is totally devoid of meaning. Mill sums up his teaching on this subject as follows: "As body is the insentient cause to which we are naturally prompted to refer a certain portion of our feelings, so mind may he described as the sentient *subject* (in the Scholastic sense of the term) of all feelings: that which has or feels them. But of the nature of either body or mind, further than the feelings which the former excites and which the latter experiences, we do not, according to the best existing doctrine, know anything at all" (*Logic*, Bk. I., ch. iii., § 8). As regards the notion of cause, the doctrine of this school follows the same lines. A cause, we are informed, is that which experience shews to he the regular antecedent of anything. There is no philosophical basis for the view which would see in a cause *that which makes a thing to be what it is*. Our senses merely perceive one thing precede and another follow. We cannot see one thing impart being to another. We have, then, no right to introduce such a conception, and to say that the existence of the consequent is determined by the antecedent. The passage in which Hume propounds this conclusion is well known, and deserves to be cited here. He says:

"After one instance or experiment, where we have observed a particular event to follow upon another, we are not entitled to form a geheral rule, or foretell what will happen in like cases: it being justly esteemed an unpardonable temerity to judge of the whole course of nature from one single experiment, however accurate or certain. But where one particular species of events has always in all instances been conjoined with another, we make no longer any scruple of foretelling one upon the appearance of the other, and of employing that reasoning, which can alone assure us of any matter of fact or existence. We then call the one object cause, the other effect. . . . But there is nothing in a number of instances different from every single instance, which is supposed to be exactly similar: except only that after a repetition of similar instances the mind is carried by habit, upon the appearance of one event, to expect its usual attendant, and to believe that it will exist. This connection, therefore, which we feel in the mind, this customary transition from one object to its usual attendant, is the sentiment or impression from which we form the idea of power or necessary connection. Nothing further is in the case. . . . The first time a man saw the communication of motion by impulse, as by the shock of two billiard-balls, he could not pronounce that the one event was *connected*, but only that it was *conjoined* with the other. After he has observed several instances of this nature, he then pronounces it to be *connected*. What alteration has happened to give rise to this new idea of connection? Nothing but that he now feels these events to be connected in his imagination, and can readily foretell the existence of one from the appearance of the other." (*Inquiry concerning the Human Understanding.* Section vii., p. 2).

Such in outline is the teaching of the sensationalist school on causality. Substantially, it has not altered since the days of Hume. Spencer, it is true, modifies it in one respect. He attributes our conviction that the same cause will produce the same effect, not merely to the experience of the individual, but to that of the race. The experience of past generations, he holds, has gradually stamped itself upon the brain, so as to establish 'forms of thought.' Hence from the dawn of reason we are led to anticipate that the law of uniformity will prevail in nature, and that the same antecedent will be followed by the same consequent. As regards the point which concerns us at present this modification of sensationalist doctrine is immaterial.

It is manifest that if things really are as this philosophy represents them, the arguments for the existence of God as the First Cause of all things are utterly worthless. The principle of causality lacks all necessity: we have no right to affirm that whatever comes into being must have a cause. As far as our limited experience goes, every event has been preceded by an antecedent with which we connect it. But we are not justified in asserting that this must of necessity be so, except in so far as all sensible experience takes place in time, and time involves succession. We have no ground, as Mill frankly owns, for supposing that there is an ontological connection between antecedent and consequent.[1] Indeed, even if the universality of the principle of causality be admitted, it would not carry us to a First Cause, but to an infinite series of temporal antecedents. Mill is absolutely true to sensationalist principles when he says: "The cause of every change is a prior change; and such it cannot but be; for if there were no new antecedent, there would not be a new consequent. If the state of facts which brings the phenomenon into existence had existed always or for an indefinite duration, the effect would always have existed or been produced an indefinite time ago. It is thus a necessary part of the fact of causation, within the sphere of our experience, that the causes as well as the effects had a beginning in time, and were themselves caused."[2] The very notion of God, as we conceive Him, is, on the principles of this school utterly irrational. For how else can we conceive of God than as the Supreme Substance, infinite in all perfections and existing from all eternity? But sensationalism declares that substance is a meaningless word: that all we can know or ever hope to know either of bodies or of minds are states -- ever-changing states. To assert, therefore, that the existence of finite substances enables us to conclude to an Infinite Substance is simply to juggle with words. No significance whatever can be attached to either of the two terms in the theory under consideration.

We stated above that, great as is the difference between the philosophy of M. Bergson and sensationalism, his attitude to the proofs of God's existence is practically the same. According to him, change, becoming, movement, is all there is. The universe does not consist in changing things: it is itself change, life. It is not a living thing: it is the actual process of life. We ourselves seem to be permanent beings endowed with life; but it is not so in reality. We are partial manifestations of the universal flow. And if it he asked what are the substances, to whose existence our external experience seems to testify, the reply must be that they are, so to speak, 'sections' taken in the flux by the intellect for practical ends. Life demands action, and action is impossible unless we stabilize our view of the flow by thus cutting across it and treating what in fact is moving -- or to speak more accurately, motion -- as though it were fixed and abiding.[3] So, too, the separation of cause and effect is wholly the work of the mind. The stream of life is one and indivisible. Cause and effect are partial views, which the limitations of our intellect compel us to take as the condition of our activity. [4]

It is manifest that the proof of the existence of God fares no better in this system than in the sensationalist philosophy. The objective validity of the concept of substance and of the principle of causality is rejected: both are declared to be creations of the mind. In consequence, every argument which relies on them is worthless.

2. *The concepts of substance and cause in the light of experience.* The work of a philosophy lies in its ability to account for facts. It claims to give us the

explanation of facts: to tell us what in their ultimate analysis the data of experience involve. If then a system fails to give us such an explanation, if the solution which it provides is wholly inconsistent with our experience, that system has no claim on our acceptance. It may be ingenious: it may suggest novel objections against current theories; but it has failed to make good. Properly speaking, it has no right to be termed a philosophy. Sensationalism certainly is open to this reproach. It is in flagrant contradiction with facts. Nothing is more evident than that we possess a direct and immediate knowledge, not merely of thoughts, volitions and emotions, but of a subject which thinks, wills and feels. We are not first conscious of a thought, from which by a subsequent inferential process we conclude to the existence of a thinking subject: we are not conscious of the bare thought at all, but of *ourselves as thinking.* In other words, our consciousness of the thinking, willing subject is direct, not indirect, immediate not mediate. Do we not, each of us, spontaneously speak of *my* thoughts, *my* desires, *my* feelings? Every time we so speak we bear witness that we are conscious of ourselves as substances, and of our thoughts as accidental determinations of the subject self.

Sensationalism refuses to admit this consciousness of a subject, and declares that we know nothing save a succession of states. In other words, it denies that we are aware of an *ego* to which these states appertain, and to which they must be referred. [5] In this, it is plain, it is altogether in conflict with one of the most certain facts of experience. We may note further that since consciousness shews us that thought is essentially the action of a thinking subject, it follows that thought without a mind is a sheer contradiction in terms. There cannot be action without an agent. Action is a determination of the thing that acts: and we cannot have a determination apart from the subject which it determines.

Again, the power of memory enables us to say *I thought.* When we so speak, we recognize that, while the thought is transitory, the subject remains one and identical. I, who am now looking back on past events, am the self-same person who then thought and willed in such and such a way. Each time we exercise the power of memory we distinguish the enduring substance from its transient determinations: we have knowledge of the former as well as of the latter. Indeed, the very existence of this faculty affords a conclusive proof that the mind persists through time as the same reality. If our mental life consists simply of passing states, existing of themselves without any permanent and substantial *ego*, how does it come about that they do not utterly perish as one by one they make way for the next in the long series? How can one state reach back into the flow and recall another which has long ceased to be? Recollection is not merely inexplicable, but impossible, unless we admit the identity of the subject who remembers with the subject whose states he is recalling.

Nor is the appeal to experience conclusive only as regards the concept of substance. It is no less decisive as to the validity of the notion of cause. I am aware beyond the possibility of doubt that I can produce thought. I can direct this activity into a particular channel, and produce thoughts about such matters as I wish. In other words, the mind has direct experience of causation: it is conscious that it gives being to the thought, and makes it to be what it is. Here the attempt to explain away causality as mere succession breaks down hopelessly. Not merely am I conscious of causation properly so called, but this causation is not exercised by the antecedent mental state at all. What no longer exists cannot exert causality. It is the mind which is the cause alike of the previous and of the subsequent state. And the action of the mind is not previous to, but simultaneous with the thought which it produces.

When these facts are duly weighed, it becomes evident that a philosophy which maintains that we have no experience either of substance or of causation, that these are mere terms to which nothing objective corresponds, stands self-condemned.

It may, perhaps, he said that our appeal has been to internal experience alone; and that we have no right to apply concepts derived from internal experience to the external order. It will, however, appear that the data of our experience regarding the external order are no less incompatible with sensationalism than are the facts of our mental life.

The sensationalist appeals to his chosen illustration of the two billiard balls. What we see here, he says, is succession, and succession alone: the impact of one ball is *followed* by the motion of the other. And he claims that, so far as experience is concerned, our knowledge is limited to this: that the notion of causation is a gratuitous addition of our own. "All events," says Hume, seem entirely loose and separate. One event follows another, but we can never observe any tie between them. They, seem *conjoined* but never connected" (*l.c.*). We may readily admit that the example selected lends some colour to the statement. But is this single example really adequate? When I watch a potter mould the yielding clay with his hand, do I not see the clay actually *receive its determination* from his fingers? Here, surely, there is much more than succession. Indeed, succession does not enter into the case: for no interval of time separates the pressure of the finger from the shape newly taken by the clay. No one, we believe, will maintain that when we affirm that we see the hand communicate its shape to the clay, we are introducing a new notion in no way gathered from experience. I could not, if I would, leave this notion out. True, I do not see with my eyes the abstract idea of causation, for the simple reason that the eye does not see abstract ideas, but concrete facts. But it is clear that the connection between cause and effect is no product of the imagination, but is immediately apprehended as given in experience. In other words, the sensationalist contention that our experience can never shew us anything hut two events conjoined by a temporal sequence, is altogether at variance with the facts: and this alone is sufficient to shew the falsity of the theory.

Once again, is it really the case that external experience is limited to sensible qualities and has nothing to tell us as to substance? What is, in point of fact, the object of experience? Do we perceive mere colour or that which is coloured? mere hardness or that which is hard? *color* or *coloratum, durities* or *durum*? It will hardly be denied that whiteness and hardness and sweetness are mental abstractions, and that the real datum of experience is the concrete object, the hard, white, sweet thing. If so, experience gives us something more than sensible qualities: it gives us the thing or substance. Of course, the external sense does not apprehend the substance as such. We shall deal later in this chapter with the manner in which we know it. Here we are only concerned to point out that the sensationalist analysis of experience is inadequate: that when we perceive an external object, we apprehend something beyond its mere sensible qualities: and that this element, of which these philosophers take no account, is precisely what we signify when we employ the term *substance*.

3. *Philosophical vindication of these concepts.* There is, then, no shadow of ambiguity in the answer elicited by our appeal to experience. It testifies decisively that substance and cause are realities not figments. Under the circumstances it might, perhaps, seem that no more need be said on the matter. Yet in view of the fact that both sensationalism and Kantianism deny the worth of these concepts on grounds of abstract reason, it appears desirable to examine the point somewhat more closely. In the present section we shall shew that the principles of a sound philosophy compel us to admit that these concepts are valid representations of reality.

We have seen that the sensationalists limit our knowledge purely and entirely to the perceptions of sense. They overlook the fact that sense and intellect are distinct faculties, and that it belongs to the intellect to apprehend certain features of reality which lie beyond the scope of sense. Each cognitive faculty reveals to us a special aspect of reality, the aspect apprehended by one being diverse from that apprehended by another. Colour is the object of sight. The eye knows things in so far as they are coloured. Sound is the object of the sense of hearing: odour is the object of the sense of smell. The intellect, too, has its proper object. In knowing anything it apprehends it in so far as it is a *being* or *thing*. Its object is *being* and those notions which stand in immediate connection with *being*, such as, *e.g.*, unity, multiplicity, efficient causality, finality, etc., etc. Just as sight shews us of what colour a thing is, so the intellect shews us *what it is* -- its essential nature. It distinguishes, as sense cannot do, between things which are such as to subsist upon their own account (substances), and those which like light or colour are mere determinations of substance (accidents). It apprehends the constitutive principle which makes its object the kind of thing it is, the principle which is the root whence its properties proceed. Take the case of a mathematical figure, *e.g.*, a circle. The eye perceives a particular circle of a certain size and colour. The intellect shews us something over and above this. It apprehends what a circle is -- its *quidditas*, as the Scholastics said -- and expresses this in the definition with which Euclid has made us familiar. That formula is not concerned with size or colour: it is concerned with the constitutive principle of the circle, it shews us its essential nature. Again, take our knowledge of some concrete object designed for some special purpose, *e.g.*, a clock. The difference between the apprehension of sense and of intellect is immeasurable. Sense perceives the face of the clock, and the hands progressing round it at different rates of speed. But the eye as such knows nothing, and can know nothing as to the purpose of the clock, the purpose which is the determining principle of its every detail. For that we depend on the intellect. It is through the intellect we know that the clock is so constructed that the progress of the hands stands in a definite relation to the period of time which we term a day, and that the motion being uniform, we can by the help of the clock determine the precise point of the day's time, at which an event takes place. Sense cannot apprehend this relation to the sun's diurnal course. Yet this is the constitutive principle of the clock as such. The mechanism of clocks may vary: one may be driven by weights, another by a spring. It is the relation to time which makes the thing a clock.

How absolutely different is the abstract idea -- the work of the intellect -- from the picture which we form in the imagination! The one shews us the sensible appearances and these alone: the other shews us what the thing *is*. Yet according to the sensationalist philosophy the abstract idea of a thing is nothing but an individual image coupled with a general name. On this subject Mill is explicit:

"The Concept is either a mere mental representation of an object differing from those copied directly from sense only in having certain of its parts artificially made intense and prominent: or it is a *fasciculus* of representations of imagination, held together by the tie of an association artificially produced. When the mental phenomenon has assumed this . . .

character, it comes to be termed a Concept, or more vaguely and familiarly, an Idea."[6]

It is little wonder that a philosophy vitiated at its very source by an error so profound should lead us in the issue to scepticism. For it will hardly be denied that such is the inevitable conclusion of a theory which regards the notions of substance and cause as mere figments.

The idea is frequently distinguished from the image on the score that the former is universal, the latter particular. This is true. The intellectual concept does not rest in the particular: it seizes the type. The definition of a circle is applicable to every circle that ever existed. But the difference to which we have adverted is yet more fundamental, viz., that the image exhibits the object in its sensible determinations, while the intellect views it as a *being* or *thing*, and shews us what it is under that aspect.

The point with which we are dealing is of such vital importance for the vindication of our primary notions, and in consequence for the proofs of God's existence, that it will not be superfluous to offer yet another argument for the same conclusion.

Of the three operations of the understanding, conception, judgment and reasoning, the first place is rightly assigned to judgment. Judgment is the term of the mind's activity. Both conception and reasoning are of value to us, because through them the mind arrives at judgment. Now judgment deals with beings and with nothing else. The sign of a judgment is the verb 'to be' functioning as the copula between subject and predicate. The subject is the thing with whose being we are concerned. The predicate expresses some particular determination of being belonging to the subject.[7] It may inform us regarding its substantial being, as when I say: 'Caesar is a man'; or about some accidental mode, as in the proposition: 'Caesar is in Rome'; or it may be a mere negation conceived by the mind as though it were a mode of being, as when we say of some one: 'He is a nonentity.' But whatever be the nature of the judgment, it is of necessity concerned with the being of the subject. It is a standing proof that, over and above sense, we possess a faculty of another order: and that it belongs to this faculty to know, not merely those modes of being with which sense is concerned, but also that substantial being, of which they are but the accidental determinations. The tale of the philosopher who declared that on the day when a pig could say, 'I am a pig,' he would hold himself bound to take off his hat to it, is familiar to all. There was reason in what he said. To arrive at this knowledge of its own nature, the pig would need something far beyond that sense-perception with which the brute-creation is endowed. It would need an intellect enabling it to know the being of things, to distinguish substantial being from its accidental determinations, and to refer these various modes of being to itself as their conscious subject. Such an agent would be an *animal rationale* like ourselves, and might justly claim to be treated with a similar regard.

Our conclusion, that just as vision perceives the colour of things, so does the faculty of intellect apprehend their being, may, however, appear open to a serious difficulty. It is true that we apprehend the essence of a mathematical figure, and can give a definition from which its properties can be deduced. But this is not the case as regards the things of nature. It would seem that where they are concerned the scope of intellect is very limited. It can discern between substances and accidents, and as regards substances it can grasp the distinction between the living and the inanimate, between those which are endowed with sense-perception and those which lack this endowment, between the rational and the irrational: and it can deduce the properties consequent on these broad divisions. But here apparently its powers stop short. If we wish to define any specific class which falls under one of these heads, *e.g.*, a lion, the only way is to enumerate the most characteristic determinations which sense-perception exhibits, and to define it as a sentient substance (an animal) characterized by these attributes. We certainly do not apprehend the specific essence of these things, as we do in the case of mathematical figures.

The limitation here noted must be admitted. The fact is that only those aspects of being are fully intelligible which can be entirely abstracted from matter. Such, *e.g.*, are substance, accident, cause, life, unity, etc., etc. The more any nature is involved in material conditions and incapable of such abstraction, the less of intelligibility does it possess.[8] In this lies the reason why our knowledge as to the concrete things of nature is so restricted. The essence of these things -- the constitutive principle on which their properties depend -- is so bound up with matter that the intellect cannot know it. We must be content with a knowledge of the sensible qualities: and the only abstraction possible in their regard is that by which from the qualities as found in the individual, we form a general concept applicable to all the class. In mathematics a higher degree of abstraction takes place: for in that science we are no longer concerned with sensible qualities, but only with quantity, discrete or continuous, as the case may be. But, as we have already said, a still fuller measure of intelligibility belongs to those aspects of being which admit of entire abstraction from all material conditions whatsoever.

We embarked on this discussion with a view to establish the validity of the notions of substance and cause. And the bearing of our conclusions upon this question will easily appear. By a 'substance' is signified that which exists as an independent thing, and not as a mere determination -- that which is in the full sense of the word. For the independent entity is termed a being in a sense to which its accidental determinations have no claim. Although they, too, are said to be, yet being is predicted of them, not with the same signification which it bears in regard to substance, but analogously. A man, a horse, a tree, are substances: so too are iron, gold, water. It should be observed that by 'substance' we do not denote the mere material substratum which may be at one time the earth, then become vegetable tissue, then be transmuted into human flesh, and afterwards return once more to its original form.[9] A 'substance' is a complete nature. It is substance *because it exists in its own right, and not as a determination of another entity.*[10]

This notion of substance is a primary apprehension of the intellect. No inference is required to arrive at it. Our sensitive faculties perceive the sensible qualities of the objects presented to them -- their colour, shape, etc. -- and gather them together in their relation to one another. The data thus obtained are seen to fall into separate groups, acting as independent units. Wherever this is the case, the intellect conceives the object as a substance. What acts as a single unit, is *one*, notwithstanding the variety of its attributes. It is *a thing*: its attributes are mere determinations of that which properly speaking *is*.

Of course, in saying that the intellect immediately knows the object as a substance, we do not mean that from the first it has a clear-cut abstract notion of substance, such as we have given. It first apprehends the object confusedly as a thing with these or those attributes. Only later by reflection does it come to an explicit recognition of the distinction between the attributes, which are many, and the subject to which they belong, which is one. But we contend that even in the earliest confused apprehension, the notion of substance is implicitly present. All that is needed is the reflective operation of the mind upon its own concept, and its true character will make itself known.

That this concept of substance is utterly different from any datum of sense is abundantly clear. The substantial nature is whole and entire in each part of the object. It does not increase or diminish with the object's size. Every particle of an oak-tree has the substantial nature of oak. A small piece of the wood is just as truly oak as is the whole trunk. The tree may increase in bulk: or on the other hand, the branches may be lopped off. In either case the substantial nature remains what it was. Moreover, as was said above, the substance is one, though the attributes are many. And, further, the substance remains permanently the same even though the attributes display numerous changes. A reality with characteristics such as these lies outside the scope of sense perception. The intellect, and the intellect alone, has power to make it known to us.

Substance and attribute are by no means the only notions which are directly apprehended by the mind from the objects of sense without the need of any kind of inference. To this same class of apprehensions belong, *e.g.*, unity, multiplicity, causality, finality, truth, goodness. All of these stand in immediate relation to being. Thus unity is being as undivided: multiplicity is a plurality of undivided things: a cause is that which gives being to a thing: finality is the purpose of a being: truth is the conformity between thought and that which is: goodness is the relation which being, as an object of desire, bears to the will. Of these we are here concerned only with the notion of cause. Just as it belongs, not to the eye, but to the intellect to know anything as a substance, so the intellect is needed to apprehend an object as *that which confers being*, a cause. It is this which explains the error of the sensationalists. Holding that there is no other knowledge save that of sense-perception, and seeing clearly that the notion of causality is not a thing which the eye can see, they maintained that it is a mere word devoid of any corresponding idea. Yet nothing can be more evident than that not merely have we the idea, but that the mind can no more avoid it than the eye can avoid seeing and recognizing the colours of the objects of vision. Granted appropriate objects, the mind instantly, and apart from all inference, knows the one as cause and the other as effect. The sensationalist difficulty disappears as soon as the spheres of sense and intellect are distinguished: the faculty whose proper object is being must be capable of apprehending in the data afforded by sense that which is the source and that which is the recipient of being.

Doubtless we sometimes err, and judge that to be the cause of a thing which in fact is not so related to it. But this is a case in which our error bears witness to the validity of the concepts in question. It is because we are so familiar with real causes and effects that we occasionally allow ourselves to be misled, and conclude that some event which follows immediately on another must needs be related to it as its effect.

It may perhaps seem that we have given an undue amount of attention to the defence of these concepts. Yet a somewhat full discussion, we are convinced, was absolutely necessary. The principal objections now urged against the proofs for God's existence are based, as we have already said, on the contention that substance and cause are meaningless terms to which no objective reality corresponds. Until this fundamental fallacy should have been refuted, the whole value of the proofs must have remained in question.

4. *Philosophical vindication of first principles.* Now that we have shewn that the primary concepts of the intellect are valid, no great difficulty will be presented by the defence of first principles. These arise immediately from

a comparison of two such concepts, the mind pronouncing judicially in their regard whether the one necessarily excludes the other, or, on the other hand, necessarily involves it. It will be sufficient here to deal with two principles only, viz., the principle of contradiction, the most fundamental of all judgments of the understanding, and the principle of causality, the basis of our proofs of God's existence. Those against whom we are contending deny the worth of both.

(a) The principle of contradiction tells us that 'the same thing cannot both be and not be, at the same time and in the same respect.' We reach this judgment by a simple comparison of the concepts of being and not-being. Being, as we have seen, is the first of all concepts. The mind knows all its objects under this aspect -- as things which *are*. The task which lies before it, often a most laborious one, is to determine exactly *what* they are. But the notion of 'being' -- of *that which is* -- is plain from the very dawn of intelligence. We cannot explain it by any that is simpler: for its simplicity is ultimate. This notion is followed by that of its opposite, 'not-being.' The mind recognizes the incompatibility of the two, and judges that, 'it is impossible for the same thing both to be and at the same time not to be': or, as it may be stated in a slightly different form: 'It is impossible for the same attribute both to belong and not to belong to the same thing at the same time.'

The absolutely necessary character of the judgment is manifest from the direct opposition between being and not-being. It is for this reason that the mind does not merely assert its contradictory to be untrue, but finds itself impelled to state the proposition in a modal form and to declare that it is *impossible* that it should be true.

It is plain that if this principle were dubious, all search after truth would be futile: for no statement of any kind could be made which might not be simultaneously both true and false. Indeed, it might have seemed impossible to call it in question. Yet, in the philosophical confusion of the present day, this has been done. The pragmatists, who regard reality as plastic, and hold that we ourselves establish the objective order by stamping upon it those principles which we find most convenient to the conduct of life, will not lower their flag even to the principle of contradiction. Mr. Schiller has the courage to maintain that this is not, as we fondly imagine, a self-evident truth, but a postulate which we impose on reality, because it is useful. Indeed, to him, as to Heraclitus of old, it can never be true to say of anything that it is. All things are in flux: all is *becoming.* "In strict fact," he says, " nothing ever is: everything *becomes* and turns our most conscientious predications into falsehoods" (*Axioms as Postulates,* § 34). He fails to see that though the material world is subject to unceasing mutation, so that the object of sense-perception is altering even while we perceive it, yet the intellect can give us knowledge of that which *is.* Not merely does it apprehend the substance, which remains permanent notwithstanding the changes in its sensible attributes, but from perishable individuals it abstracts the notion of the type. Indeed, it is only through this power of abstracting the stable type that science is possible to us. For the object of science is to be found, not in the singular as such, but in singulars just so far as the type is realized in them.

M. Bergson, similarly failing to recognize the essential difference between the object of sense and the object of the intellect, also conceives reality as an ever-flowing stream, whose constant changes afford us no ground for the apprehension of any stable truth. He, too, rejects the notion of being, and contends that there is no reality save becoming. In this system also, where of nothing can it be said either that it is or that it is not, there is no room for the principle of contradiction.[11]

(b) We now pass to the consideration of another principle for which self-evidence is claimed, the principle of causality.

It was stated above that the notion of cause, in the sense of that which makes a thing to be what it is, is one of those which are so intimately related to that of being, that reason apprehends them as soon as it begins to operate at all. But the mind soon realizes that there is more than one sense in which we can say of a thing that it makes something else to be. It distinguishes four kinds of cause, two of them extrinsic to the effect, viz., the efficient and the final: and two intrinsic, viz., the material and the formal. Thus, to use a familiar illustration, when a potter shapes a vessel, say a bowl, the efficient cause is the workman himself: the final cause is the purpose for which the vessel is made, in this case to hold food: the material cause is the clay out of which it is formed: the formal cause, the shape given to the matter by the agent. Each of these four principles of the thing's being is rightly said to be a cause of the thing. Of each it may be truly affirmed that it makes the thing to be what it is. But the senses in which the term is applied are not identical: the four kinds of causation are distinct each from the others. The principle of causality with which we are here concerned has reference not to all of these, but only to efficient causation.

The principle is stated in various ways. Of these we may notice two: 'Whatever begins to be must have a cause': and 'All contingent being must have a cause.' The first of these is a more popular, the second a more accurate and philosophical expression of the truth in question. The term 'contingent being' signifies that which is capable of non-existence. It stands in direct opposition to 'necessary being,' a term only applicable to God. The principle as affirmed in regard of contingent being is wider in its application than in the first of the two forms given. For it is a point in dispute among philosophers whether God, had He so willed, might not have created things from all eternity, in such wise that the universe should have known no beginning, but that the years should stretch back in an infinite series. It is plain that, if this supposition be entertained, there would exist created being which never began to be, inasmuch as *ex hypothesi* the universe is eternal. Nevertheless, what has been created even *ab aeterno* is capable of non-existence: it is contingent being.

When we assert that a proposition is self-evident, we signify that its truth appears from the mere comparison of the concepts which constitute the subject and the predicate: that there is no need to have recourse to experience to discover whether or not the predicate will be found in the objects denoted by the subject: but that the simple consideration of the two concepts suffices to shew us that the presence of the one involves the presence (or absence, as the case may be) of the other. Thus, we saw just now that the principle of contradiction was self-evident, because the concepts of being and not-being are mutually exclusive, so that in no case is it possible that what is known to *be* should in the same respect *not be*. In the same way the principle of causality is self-evident, because when we consider the notion of 'contingent being' and that of 'a thing which owes existence to an efficient cause,' the mind recognizes a necessary agreement between them, and sees beyond all possibility of doubt that what is contingent must be a thing owing existence to an efficient cause. It is manifest that what is capable of not-being is not self-existent. What is self-existent is necessary: to exist is part of its nature. We might as well try to suppose a triangle having only two sides as a self-existent being which should not exist. It is also clear that whatever exists must either receive its existence from itself or from some other being. There is no *tertium quid* possible: it cannot have received existence from nothing. Therefore, as contingent being does not receive existence from itself -- otherwise it would be, not contingent, but self-existent, and therefore necessary, being -- it must receive existence from some other being. But to receive existence from another being is to have an efficient cause. The principle, therefore, is self-evident. It cannot be proved by an appeal to some higher principle from which it is derived, for the simple reason that it is itself in the full sense of the word a first principle: its truth is involved in the very terms of which it is composed. The only proof of which it is susceptible, is that which is proper to first principles, viz., a *reductio ad absurdum*, in which it is shewn that a denial of this truth involves a denial of the principle of contradiction, inasmuch as we cannot suppose a thing to be contingent and yet uncaused without maintaining that it can, at one and the same time, both be, and not be, contingent.

5. *Kant's teaching.* Kant assures us that by the very nature of the case it is impossible that we should know realities unmodified by the mind -- things as they are in themselves, noumena. This he regards as in need of no proof, since he starts from the assumption that the immediate objects of experience must be internal to the mind. For that reason, he contends, our knowledge is, of necessity, confined to phenomena -- mental representations. These, as presented to our knowledge, have been refashioned according to the laws of our mentality. The raw material of experience consists of disconnected sensations; but by our cognitive

faculties these are transformed into a world which is apparently external to us. It seems to us that we know things as existing in space and time. But in point of fact space and time are our own contribution. They are the 'form' of our sensibility: and they do not belong to things in themselves, which are out of all relation to such purely subjective conditions. As sensibility has its forms, so too has the understanding. Kant enumerates twelve. These are, so to speak, the moulds through which sensation passes on entering the mind, and by means of which the world of experience is rendered intelligible. Substance and causality are of their number. We conceive things as substances, and we conceive them as due to causes. But these notions of the understanding, like space and time as regards sensibility, are in no way derived from the noumena. They are merely schemata according to which the mind organizes its objects.

The principle of causality Kant declares to be a synthetical *a priori* judgment. His division of analytical and synthetical judgments differed from that in use among the Aristotelian logicians. According to him, analytical judgments are those alone in which the predicate can be found in the concept of the subject, as when, *e.g.*, we assert that a triangle is a plane figure. In synthetical judgments, on the other hand, the predicate adds something to the subject-notion, and is not contained within it.[12] He further distinguished between judgments *a posteriori* and *a priori*. By *a posteriori* judgments he signified those which are gathered from experience; by *a priori* judgments those which are wholly independent of experience, and must be attributed to the operation of the mind. All analytical judgments are *a priori*, since, although the subject-notion may be drawn from experience, no experience is needed to arrive at the connection between subject and predicate. But he maintained that many synthetical judgments too belong to this class. Wherever a judgment possesses the notes of universality and necessity, there, he contended, we have an *a priori* judgment. Such a judgment cannot be due to experience: it must, in consequence, be attributable to the subjective laws of our own mind and be *a priori*. To this class he assigned first and foremost all mathematical judgments, save those in which the predicate is actually part of the definition of the subject. No experience, he maintains, can ever afford us justification for asserting that all triangles without exception must necessarily have their interior angles equal to two right angles: for experience can only inform us regarding those individuals which we have actually seen. The element of necessity must be derived from our own minds. The explanation of such propositions is that the intellect in forming its judgment applies to it the subjective categories of 'universality' and 'necessity,' and judges that '*every* triangle *must* have its interior angle equivalent to two right angles'; but we have absolutely no guarantee that this is the case as regards things in themselves. It must be reckoned to Kant's credit that he recognized that a vast number of our judgments are characterized by *necessity* and *universality*: and that these features call for philosophical explanation. Empiricism can offer no rational account of them. Kant, at least, makes the effort to do so. But the answer which he gives to the problem has little to recommend it.

The whole of this theory rests upon the contention that a judgment must either be derived immediately from sensible experience or be wholly due to the internal constitution of the mind: that no other alternative is possible. This he assumes: he offers no proof. Yet, as a matter of fact, the Aristotelian philosophy provides an explanation of our knowledge which satisfactorily accounts for the universality and necessity of these propositions, quite apart from the alleged subjective categories. According to that system, as we have already explained, when the sense perceives the individual concrete triangle, the intellect apprehends its essential nature. It understands what the triangle is, and what are the relations which attach necessarily to a three-sided plane figure. Moreover, the apprehensions of the intellect are not confined in their scope to the particular individual: they relate to the universal type. The mind, in forming its concepts, abstracts the general notion from the singular instance: it knows the triangle *as such*. Hence it is able to enunciate propositions, which are true of each and every triangle: for in every individual the general type is realized.

It is, moreover, to be noted that Kant's theory is altogether inconsistent with the facts of experience. It is manifest that when we affirm a judgment to be necessarily and universally true, we do not do so in obedience to a spontaneous action of the understanding for which no reason can be assigned in the real order, but that we so judge because our intelligence recognizes the objective ground of the connection between subject and predicate. We understand why this predicate must of necessity accompany this subject. We see that objectively considered the one involves the other: and that the connection between the two follows from the very nature of the things in question. To attribute the element of necessity to a subjective 'form' of the mind, and not to the objective nature of things, is contrary to the most direct testimony of consciousness. It is not to explain facts, but to set facts aside in favour of a theory. In regard to the workings of our mind the testimony of consciousness must be final. And on this point its verdict is unambiguous. It is simply untrue to say that the mind constrains us, we cannot say why, to affirm this proposition under the category of necessity, that other under the category of possibility, and a third under the category of existence. In each instance we know perfectly well why the judgment assumes its particular character: and we know that the reason is found, not in any law of our mentality, but in the objective data of knowledge. Yet according to the Kantian theory our predications are blind: and no cause can be assigned why we should apply one category rather than another in any given case -- why we should, *e.g.*, judge one phenomenon to be substance and another a cause. The whole process must be attributed to a subjective law, about the working of which we cannot even hazard a conjecture. Again, Kant's whole theory is based upon the supposition that noumena -- things in themselves -- are the cause of those sensations which by means of the categories we organize into phenomena. We cannot know these noumena; but we are bound to postulate their existence. Otherwise, the raw material of our knowledge remains unaccounted for. Here, as has often been pointed out, we have a flagrant contradiction. On the one hand, causality is declared to be a mental 'form' -- a scheme under which we view the objects of knowledge, but regarding whose validity in the noumenal world we have no means of judging. On the other, noumena are held to exercise a veritable causality by producing sensations antecedently to the mental operation which organizes these sensations into phenomena. Similarly, it is assumed that the categories themselves are true causes: for they are held to shape the transient sensation into what seem to be stable objects other than ourselves. They could not do this if causality were not to Kant's mind something far more than a mere form under which certain phenomena are presented to the mind.

Nor is it more easy to get rid of the notion of substance than of that of cause. For how, it may be asked, does Kant conceive the subject of knowledge, the mind in which the categories inhere? Is it a reality or not? Manifestly he regards it as a really existing thing. It is, in his theory, something over and above the categories themselves: it is that to which they belong. It is not, like them, a determination of an already existing subject; but it exists in its own right, as an independent entity. But what is this except to conceive it as a substance? In view of these facts we are justified in maintaining that there is nothing in Kant's theory to shake our conviction as to the validity of our primary notions and the truth of those fundamental first principles which form the very basis of our knowledge.

6. *Neo-hegelianism*. The neo-hegelian doctrines which in one form or another have in recent years enjoyed so wide a vogue in England, will claim a somewhat full consideration in a later chapter (chap. xv.). Hence we shall confine our remarks on them here within the very briefest compass, reserving our criticism till it can be given in the light of a fuller exposition. There are, it is true, many varieties of opinion within the school to which we refer, so that it is difficult to make general statements without seeming unjust to some individual or other. But it may fairly be said that in this system there is no room for the notion of substance. What appear to us to be substances have no right to be so considered. They are not subsistent units, nor independent sources of activity. This is true even in regard to ourselves.[13] Whatever may be the testimony of consciousness, we are 'adjectival to reality,' not substantival entities. Nor is the one reality to which we are thus subordinated a substance: it has no being outside the ever-evolving modes in which it manifests itself. The notion of cause fares no better. To the neo-hegelian there are not two orders, an objective order of reality and a representative order of thought. There is but one, and that is intellectual. It follows that there can be no

question of real dependence of effect from cause, in the sense that the action of cause makes the effect what it is. In the intellectual order there is no such thing as efficient causation: we are concerned, not with cause and effect, but with premises and conclusion. In this system these totally different relations are identified. We are told that the effect does not depend on the cause any more than the cause upon the effect: they are simply the terms of a relation. Mr. Bosanquet expressly assures us that apart from temporal succession, which is "the natural differentia of causation," he "cannot see how the relation of conditioning differs from that of being conditioned."[14] It is needless to say that there is no room here for a principle of causality or for an argument to a first cause.

We have here only said just sufficient to shew in bare outline how this philosophy deals with those fundamental notions and principles with which we are concerned. But it will, we think, be felt that a system which leads to conclusions so much at variance with reality cannot be other than fallacious.

NOTES

{1} *Logic*, Bk. III., c. xxi., §I.

{2} *Three Essays on Religion*, p. 144.

{3} Choses et états ne sont que des vues prises par notre esprit sur le devenir. II n'y a pas de choses, il n'y a que des actions. . . . Que des choses nouvelles puissent s'ajouter aux choses qui existent, cela est absurde sans aucune doute, puisque la chose résulte d'une solidification operée par notre entendement, et qu'il n'y a jamais autres choses que l'entendement a constituées " (*L'Evolution Créatrice*, p. 270, 7th ed., 1911).

{4} Originellement nous ne pensons que pour agir. . . . Or pour agir, nous commençons par nous proposer un but: nous faisons un plan, puis nous passons au détail du mécanisme qui le réalisera. Cette dernière opération n'est possible, que si nous savons sur quoi nous pouvons compter. Il faut que nous ayons extrait de la nature des similitudes qui nous permettent d'anticiper sur l'avenir. Il faut donc que nous ayons fait application consciement ou inconsciement de la loi de causalité" (*ibid.*, p. 47).

{5} M. Bergson is of the same mind. After maintaining that the expence which constitutes our psychological life does not really consist of distinct states, but is a continuous flow, he proceeds: "Mais comme notre attention les a distingués et séparés artificiellement, elle est obligée de les réunir ensuite par un lien artificiel. Elle imagine ainsi un moi amorphe indifferent immuable, sur lequel défileraient ou s'enfileraient les stats psychologiques qu'elle a erigés en entités indépendentes. . . . Force lui est de supposer alors un fil non moins solide, qui retiendrait les perles ensemble. . . . Quant à la vie psychologique telle queue se d,roule sous les symboles qui la recouvrent, on s'aperccedil;oit sans peine que le temps en est l'étoffe même " (*op. cit.* pp. 3, 4).

{6} *Exam. of Hamilton* (2nd edit.), p. 394. Cf. also p. 321. "General concepts, therefore, we have, properly speaking, none; we have only complex ideas of objects in the concrete; but we are able to attend exclusively to certain parts of the concrete idea." M. Bergson is in full agreement: "Quand les images successives ne diffèrent pas trop les unes des autres, nous les considérons toutes comme l'accroissement ou Ia diminution d'une seule image moyenne, ou comme la déformation de cette image dans des sens différents. Et c'est à cette moyenne que nous pensons quand nous parlons de l'essence d'une chose " (op. cit. p. 327).

{7} It is doubtless the fact that certain modern logicians, *e.g.*, Mr. Bradley and Professor Bosanquet reject the traditional analysis of the judgment, and so explain its import as to deprive the copula of all significance. To anyone, however, who is not committed to their particular philosophical presuppositions, the mere fact that man, whatever be the language he employs, is forced to use the verb to be to enunciate his judgment, affords a sufficient refutation of their theory. On the the analysis of the proposition see the present writer's *Principles of Logic* (3rd edition), c. iii., § 2; c. ix., § 4.

{8} We are here, it must be observed, speaking of intelligibility in the abstract, not in relation to human faculties. A nature such as ours, which acquires its knowledge by sensible perception and by discursive reasoning from the data thus obtained, arrives with more facility at some measure of knowledge, however inadequate, regarding sensible things, than regarding the abstract notions of cause and substance. But viewed in themselves sensible things do not admit of knowledge in the same degree as do those realities into which sense-conditions do not enter. On the lack of intelligibility in matter, see below, c. x., § 3.

{9} We call attention to this point, since even such an able writer as Lord Balfour so entirely misunderstands the Aristotelian doctrine of substance, as to interpret it of the material substratum, which passes from one entity to another. See Theism and humanism, p. 231. Lord Haldane offers us an error of another kind, but no less fundamental. The conception of substance, he says, " has meaning in relation only to accidents or properties. To define God as substance would therefore be to define Him as something relative" (*Pathway to Reality*, I., p. 28). The definition which asserts that a substance exists in its own right and not as a mere determination, is so framed that the idea of a necessary relation to accidents is not included in it.

{10} Aristotle alleges this as the reason why substance constitutes the primary object of metaphysics. The science of being finds its proper object in that which is in the full sense of the term. Accidents only have being in so far as they are determinations of what truly is. *Metaph.*, IV., c. ii. S. Thomas Aq. *in Metaph.*, IV., lect. (cf. also *Metaph.* XII., c. i).

{11} In *Metaphysics.*, iv., c. iii., Aristotle points out that the principle of contradiction is the first of metaphysical principles, and that it is the most certain of all truths, inasmuch as it is impossible for any man to hold that the same thing can both be and at the same time not be. He is not unaware that some have questioned its validity, but remarks on this subject that 'what a man says he does not necessarily believe' ().

In ch. iv. he rejects the claim for a direct demonstration: "Some indeed demand that even this shall be demonstrated, but this they do through want of education: for not to know of what things one may demand demonstration, and of what one may not, argues simply want of education. For it is impossible that there should be demonstration of absolutely everything: there would be an infinite regress, so that there would still be no demonstration" (Oxford University Translation), It admits, he adds, of 'negative demonstration,' *i.e.*, by a *reductio ad absurdum*. Cf. also St. Thomas Aq. *in Metaph.* IV., lect. 6.

{12} The Aristotelian logicians counted as analytical propositions nor only those in which the predicate forms part of the subject-notion, but those in which it is connected with it by necessary relations. Thus a proposition such as, 'every triangle has its interior angles equal to two right angles,' is by them termed analytical. Kant's division labours under the grave disadvantage that it reckons together as members of one class mathematical judgments such as the above and empirical judgments such as 'Socrates is running.' Philosophically it is not merely valueless but misleading.

{13} Thus Prof. Bosanquet, arguing on behalf of his contention that the ultimate subject of all predication is Reality -- 'the one true individual' -- says: "It is to me quite astonishing that an appeal in favour of independent substances should be made on the ground of our experience of ourselves. What all great masters of life have felt this to reveal has been a seeking on the part of the self for its own reality, which carries it into something beyond." (*Logic*, 2nd edit., II., p. 255). This is to give us metaphor in place of argument. The self does not seek for its own reality (*esse extra causas*), but for its qualitative perfection -- a very different thing.

{14} *Op. cit.*, II., pp. 262, 264. Similarly, Lord Haldane an adherent of the same school of thought, informs us in his Gifford lectures that God "cannot stand to the world in the relation of Cause. For He must be independent of Space and Time, and we can attach no meaning to a Cause excepting as operative within Space and Time" (*Pathway to Reality*, I., p. 20). Later he enunciates the principle of causality as: "The principle that every change must be due to some event anterior to it in time and separate from it in space' (*ibid.* p. 214). As we have seen, the notion of cause has absolutely no connection with the notion of time or of space.

Chapter III. Proofs of God's Existence (i. Metaphysical proofs).

1. The Cosmological Argument (God as the First Cause).

2. The Argument from Contingency (God as Necessary Being).

3. The Argument from Motion (God as the Prime Mover).

4. The Henological Argument (God as the One and the Perfect).

We treat in this chapter of the proofs of God's existence derived from efficient causation, from contingent being, from motion, and from the multiplicity and limitation of finite things. Among the many arguments by which our conclusion may be established these have an indisputable right to priority. They are in the strictest sense *metaphysical* demonstrations. They rest directly on primary principles of reason, so that it is impossible to reject them without at the same time calling in question the validity of human reason itself. Furthermore, in them our appeal is not to the witness afforded by physical law, nor to the nature of man as a moral agent, but simply to the nature of finite being as such. Any finite substance whatever is capable of furnishing the data for the reasoning. Natural Theology, viewed as a science, is, as we saw in chap. i., § 2, a part of metaphysics. It follows that the demonstrations on which it rests. must be metaphysical. The physical and moral proofs to be considered in the two following chapters are subsidiary in character. Those with which we are here concerned form the essential basis of the whole treatise. It must not, however, be imagined that the physical and moral arguments, because subordinate to the metaphysical, are therefore devoid of importance. Natural Theology cannot afford to overlook them. It is manifest that, where the same conclusion can be reached by very different paths, some minds will be more influenced by one argument, others by another. And it is often the case that reasoning which can be variously illustrated from the field of experience is more efficacious to convince the understanding than such as is immediately based on first principles.

I. *The cosmological argument.* In this first proof we shew that it is necessary to admit the existence of a first cause of all finite things, and that this cause is intelligent and personal. We are here, be it noted, concerned with *efficient* causation, an efficient cause being that whose action makes the thing what it is. The point is of importance as the term 'first cause' may be employed in another sense. When, *e.g.*, the materialist says that no other first cause of the universe need be postulated save ether,[1] he is in fact asserting that a material cause is sufficient, and that we may dispense with efficient causes altogether. We must, further, by way of preliminary, call attention to another distinction, this time among efficient causes themselves, viz., that between a cause *in fieri* and a cause *in esse*. A cause *in fieri* is the cause of the thing's *becoming* what it is: a cause *in esse* is one whose action sustains the thing in *being*. If a smith forges a horse-shoe, he is only a cause *in fieri* of the shape given to the iron. That shape persists after his action has ceased. So, too, a builder is a cause *in fieri* of the house which he builds. In both these cases the substances employed act as causes *in esse* as regards the continued existence of the effect produced. Iron, in virtue of its natural rigidity, retains in being the shape which it has once received: and, similarly, the materials employed in building retain in being the order and arrangement which constitute them into a house. It may, perhaps, be asked whether in these examples we are dealing with efficient causation. Can iron be said to be an efficient cause of the conservation of the shape, as the smith is the efficient cause of its origination? Do the building materials really exercise an efficient causality in regard of the permanence of the structure? Reflection will shew that the question must be answered in the affirmative. Inasmuch as the persistence in being of the accident supposes a continuous exercise of conservation on the part of the substance, it stands to the latter in the relation of effect to cause.[2]

There are, however, certain effects which require the continued action of the same cause which first produced them. In this case we have a cause which is at one and the same time a cause *in fieri* and *in esse*. Thus not only does a candle produce light in a room in the first instance, but its continued presence is necessary if the illumination is to continue. If it is removed, the light forthwith ceases. Again, a liquid receives its shape from the vessel in which it is contained; but were the pressure of the containing sides withdrawn, it would not retain its form for an instant. Similarly, a certain measure of heat was needed that the icecap, which once covered northern Europe, should melt, and the soil become capable of supporting vegetation. But the same cause must remain in operation if the effect is to continue. If ever the temperature of these regions should sink to its former level, Europe would again become icebound. In all these cases we have causes *in fieri et in esse* .

It must not be imagined that we wish to maintain that the cause *in fieri* is altogether unconnected with the being of the thing which it produces. Becoming is the passage from potential to actual being. The cause which affects the transition -- the process of change from the potential to the actual -- is indirectly the cause of being also. But its direct effect is limited to the process: and the cause of the thing's continuance in being must be sought elsewhere.

In the present proof we are concerned only with causes *in esse*: the question of becoming -- of the origination of things -- does not come under consideration.

The preliminaries of our argument are, however, not yet complete. Besides the vital distinction which we have just noticed, two philosophical principles bearing on causation claim our attention.

It must be observed, first, that an effect properly so called demands the actual operation of the cause of which it is the effect, and ceases with the cessation of that action. The horse-shoe, it is true, continues to be, long after the smith has ceased to act; but this is simply because it is not the effect of his action as regards being, but only as regards beeoming. Had he stopped work during the process of becoming, that process would have ceased likewise. Precisely the same is true as regards the cause *in esse*. Were the substance iron to lose those natural qualities of rigidity, etc., which conserve the shape once given to it, that shape would disappear. This truth was expressed in the saying, *Cessante causa cessat effectus*[3]

The other point which calls for notice is this: that whatever demands a cause *in fieri* demands also a cause *in esse*. It is absolutely impossible that a thing, which requires a cause to bring it into being, should remain in existence independently of a cause *in esse* retaining it in being. At first sight this truth may present some difficulty. We are accustomed to regard substances as enjoying an absolutely independent existence in their own right and apart from any conserving force, so soon as the process of becoming is complete. When the bird develops from the egg, or the oaktree from the acorn, or when a human being, complete as a member of the species, though as yet far from full maturity, is produced by generation, we readily recognize that the transition from potentiality to actuality demanded a cause *in fieri*; but the idea that the completed entity needs to be sustained by a cause of its being strikes us as strange. Yet it may easily be shewn that so it is. For to what is the existence which the thing possesses due? This existence requires, we admit, a cause to bring it into being, and can only be explained by reference to this efficient cause. But viewed as a fully constituted and enduring substance, it does not depend upon the cause *in fieri*. That cause, as has been pointed out, only effects the process of becoming. Moreover, it is no longer operative: and what is no longer operative cannot be now exercising causality. But, most assuredly, the persisting existence calls for explanation no less than does the original passage into existence. The nature is not the sufficient reason of its own reality in the full sense of the term. That which even for a single instant is the sufficient reason of its own existence is self-existent. But a nature which is capable of self-existence needs not to wait for the action of an efficient cause in order to exist; it must have existed from all eternity. Probably most people imagine that, once constituted, the substance can somehow conserve itself unless brought into contact with hostile agencies which are too powerful for it. Yet to say that a thing conserves itself is to say that its persistence through each successive moment is to be attributed to its own existing nature. But the existing nature is the precise thing which we are seeking to explain. We are thus driven by sheer logical necessity to admit that the finite substances of this world, inasmuch as they require a cause *in fieri*, depend for their present actual existence upon a cause *in esse*, even though that cause is not an object of sensible experience.

We pointed out just now, in regard to the shape of the horse-shoe, that were the iron to lose the qualities which are the cause *in esse* of that shape, it would cease to be. Its permanence in being, as well as its origination, demand a cause: and the permanent existence being a present effect must be due to the operation of a present cause. What is true of the accident is no less true of the substance. The blacksmith and the horse, as well as the shape of the horse-shoe, need a cause *in esse*. The greater difficulty which we experience in grasping this truth where substances are concerned is due to the fact that sense does not assist us to realize the dependence of substances, as it does the dependence of accidents. But the verdict of reason is conclusive.

Nor can the materialist invalidate this argument by contending that the elementary constituents of which, *e.g.*, the man or the horse are formed, when once they have received the requisite collocation, will retain it much as the building materials secure the permanence of the house when once built.[4] Such an objection supposes that man is not an independent being at all: that he is merely an accidental arrangement of atoms: that he possesses no more true unity than does a house. This is in open contradiction with the facts. Man *acts* as a single whole. Whether there is question of thought or feeling or of external activity, it is the man as such, not the individual particle, who is the true agent. That which acts as a unit is a unit. Man, in other words, is a single *substance* -- a reality of a higher order than the material constituents which go to form his body. *A fortiori* the efficient cause which sustains him in being is of a higher order than they.

It appears, then, that all those things which experience makes known to us, substances and accidents alike, are dependent on an efficient cause without whose action they could not continue in being. Just as the building of a house would be at a standstill, if the builder ceased to work, so the builder himself would cease to exist if the cause *in esse* on which he depends were not to exert its causality. What that cause is does not here concern us. It is enough to note that we are speaking of an efficient cause, not a material or a formal cause, and with a cause which is actually *hic et nunc* operative in regard of its effect. We are now in a position to consider the argument by which the existence of God as the First Cause is established : --

We see all around us things, both substances and accidents, coming into being through the action of efficient causes. Reason assures us that what commences to exist through the operation of a cause is similarly dependent on a cause for the continuance of its existence: that it can never be the sufficient reason for its own being. The cause which is actually operative in regard of the effect in which we are interested, may itself depend for its existence on a higher cause, and this on another, and so on. Thus, in the example which we have already employed, the form of the horseshoe is the immediate effect of quantitative extension combined with certain qualitative properties such as rigidity, etc.: quantity and the properties in question are the effect of the substantial nature of iron: and, finally, the substance itself supposes an efficient cause. But it is impossible that a series of causes, of which each is dependent for its being on the cause above it, should be infinite. It follows that we must admit the existence of a first cause, itself uncaused and self-existent. This first cause can be none other than God: for (as will be shewn) a self-existent being is, of necessity, infinitely perfect, immaterial and intelligent.

It will be observed that the key-stone of the argument is to be found in the assertion that an infinite series of efficient causes *in esse*, each essentially dependent on the actual operation of the cause above it, is impossible. The truth of this is evident. If no member of the series possesses being otherwise than in virtue of the actual present operation of a higher cause, it follows that in default of a first cause there can be no secondary causes in existence.[5]

It is manifest that the reasoning which we have employed is quite independent of the vexed question whether an infinite series of causes *in fieri* operating successively is possible. We do not base our proof on the alleged impossibility of an infinite number. Our argument is not that the world must have been created, inasmuch as, had it existed from all eternity, we should be forced to admit an infinite succession of causes and effects. In the last two or three centuries, it is true, the proof has not infrequently been presented in that form: and we shall return to the point very shortly. Here it is sufficient to note that such is not the true scope of the traditional argument for the necessity of a first cause. Even though it should be true that reason cannot demonstrate that an infinite number of successive causes *in fieri* is repugnant, our proof that there must be a first cause actually operative in giving existence to all things which depend on efficient causation retains its full force.

An illustration may serve to make this point clearer. The movement of a clock's hands is caused immediately by wheels, of which there may be more or fewer, but which are ultimately dependent, as regards their action, on the spring. If there be no spring to start the motion not a wheel will move. Unless there be a cause which Originates the movement, none will ever take place.

Nothing is gained by supposing the wheels multiplied to infinity. An infinity of subordinate agents is as incapable of initiating action as is one alone. But the same reasoning will not prove that the number of times which the clock has been wound up is necessarily limited. It is a matter of indifference to the actual working of the clock whether this number be finite or infinite. The movement of the hands has no essential dependence on past windings. We may imagine, if we will, that these form an infinite series, and have gone on through infinite time. Whatever supposition we make regarding them, the causes on which the movement of the hands, as a present fact, essentially depends, must be finite in number, and the first of them -- that to which the others are subordinate -- must be an originating principle of activity.[6]

St. Thomas Aquinas supplies us with a similar example.[7] When a carpenter is at work, the series of efficient causes on which his work depends is necessarily limited. The final effect, *e.g.*, the fastening of a nail is caused by a hammer: the hammer is moved by his arm: and the motion of his arm is determined by the motor-impulses communicated from the nerve-centres of the brain. Unless the subordinate causes were limited in number, and were connected with a starting-point of motion, the hammer must remain inert: and the nail will never be driven in. If the series be supposed infinite, no work will ever take place. But if there is question of causes on which the work is not essentially dependent, we cannot draw the same conclusion. We may suppose the carpenter to have broken an infinite number of hammers, and as often to have replaced the broken tool by a fresh one. There is nothing in such a supposition which excludes the driving home of the nail.[8]

It should be noticed that from the fact that substances require a cause *in esse* we cannot forthwith draw the conclusion that their existence is immediately due to God's causal action. The argument throws no light on the question whether He is an immediate or a remote cause. So far as it is concerned the immediate cause of material substances might be a subordinate agency. Indeed, at one time it was held by a certain school of philosophers that each natural species postulated such a cause, the *causa totius speciei* -- a theory now almost forgotten. We merely argue that whether the series of causes be long or short, it must ultimately rest on the action of a First Cause.

It is sometimes urged that the proof which we have given fails to shew us that the cause is intelligent and personal: and that, this being so, it does not establish the existence of God at all.[9] To this it may be replied that, in the nature of the case, the consideration of the properties of the First Cause must follow after the proof that such a Cause exists: the two points cannot be taken together. Only when the existence of a self-existent being has been demonstrated, can we proceed to the discussion of His attributes. To shew that He is a Person possessed of intelligence and free-will is logically complementary to the demonstration which we have given. This complement, it is true, is sometimes taken for granted: since it is felt that the main issue has been decided, when the existence of a First Efficient Cause has been made good. Still, it is reasonable enough that some treatment of the point should be required here. There are two ways in which the conclusion may be reached. We may argue *a priori* from the essential attributes of a self-existent being: or we may adopt the *a posteriori* method, and reason from the perfections found in the effects to those which must belong to the cause. In this chapter we shall employ the latter proof. The former will be made good later, when we shall shew in a series of detailed arguments that to the self-existent being belong all those attributes which reason assigns to a Personal God. Here we shall merely indicate the general line of this demonstration.

It will appear that the self-existent nature must, as self-existent, be infinite, possessing or, rather, itself being the plenitude of all perfection. Both intelligence and volition must, therefore, be of the number of its attributes. Moreover, there cannot be such a thing as a nature apart from the individual subject (or subjects) to which it is referred: the ultimate subject alike of predication and action is the individual. It follows that in God there must be personality in the strict sense of the term. For by the term 'person' is signified nothing else than an individual endowed with intelligence and will.

Such in bare outline is the first of the two proofs which we have mentioned. Its various parts will receive full treatment in the course of the work. But in view of our statement that any finite thing would serve as a basis of our whole argument, it seemed desirable to indicate at least in general how, when once the existence of the First Cause is proved, it may be shewn on *a priori* grounds that that cause is none other than a personal God.

The *a posteriori* proof is of a less abstract character and presents little difficulty. It may be briefly stated as follows: An effect cannot contain any perfection which is not found in its cause: and among the effects produced by the First Cause are immaterial beings possessed of intelligence and free-will; it follows that the First Cause must Himself be an immaterial being, intelligent and free. The statement that every perfection belonging to the effect must be found in the cause is an immediate deduction from the principle of contradiction. A cause is that which makes its effect to be *what it is* -- which gives to it that actuality or perfection in respect of which it is termed its cause. If it does not itself possess that actuality, it cannot confer it on another. None can communicate what it has not got. To hold the contrary is to assert that nonentity can produce being: and this is equivalently to deny the principle of contradiction.

It is perfectly true that everyday experience seems to bring us across many cases in which a cause certainly does not contain the perfection which it appears to confer. An engine-driver turns a handle and thereby gives motion to the locomotive; but he has no motion himself save that which the locomotive may be giving him. And countless other examples occur to the mind. How then is it possible, it may be asked, to lay down the principle as a general truth? We will endeavour to deal shortly but sufficiently with the difficulty. In the first place it is necessary to distinguish the *causa per se* from the *causa per accidens*. A cause *per se* is a cause which contains in itself the explanation of the effect. Thus a seal is the cause *per se* of the impression which it leaves on the wax: a father is the cause *per se* of the human nature in his son. Such alone are causes properly so called: and our principle has reference alone to these. A cause *per accidens* is an agent whose action allows the true causes to exercise their causal efficacy. The engine driver is a cause *per accidens* in regard to the motion of the train. His action allows the steam to produce its due effect on the machine which he directs. It is clear that the cause *per accidens* is only termed a cause by analogy, and that it is very far from being a cause in the full and adequate sense of the word. It does not really make the thing to be what it is. Further, it is by no means necessary that the perfection which the cause *per se* communicates to its effect should exist in it alter the same manner in which it exists in the effect. The carpenter is the cause *per se* of the table which he makes: the sculptor the cause of the statue. In a true sense they possess the perfections which they confer. The sculptor could not transform the rude block of marble into a statue, unless the form to be communicated to it existed in his mind: and the same is true of the more modest achievement of the carpenter. In these cases the perfection conferred belongs to the physical order, whereas in the efficient cause it exists in the order of thought. But this latter mode of existence, it must be noted, is not the less perfect, but the more perfect of the two. It is spiritual, not material.

We have already referred to the fact that some writers give the argument for a First Cause in a very different form. The series of causes which they consider does not consist of such as are essentially dependent, one on another, for the actual exercise of causality, but of such as succeed each other in time. The universe in which we live, they say, is one in which all things owe their origin to a cause. The son takes his being from his father, the oak-tree from the acorn, etc., etc. However far back we go, the same must hold good. Now a series which stretches back to eternity is, they urge, an impossibility. The world certainly began, and, therefore, must have had a first cause to give it being. And this first cause must have been a Creator.

It is in this form that the argument is commonly criticized by its assailants. Yet the demonstration as given by the great Scholastic philosophers has nothing whatever to do with these successive causes *in fieri*, but is wholly concerned with causes on which the effect is actually *hic et nunc* dependent. Indeed, St. Thomas Aquinas in more than one of his works is insistent in affirming that we cannot prove by reason that the world has not existed from eternity. We can shew that it was created, he contends, by many lines of proof; but we cannot prove that God could not, had He so wished, have created it from all eternity. That He did not do so is known to us by revelation. It cannot be established by philosophical demonstration.[10]

It would carry us beyond our limits to enter at any length into the question of the abstract possibility of creation *ab aeterno*. But it may be said that, philosophically, there does not appear to be greater impossibility involved in the notion of an infinite series in the past, than in that of an infinite series in the future. All those who believe in the immortality of the soul admit the latter notion: holding, as they must, that the series of our intellectual acts will endure for all eternity. In both cases the series is *innumerable*. It lies outside the category of number; for number is multitude measurable in units (*multitudo mensurata per unum*). Such a series is a multitude, but a multitude to which no measure is applicable. Our difficulty in grasping the notion lies partly in our failure to distinguish the two ideas of multitude and number. It is objected that the future series, when computed from the present, never reaches infinity. Whatever point it may have reached in future time, the series is finite. But to this it may be replied that, similarly, whatever point we take in past time, the series between now and then is finite. Just as we cannot actually reach infinity in the future, so, no matter how far back we go in thought, we cannot indicate a point at which the series between that moment and the present is not a finite series. The two cases are absolutely parallel. If we admit that there will be an infinite series in one direction, it seems necessary to allow the abstract possibility of such a series in the other. The same difficulty is sometimes urged in another form. If the world had no beginning, it is said, it is hard to see how we could ever have reached the present point. We should be supposing that a journey *ex hypothesi* infinite had nevertheless arrived at its term. But to this it is replied that in judging of the possibility of traversing any distance, we must count from point to point. If the distance between the *terminus a quo* and the *terminus ad quem* is infinite, then, manifestly, starting from the former we shall never reach the latter. But if there is no *terminus a quo* no reason can be assigned why in an infinite progress we should not pass any given *terminus ad quem*. As soon as we fix on a *terminus a quo* in our series, no matter how remote, the distance between then and now is a limited distance, and can in consequence be traversed.[11] Notice must also be taken of an argument not infrequently found in recent Scholastic works, that an infinite series in the past is impossible, because it is a contradiction in terms to suppose that the infinite can be increased. That which can be increased is not infinite. Yet the series of causes *in fieri* is constantly receiving increments. This reasoning we believe to be quite unsound. It is, of course, impossible that the infinite can be increased, if by the infinite is signified the fulness of all being, the sum of all reality. But we are here using the term in a wholly different sense, viz., to signify a series of units which had no beginning. To say that such a series is incapable of increase is the merest assumption. The syllogism, in fact, has four terms, and would seem to be a pure sophism.[12]

Before bringing our treatment of the argument for a First Cause to a close, it will be well to consider a criticism of it from the empiricist standpoint. J. S. Mill has devoted a chapter in his *Three Essays on Religion* to the subject,[13] and there contends that it is valueless as a proof of God's existence. He maintains that the evidence at our disposal does not enable us to conclude to any other ultimate causes than matter and force.

"There is," he says, "in Nature a permanent element and a changeable: the changes are always the effect of previous changes: the permanent existences, so far as we know, are not effects at all. . . . That which in an object begins to exist is that in it which belongs to the changeable element in Nature: the outward form and the properties depending on mechanical or chemical combinations of its component parts. There is in every object another and a permanent element, viz., the specific elementary substance or substances of which it consists, and their inherent properties. These are not known to us as beginning to exist: within the range of human knowledge they had no beginning, consequently no cause." As regards the changes which take place in nature, these, he holds, are adequately accounted for by force. While in regard to the reasoning by which the existence of the human soul is made the basis of argument for an intelligent and personal Cause, he says: "The notion seems to be that no causes can give rise to products of a more precious and elevated kind than themselves. But this is at variance with the analogies of Nature. How vastly nobler and more precious, for instance, are the higher vegetables and animals than the soil and manure out of which and by the properties of which they are raised up." In view of what has already been said in this section, little need be added to shew that these criticisms are devoid of philosophical value, and fail to touch the argument. We have already adverted to the absurdity of regarding the specific types of nature as mere combinations of chemical elements without unity of their own. An animal is more than the simple aggregate of its material constituents. There is in it a principle of unity, the source of its characteristic attributes, constituting it as a single substance, a special type of perfection. It is for the philosopher to provide some explanation of these substantial perfections which are the true units of the natural order. They must, as we have maintained, be referred to the operation of an efficient cause. Otherwise their existence is inexplicable.

It is assuredly no explanation whatever to say, as does Mill, that they are adequately accounted for by their material constituents as affected by 'force' -- a notion which he does not attempt to explain, but which is apparently understood as a principle of local motion operating blindly, and directed to no particular end. Moreover, it is to be observed that Mill does not dispense with the notion of a self-existent first cause. He merely asserts that matter will serve the purpose, whereas, as we have contended above, it may be demonstrated *a priori* that self-existent being is, as such, infinite in perfection, immaterial and intelligent. Mill does not deal with this difficulty at all. Had he been aware of it, he could hardly have assumed without proof the possibility of self-existent matter. He does, however, touch upon the *a posteriori* argument from the existence of the human soul, saying that he regards it as invalid, since experience seems to shew that effects can be more perfect than their causes. We have already pointed out that this is tantamount to saying that being can spring out of nonentity: and that in the numerous cases in which the effect appears at first sight to surpass the cause, this is only because the cause which we are contemplating is either a partial cause or a mere *causa per accidens*. It is utterly impossible that an effect can ever surpass its total cause. Thus, to employ Mill's own illustration, the soil and manure are not the total cause of the plants and animals into which their constituent elements may eventually enter. The perfection of the total effect is attributable in a far higher degree to the efficient than to the material cause.

It is further to be observed that, as Mill was considering the argument in the form in which it regards, not causes *in esse*, but successive causes *in fieri*, it was imperative that he should face the question whether an infinite series of changes succeeding each other in time, such as is involved in his supposition of self-existent matter and force, is or is not a contradiction in terms. Yet not a single word is said on this essential point. He had not even taken the trouble to make himself acquainted with the argument which he undertook to refute.

2. *The argument Irom contingency.* The argument from contingency is closely related to that from efficient causation. It is indeed more accurately described as the same proof viewed under a new aspect and treated in a

different manner than as an independent demonstration. Yet among Scholastic writers the custom has grown up of presenting the two forms of the argument separately. And as the conceptions employed are not the same, this course has much to recommend it. By a contingent being is signified one which need not exist. It may be, but it also may not be: existence is in no sense one of its essential predicates. It stands in direct opposition to necessary being -- being, that is, which is incapable of not existing. Actual existence belongs to the nature of necessary being, just as to be three-sided belongs to the nature of a triangle. It is one of its essential attributes. Such a being must be either self-existent, or (if the supposition be admitted for a moment) some self-existent being must be determined by nature to its production. With this brief explanation of terms we may state the proof as follows: --

Experience shews us that contingent beings exist. We see things come into existence and pass out of it. Animals and plants have their period of life and then die. Inanimate substances enter into composition, forming a new substance with properties different from those of its constituents: and after a time the compound is again resolved into its original elements. Now the existence of contingent beings involves the existence of necessary being, and is inexplicable without it. Therefore a necessary being exists: and this necessary being can be none other than a personal God.

Such in briefest outline is the argument. The value of the conclusion depends, it is evident, on the statement that the existence of contingent being involves that of necessary being. If this can be established the proof holds good. There is no occasion for us to shew that necessary being can only be realized in a personal God: for here the same reasoning may be employed which we used to complete the cosmological argument.

Since contingent being may either exist or not exist, it is evident that it does not account for its own existence. It is not the sufficient reason for that existence. Were it so, it would be impossible for it not to exist: in other words, it would not be contingent. Consequently we must seek an explanation for it elsewhere: some sufficient reason for it there must needs be. If a thing be not self-existent, its existence must be due to a cause external to itself. The conclusion is the same, even if we suppose a contingent being to have existed from all eternity. Once admit that a thing is capable of non-existence, and it follows of necessity that it owes its existence to something else: and this in the last resort must be necessary being.[14]

It may, perhaps, be objected that even a materialist or a pantheist would go as far with us as this, and would be prepared to own the existence of necessary being: that the real question at issue is what that necessary being is. The materialist will urge that, though the individual substances are contingent, yet the whole vast series of such substances, taken in its entirety, should be regarded as necessary: or he will contend that the material substratum, which is common to all, is the necessary being whose existence has been established. The pantheist will maintain that the necessary being is in fact the Absolute, of which contingent beings are but manifestations: and that this is very different from a personal God. We shall deal with each of these points.

It may be easily shewn that no series of contingent beings, even were it infinite as regards time or spatial extension, could ever constitute a necessary being. If each individual member of a collective whole is such that it cannot account for its own existence, the same must be said of the whole collection, no matter how immense it may be. Inasmuch as it does not contain within itself any sufficient reason for its existence, it cannot be self-existent. To put the matter in a somewhat more technical form: contingency is an attribute belonging to the essential nature of the object of which it is affirmed: and such attributes are predicable, not merely of individuals, but of the whole body. Since individual men are rational in virtue of their essential nature, it follows that rationality is rightly predicated of a collective body of men. It has been aptly said that we might as well say that, although one idiot is not reasonable, a million idiots would suffice to form a reasonable being, as to maintain that an infinite number of contingent substances would constitute necessary being. Or to employ another illustration: those who contend that while the existence of each substance in a collection is contingent, the collection as a whole may be necessary, are asking us to believe that although each link in a suspended chain is prevented from falling simply because it is attached to the one above it, yet if only the chain be long enough, it will, taken as a whole, need no support, but will hang loose in the air suspended from nothing. It is, of course, true that there are some attributes which, though they are predicated of the several parts, cannot be affirmed of the whole. But these are those which relate to the thing in its quantitative aspect. We cannot conclude, because A, B and C, taken separately, each weigh an ounce, that therefore the three together will weigh the same amount. It is needless to say that contingency has no connection with quantity.

Can it be maintained that matter, understanding that term in the sense of the material substratum common to natural substances, is necessary being? We have seen that Mill entertained this idea. And we imagine that many materialists take the same view. Yet such a supposition involves us in numerous impossibilities. Matter, it is plain, is capable of receiving perfections which are not among its essential attributes. It becomes man: or gold: or a flower: and in each of these substances is endowed with distinctive properties. They are not essential to it; for what is essential to a nature is inseparable from it: the nature is never found without it. Whence then do they come? We answer that since they are not essential, there is no avoiding the conclusion that they are due to the operation of an external cause. We are here brought across a metaphysical principle of primary importance, viz., that whenever two things essentially distinct the one from the other are found in union, this must be due to the operation of an efficient cause other than the things themselves.[15] A little reflection will shew that this is a necessary and self-evident truth. To affirm the opposite would be to assert that something could take place without a sufficient reason. If A and B, things essentially distinct, are found united, the reason cannot be found in A. For A is the sufficient reason only for itself and its own essential attributes. For the same reason it cannot be found in B. No cause, for instance, is needed to explain why a triangle should have three angles. The attribute of having three angles results immediately from its essence as a plane figure bounded by three straight lines. If it had not three angles, it would both be and not be a triangle. But if there is question of a wooden triangle, we have a right to say that a cause is requisite to explain this union. Wood is not triangular *per se*: nor is a triangle *per se* wooden. The composition of diverse elements of necessity supposes the operation of an efficient cause other than the elements themselves. Now no agent can exist capable of conferring perfections upon necessary being. For that agent, since it is other than necessary being, must be a contingent being. But whatever contingent beings possess they owe in the last resort to necessary being. They have nothing which is not already found in it: they can add nothing to it. It follows that matter, the common substratum, which is a mere recipient for perfections, is not necessary being.

It may perhaps be urged that the reasoning just employed is open to a serious objection: since, granted the existence of a plurality of necessary beings, there does not appear to be the same difficulty in the hypothesis that one such being may receive perfections from another. This objection will receive its full answer, when in a later chapter we establish the essential uniqueness of necessary being, shewing that in the very nature of things it can be but one. Here it must be sufficient to point out that no metaphysician of real weight regards the supposition of a plurality of necessary beings as other than a paradox. All have recognized that the self-existent can be one only.

Equally invalid is the pantheist contention that contingent beings are merely modes of the one and all-inclusive Absolute: that they are manifestations of necessary being, and not entities possessed of a distinct though dependent existence. Here we may make appeal to the argument which we have just employed in regard of material substances. The contingent beings of experience are constantly undergoing changes and acquiring new perfections. This alone establishes that they are not modes of necessary being. A sheer contradiction is involved in the supposition that an agent exists, which can confer perfections on necessary being. Yet the acquisition of a perfection apart from an agent is, as we have seen, a metaphysical impossibility. We may, too, reach the same conclusion by another path. We have stated in the argument to the First Cause that it might be proved that the self-existent being -- and this concept includes necessary being as well as the First Cause -- is infinite in perfection. From this, as we shall also shew, it follows that He is immutable. But that which is immutable cannot be identical with the transitory contingent beings of experience.

3. *The argument from motion.*[16] As the cosmological argument is founded on finite substances statically regarded, so the argument from motion is based on them in their dynamical aspect. Of the five metaphysical proofs which St. Thomas gives, he assigns to this the first place, as being the simplest and easiest to grasp. Latterly it has suffered an eclipse owing to a belief that it depends upon a principle which physical science has shewn to be untenable. As a matter of fact, the prejudice against it is due, as we shall see, not to any of the results which physical science has achieved in recent times, but to an erroneous philosophy of motion, introduced by Descartes, which has widely affected current modes of thought. A careful consideration of the proof will shew its apodictic character. It is securely based on those fundamental first principles, which no physical discoveries can invalidate.

The term 'motion,' as here used, is not, it should be noted, restricted in its significance to local motion. This is but one of several distinct kinds of motion. By motion (**kinêsis**) is signified the process by which a potency is realized. It may be defined as the energetic and therefore incomplete actualization of a potency belonging to some form of being. The end towards which the process tends may be a new quality: or an increased quantity: or, again, a specific nature as is the case in the development of a seed or an embryo. Among the various kinds of motion which experience makes known to us local movement holds an important place. By reason of its universality it forces itself more than any other upon our attention: for physical change of every kind involves local movement at least in the constituent parts of the thing changed. Viewed, however, precisely in its aspect as change, it is similar to those other kinds of motion which we have just mentioned. It is a process by which a natural potency is realized. *To be in a given place* is the actualization of a natural potency of a material body -- an actualization requisite for its complete determination. It is, it is true, an extrinsic, not an intrinsic determination; but one which is none the less essentially requisite if the substance is to take place as an integral unit in nature. Certain special difficulties connected with this form of change we reserve for treatment in a separate note.

Before proceeding to our proof we must state with some degree of philosophical accuracy what motion is.

Motion is not a form of being. It is something very different, namely, the transition from one form of being to another. This is well illustrated in the case of a chemical compound. When, *e.g.*, hydrogen and oxygen are brought together, and combine as water, the process of change begins and ends with definite forms of being. But in none of the intermediate stages have we a natural entity capable of subsistence. Sometimes it is true the process of actualization may be arrested, as in the case of a fertilized cell. But the result is not a natural entity -- a complete unit in the order of nature: it is a frustrated beginning of such a unit -- not a *being* properly so called, but a *might-have-been*. Aristotle's insight was too sure for him to reckon motion as a mode of being. It is not found among the nine categories into which he distributed the accidental perfections of substance. For it is *becoming*, not being -- *fieri* not *esse*.

Motion possesses certain special characteristics which should be most carefully observed. First, it is always *on the road to* realization. So long as the process endures the potency is still passing into act: it is not completely actualized. Strange as it may appear, motion, as such, never attains full actualization: for when it has reached its term, it has, as motion, already ceased to be.[17] Secondly, it is divisible *in infinitum*. Each part, however minute, being just as truly motion as is the whole. Yet these parts are all different one from another: and, what is more, they are not interchangeable. They occur in a definite order, all the previous portions being neeessary in any given process of change that the one next in order may take place.[18]

These facts regarding motion bring us to a conclusion of the highest importance. It is this. All motion demands the continuous operation of a cause *in fieri* producing it: without such an influx of causality motion is impossible. At every stage of a movement, and at every fraction of every stage, there is the emergence of something new. There is the continuous passage from being potentially in movement to being actually in movement: and, as we have just noted, each part of a movement differs from every other part, the previous portions being a necessary condition to the production of the later ones. This continuous production of new reality postulates a sufficient reason: and this can only be the actual and constant operation of an efficient cause. In other words motion is not a stable entity which can be produced once and for all, and then only needs to be conserved in being by a cause *in esse*. It demands a cause *in fieri* -- a cause continuously productive of a new effect. This truth was expressed by the Schoolmen in the saying, *Quidquid movetur ab alio movetur*, 'Whatever is in motion is being moved by something other than itself.' The immediate agent of motion need not indeed be external to the substance in which the motion takes place; but it must at least be external to the part which is the immediate subject of change. If a thing is destitute of a particular form of being, it cannot be itself the source from which it receives the actualizing process by which that form of being is attained. *Nemo dat quod non habet.*[19]

The principle we have enunciated (*Quidquid movetur ab alio movetur*) does not of course deny the essential difference between those recipients of motion which possess active powers of their own and those which are devoid of any such endowment. It is plain that the 'motion' of a growing tree is very different from that which the hand communicates to the pen which it is guiding. In the former case the subject of motion receives from the superior agent the ultimate complement of active powers really internal to it, in default of which these powers would remain inert. In the latter case the subject acts instrumentally, *i.e.*, its motion is not determined by its own powers but by an efficient cause.

We are now in a position to propose our argument:

The existence of motion in the world is undeniable. It meets us on every side. Now it is a certain and evident truth that whatever is in motion is being actually moved by an agent other than itself. The effect now coming into being demands the actual and present efficiency of a cause.

If this efficiency requires motion in the agent itself, the principle which we have invoked compels us to admit that this change in its turn must be due to the actual efficiency of another agent, and so on. But however many of these antecedent agents we suppose, we must of necessity come to a first of the series -- an agent which has the power to produce motion without any change taking place in itself -- *a primus motor immobilis*.

Were there no prime mover, but only a series of secondary agents, there could be no motion. For a secondary agent cannot of itself pass from potency to act. Its activity from moment to moment is due to the influx of a higher cause. If then the higher causes are themselves one and all secondary, and there be no prime mover, the sufficient reason for its own action, no motion will ever arise. To use an illustration already employed, to maintain that a series of secondary agents can produce motion without the influx of a prime mover is comparable to saying that no spring is needed to account for the movement of a clock's hands: that a series of wheels, if only it be long enough, affords an adequate explanation.

Yet here there is a difficulty to be met. It is maintained by some that the notion of an immutable mover, a cause which produces its effects without undergoing any change in so doing is self-contradictory: that causation necessarily involves a transition in the agent. The production of an effect, it is urged, is an activity: and an activity implies a change -- the actualization of potency. The objection was, in fact, raised by Kant. He reckons it as one of the antinomies of the human reason that, on the one hand, it leads us to refer finite existences to an Infinite Cause, and, on the other, compels us to admit that every change supposes a previous change in endless regress so as to exclude the supposition of ever arriving at an Infinite First Cause.[20] Now it is, of course, true that the causes of which we have experience, can only produce an effect in virtue of a change realized in themselves. But so far is this from being involved in the essential notion of causality, that it is due to the fact that finite agents are not causes in the full sense of the word. They have the potency of becoming causes, but that potency is incompletely actualized. An *internal* complement is needed before they are fully constituted in the actuality which will render them the sufficient reason of a given effect. But where the Infinite Being is concerned this is not so. Inasmuch as He is infinite, there can be no question of His reception of any complement to His actuality. He possesses in Himself the full actuality requisite for causal efficiency from all eternity. Moreover, as He is not a necessary agent but endowed with freedom, His effects proceed from Him at such time as He has from eternity determined. The full discussion of this point must wait for a later chapter (chap. xiv., § 3) since it presupposes the treatment of the Divine infinitude, of the Divine free-will, and of creation. But what we have here said will suffice to shew that the notion of the Unmoved Mover, the changeless cause -- a concept which the sheer necessity of reason compels us to accept -- involves no contradiction, but is verified in the Infinite Being, God.

Note on local motion. (a) *The Cartesian philosophy of motion.* We have contended in the previous paragraphs that local motion, viewed philosophically, is, like other forms of change, a transition by which the object moved acquires the actualization of a natural potency. A body, in order to be an integral part of nature, must be *in some place*. But it has always the potency of being in another place than this: in other words, it may be moved to a new place. When this is done, it acquires a new actuality: and in so doing loses the determination which it now possesses, inasmuch as the same potency cannot be simultaneously actualized in different ways. Thus just as the change by which the fertilized cell becomes the fully developed animal is a process of *fieri* resulting in a new *substantial esse*, so too local motion is no less truly a *fieri* resulting in a new *accidental esse*.

That this, the Aristotelian account of local motion, is not the point of view commonly adopted in modern physics will be patent to all. That view is derived from Descartes -- a man whose genius was most conspicuous in his achievements as a mathematician, and who treats the subject exclusively from the mathematical point of view. Descartes denied the existence of any but local motion, believing that all change might be sufficiently explained by it.[21] For a mathematician other kinds of motion have in fact little interest. He teaches that when God created the universe, He established in it a dertain amount of movement: that this movement is still conserved in it by Him, passing from body to body, but remaining identically the same.[22] Moreover he maintains that from the immutability of God we can conclude that if motion is once communicated to a body, it will remain in it unless some external force intervenes to stay it.[23] Hence, though he styles motion a mode of corporeal substance, it is clear that in his system they are distinct realities, motion being something new added to the fully constituted substance. As a metaphysical theory these views are quite untenable. (1) Motion is not a new reality added to a fully actualized entity. It is, in all its forms, in this no less than in the others, a passage to complete actualization. The mere fact of change shews that complete determination is not yet obtained. (2) Further, he considers motion, not as does the metaphysician, in regard to *being*, but in regard to *rest*, this being the point of view most suitable for the mathematician. For his purpose the *terminus a quo* and the *terminus ad quem* are both regarded under this aspect. The state of rest, however, of the *terminus a quo* is manifestly inferior to the process of change: since a mere potency is inferior to that potency as already on the road to actualization. Hence it is not surprising that he should treat motion as something additional to the constituted substance. The metaphysician, on the other hand, necessarily treats motion in its relation to being, since metaphysics is the science of being. And for this very reason it is impossible for him to restrict his consideration of it to a single kind of motion. His theory must be valid for all species, for the motion by which an acorn becomes an oak, no less than for the passage of a stone through the air. And, viewed in relation to being, motion is essentially the transition from potency to act, the *terminus ad quem* being the perfected act. (3) Again, the mathematician may for practical purposes regard motion as a *state*. Philosophically the concepts of movement and of a state are mutually exclusive. A state is a condition of stable being, while motion is a condition involving continuous transition. (4) Once more, the idea of motion as a thing which passes from body to body is a philosophical absurdity. One moving body can start movement in another; but movement is not an entity which can travel from subject to subject. Hence although the Cartesian views may be perfectly compatible with the calculations of physicists, if introduced into metaphysics, they are prolific of the gravest errors. We have judged it necessary to touch upon them here, since they still enter largely into philosophical thought. Yet they are wholly incompatible with the metaphysical principles which we are maintaining: and unless the mind is disabused of them, it is impossible for it to appreciate the cogency of the present proof.[24]

(b) *The principle 'Quidquid movetur, etc.,' and Newton's first law.* The difficulties bequeathed to us by the Cartesian philosophy are not the only ones in our path. The assertion that motion depends on the continuous operation of an efficient cause other than the actual subject of motion, seems at first sight to conflict with Newton's first law. This assures us that a body in a state of motion persists in that state unless it is subjected to the action of some external force. Is not this equivalent to saying that no agency is needed for the continuance of a motion once originated -- that a body once started will go on *of itself?* Moreover there are certain facts of experience which appear to lend colour to this view. When a billiard-ball is travelling over the table, or a stone has been flung through the air, where is there any external agency at work? Is not the force initially communicated the adequate explanation of the subsequent movement? Do we not render a full account both of the motion of the ball and its eventual rest, by saying that in virtue of the blow given by the cue it would go on indefinitely, were it not gradually stopped by the friction of the table and the resistance of the atmosphere.

Reflection will, however, shew us that, though appearances seem unfavourable to our contention, there is no escape from the conclusion that the motion of the ball involves the continued application of an external force: that apart from the operation of such an agency we are involved in a series of impossibilities. For if the efficient cause of the motion is not external, two hypotheses are possible. The sufficient cause of the effect is either to be found in the moving body itself, or in its past motion. We shall examine both alternatives: and it will appear that both must be rejected.

We take, first, the explanation which would attribute the effect to the past motion of the body. We are dealing, it must be remembered, with actual motion. For this actual effect we require an actually operative cause. The past motion of the body has ceased to exist. What is no longer existing cannot be actually operative. The past motion was needed that the body might reach the spot where it now is; but in this its office ,was exhausted. It has now ceased to be, and is totally incapable of producing the new effect which is at each successive instant coming into being.

If the other alternative be adopted, the result is no more satisfactory. Here, when it is said that the ball accounts for its own movement, it cannot be meant that the reason why it moves is that it is in motion. This is simply to say that it moves because it does move -- an assertion which will not carry us far. The statement, however, may be taken in another sense. It has been held by a certain number of recent Scholastic writers that when movement is initiated, the cause which puts the body in motion communicates to it a new quality, which, so long as it endures is productive of local movement. This quality they term *impetus* or *impulsus*: and the degree in which it is communicated is, it is held, in proportion to the efficiency of the originating cause. When the *impetus* is exhausted the motion ceases. This theory is defended among others by Fr. T. Pesch, S.J., and Fr. Garrigou-Lagrange, O.P. Difficulties of a grave character, however, may be urged against it: (1) Unless we are prepared to deny all validity to the first law of motion, we must admit that if a body is once set in motion, this movement would never cease, were it not for the action of impeding forces: as regards duration it would be infinite. Yet a corporeal quality which is a principle of movement without end appears to involve a sheer contradiction. An accident is necessarily proportioned to the substance which it qualifies and in which it inheres. But according to this hypothesis, a finite substance is the subject of a quality, which in one respect, at least, is infinite. (2) Further, even if this be supposed possible, another difficulty presents itself. The inherent *impetus* must constantly produce new effects: for, as we have pointed out, the parts of any given motion differ one from another, occurring, as they do, in a definite order, the previous stages being prerequisites to the production of each subsequent one. But it is manifest that the same quality cannot be continuously modifying its efficiency unless it is undergoing change itself. We have, in fact, merely shifted the difficulty from the motion to the alleged quality which produces it. We must provide an explanation for the change in the quality. (3) Again: the *impetus*, if it exist, is actually operative, and in consequence not indeterminate but fully determined. Yet we are required to regard this fully determined quality as being a principle of motion which is indifferently of any velocity and of any direction. According to the laws of motion a body in constrained motion will leave its path and fly off at a tangent at whatever point of its course the constraint is removed. Now there is no need that the constraint should be due to a single force acting from one centre. Successive forces may have been brought to bear upon the body from widely different quarters. But, if we accept the theory in question, it is reserved for the last of all to determine the velocity and the direction of the effects of every one. Such a result seems wholly irreconcilable with reason.

We are driven then to the conclusion that all motion requires the continuous action of an external force to explain its persistence: and that without such agency the motion must cease. Reason compels us to admit that Aristotle and his Scholastic disciples were not deceived when they laid down the principle that whatever is in motion is being moved by something other than itself -- *Quidquid movetur ab alio movetur.* Nor does this involve any contradiction with Newton's first law of motion. Newton, indeed, says that a body in motion will continue to move uniformly in a straight line, unless acted upon by external forces. But we need not understand him to deny that the uniform movement itself is due to an agency acting *ab extra*; but merely that it is produced by an agency belonging to that category of agents which he denominates "external forces." We shall point out in a moment how entirely the agency, for which we are contending, differs from these forces whose action in each case is of necessity confined to a particular direction and velocity.

There is, however, a point which calls for previous consideration. The doctrine that every change in the direction or velocity of motion is due to an external force takes it for granted that whenever a plurality of forces is brought to bear upon a moving body, their effects will coalesce into a single motion. This, of course, is the case, as experience abundantly shews. But the fact is one involving important deductions. For it is philosophically certain that where many agents combine in the accomplishment of a work which has a true unity of its own, the work must be attributed to a single principal agent who has employed the more immediate agents instrumentally -- unless, indeed, the unity be a mere matter of chance. The agents would not be at one in the production of the result, were they not subordinate to a single directive cause.[25] Thus when the united labours of bricklayers, carpenters, and masons, etc., etc., result in a house -- an effect which, though not *unum natura*, is *unum ordine* -- we know from the unity of the work produced that their operative action was directed by a cause of a higher order. They are instruments, not prime agents. The prime agent, the principle of unity -- in this case the architect -- elevates the work of the immediate contributors to a higher plane, enabling them to produce something, which, without his action, was altogether beyond their powers. Now, when the effects of various moving forces combine in a single local motion, the unity is no matter of chance. Otherwise it would not occur in every such case. It is characteristic of casual results that they only happen in a very small minority of instances. The conclusion is inevitable that the agent which brings about the combination of the different effects, employs the contributory forces instrumentally. In other words, *the phenomena of local motion reveal the existence of two orders of movers, Newton's external forces being the lower of the two.*

The objective reality expressed by Newton's first law is, in fact, this equivalent conservation of every change, whether in the direction or the velocity of a movement, throughout all its subsequent parts. The law, as it stands, is, of course, incapable of experimental verification. No material body can be absolutely withdrawn from the action of all other forces except that which originated the movement. We can remove certain disturbing factors; but so long as our experiments are performed in this concrete world, it is idle to imagine that we can realize the conditions supposed in the terms of the law. Hence some writers have declared

Newton's law to be an hypothesis suggested by the facts. It seems to us to be more accurately described as a logical abstraction based on a wide induction. For an induction of immense range assures us of the equivalent conservation of all the changes to which a movement may be subjected. And this, as we have said, is the objective fact to which the law gives expression. It follows that the first law as manifested in external phenomena provides the most cogent evidence for the truth of our thesis. We must either admit the existence of a higher mover or declare that the oneness of a work affords no proof that it is due to one agent: in other words, that multiplicity can be the source of unity.

We are now in a position to draw some conclusions as to the nature of this mover: though these will be of an extremely general character. It is manifestly a force which is not confined to any particularity of direction or velocity, but is of an altogether superior order to the mechanical forces which are the immediate agents of motion. These are instrumental in its regard. And as such, it must he carefully noted, they are not to be reckoned as mere occasional causes exerting no real efficacy of their own on the effect. The resulting motion is really produced by them: for in every case of instrumental causality the total effect is in the truest sense the work of the instrument as well as of the principal cause. The painting on the canvas proceeds in its totality alike from the directing mind of the artist and from the brush with its pigments. Although the finished work is primarily due to the intelligent principal cause, it is none the less produced in every detail by the instrument which he employs. Both causes are indispensable: for each has its own proper efficacy. The agency of both is requisite for the total result. The activity proper to the mechanical agents of motion is to determine the velocity and direction of the movement: and the total effect consists entirely of their contributions. But their efficiency is confined to the period of time and extent of space in which they are actually operative.

Just as they themselves could never have passed from potency to act save through the agency of a higher mover, so the same agency is required for the actualization of the motion which they produced. As the writer, to whom I have acknowledged my obligations at the commencement of this proof, has well said: "The agency required is of a higher and more universal order than that to which mechanical forces belong. It transcends the possibility of measurement in terms of time and space. It is continuously at work in moving bodies, reducing or tending to reduce the manifold to unity, the variable to uniformity, and that which is liable to fail to indefectibility: in one word, reducing potentiality to act, and so establishing and crowning the results achieved by the agency of material things" (*Month*, CVIII. 434).

And here we may notice another point confirmatory, at least, of what has been said. Motion in a straight line and of uniform velocity is not the only kind of uniform motion. This is uniform motion in one dimension. Motion which is of two or of three dimensions may also be uniform. Thus we have uniform motion of two dimensions when the movement of a body round a point is such that equal areas are swept by the *radius vector* in equal times. No one questions that uniform motion of two dimensions demands an external agency for its realization. It seems difficult to explain why, if a regulating cause is requisite in the one case, it is not equally necessary in the other. Again: we are familiar with the phenomenon of uniform acceleration with regard to time. The motion of a falling body increases in arithmetical progression. Here, too, we postulate an external cause, without which the acceleration is declared to be inexplicable. But it may be questioned whether uniformity of velocity is really a whit more intelligible apart from the efficiency of an agent actually present than is uniformity of acceleration.[26]

When it has once been shewn that local motion is incomprehensible apart from actual efficiency exerted by an external cause, the chief difficulty in the way of our proof is removed. Common facts of everyday experience, such as the continued flight of a stone after it has left the hand, seemed incompatible with the principle *Quidquid movetur at alio movetur*, however weighty the metaphysical reasons which were urged on its behalf. We have seen that this is not so: and the full force of the reasoning must be admitted. Does the agent whose existence we have established require to be moved from potency to act? If so, we must suppose a higher cause to effect this. But the series of such agents must, as we saw, be limited. We are driven back upon a first agent, whose activity is uncaused -- the *primus motor immobilis*.

4. *The henological argument.* The henological argument is so called because in it we reason from multiplicity to unity (**hen**, *unum*): from goodness, truth, reality in the various forms in which experience makes them known to us, to a Being who is the Good, the True, the Real. Its scope is to shew that the limited and partial manifestations of these perfections compel us to admit the existence of a Being in whom they find their complete realization: that multiplicity and imperfection are wholly inexplicable apart from unity and perfection: and finally that the One and Perfect is, in fact, a Personal God.

For the understanding of the argument it is essential first to call attention to certain special characteristics of the perfections with which we are here concerned, viz., reality, goodness, truth, unity. Other attributes than these denote some particular generic or specific perfection within one of the ten categories: they express either the substantial nature of the subject, or some quantity, quality or relation, etc., etc., belonging to it. But the perfections of which we are speaking are applied in all the categories equally: nor is the application confined to any special part, be it genus or *differentia* of the nature. There is no nature and no part of any nature of which they may not be predicated. The animality and the rationality of Socrates are alike *real*: so too are his qualities, his quantity, etc., etc. In the same way *goodness* may be predicated of all these. Manhood is a good thing: so is strength: so too the size due to a human body: so also the relation of paternity. Again, one and all these things are capable of becoming the object of intellectual knowledge. They are therefore *true*. This peculiarity has, in the Scholastic philosophy, given to these attributes the name of *transcendentals*, inasmuch as they transcend the limits which restrict all other perfections to one or other of the great divisions of being. This terminology, which we shall employ throughout this work, should be carefully noted. For Kant gave to the word transcendental a new sense, entirely unconnected with its traditional signification: and since his time his use of the word has been adopted by all philosophical writers except those who adhere to the Scholastic system.

The transcendental character of these attributes carries with it two very important consequences. The first of these is that they do not connote any limitation or imperfection. An attribute, which of its essential nature is restricted to a particular mode of being, be it substance, or quality, or quantity, inevitably involves imperfection, because in virtue of this restriction it is essentially finite.[27] But when an attribute does not imply any one of the divisions of being, but transcends the limits which they impose, there is no reason why such a perfection should not be found in the Infinite Being Himself -- why it should not be predicable of God as well as of man. The second consequence is closely connected with the first. It is that these terms are *analogous* and not univocal. A generic or specific attribute is always univocal. It has the same signification in all the subjects of which it is predicated: the notion which it expresses is always identically the same. Thus the term 'animal ' denotes precisely the same characteristics, whether it is affirmed of a man or of an insect. So far as this term is applied to them, the differences of the two classes, however fundamental, do not come under consideration. Similarly 'spatial extension' has always the same meaning, the notion of extension as such prescinding from the question whether the extension be of one or two or three dimensions. It is otherwise as regards analogous terms. The notions which these signify are not identically, but proportionally (**kat' analogian**)the same. The goodness of a man is not identical with the goodness of a horse, nor can the two kinds of goodness be expressed by a concept which remains the same as applied to each of them. Yet there is a proportionate resemblance in the two cases. A good man and a good horse are each understood to have that which constitutes the perfection of their respective natures. In the one case the requisite qualities are moral: in the other physical. H ere we see how it is that the transcendental perfections can be affirmed of God. When from the goodness of the creature we conclude to the goodness of the Creator, we do not imply that the goodness is in all respects the same in the two cases. There is always analogy when we pass from the finite to the Infinite. Being or reality, goodness, truth, unity, are found in God, not in the same manner, but after an infinitely higher manner than they are found in the creature.

It seemed necessary to say at least thus much on this point at once. The further discussion of our analogical knowledge of God must be reserved for the chapter in which we treat at length of that subject (chap. viii.). There too we shall explain how it comes about that we are able by analogy to affirm of God certain other attributes (causality, will, intelligence, life) which are not themselves reckoned among the transcendentals. We may now pass to the consideration of the argument itself. It may be stated as follows : -- When one and the same perfection is found in different beings, it is impossible that they should possess it independently; all must have received it from one and the same source. And if the perfection in question is one, the idea of which connotes no imperfection, the source from which it is received is none other than the perfection itself, subsisting as an independent being. Now the things of our experience possess in common the perfections of being or reality, of goodness, of truth, and of unity: and these are perfections which involve no idea of imperfection. Hence we must admit the existence of the Real, the Good, the True, the One. Moreover, it may be shewn that these are not distinct the one from the other, but are one supreme and infinite Being.

It is manifest that each of the two assertions which form the major premiss of this argument call for proof: neither is immediately evident. On what grounds, first, is it declared that when the same attribute is found in a plurality of individuals, it is impossible that it can belong to each of them in its own right and in virtue of its being the particular thing which it is (*per se et secundum quod ipsum*): that even if there be but two such entities, either the one must have received the perfection from the other, or both must owe it to a cause belonging to a higher order: that the explanation of the manifold must necessarily be sought in the One?

We reply that this follows as a certain conclusion from a metaphysical principle which we have already had occasion to employ, viz., that wherever we have a union of diverse elements, that union postulates the action of a cause.[28] When we previously appealed to this principle, we were dealing with the case of the combination of different elements in a concrete thing. Here we are concerned with another kind of union -- that of separate individuals in a single class. It is undeniable that this is a true union of the diverse. The individuals, *e.g.*, who form the class of men, are in virtue of their individuality utterly distinct. Yet their common nature makes them specifically (not numerically) one: and a series of propositions can be framed regarding the abstract subject Man, which are verified of every individual in the Class. We cannot explain this unity apart from a common cause. We cannot say that each member of the class is a man in virtue of his being himself, and because he is the individual which he is. Things are not united by the very thing through which they differ: the principle of diversity is not, and cannot be, the principle of unity. Individuality is the principle of diversity. It follows that the perfection held in common must have been received from another. And as diversity will never account for unity we are driven back at last to a single cause to which that common perfection must be referred. [29]

It might seem that we are drawing dangerously near the Platonic theory of ideas. Plato, as we know, held that wherever material objects exhibit similar properties and thus form a class, we must needs refer the common effect to a single cause, the source and origin of the properties in question: and that we are thus compelled to admit that there exists a world of immaterial essences, the archetypes and causes of all sensible objects, but belonging to a higher and supersensible plane of being. The theory involves many impossibilities. It is sufficient here to note that, as Aristotle points out, there can be no such thing as an immaterial essence of a material nature. Matter is part and parcel of the essence of such things. An immaterial essence of a horse or of a tree, subsisting as an individual thing, is a sheer contradiction in terms. Such natures can exist apart from matter as concepts of the mind: but not *in rerum natura*. Yet the Platonic theory supposes that the archetypes, which are the causes of the things of sense, are subsistent entities. Our argument, on the other hand, does not involve us in this absurdity. It does, it is true, conclude that when the same specific nature is found in many individuals, we must needs refer this similarity to a single cause. But we do not look for these causes in immaterial essences specifically the same as the material things themselves. We look for them, as will appear later, in a series of archetypal ideas in the Divine mind.

Transcendental perfections, however, stand on a different footing. Matter is no necessary part of their essence. 'Being' or 'goodness,' considered in their essential nature, involve no limit, no imperfection. The concept of goodness as such expresses goodness in an infinite degree. If we desire to conceive a finite and restricted goodness we must ourselves introduce the note of limit. It is true that, as we have experience only of finite things, our knowledge of goodness is necessarily of a goodness which is limited. But this does not affect the significance of the term. For the transcendentals are analogous: and hence the terms expressing them signify the perfection, but do not connote the particular mode in which it is found in this or that subject.

From this we draw a weighty conclusion. The perfections of being, goodness and truth, as they are known to us in experience, must, as we have seen, be referred to a single cause of a higher order. Now, when we were considering material essences, we recognized that this immaterial higher cause could not be something of the same specific nature, since such a nature can only be found upon the plane of material existence. The higher cause which confers a material perfection must be of an altogether different kind. It must, indeed, somehow contain the perfection which it confers, or it could not give it. But, to employ Scholastic terms, it contains it *eminently* and not *formally*.[30] As regards transcendental perfections the case is otherwise. Goodness and reality are not perfections proper to a lower plane of being. Here there is no question of a cause which only contains the perfection which it gives, eminently. Goodness and reality will be found *formally* in the cause producing them. The cause of goodness will itself be good: the cause of reality will be real; though the mode in which these perfections belong to it will not be identical with, but analogous to, the same perfections as found in its effects.

We may go yet further. In the ultimate resort the cause must be the perfection itself as a subsistent entity. The cause of goodness will not be something which possesses goodness, but is not identical with goodness. It must be none other than subsistent Goodness. Were it otherwise, we should again be face to face with a thing composed of diverse elements, and be compelled to seek for the cause of the union. We should have to refer the goodness possessed by this thing to some higher cause which had conferred it: and thus we should at last be driven back to a cause identical with goodness. And the same reasons hold good of the other transcendentals.

But goodness itself -- absolute goodness -- is not goodness restricted to some particular mode. It is goodness in its fullness: in other words, infinite goodness. For we are *ex hypothesi* dealing with a goodness which has no cause higher than itself. But, as we have seen, wherever we find a limited perfection, that perfection involves the presence of two principles distinct from each other, the principle of perfection and the principle of limit. The entity is therefore composite, and is the result of causal efficiency. It follows of necessity that the goodness with which we are dealing knows no limits.

It only remains to point out that the Good, the Real, the True, the One, are but one supreme Being, whom we term God. Pure goodness, as we have seen, is absolutely simple and is uncaused. It is at the same time *real*. Hence it is not merely uncaused goodness, but uncaused being. It does not possess being; but it *is* being. It is therefore infinite being as well as infinite goodness. So, too, in regard to truth. The True is an absolutely simple and uncaused perfection. Moreover, like the Good, it is real: otherwise it would be nonentity. It, therefore, also is identical with uncaused and infinite being. And a precisely similar argument gives us the same conclusion regarding the other analogous perfections which we mentioned, Unity, Intelligence, Will. They are identical one with another, coalescing into one simple Being. But this Infinite Being, Who is at the same time Infinite Intelligence, Infinite Will and Infinite Goodness, is manifestly what we signify by the name God.[31]

NOTES

{1} "We regard ether as the fundamental cause or agency in nature, and are not compelled to look for anything beyond it. As far as the arguments for a first cause goes, the first cause may be material " (*The Existence of God*, by J. McCabe, p.41).

{2} Between a substance and its accidents there is reciprocal causation in different orders of causality. While the substance is the efficient cause of the accident, the latter exercises formal causality in regard of the former, giving it an accidental determination which it would not otherwise possess. Reciprocal causation in the same order of causality would, of course, be a contradiction in terms. Aristotle takes note of reciprocal causality in *Metaph*. V., c. ii., 1013b9. See also St. Thomas in *Metaph*. V., lect. 2. 'Dicit quod etiam contingit.'

{3} "Omnis effectus dependet a sua causa, secundum quod est causa ejus. Sed considerandum est quod aliquod agens est causa sui effectus secundum fieri tantum, et non directe secundum esse ejus: quod quidem convenit et in artificialibus et in rebus naturali us. Aedificator enim est causa domus quantum ad ejus *fieri*, non autem directe quantum ad *esse* ejus. Manifestum est enim quod *esse* domus consequitur formam ejus: forma autem domus est compositio et ordo: quae quidem forma consequitur naturalem virtutem quarundam rerum. Aedificator facit domum adhibendo caementum, lapides et ligna, quae sunt susceptiva et conservativa talis compositionis et ordinis. Unde esse domus dependet ex naturis harum rerum, sicut fieri domus dependet ex actione aedificatoris. . . . Sicut igitur fieri rei non potest remanere cessante actione argentis quod est causa effectus secundum fieri: ita nec esse rei potest remanere, cessante actione agentis quod est causa effectus non solum secundum fieri, sed etiam secundum esse" (St. Thomas Aq., *Summa Theol.*, I., q. 104, art. 1).

{4} It is hardly needful to point out that the building-materials need a cause*in esse* just as does a man. But these materials, in virtue of their respective qualities, are able to act as a permanent cause of the organized arrangement in which the house, as such, consists.

{5} Dr. J. Caird urges the following strange objection to the cosmological argument: You cannot in a syllogistic demonstration put more into the conclusion than the premisses contain. Beginning with an infinite or absolute cause you might conclude to finite effects, but you cannot reverse the process " (*Phil. ol Religion*, p. 128). He seems to regard the finite causes of experience as actually constituting the premiss of the syllogism. As a matter of fact, the two premisses are self-evident propositions. The existence of a finite cause is simply that which enables us to apply our *a priori* reasoning to the world of fact, and conclude to the existence of a First Cause. This becomes perfectly clear when the argument is thrown into strict logical form, as follows: "Every causally produced substance demands a cause *in esse*: and this cause (if itself causally produced) demands a similar cause, and so on: But a series of causes, each of which is dependent for its existence on the one which precedes it in the series, is impossible apart from a self-existent first cause: Therefore every causally produced substance demands a self-existent First Cause: But there are such things as causally produced substances: Therefore a First Cause exists." The same sophistical objection occurs in Illingworth, *Personality, Human and Divine*, p. 92.

{6} The illustration is from Garrigou-Lagrange, *Dieu, son existence et sa nature*, § 10 (Paris, 1914).

{7} *Summa Theol.*, I., q. 46, art. 2, ad 7.

{8} Aristotle establishes the necessity of admitting a first cause in connection with his statement that the science of metaphysics deals with primary principles. And it is noteworthy that he illustrates the impossibility of an infinite series by an example in which each cause is essentially dependent for its operation on the one immediate preceding. **oute gar hôs ex hulês tode ek toude dunaton ienai eis apeiron . . . oute hothen hê archê tês kinêseôs, oion ton men anthrôpon hupo tou aeros kinêthênai, touton d' hupo tou hêliou, ton de hêlion hupo tou neikous, kai toutou mêden einai peras.** (*Metaph.* II. c. ii.) St. Thomas comments as follows: "Secundo exemplificat in genere causae efficientis ; dicens quod nec possibile est ut causa quae dicitur unde principium motus in infinitum procedat: puta cum dicimus hominem moveri ad deponendum vestes ab aere calefacto, aerem vero calefieri a sole, solem vero moveri ab aliquo aijo, et hoc in infinitum."

{9} Cf. *e.g.*, Martineau, *SeaL of Authority in Religion*, p. 312. "The theist deceives himself by secreting in his premisses more than he supposes them to contain, the additional element being no other than the conclusion itself: for whether he works from the principle of causality, or from the signs of a perfection higher than the realized world, he hides within them the assumption of living will, of supreme excellence, of eternal authority, which come out at last in concentrated form under the name God."

So, too, Mr. McTaggart, *Some Dogmas of Religion*, § 156, who adds strangely enough, "Thus the argument could not reach the desired conclusion without calling in the aid of the argument from design." Why it should be necessary to appeal to the argument from design does not appear.

{10} *Summa Theol.* I., q. 46, art. 2; *Con. Gent.*, II., c. xxxviii; II. S., d.1, q. 1, art. 5; *Opusc.* 23 *De aeternitate mundi.*

{11} It is one thing to say that God might, had He willed, have created *ab aeterno*. It is another to say that the phenomena of experience must form an infinite series. The former statement is, as we have seen, defensible. For the latter no valid reason can be assigned. Yet where the authority of Kant holds sway, it is confidently asserted. Thus Professor Pringle-Pattison writes: "As Kant no less than Spinoza clearly saw, God cannot be reached at the farther end of any chain of phenomenal antecedents and consequents. To imagine that He could be reached in that way is to treat God and the divine action as a particular fact, one more phenomenon added to the series. But to talk of a first cause in that sense is a contradiction in terms: once embarked on the modal sequence, we are launched on an infinite regress" (*Idea of God*, p. 302).

{12} Cf. P. M. Périer, *A propos du nombre infini*, in the *Revue pratique d'apologétique*, Aug. 1919, p. 526.

{13} *Three Essays on Religion*, pp. 142-154.

{14} "I cannot see why it should be said, of three substances existing in time, that God did not need a Creator, but that a man and a pebble did" (McTaggart, *Some Dogmas*, etc., § 158). The question of time is here quite immaterial. The man and the pebble need a Creator because they are not the sufficient reason for their own existence; in default of certain definite conditions they cease to exist.

{15} Quae secundum se sunt diversa non conveniunt in aliquod unum nisi per aliquam causam adunantem ipsa." St. Thomas Aq., *Summa Theol.*, I., q. 3, art. 7; *Con. Gent.*, I., C. xviii., n. 4.

{16} In my treatment of this proof I am under great obligations to a short article by the late Fr. T. Rigby, S.J., "Aristotle and the First Law of Motion," which appeared in the *Month* (Oct. 1906), and to two letters addressed by the same writer to the *Tablet* (Nov. 10 and Dec. 1, 1906).

{17} Hence Aristotle defines motion as "the act of that which is potential inasmuch as it is potential " (**hê tou dunamei ontos entelecheia hê toiouton**). In other words, motion does not actuate the subject in respect of its potency to be at the term of its movement, seeing that this remains throughout to the end of movement unactuated; but in regard of the potency signified when we say that the thing is movable, *i.e.*, capable of being subjected to motion.

{18} Motion, of course, like time, is continuous; it does not consist of discrete parts. It seems worth while to call attention to this in view of Mr. Bradley's attempt to shew that motion is self-contradictory, and therefore can only be appearance not reality (*Appearance and Reality*, c. v.). His chief argument is found in the contention that the unity of any motion demands that the time in which it takes place should be one. But, "no duration is single: the would-be unit falls asunder into endless plurality." The fallacy is patent. A given duration being continuous, does not 'fall asunder.' It is one.

{19} In regard to the principle *Quidquid movetur ab alio movetur*, Aristotle's teaching in *Physics*, III., c. iii., is in the highest degree illuminating. He there points out that when the mover energizes as such -- when it is actually exercising its efficient powers -- its action is simply the motion effected in the moving body. The process of change (**kinêsis**) taking place in the subject of motion may in fact be viewed under two aspects. On the one hand, it is the action of the mover received by the patient. On the other, it is the actuation of the potentiality of the movable subject. In relation to the mover it is *actio*: in relation to the movable body it is *passio*. He says: "We have now solved the difficulty, and shewn that motion is in the thing moved. For it is the act of this latter effected by the agency of the mover. And the act of the mover is not something other than it. For it must of necessity be the act of both. For the mover (**kinêtikon**) is so termed by reason of an active power which it possesses: and it is said to be 'moving' (**kinoun**), because it exercises that power. But it exercises it in the thing moved. So that the act of both is one and the same. Just as the difference between one and two is the same as that between two and one, and uphill and downhill are the same reality.

{20} Mr. McTaggart states the objection with great confidence: 'An event happens, and makes the state of the universe different from what it had been before. The cause is said to be God's timeless nature. That nature is the same, however, both before and after the event. . . . Then there is nothing in that nature which accounts for the change; and it cannot be the cause. If while the so-called cause remains the same, the effect varies, it is clear that the variation of the effect -- that is, the event is uncaused. . . . The position we are discussing maintains that God is changeless and a cause. . . . This means that a cause may be what our reason says it cannot be" (*Some Dogmas of Religion*, § 159).

{21} *Principia*, II. 24.

{22} *Ibid.* n. 42.

{23} *Ibid.* n. 37.

{24} There is another point on which the modern conception of motion differs from the Aristotelian, to which it may be well to call attention. In modern mechanics motion is viewed purely as relative to a closed system, understanding by that term a system of bodies and forces so ordered that it may be considered as an integral whole, prescinding from all forces external to it. In regard to any particular body which appears to be in motion it remains an open question, whether its movement is real or only apparent. All that matters is its change of position relative to the other members of the system. Viewed absolutely it may be undergoing no transference in space. It may, therefore, be objected that we are reasoning at cross purposes, since the Aristotelian assumes that a given motion is a veritable transition from point to point in space, whereas the modern scientist neither can nor does affirm anything of the kind. The difficulty, however, does not really affect the value of our argument, since relative motion necessarily involves absolute motion. If a body A, which is moving relatively to the other members of the system to which it belongs, is, absolutely speaking, stationary in space, it follows that the rest of the system is moving with real motion. There cannot be relative movement without absolute movement somewhere. The Aristotelian is indifferent on which side the real movement is found. He sees that there is motion in the universe. This is sufficient for his purpose. From this he will demonstrate the existence of the *motor immobilis*. Moreover, there are many cases of local motion in which we can discard the whole question of absolute position in space, such, for example, as the motion which takes place when a man moves his limbs in walking. And, further, as we have pointed out already, the argument is based not on the phenomenon of local movement as such, but on the fact of *motus* in its widest sense, including change in all its different species.

Latterly, however, the doctrine of relative motion has been made the basis of a more fundamental objection. Einstein contends that the very conception of absolute motion is a chimera: that the terms motion and rest are significative simply of certain relations between bodies as observed. According to him, the motion which we believe ourselves to perceive in a body, is no positive determination inherent in that object, but consists solely in the relations between it and ourselves as observers, and is dependent on the subjective conditions of observation. We note once more that this theory treats of local motion alone in abstraction from all other kinds of *motus*, and that it does so entirely from the abstract standpoint of the mathematician to the exclusion of all other aspects of reality. The metaphysician, on the other hand, views the motion of a billiard-ball, not simply in its spatial relations, but as a new *fieri* resulting from the action of an efficient cause -- as a new actuation of a subject previously in *potentia*, and, further, as manifesting the characteristics common to change as such. When thus considered the plausibility of Einstein's theory disappears.

{25} *Ex multis enim non fit coordinatio nisi per aliquem ordinantem: nisi fortasse multa casualiter in idem concurrant* (St. Thomas Aq. De Pol., q. 3, art. 6).

{26} [For my opponent] the quantity of movement would appear to be indistinguishable from the momentum of the body in motion, it follows from this that uniformity in the quantum of motion can have no other meaning for him tban uniform velocity. A truer conception, as I think, would identify quantity of motion with momentum of movement -- a thing altogether independent of the mass in motion. It is a conccption, which opens our eyes at once to the absurdity of measuring motion round a point by units of motion towards a point, the latter being of one dimension only, while the former is manifestly of two. It reveals the true conditions of uniformity in each of the three orders of motion. In the measure of motions towards a fixed point the only variable is the distance covered by the moving body in a unit of time, *i.e.*, the measure of its velocity. Therefore uniform motion, in this order, means uniform velocity. But the measure of a turning movement should be a unit of revolution, in which two variable factors are involved; and all that is required for the maintenance of uniformity in this second kind of motion is that these factors should vary inversely. Such is the case when the law of equal areas swept by the radius vector in equal times is seen to hold. Thus movement in a circle, or in an ellipse, or in a parabola, can be just as uniform as motion in a straight line. If the one needs no external agency to keep it uniform, neither should the other.

But is uniform motion towards a fixed point a proof of actual external agency? Most decidedly, yes; for there is nothing, either in the moving body, or in its past movement, to account for any further realization of uniformity as time goes on. Assuredly agency is as much needed to keep movement straight as to confine it to any other orderly course. The moving body cannot choose its own course. Its past movements are no longer in existence, and therefore cannot be the agency we require. In fact, all that can be affirmed of movement is that it has been, or that it will be never that it is. How, then, can it be either an agent or its agency? It seems to me that, on this point, modern science has something to learn from the Aristotelian physics. Aristotle knew better than to put motion in his list of Categories of Being (Fr. T. Rigby, S.J., in the *Tablet*, Nov. 10, 1906, Vol. CVIII., p. 739).

{27} It may here be noted that the term 'substance' has not precisely the same signification when applied to God and when applied to creatures. In both it signifies a nature possessed of existence on its own account (*per se*). But the sense in which this is said of God is not identical with that in which it is affirmed of creatures. God exists on His own account as being Self-existent: created substances as being natures which are capable of receiving existence as independent realities, and not as mere accidental determinations. The two ideas are radically different. Hence God is not included in the Aristotelian category of substance. The beings which fall within the category form a class, the generic term being affirmed of all alike in precisely the same sense. The Infinite cannot belong to the same class as finite creatures: and when we term Him a Substance, we do not attribute to Him a limited and restricted mode of being. See St. Thomas Aq., *I. Sent.*, d. 8, q. 4, art. 2.

{28} *Supra.*

{29} Cf. St. Thomas Aq., *Summa Theol.*, I., q. 65, art. I. "Si diversa in aliquo uniuntur, necesse est hujus unionis causam esse aliquam: non enim diversa secundum se uniuntur. Et ideo est quod, quandocunque in diversis invenitur aliquod unum, oportet quod illud unum ab aliqua una causa recipiant. . . . Hoc autem quod est *esse* communiter invenitur in omnibus rebus quantuncumque diversis. Necesse est ergo esse unum essendi principium a quo esse habeant."

De Pot., q. 3, art. 5: "Oportet si aliquid unum in pluribus invenitur quod ab aliqua una causa in illis causetur: non enim potest esse quod illud commune utrique ex seipso conveniat, cum utrumque secundum quod ipsum est ab altero distinguatur: et diversitas causarum diversos effectus producit. Cum ergo *esse* inveniatur omnibus rebus commune, quae, secundum illud quod sunt, ad invicem distinctae sunt, oportet quod de necessitate eis non ex seipsis sed ab aliqua una causa *esse* attribuatur."

{30} A thing is said to contain a perfection *formally*, when the perfection in question is found in it with the same essential characteristics, which are expressed in its definition. It contains it *eminently* when the perfection exists in it in an altogether higher manner, in such wise that the same definition is not verified in the two cases.

{31} St. Thomas in the *Summa* states the henological argument in a somewhat different form. We find, he says, that in the world of experience some things possess more, some less of goodness, truth, unity and being. But we cannot speak of more or less of any perfection unless that perfection is, somewhere or other, realized in its fullness: and as thus completely realized it must be the cause of all its inferior exemplifications. It follows that being exists in absolute perfection, and as the cause of all finite things. The assertion here made that being is found in a diversity of grades is established from the correspondence of being with the attributes of goodness, unity, etc. The measure in which a substance possesses these attributes is the measure of its being. Unity will serve as an illustration. Substances, it is evident, exhibit this attribute in very different degrees. An organized animal is more perfectly one than a plant, which can often be multiplied by mere division: and a plant is a truer unit than a fragment of some inanimate substance. Man, on the other hand, in virtue of his self-consciousness, is more perfectly one than any of the lower animals. A pure spirit is a more perfect unity than man. The more fully a thing is a unit, existing in and for itself, the greater is the degree in which it possesses substantial being. Only the individual substance is properly said to *be* (*infra*): and our argument shews that this substantial being is realized in many different grades. Moreover, these grades demand the existence of a highest grade in which the perfection is fully realized. Were there not such a supreme realization the terms more or less would be meaningless The various manifestations can only be grouped together as possessing a common nature, if there is an ultimate norm to which the several individuals approach more or less closely. This may be exemplified in the case of a circle. We should have no right to group circles together in a class and call them by a common name, did not the circles which we draw, approach, however imperfectly, to an ideal type, which the mind can apprehend, though concrete matter does not admit of its perfect realization. What has been said in the text will shew why the argument enables us to conclude to the real existence of the supreme degree of being, goodness, etc., though only to the ideal existence of those inferior perfections, which demand material embodiment. The argument was derived by the Schoolmen from St. Augustine. He thus establishes the existence of God in *De Civ. Dei* viii c.6. *P.L.* 41, col. 231. Cf. *De Div. Qq.*, lxxxiii., q. 45; *De Doct. Christ.*, c. 38; *De Trin.* V., c. 10, n. 11. The proof in this form is generally called the argument from the degrees of being.

Chapter IV. Proofs of God's Existence (ii. Physical Arguments).

1.   The Teleological Argument.

2.   The Argument from Life.

1. *The teleological argument.* In the two arguments treated in the present chapter we start, not from the primary attributes proper to all finite being as such, but from the order of nature as manifested in the universe. We shew that the world in which we live possesses certain characteristics, which compel us to admit that it is the work of God. As proofs, therefore, they fall into a different category from those which we have been considering in the foregoing chapter. They are termed, not metaphysical, but physical arguments for God's existence.[1]

The proof from final causes may be thus summarized: -- The adaptation of means to ends is an evident sign of an intelligent cause. Now nature offers us on every side instances of the adaptation of means to ends. Hence it follows that nature is the work of an intelligent cause. But this can be none other than God.

Before entering on the proof of these statements a word must be said on the signification of the term 'means.' A cause is only termed a means to a particular result, when its action has been determined in view of that result as an end. If an effect follows from the operation of a cause in such a manner that there is no need to suppose a direct reference of the cause to its production, we do not regard the latter as a means. Thus, if a high wind results in the fall of some trees, we do not speak of it as a means to the fall of these trees. On the other hand, works of human industry are as a rule means. The bit in the horse's mouth is a means to its control: the railway-engine is a means to the propulsion of rolling-stock.

We affirm, then, that the adaptation of means to ends is an evident sign of an intelligent cause. The statement hardly calls for formal proof. Means, as we have said, are such in virtue of being determined in view of the end. They are directed to it: and apart from their relation to it, it would not be an end. Now only an intelligence has power to apprehend the relation of one thing to another -- to understand the proportion of a means to its end -- the 'reason why' of this means. It follows that only an intelligent cause can set one thing in relation to another as its end -- can employ it as a means. Wherever, therefore, we find the adaptation of means to an end, there we have evidence of a directing intelligence. The point on which we are insisting, viz., that only an intelligent cause can employ a thing as a means, is illustrated in the familiar definition of man as a 'tool-using' animal. The employment of instruments supposes intelligence. Since man alone among the animals possesses intelligence, he alone knows how to fashion and make use of tools. He is *animal instrumentificum* because he is *animal rationale*.

The same result may be reached in another way. If the means are really determined by the end, it is certain that this latter must have some sort of being. A nonentity could not exert a determining influence on the physical causes. If the house about to be built actually determines the cutting of the timber and the shaping of the stones which are to form it, that house in some manner actually exists. But *ex hypothesi* it does not yet exist in the real order. Hence, in so far as it determines the means, its being must lie in the ideal order. Now nature does in fact display countless instances of the adaptation of means to ends. It follows, therefore, that the cause of nature is a being endowed with knowledge.

It is evident that a pantheism, such as that of Hegel, which holds that there is but one Absolute Substance, of which all finite things are manifestations, but which only attains full self-consciousness in the human spirit, must of necessity reject our conclusion. It has no place for a prior efficient cause to whose intelligence the adaptation of means to ends in the realm of nature is due. In view of the influence which Hegel's system exerts at the present day, something must be said of his treatment of this subject. He held strongly that finality was present throughout the whole world process, but was emphatic in denying that there is any need to refer it to a separate efficient cause. The finality of the world, he urges, is immanent. It may be best understood from what we see take place in a living organism. There the idea is present from the beginning, governing the whole process of development, until it attains its full realization. The goal is not reached through means which are external to the organism; but all its parts are reciprocally ends and means to each other: and all in combination work for the final end in view. So it is in the universe. The universe passes on to its own realization. Cause, means and end are not separate things as in the works of human industry. The end realizes itself.

This explanation of the finality in nature will not bear the test of a critical examination. There are no grounds whatever for saying that immanent finality dispenses with the action of an intelligent efficient cause. It is, of course, true that in this case the principle of development exists within the substance, determining all its parts in such wise that they contribute to each other's perfection and cooperate to the ultimate result. But how is this determination to be explained? It is clearly false to say that the end as actually realized is operative throughout the process. The process takes place in time: and, until it is past and gone, the end as actually realized has no existence. What does not exist certainly cannot operate. It would be as reasonable to say that the ultimate form of a statue was operative in bringing itself into being, as to hold that the acorn becomes the oak through the causality of the as yet unrealized tree. Yet it is not to be denied that the final result does in some manner determine the contributory agents to its own production. There is no possible way in which it can do this, except in so far as it has a prior ideal existence in an intelligent efficient cause. It seems indeed to be imagined that an immanent activity is in some way exclusive of a distinct efficient cause: that this latter is only to be supposed when we are dealing with means directed to an external end. This is a mere assumption. Man, it is true, cannot give life to his productions, and endow them with the power of self-development. But no impossibility is involved in the idea of such efficiency.

The Hegelian theory involves another fallacy, which it will be sufficient merely to mention, as we shall have occasion to deal with it later. It treats of the world as though it were an organism, endowed with a life of its own, and actuated by a principle of internal evolution. This is a thoroughly misleading conception. The universe is built up out of many substances. Undoubtedly it possesses a unity of its own. But this is not the unity of a single substance: it is a unity of order, all the diverse substances being so related to each as to form an organized whole.

We may now pass on to the consideration of the other premiss of our argument, and ask: Does nature really afford us instances of the adaptation of means to ends? The fact, indeed, might seem hardly to need proof, so abundant appear the examples of design in things around us. What, it may be asked, can be more manifest than that the ear is fashioned to hear, the eye to see, and the hand to work? Yet it is maintained by many that we are mistaken in attributing any finality whatever to nature. The natural order, it is contended, is sufficiently explained by efficient causality alone. The physical agents of which the universe is formed have operated each after its kind, and in so doing have realized certain results. But this action was not guided by a set aim: it was not determined in view of the attainment of a particular end. Man, indeed, acts in this way, for man is conscious. He proposes an end to himself, and directs his action towards its realization. But we have no reason to attach this conception to the works of nature: the analogy between human industry and the action of physical causes is illegitimate; and instances adduced in proof of finality have again and again turned out illusory. Wheat does not grow that man may have bread; but man makes and eats bread because there is such a thing as wheat. The bird does not possess wings in order that it may fly. It flies because physical causes have given it wings.

It will be observed that there is a marked difference between these two examples. In the one case we are concerned with external finality: in the other with internal -- the actual operation of the organ in question. It is plain that in nature internal finality is far clearer than external. It is frequently rash to assume, because a substance is useful for a particular external purpose, that it exists for that end. We cannot affirm that the papyrus plant exists that man might be provided with paper: though probably this belief prevailed in ancient Egypt. But where internal finality is concerned there is not the same difficulty. Our argument will therefore rest primarily on internal finality. Of external finality we shall say something afterwards.

Our first proof that there are in truth ends in nature is drawn from the undeniable fact that our intellect recognizes, and cannot avoid recognizing, finality in nature's operations. Finality, we contend, is one of those features of reality which form the proper object of the intellect. It falls within the scope of that faculty to apprehend it. And if, after due consideration, it judges a given effect to be the final cause of certain antecedent phenomena, it is not mistaken. We said in chap. ii. that the object of the intellect is being and those notions which are immediately connected with being: and amongst these we included the notion of finality. Just as, where the requisite conditions are present, the mind pronounces infallibly of a given antecedent that it is an efficient cause, so it can affirm of a given consequent that it is a final cause. The mind apprehends what the thing is and *why* it is -- elements of reality which are outside the scope of sense. It judges of the efficient cause, the formal cause, the material cause, and the final cause. In the example which we gave in chap. ii. we dealt with an artificial product -- a clock. Just as the mind can grasp the purpose of a clock, so it can grasp the purpose of a bird's wing. Indeed, the finality of the latter is much more evident than the former. A clock's finality is external: and though there is an accurate proportion between the movement of the hands and the daily motion of the sun, the machine might conceivably have been intended for another end. But to fly is the actualization of the natural potentiality of the wing. And where this is the case, we judge unhesitatingly that the wing exists in order to fly. We may take another example. In the class of *mammalia* the female is endowed with certain glands, which at the period of parturition, and only then, secrete milk. This substance is that which of all others is the best adapted for the nourishment of the newly-born offspring. The intellect recognizes, without the possibility of doubting, that nature has provided the mother with milk *in order* to nourish her young. It cannot, save by doing violence to its own clear perception, adopt the alternative hypothesis, and hold that the mother feeds her young on milk, because it so happens that certain physical causes, acting without reference to her condition, have provided her with this liquid.

In saying that, given adequate data, the mind's judgment regarding final causation is infallible, we do not, of course, assert that we never err in these matters. We frequently judge on insufficient grounds, and see finality where there is none, precisely as we sometimes form a mistaken estimate about efficient causality. Yet although we occasionally misinterpret the data before us, it remains true that there are many cases where the evidence is such that a mistake is impossible. Our other cognitive faculties are equally liable to errors from this source. Our first estimate in regard to colour or shape or sound often turns out to be inaccurate. Yet we know that, under due conditions, the witness of the senses regarding their appropriate object is beyond all question. And precisely the same holds good of the mind's judgment concerning these aspects of being which are its special province.

Our principal argument, however, must, of course, be taken from the actual facts of nature, and the conclusions which these impose upon us. We urge, then, that the function of an organ is a single perfection. The unity of the act of flight, of the acts of vision and of hearing, is irreducible. It is not a unity of composition, but absolutely simple. It is *unum per se*, not *unum per accidens*. The organ, it is true, is a highly complex thing: its constituent elements are very numerous. Those who reject final causation contend that these constituent parts, acting separately and independently, result in a combined effect; but such an explanation is philosophically impossible. There must, of necessity, be in them a veritable principle of unity: otherwise they could not be the seat of a single activity. A plurality of causes acting independently may be imagined to unite by chance to produce a composite result. But only in virtue of an objective principle of unity can diverse agents energize as a single cause productive of a perfection which is not complex but simple. What, then, is this principle of unity? The only answer is that it is a principle consisting in a relation to the end to be realized. Only in virtue of such relatedness could the manifold elements of the organ issue in an activity which is one: the office of the relation being to determine the separate agents to the production of this end. In other words the agents are determined in view of their final cause.

This becomes still more manifest, if we consider what is involved in the rejection of our conclusion. In that case, the multiple physical agents operating each according to its own specific nature, and without any determination towards the ultimate result, select out of the million alternative courses open to them precisely that particular combination which is requisite for the activity in question. Now order is a perfection, and like every perfection, demands a cause. From chaos nothing but chaos can emerge. It is wholly impossible that without the intervention of an adequate cause it can issue in cosmos. The wing of a bird will afford an instance in point. We need not enter into the details of its anatomy. Even given the requisite formation of the anterior members, which enables them to act as wings, the problem of aerial flight is still far from being solved. The surface of the members must be greatly extended, yet without adding materially to their weight: and the body must be provided with a covering, which shall keep it at a nearly equal temperature, while not impeding flight. If, then, final causation be a figment, and nothing be at work save physical causation, how amazing is the solution which nature affords. The hair which, clothes other animals is here replaced by feathers -- a covering which is extremely light and at the same time is an effective protection against cold: while the greater feathers are of such proportions that they give to the wings the extension which they require. Nor is this all. Were feathers liable to become saturated with rain, flight would be only possible under very restricted conditions. But we find, in fact, that the bird is provided with a special gland secretive of an oily substance, with which it covers its wings, and which has the property of rendering them altogether impermeable to water.[2] We may well here cite some words which M. Janet employs in regard to another of the illustrations which he gives:

"How is it conceivable that so many diverse causes acting without an end, should coincide so well in their common action with that end? Remember, we have the right to say here, as men of science do in similar circumstances, that all takes place as if the cause of these phenomena had foreseen the effect which they behoved to produce: would it not be strange if a blind cause should act precisely in the manner in which one not blind would do? Consequently unless it be proved that such facts have not been foreseen, the presumption is that they have been. It lies with those that deny it to furnish the contrary proof: *Neganti incumbit probatio.*"[3]

The finality of organ in relation to function is a finality of action. There is another kind of finality, viz., that which appears in the symmetrical order -- the plan -- of a thing. Organic nature falls into four great divisions according to the four types of symmetry upon which living things are constituted. We have 1) the *radiated* type, as in *radiata*, which shews us homogeneous parts grouped round a common centre: 2) the *branched* type, which is exhibited in plants and in polyps: 3) the *serial* type, a symmetry of successive parts from head to tail: 4) the *bilateral* type, which appears in the higher animals and man.[4] The limits of space prevent us from developing the argument which may be drawn from the marvels of harmonious arrangement which these types afford, and which are inexplicable save as the work of an ordering intelligence. But under this head must be reckoned aesthetic finality, and of this subject we propose to say something.

Beauty is present everywhere in nature. Whether we look at the sky above us, or at the earth below, or at the wide expanse of waters, all manifest it. They display it in all their parts and under all their aspects. It is seen in the smallest flower, no less than in the forest as a whole: in the icebound regions of the pole, and in the sandy deserts, as in the glories of the tropics. A recent writer on this subject says with truth:

"To produce a good colour scheme is not easy, as everyone knows who has tried to do it. Yet Nature surmounts this difficulty daily. The colour schemes of Nature are not all of equal beauty. But even the worst are good, and stand in strong contrast, as objects of study and imitation, with some of the products of human manufacture and art. Each year the Royal Academy, in spite of the exercise of much selective skill, exhibits many schemes of colour, which are worse than any which a critical observer can find in Nature in a life-time."[5]

Nor is it colour alone that is in question. The forms of nature possess the same quality. The outlines of the different kinds of trees, the configuration of their leaves, the varied curves of their branches, are as perfect in their way as is the colouring of the flowers. Of the innumerable species of animals, which people earth and air and sea, there is hardly one which does not arouse our wondering admiration, some by their grace, some, like the lion and the elephant, by their grandeur. Moreover, the sense of hearing, no less than that of sight, acknowledges the perfection of nature's handiwork. The song of the birds, the music of the waters, the sound of the breeze among the trees, attract and delight us. We recognize beauty as the authentic note of nature in all its works.

The argument is, perhaps, most forcible if it is based on the beauty displayed by individual substances rather than on that of nature in its wider aspects. We say, then, that in nature each individual thing is endowed with a high degree of aesthetic perfection: exceptions -- of which we shall speak later -- being so rare, that we can here afford to neglect them. In regard alike of colour, form and sound, they display a harmony determined by aesthetic principles, and surpassing by far the highest achievements of human art. This beauty, we urge, can only have arisen by design. To attribute it to chance is a plain contradiction of the principle of sufficient reason. Every perfection demands a cause. As we have already said, order does not arise from disorder. Here we are in presence of a perfection so striking as to challenge the consideration of every thoughtful mind. Here is an art which never fails of its aim: which sets itself millions of tasks, and reaps a success in every one. There can be but one conclusion, that nature is the work of a Master-Artist to whom this perfection was an end to be attained. In other words, the beauty of nature affords a manifest instance of final causation.

Our conclusion may be enforced by another consideration. Though beauty is universally present in nature, its distribution is not uniform, as though it were determined by some general law. From time to time it acquires a special intensity. Cases occur in which ornament and variety appear to have been introduced for their own sake, and apart from any other reason than their aesthetic value. A conspicuous instance in point is afforded by the humming-birds of America. Of these the Duke of Argyll writes:

"Different parts of the plumage have been selected in different genera as the principal subject of ornament. In some it is the feathers of the crown worked into different forms of crest; in some it is the feathers of the throat, forming gorgets and beards of many shapes and hues ; in some it is a development of the neck plumes, elongated into frills and tippets of extraordinary form and beauty. In a great number the feathers of the tail are the special subjects of decoration, and this in every variety of plan and principle of ornament. . . . It is impossible to bring such varieties into relation with any physical law known to us."[6]

Facts such as these seem to force the reasoning mind to admit that the beauty of the world is the work of a Designer who Himself delights in the gift which He bestows with such lavish generosity.

The argument from final causes has not been allowed to pass unchallenged: and due consideration must be given to the objections urged against it. It has been frequently asserted that the ultimate ground of our conclusion lies in an analogy between man's own works and the works of nature: and that the use of analogy in this case cannot be justified. Such is the contention of Hume: of Kant in the *Critique of Judgment*: and of those thinkers who have drawn their inspiration from Hegel. It is urged that analogical reasoning is always wanting in conclusiveness: and that when employed to argue from the special mode of human activity to the action of physical nature, it is wholly arbitrary. To this it may be replied that those who raise this objection have misunderstood the character of the argument. Our proof is not based on analogy. We contend that the facts of nature are wholly inexplicable apart from finality. We have seen that again and again a multiplicity of physical agents possesses a unity of action which is only intelligible if attributed to their relation to an end. Efficient causes capable of a million chaotic combinations adopt that one combination in which they cooperate harmoniously to bring about a result of essential importance to the subject in which they are found. In many cases they are so unified that the act to whose production they are contributory is absolutely simple of its kind. Moreover, on all sides of us we observe that things are so fashioned as to conform in an admirable manner to aesthetic principles and to delight us with their beauty. It is impossible that these things could be, unless the action of the physical causes were guided in view of the end: and guidance in view of the end supposes a conscious intelligent cause, who knows the end and directs the physical agents to its realization. The reasoning here employed is not the loose method of analogy, but a rigid deduction from principles indisputably true.

It is, of course, the case that in judging of particular phenomena we often argue by analogy. We cannot do otherwise. When, *e.g.*, we see the hair or fur which covers an animal, we conclude that the purpose of the covering is to protect it from the cold. The analogy with human needs is so close that we feel no hesitation in judging to this effect. We followed this method when just now we appealed to the variety of ornament displayed by the humming-birds as affording proof that the Cause to whom they are due is One who delights in beauty. Yet though such analogical reasoning is perfectly legitimate, it may be abused. There is no doubt that misleading analogies have often been drawn, and been made the basis of false and even extravagant conclusions. But the point on which we desire to insist is that analogy is not the ground of our conviction that nature is throughout teleological.

The theory of Natural Selection set forth by Darwin disputed the finality of Nature on new grounds. And so widespread was the acceptance of his views, that the denial of finality was for a time a commonplace of scientific thought. He maintained that every instance of adaptation to purpose could be adequately accounted for without introducing the notion of conscious design: that the various contrivances which had hitherto been attributed to purposive intelligence owed their existence to the fact that they gave to their possessors an advantage in the struggle for existence. The offspring alike of plants and animals is subject, he urged, to fortuitous variation from the normal type: and those individuals which in virtue of some such difference were more fit for the battle of life than their fellows, would naturally survive and would tend to transmit their advantageous variation to their progeny. The next generation would see a further development of the gain thus secured. And in this way, by gradual and successive advances, might reasonably be explained the origin of all those organs -- the eye, the ear, the heart, etc. -- which had been hitherto regarded as standing proofs of the creative skill of God. The theory of Natural Selection, he contended, accounts for the production of nature's works by the sole operation of physical causes without the need of any recourse to finality. It is a *vera causa*[7]: and given sufficient time, is adequate to the results achieved. The influence exerted by these views was, as we have said, enormous. The majority of scientists, even though they might not accept Darwin's theory in its entirety, followed him in the rejection of final causes. Professor Romanes probably does not overstate the case when (writing in the eighties of the last century) he speaks of the "gradual, successive and now all but total abolition of final causes from the thoughts of scientific men."[8]

Yet the explanation of nature's contrivances here offered is wholly inadequate. The causes alleged are incapable of producing the results attributed to them. For according to this theory, nature s causes operate blindly: there is not in them any inherent determination guiding them in one direction rather than another. They vary in all directions: and every variation, whether favourable or unfavourable, is absolutely fortuitous -- a matter of pure chance. This being so, it is, we maintain, a sheer impossibility that the ordered harmonies of the actual world should ever have come to pass. Darwinians would have us believe that these are favourable variations which have been perpetuated through the struggle for existence. But we deny that they could ever have arisen. In order that a thing may be perpetuated it must first be: and fortuitous variation could never have brought such effects into being. As we have already contended, order cannot result from disorder, nor unity from multiplicity. The imperfect cannot spontaneously produce the perfect. Diderot maintained that if a case of type were emptied out a sufficient number of times, the letters might at last so fall as to give the text of the *Iliad* or the *Henriade*. We know that such an idea is preposterous. The type might be poured out through all eternity, and no such result would ensue. And the reason for the impossibility lies in the principle just enunciated, that where there is order, that order must have a sufficient reason.

The proof here given is valid in regard of order in all its aspects, and is not peculiar to that which involves finality. But the impossibility of which we have spoken is nowhere more conspicuously exemplified than in those instances of organization, in which numerous parts cooperate in a function in such wise that not merely must each part do its own work, but must so do it as to further the action of all the others. The human eye affords the classical example. The organization of the retina alone is so exquisitely elaborate that it baffles our powers of comprehension: and the retina is but one out of many distinct parts, each made up of others more minute, which combine to produce the act of vision by a reciprocal adjustment of extraordinary complexity. It has been often said that millions of combinations were requisite to the production of the organ. It is manifest that the indeterminate variations of the several parts -- variations having no relation to the other parts -- could never have resulted in a state of things in which the operation of every constituent factor is proportioned with infinite nicety to the operation of every other -- the proportion being essentially related to the exercise of an unrealized function.

The explanation of adaptations by Natural Selection is open to objection on another score, which claims mention here. For the validity of the theory it would be necessary that in the gradual development of an organ, each successive stage should confer on its possessor some advantage in the struggle for existence. This advantage is assigned as the sole and sufficient reason for its preservation. Now it has often been pointed out that in the development of a new organ the initial stages would be of no service whatever, but only the completed result. If wings, for example, were gradually evolved, the earlier variations destined ultimately to become an apparatus for flying would have been an encumbrance rather than a gain. Granting, then, that the evidence at our disposal points to the evolution of one species from another, some influence other than Natural Selection must be postulated to account for the new type. And reason declares that that influence can only have been the operation of final causality.

Natural Selection is equally at fault in providing an explanation for the beauty of the universe. It is, of course, impossible that the physical agents of the universe should through absolute chance have produced results, which, while infinite in variety, conform in all cases to aesthetic standards. Darwin has no resource but to deny the objective value of aesthetic principles. "The sense of beauty," he says, "obviously depends on the nature of the mind, irrespective of any real quality in the admired object: . . . the idea of what is beautiful is not innate or unalterable."[9] And he appeals for proof to the fact that the men of different races admire a different standard of beauty in their women. The conclusion, we feel, is manifestly false. We are certain with an assurance which admits of no doubt, that the principles of beauty in colour, in form, and in sound, are as objectively real as the principles of mathematics. We may not be able to enunciate them in the same compendious manner. They may elude our analysis by reason of their complexity. But we cannot question their reality. When we admire a beautiful object, it is not merely that our sensibility is gratified: we recognize in it the specific quality of aesthetic excellence. Indeed, were beauty a mere matter of subjective feeling, no education would be needed to cultivate an accurate taste. Yet we know well that to possess a true appreciation of the beautiful, much training is required. In this, as in every other branch of knowledge, prolonged labour is requisite before we can judge aright. Nor is the argument from the different standards of female beauty of any weight. There are various types of physical beauty. The men of a particular race will be appreciative of one type, rather than of others. But it does not follow that the others have not their peculiar excellence.[10] It is, however, claimed for Natural Selection that it affords an adequate account of the bright colours of flowers, the brilliant plumage and musical song of birds, and of the beauty and grace visible in so many of the tribes of animals. The conspicuous colours of the flowers has served, it is said, to draw to them the insects which effect their fertilization: and it is by this means that they have been developed. The plumage and song of the birds and the singular perfection in form or colouring of many other animals are due to sexual attraction. During the long ages the females have consistently preferred males endowed with these qualities. Such an explanation is palpably insufficient. In flowers it is not the bright colouring alone which is in question, but the perfect harmony of each separate colour-scheme. It will not be contended that the insects were appreciative of this. Besides, beauty is by no means the prerogative of plants fertilized by insects. It is no less present, though frequently in a more humble form, in those whose propagation is otherwise effected. So, too, the results attributed to the sexual attraction of animals are quite disproportionate to the alleged cause. It can hardly be seriously maintained that female birds possessed an accuracy of musical taste uncommon even in civilized man. Yet this must be admitted, if the song of the male bird really has the origin ascribed to it. And what is true of song holds good likewise of beauty of form and colour. Is it credible that beast and bird and fish, and even reptiles and butterflies possess an appreciation of aesthetic excellence which man endowed with reason can only emulate after long and careful training. No explanation, in fact, is possible of nature's inexhaustible loveliness, save that it is the purposed work of One whose wisdom conceived it, and whose power was capable of executing His designs.

There are, it is true, a few animals which form an exception to the general rule. Some of the bats, and certain tribes of fishes, repel us by positive ugliness. These are sometimes held to constitute an objection to the argument. Yet they will not appear as such, if only attention is paid to their proportion to the whole. Beauty possesses so overwhelming a preponderance in the world that the argument retains its full force even in the presence of these singular exceptions. The only conclusion to which we can come is that they have their place in the scheme taken as whole. It may well be that the contrast which they afford is intended to bring home to us what otherwise we might have failed to realize, that beauty is no necessary element in material things, but an added perfection with which they have been enriched.

Moreover, in our judgments regarding the grace or the deformity of creatures, we must view them in the setting which Nature herself has provided, not in artificial conditions which we have selected. When this is borne in mind, we see that the exceptions to which we have adverted, are apparent rather than real. It is not in the intention of Nature, if we may so say, that either the bats or the fishes which so excite our repulsion should be inspected in the broad light of day. She veils the former with darkness, and to the latter has given the deep water as their home. In that environment they, too, are not without a grace of their own. Professor J. A. Thomson invokes this principle most appropriately on behalf of another animal, which at first sight might seem to have little claim to beauty of any kind:

"If we are to appraise rightly we must see the creature in its native haunts -- in the environment to which it is adapted, which is in a sense its external heritage, which it has in some cases sought out. The hippopotamus at the zoo may fail to excite aesthetic emotion; but that this is our misfortune not Behemoth's fault is evident from the book of Job. We have to see him as the author of that poem saw him, with his ruddy hide in the shade of the lotuses, in the covert of the reeds and the f ens." (*System of Animate Nature* I., 267.)

A somewhat similar explanation will cover the case of some of the animals most serviceable to human needs. Their present condition is not that which nature gave them: it has been imposed upon them by man. If they lack beauty, this is because man has interfered with nature, and in doing so has marred her work.

Our attention has hitherto been confined to instances of internal finality, viz., the finality in which the end is some perfection of the same subject which furnishes the means. These instances have afforded us a clear and conclusive proof that the world has been organized by an intelligent Cause. We are now in a position to consider the part played by external finality, in which the means and the end are distinct and separate substances. We have only to consider the constitution of things to recognize the existence of such finality. Every living being displays internal finality, and is, in its measure, a true end. But living substances are not self-sufficient. They are sustained by substances external to themselves, which they employ as means: and in so doing they are putting these things to an entirely natural use. "How could internal finality be maintained," most rightly remarks Janet, "without admitting at the same time an external finality which is its counterpart? How could it be said that nature has made the herbivora to eat grass, without admitting that the same nature has made the grass to be eaten by the herbivora? "{11}

A. due consideration of the world reveals that the component substances exercise a wonderful interplay of reciprocal activity in virtue of which they become means and ends in relation to each other. Air and water are the media in which organized life is sustained: and each of these two media exercises a necessary function in regard to the other. The two great kingdoms into which living substances are divided -- animal and vegetable -- respectively give back to the air the chemical constituents consumed by the other. The vast insect world fulfils an essential office by destroying putrefying matter, and thus prevents a state of things from arising in which all life would be poisoned. The theme might be developed to any extent. It is harder to obtain full certainty in regard of external finality than of internal, for the simple reason that it is not, like internal finality, apparent in the very constitution of a substance. But it is by means of external finality that the parts of the world are linked together in an interdependence so intimate that the unity of the whole, though but a unity of order, bears a veritable analogy to the substantial unity of a single organism.

Yet these substances, which thus serve each other as means, differ widely in worth. Living Organisms rank above inanimate matter. We rightly view inanimate matter as being for the use of living things, not living things as existing for what is inanimate. Again, among living substances, animals are more truly ends than trees or plants. In virtue of their sensibility, they exist for themselves in a measure impossible for things which possess only a vegetable life. Man, in fine, as endowed with reason and will, stands on a higher plane than any. He justly holds all other things to be mere means in his regard, and claims the right to dispose of them for his

good. He is, it is true, a part of nature, but he is none the less the end of
nature. Those only fail to realize this who make space and duration their
measure of value. The Cause Who made the world, made it for man.[12]
When this truth has once been grasped, we obtain, a new view of external
finality. Wherever in the universe a thing operates in some striking
manner for man's advantage, we are justified in concluding that it was so
constituted for man's sake. Many theistic writers have scanned nature
under this aspect, and have enumerated a vast number of facts pointing
to the purposive care of the Author of nature on man's behalf. To take
but two examples out of very many, they hate instanced how necessary to
man is the provision in virtue of which the earth revolves upon its axis,
instead of continually presenting the same hemisphere to the sun, as does
the moon to the earth: and how immense is the benefit resulting to us
from the inclination of the earth's axis to the plane of the ecliptic, without
which we should have enjoyed no change of seasons, while those
temperate regions which are now the best adapted for human life, would
have been covered with perpetual ice. To those who regard man's part in
the universe as insignificant, to instance these facts as examples of finality
will seem in the last degree fanciful. But if it can, as we contend, be
proved that man is the end of the universe, and that the earth was made
with man in view, such conclusions are legitimate. We may not possess
apodictic certainty that such was the intention with which nature was thus
organized. But the theist who holds it to be extremely probable that this
is a true case of finality, does not lack solid grounds for his opinion.

Our argument has shewn that nature is the work of an intelligent Cause.
But a Cause possessed of intelligence must be immaterial and personal,
and hence distinct from the world itself. We have, therefore,
demonstrated the existence of a Personal Being endowed with intellect
and will, the Author of nature. This Personal Cause is therefore the Lord
and Master of man, with a claim on him for his service and homage.
Since the time of Kant, it has been customary to maintain that the proof
only carries us to an architect of nature, not to God. We defer the full
treatment of Kant's objections till we reach the chapter devoted to the
consideration of his criticisms. We shall there shew that, save as regards

this particular point, the difficulties which he raises against this argument are devoid of validity. It is, however, certainly the case that our proof does not directly establish that the Author of nature is the supreme, self-existent Being. Yet the value of the argument is not really affected. In the first place, no one who grants our conclusion will have any doubt that he has proved the existence of God. He will recognize that He Whose wisdom and power fashioned the order of nature, can be none other than the self-existent God. We shall search in vain for a thinker who admits such an ordering Intelligence, and yet remains in doubt whether there be a God or not. And, secondly, should anyone choose to entertain the extravagant hypothesis of a subordinate agency, the immediate cause of nature, it may legitimately be contended that our argument does not necessarily rest in this agent: that it has regard to the first source of all order: and that this first source of order can only be the self-existent Being. If the immediate agent be not unconditioned, it is manifest that the order which he institutes must itself be derivative: that the finality of nature points to a yet remoter source whence order takes its rise: and that this source is the Absolute, in other words, God Himself.

It has been contended by some that to suppose God to carry out His purposes by the use of means is implicitly to deny His omnipotence.[13] Finite creatures, it is urged, attain their ends by means. What they cannot achieve directly they can often accomplish by a right use of the materials at their disposal. But to represent God as thus acting is sheer anthropomorphism: and, more, is incompatible with the essential attributes of the Deity. The objection is so purely sophistical that it is difficult to realize how a competent thinker can propose it. We do not represent God as dependent on the means which He employs. It surely is not incompatible with His omnipotence that He should have willed that oaks should spring from acorns, and birds emerge from the egg. He could, had He chosen, have created each oak-tree and each bird separately. He preferred to form a nature in which creatures should exercise a veritable causality, so that each created cause should be a true means to the realization of its effect. No theist ever suggested that God so ordered nature, because He could not attain His ends otherwise than through the employment of created instruments. That He should effect His designs through causes which are proportioned to them, and which He has instituted for this purpose, so far from implying impotence, is a singular manifestation of His wisdom and His power.

2. *The argument from life.* The existence of life on the earth affords us yet another proof of our thesis. There was a time when there was no life upon this planet. Geology tells us of a period, when the rocks which form the surface of the earth were molten, so that no living thing could have endured upon it. The fossil remains of organisms first appear in the strata which were deposited when more temperate conditions prevailed. In the igneous rocks, as we should expect, no trace of living forms is found. How, then, did life appear? It cannot have arisen through any natural development of the forces inherent in matter. The living thing is, it is true, formed of material constituents. Yet the activities characteristic of life-activities which are displayed -- even by the unicellular organism only visible under the microscope -- are fundamentally different from those of inorganic matter. There is no question here of classes, whose perfections, though differing to a degree which places one far higher than the other in the scale of being, are nevertheless perfections of the same order. We are in the presence of mutually exclusive contraries. The living thing possesses a series of attributes, which sever it from the inorganic by a chasm across which there is no bridge. Hence, to account for life we are compelled to admit that a power outside and above nature intervened to produce upon the earth this strange new factor, which while employing inorganic elements, turns them to such new ends. Moreover, a consideration of the living forms themselves throws a certain light upon the nature of that power. For since amongst them are found some, in whom life, passing beyond the order of the merely physical, carries with it the gifts of intelligence and personality, it follows that the Cause which placed it upon earth must likewise be intelligent and personal.

Before we speak of the special activities of life, we must first call attention to the fact that the individual living substance, though often highly composite in its formation, is a true unit. Whatever the multiplicity of its parts or the complexity of its structure, it is *one thing*. Its activities all subserve the good of the whole and not that of the particular part which may produce them. And, as we have already had occasion to urge, that which acts as one is one: the action of a thing is the expression of its substantial nature. There is nothing like this in inorganic matter. If gravitation or some other motive force were to bring together a diversity of elements, they would never form a single individual thing. The result might be juxtaposition, or it might be chemical combination. But under no circumstances could it be a natural unit -- -a thing complete in itself, distinct from all other beings, exerting its activities in such a manner that all the parts should operate for the good of the whole. It is no answer to this to point out that a machine acts as a unity. A machine is not the product of inorganic nature: it is the work of human intelligence. Man, the highest of all the living beings on this earth can so dispose inorganic matter that it effects *his* purposes after a fashion somewhat analogous to that in which an organism effects *its own*. Moreover, it is easy to shew how immeasurable is the difference between the living organism and a mere machine. Of the various processes which distinguish life from non-living matter it will be sufficient for our purpose to call attention to two -- assimilation and regeneration.

The living substance has the power to lay hold of its appropriate nutriment, to dissolve it, and to incorporate it into itself. In this way it builds up its tissues and gathers fresh stores of energy for the exercise of its active powers, at the same time casting away those elements which are useless or deleterious to it. It thus attains its natural perfection and realizes its proper end by a process which is initiated and carried out by itself. Inorganic nature exhibits nothing of this kind. In the case of a chemical combination two substances, if placed in suitable circumstances, will unite to form a third. But no one ever heard of an inorganic substance which set on foot a series of operations tending to the attainment of its connatural perfection. Some writers, it is true, have claimed that the phenomenon of crystallization affords a kind of parallelism with the process of assimilation. But the comparison serves only to emphasize the fundamental difference between the operations of the organic and the inorganic. A crystal is formed by the cohesion of material of the same kind. If it increases, it does so by receiving a fresh layer of similar particles. A minute crystal placed in a solution of the same chemical character will gather round it a fresh deposit of crystals, and may thus be said to grow. But where assimilation takes place, how different is the manner of growth! The matter assimilated is not of the same kind as that to which it is added. The living substance dissolves non-living matter and converts it into itself. Nor is the increment received by the deposit of a new layer. There is a veritable process of incorporation, the fresh matter being taken up into the living cells themselves. Moreover, organic growth displays the wonderful phenomena of differentiation. As the body assimilates food and grows, the cells developed are not all of one kind: they differ widely in the different organs. The cells of bone, muscle, skin, etc., etc., are utterly unlike each other. Yet one and all have been formed from an original unicellular ovum through the process of assimilation. On this subject Sir B. Windle writes as follows:

"Let us grant that the cell -- the single cell -- is a machine, for the purpose of argument. Let us even suppose that such a machine should be capable of producing, of its own mere motion, other machines like unto itself. That is a sufficiently large assumption, since no machine has ever yet been made or thought of, which does anything even faintly foreshadowing what is here imagined. Nor has any chemical compound the power of reduplicating itself by means of its own inherent forces. Supposing even that these things were believable, they are nothing to what happens in the formation of the body of an animal. For here the original cell -- or machine as some would have it -- does far more than merely reproduce itself: it makes scores and hundreds of new and quite different machines. We might perhaps imagine a lathe which could beget other lathes, but here is a lathe which begets sewing-machines, organs, quick-firing guns, dredges, railway engines, and a whole host of other complicated assemblages of machinery."[14]

In view of facts such as these it is manifest how vast is the gulf between the living thing and that inorganic matter, which, as we have said, is essentially incapable of originating any process tending to its own perfection. To affirm, as did Huxley, that the activities of life could one and all, had we but requisite knowledge, be expressed in terms of matter and motion, is surely to fly in the face of evident facts.

The other characteristic of life, of which we shall take notice, is regeneration. By this living substances are capable of repairing injuries which they have suffered, and in certain cases of replacing organs which they have lost. We see this process in operation in the healing of wounds. If an abrasion tears away a certain amount of skin and flesh, nature soon replaces what we have lost. This is but an illustration on a small scale of a power which manifests itself in far more remarkable ways in the lower animals. Thus, if the *hydra* or the little fresh-water worm called the *naïs* is cut in two, each portion turns into a complete member of the species, even the production of a new head not being beyond nature's capacity in these cases. The crayfish, if deprived of its claw, will replace the lost member. Even some of the vertebrates will reconstruct a missing limb. If the salamander loses a leg, it will grow another. It will achieve a similar feat, if its upper or lower jaw should be cut off. More astonishing still are the results obtained by Driesch in his investigations in embryology. He shewed that in certain cases, when the original ovum consists of two cells, these may be separated, and each cell will develop into a complete animal. In the case of the *ampibioxus* he proved that even at the eight-cell stage the cells might be shaken apart, and that each fragment of the broken embryo would regenerate itself into a perfect*amphioxus*. "For certain purposes," writes Professor J. A. Thomson, "it is not amiss to think of the organism as an engine; but it is a self-stoking, self-repairing, self-preservative, self-adjusting, self-reproducing engine."[15]

It would carry us beyond our limits to touch on the other distinctive characteristics of life, such as respiration, irritability and reproduction. It must suffice to say that they are no less incompatible with the essential properties of non-living matter than those which we have been considering.

Fifty years ago it was confidently asserted by a vigorous school of rationalist scientists, of which Huxley was the most notable representative, that it was an assured fact that life could develop from the inorganic. Few competent scientists, however hostile to religion, would now care to adopt such a position. Men of science are more and more inclined to insist on the principle *Omne vivum ex vivo*. Two causes have chiefly contributed to this altered attitude. First, the fuller knowledge now acquired as to the nature and activities of the cell: and secondly, the famous series of experiments carried out by Pasteur, which afforded so convincing an explanation of all the apparent cases of spontaneous generation. The verdict of scientific investigation at present is well summed up for us by the author whom we have just quoted. He writes:

"In such matters we must keep, first of all *to what has been actually achieved*, and we submit (a) that there has not yet been given any physico-chemical description of any total vital operation, such as the secretion of digestive juice or the filtering of blood by the kidney; (b) that the progress of physiology seems at present to make vital functions appear less, not more, reducible than they seemed half a century ago; (c) that we are not within sight of a physico-chemical interpretation of the most distinctively vital processes such as anabolism and growth; and (d) that even if we had a complete record of all the transformations of matter and energy that go on within the living body in its every-day functions we should not be answering the biological question. As biologists we wish to describe the activity of the creature as a whole: What is the 'go' of it, how does it keep a-going? And while the analysis of particular items in the activity clears the ground and is important for special purposes, *e.g.*, in medicine, it certainly does not give us a biological description." {16}

Whence, then, did life come? As we said above, there is no reasonable answer to this question save to admit that at some definite point in past lime it was placed upon the planet by the operation of an extra-mundane cause. So inevitable is this conclusion that Helmholtz, being unwilling to admit divine interference, suggested that the germs of life were conveyed to our earth by a meteoric stone.{17} The suggestion can only be regarded as extravagant. In the first place life, as we know it, demands definite conditions as to temperature: and there is no reason to believe that these are found elsewhere than on the earth. Secondly, even if we adopt the unlikely hypothesis that such life existed, and, what is more unlikely still, that after the cataclysmic destruction of the world in which it was found, some germs survived and were preserved on one of the fragments set adrift in space, these must needs have perished in those wide regions where there is no atmosphere. They would there have dried up and been extinguished. There is, in fact, no other possible explanation of the origin of life upon the globe than the direct action of a cause adequate to its production. That cause, as we have said, must have been living, intelligent, personal. But this can only have been God.

NOTES

{1} The teleological argument may be presented in a form which brings it fully into line with the proofs given in chap. iii. It is possible to establish that, wherever there is efficient causality, there must also be final causality: that *omne agens agit propter finem*. If this principle be assured, then an argument from finality may be derived from any substance which is subject to change (cf. Garrigou-Lagrange *op. cit.*, § 27, § 40). There is, however, no question that the manifest examples of finality which nature affords, appeal to most minds with greater persuasive force than the more abstract method here indicated, but which for that reason we do not employ.

{2} Paul Janet.*Final Causes* (Eng. trans.), p. 88.

{3} *Op. cit.* p.78.

{4} *Op cit.* p.211.

{5} C. J. Shebbeare, *The Challenge of the Universe* (London, 1918), c. vi., Beauty, p. iii.

{6} *Reign of Law* (1867), pp. 244 sqq.

{7} *Life and Letters*, vol. III., p. 25.

{8} *Thoughts on Religion*, edited by C. Gore (1895), p. 44.

{9} *Origin of Species*, c. vi., p. 160 (edit. 6).

{10} C. J. Shebbeare, *The Challenge of the Universe*, p. 123. "True beauty in a Negress is not to be looked for in her approximation to the type of the beautiful European, but in a characteristic beauty of her own, which only the minority

{11} *Op. cit.* p. 193.

{12} On man as the end for which all else in creation exists, see below, c. xvii., § 1.

{13} McTaggart, *Some Dogmas of Religion*, § 164.

{14} *What is Life?* by Sir B. C. A. Windle, F.R.S., etc., etc. (Edinburgh. 1908), p. 62.

{15} *System ol Animate Nature*, I., p. 157.

{16} Prof. J. A. Thomson, *Is there One Science of Nature* in the *Hilbert Journal*, Vol.X. (1901), pp. 113, 119.

{17}The hypothesis, it is manifest, in no way explains the origin of life. It merely sets its beginning one stage further back. It leaves the argument for God's existence unaffected. Thus Lord Kelvin, who himself somewhat favoured the theory, writes: "Even if some of the living things in the earth did originate in that way so far as the earth is concerned, the origin of the species elsewhere in the universe cannot have come about through the functions of dead matter: and to our merely scientific judgment the origin of life anywhere in the universe seems absolutely to imply creative power." *Life* by S. P. Thompson, p.1103.

Chapter V. Proofs of the Existence of God (iii. Moral arguments).

1. Argument from Conscience.

2. Argument from the Desire of Happiness.

3. Argument from Universal Consent.

1. *Argument from conscience.* Since man is possessed of intelligence, he recognizes that certain actions are conformable to his rational nature and that others are at variance with it. He sees, for instance, that gluttony, cruelty, lust, and the infringement of the rights of others, are contrary to the order of reason: that in so far as a man allows the lower part of his nature, his passions, to dominate him, or disregards the law of justice which bids him give to each his due, he is doing violence to that element in him which makes him a man. In other words, these actions are evil, and, contrariwise, temperance, kindness, continence, and justice, are good. And this distinction between good and evil has regard purely to our nature as moral agents: it is entirely irrespective of any question as to whether the act results in a balance of pleasure or of pain. Those acts are good which befit us as rational beings: those are evil which are repugnant to our nature in this respect. The supreme rule of conduct is to do what is morally good and avoid all that is morally evil. The ethical standard thus imposed is clear enough as regards its broad outlines. All men can see sufficiently for the general direction of life what acts are conformable to reason and what are not. The primary precepts of the moral law, as the Scholastic philosophers said, do not admit of mistake. It is, of course, the case that on points of detail there will be numerous differences of opinion. Problems of this kind are bound to arise, since it is frequently no easy matter to judge of the application of a general principle to a particular case. All will own that obedience to lawful authority is ethically right. But the precise limits within which obedience is due alike as regards the state and as regards the family in this or that individual instance may be an extremely delicate point to settle. Sometimes, too, it happens that what once was a right action ceases to be so owing to change of

circumstances. Thus it comes about that what was universally recognized as a duty is afterwards viewed as a breach of the moral law. Moreover, occasionally the force of custom is so strong that great numbers of men form an erroneous judgment on some matter which to the unprejudiced mind is plain enough. The Chinaman who commits infanticide may do so without realizing that the act is evil. But difficulties and discrepancies such as these do not alter the broad fact on which we are insisting, that all men without exception can and do distinguish between moral good and moral evil. Were a man incapable of distinguishing these, he would have no just claim to the name of man, for he would be destitute of that light of reason which is man's prerogative above the brutes.

It is, further, a patent fact not admitting of denial or question that men feel the moral law to be *obligatory*. They recognize it as a force which *binds* them. Its prescriptions are no mere norm for the realization of life at its best. They come as authoritative commands: and to slight those commands is to fail in a duty which we *owe*. If we act thus, we are conscious that retributive justice pronounces us deserving of punishment. *Necessity* is a primary characteristic of the moral law. The meaning of this word should be carefully weighed. The necessary is that which *must* be. We sometimes speak of physical laws as necessary. Yet it may be questioned whether we are justified in using the term in their regard. The mind does not recognize any reason in the nature of things why such and such an antecedent *must* be followed by such and such a consequent. Experience shews us that the fact *is* so, not that it *must be* so. On the other hand, mathematical relations are necessary: the square on the hypotenuse *must* be equal to the squares on the containing sides. But the necessity with which we are concerned is not mathematical: it is moral. It signifies that our will is bound by an obligation which is not conditional but absolute: that we have no choice in the matter: that no alternative course is open, which we are free to adopt if we will. It declares that we are face to face, not with a counsel, but with a command.

This sense of moral obligation cannot be resolved into a perception of expediency, notwithstanding that many have sought so to explain it. In England, Mill and Spencer, though differing on many points, were at one on this, that the sole basis of morality is expediency: that the moral law is simply the generalized result of what experience has shewn to be conducive to the public utility. Right, they held, is not absolute but relative. It is determined by the needs of the species, which are essentially variable: of no action whatever can it be affirmed that it is essentially and unalterably evil or good. Such an explanation of the moral law is manifestly inadequate, inasmuch as it wholly fails to account for that binding force which is its essential characteristic. Obligation and expediency are incommensurables: the one cannot be reduced to the other. That an act will in the long run contribute to the material welfare of the community is certainly a reasonable motive of action. It is not, and can never be, an obligation -- an absolute imperative with power to bind my will. Expediency affords no account of the word 'ought.' The conviction expressed when we acknowledge that we ought to do this or that, could never spring from that source. It cannot give it, for it has not got it to give.

Law implies a lawgiver. We cannot have a command without a superior who issues the command. It is true that Kant declared the reason to be autonomous, and maintained that its precepts must be self-imposed. He contended that unless they were regarded in this light, they lacked the essential quality of moral laws: that to treat them as commands coming from an external source, was to deprive them of their moral character. But, though many writers have adopted his views on this point unquestioningly, the position is altogether untenable. There can be no obligation where there are not two persons concerned -- a superior having authority and a subject who owes obedience to his commands. No man can impose a law upon himself. For law binds the will: and so long as no superior authority commands us, we remain at liberty to choose either alternative. I cannot owe a debt to myself. If the moral law binds us, as we know that it does, this can only be because it comes to us from one who can claim the duty of obedience from us. An essential note of morality is lacking unless we recognize that the command is imposed by an external authority, and yield obedience to it as such.

This is not to say that the moral law is arbitrary. We have seen that it is not so: that it is revealed to us by reason as the rule of life involved in our rational nature. It is *natural* law. But only if there be an authority who commands me to observe the natural order, does it acquire the character of *law*.

If, then, we ask who it is who thus commands, there can be but one answer. The moral law, as we have seen, has the note of necessity. The authority who imposes it must then be final. Only when a command issues from the supreme and ultimate authority is it in the strict sense necessary. The lawgiver who commands me is, then, the source and fountain of morality, the supreme arbiter of right and wrong. But He who possesses these attributes is God.

The proof which we have here sought to enforce, is finely expressed by Butler, in language every phrase of which bears witness to his conviction of the force of the argument. His words are all the more weighty, since no point of style is more characteristic of this great thinker than his cautious accuracy of statement and his care to avoid aught that savours of rhetorical exaggeration.

"There is," he writes, "a principle of reflection or conscience in every man, which distinguishes between the internal principles of his heart, as well as his external actions: which passes judgment upon himself and them; pronounces determinately some actions to be in themselves just, right, good; others to be in themselves evil, wrong, unjust: which without being consulted, without being advised with, magisterially exerts itself, and approves or condemns him the doer of them accordingly: *and which, if not forcibly stopped, naturally and always, of course, goes on to anticipate a higher and more effectual sentence, which shall hereafter second and affirm its own.*"[1]

It has sometimes been urged that it is impossible to feel the sense of obligation before we are aware of a lawgiver: that no man can recognize that he owes the duty of obedience, unless he already knows for certain that someone makes this claim upon him. The argument, it is contended, which professes to prove the existence of God from the consciousness of obligation is manifestly fallacious: the conclusion is presupposed in the premisses. We imagine we are demonstrating God's existence, whereas it is really assumed without proof. The objection has, it is true, a *prima facie* speciousness; but this is all. It amounts to no more than that it is not easy to see how the sense of obligation can arise: it is wholly *a priori*. On the other hand, we have but to appeal to our own experience to convince ourselves that in point of fact the sense of obligation arises spontaneously in the mind so as to afford us the basis of a legitimate argument for the existence of a lawgiver. When faced with the alternatives of right and wrong, we are immediately aware that we *ought* to choose the right. And this consciousness of duty owed is attested no less unmistakably by the character of the feelings which are consequent upon our actions. A breach of the moral law arouses in us certain affections of the mind such as shame, self-reproach, remorse which necessarily involve the presence of obligation. Cardinal Newman, when dealing with this argument in *The Grammar of Assent*, has given an admirable description of the emotions occasioned by the commission of some evil act in one whose moral sense is not yet blunted by wrongdoing. He writes: "No fear is felt by anyone who recognizes that his conduct has not been beautiful, though he may be mortified at himself, if perhaps he has thereby forfeited some advantage; but if he has been betrayed into any act of immorality, he has a lively sense of responsibility and guilt, though the act be no offence against Society -- of distress and apprehension, even though it may be of present service to him -- of compunction and regret, though in itself it be most pleasurable -- of confusion of face though it may have no witnesses. These various perturbations of mind, which are characteristic of a bad conscience, and may be very considerable -- self-reproach, poignant shame, haunting remorse, chill dismay at the prospect of the future -- and their contraries when the conscience is good, as real though less forcible, self-approval, inward peace, lightness of heart, and the like -- constitute a generic difference between conscience and our other intellectual senses" (p. 105). The value of this argument is strikingly attested by the great writers of classical antiquity. Not a few of these affirm, as beyond all possibility of question, the existence of a law, rooted in the very nature of man, immutable, universal in its obligation, and independent of all human authority. No earthly ruler, however absolute his sway, has, they declare, the power to change or override what this law prescribes, for it is divine in origin, and is imposed upon us by God Himself. Lactantius has preserved for us a passage from Cicero's lost work, *De Republica*, which is, perhaps, the most remarkable of these. It runs as follows:

"There is a true law, right reason, consonant to nature, coextensive with the race of man, unchanging and eternal. . . . It is not allowed us to make any alteration in that law: we may not take away any least portion of it: nor can we repeal it as a whole. Neither senate nor people have power to release us from our obligation in its regard. We need not search for some one to explain or interpret it. We shall not find one law at Rome, another at Athens: one now, another hereafter; but that law, one, everlasting and immutable, is binding on all races and at all times: and there is one common Master and Lord of all, God. He it is who drew up this law, determined its provisions, and promulgated it."[2]

Yet our claim that man cannot fail to refer the moral law to a Divine authority, is not allowed to pass unchallenged. Appeal is made to the notions prevalent among uncivilized and barbarous races as, *e.g.*, the Australian aborigines. More is to be learnt, it is contended, from these backward peoples than from civilized man, since they exhibit human nature in its primitive condition. We are assured by certain anthropologists that amongst these races morality is merely tribal custom, and that it is destitute of supernatural sanction. Thus Messrs. Spencer and Gillen, speaking of the precepts forming the moral code of the tribes which they describe, declare that "in no case whatever are they supposed to have the sanction of a supernatural authority."[3] A closer investigation has shewn, however, that the statement thus confidently made was based on insufficient knowledge: that on this point the native had not fully communicated his beliefs to the European. Those who have acquired a deeper insight into the mentality of these tribes, assert unhesitatingly that the Australian, no less than the civilized man, sees in the moral law the command of a Divine Being.

It may very likely be objected that, were the obligation of the moral law really inexplicable apart from a belief in God's existence, then those who deny the latter would as a consequence repudiate the former; that this, however, is most certainly not the case, for many of those who reject all belief in a Deity are forward to acknowledge the binding character of duty, and vehement in asserting that they recognize to the full the imperative nature of its commands. This is true. And it is natural that it should be so, even though it be the case that they have deprived themselves of all reasonable basis for such an attitude. Those who enunciate a revolutionary principle do not usually recognize all that is contained in it. It is left to those who come after to draw the conclusions and apply them to the conduct of life. Our militant rationalists have been educated to regard the moral law as binding. They grew up in a society where men's opinions on these matters were determined by that Christian tradition, which for so many centuries governed European thought. From their earliest years they were taught, in common with their fellows, to regard the law of right as obligatory. It has not entered into their minds to question that early teaching, or to scrutinize very closely the grounds of that obligation. They accept it as self-evident, and overlook the important fact that the reverence for the moral law, which Christian teaching enjoined, was based on the conviction that it is the authentic voice of God speaking within the soul. If there be no God, then no adequate ground for an obligation properly so called -- for a moral necessity -- exists: the sole authority to which a man owes obedience is the state. He may, it is true, see that of two courses of action open to him the one is more, the other less desirable. In this he has a motive for choice. But, as we have said above, a motive and an obligation are not the same thing. Be this, however, as it may, even if the champions of materialism fail to realize the consequences of the principle which they have adopted, their disciples will draw the inevitable conclusion. And, human nature being what it is, we may rest assured that this conclusion will be reduced to practice. Under any circumstances the passions chafe under the restraints of the moral law, and are always tending to break loose from its control. If it be deprived of that which alone gives it its constraining force, its power to rule us will be at an end: the sole barrier to the domination of passion will have been removed. In view of these facts the rapid spread of materialism suggests to thoughtful minds some very grave apprehensions for the future.

The point which we have been considering leads us naturally to the argument from the need of a sanction to the moral law. The argument is so closely connected with that from conscience, that they may conveniently be treated in the same section.

We have already urged that the distinction between good and evil is fundamental: that the goodness of an action is altogether independent of the question whether or not it will in the long run result in a balance of pleasure to the doer or to the community: and, further, that the life of virtue is the only life which befits man as a rational being. This, we maintain, is not merely the spontaneous affirmation of reason, but the verdict of all philosophy worthy of the name. Yet in face of these truths the realities of life present us with a strange spectacle. The forces which in human society make for evil are so strong, that the practice of virtue is seen often enough to involve a man in temporal misfortune. There is no need to develop a theme which is a matter of universal experience. In a world where fraud, vindictiveness and treachery are so prevalent, the man who follows after justice does not compete with his rivals upon equal terms. His faithfulness to the law of right puts him at an overwhelming disadvantage. The prizes of life tend to fall to those who are devoid of scruples. These, as a rule, are the men who "prosper in the world and have riches in possession." Even in those cases in which a man, in spite of this handicap, attains some measure of success, the practice of virtue entails tremendous sacrifices. Purity, forgiveness of injuries, integrity, are possessions which are dearly bought. They involve an uphill struggle with our lower nature, which only ends with death. Those who purpose to be faithful to the moral law must be prepared to act directly counter to their comfort and expediency, not once or twice, but again and again: and so far as this existence is concerned, to forego in most cases all hope of a compensating advantage. It is impossible for human reason to acquiesce in this state of things. It refuses to believe that where the moral law is concerned, the universe lapses into chaos. In all other regards the mind of man recognizes the presence of order in the world. In so far as that order holds sway, things attain their perfection: it is the violation of order which involves them in catastrophe. To suppose that, when we are concerned, not with physical, but with moral law, this should become otherwise, that in that sphere alone the path of order should be the road to ruin, and the contempt of order the path leading to success, is to put inconsistency at the very heart of things. It is to affirm that the universe is at the same time rational and irrational, and, what is still more incredible, that it is rational as regards what is inferior, irrational as regards its higher element. This our minds unhesitatingly reject as an impossibility. But in this case, there is but one conclusion to be drawn. It is that the end is not yet: that the wrong of this life will be righted in another: that in due time the just will be rewarded and the wicked punished. But those who grant this must go further. They must admit that there exists a Supreme Ruler of the world who has imposed the moral law upon us as His command, and has attached adequate sanctions to its observance: and that at His tribunal the actions of all men will be judged. They must allow, likewise, that He possesses the attributes requisite for such an office: that the secrets of all hearts are open to Him, and that He can judge infallibly regarding the merit or demerit of every thought, every word and every action that has ever been. To hold this is to affirm the existence of God.

2. *Argument from the desire of happiness.* The proof of God's existence drawn from man's desire of beatitude resembles that from conscience in that it considers man in his capacity as a voluntary agent, and finds in human nature viewed under this aspect data which suffice to establish the existence of God. Very briefly the argument may be stated as follows. The desire for full and unalloyed happiness, or, as it is termed, beatitude, is common to the whole race of man. It is an inborn craving of the soul. The existence of this constitutional tendency is itself a guarantee that a satisfaction corresponding to the desire is to be found. In other words, beatitude is no chimera, but it is something which the soul may attain. But the nature of the soul is such that it could never find satisfaction in any finite good. If it is to attain perfect happiness, it can do so only in the

Infinite Good: and the Infinite Good is God Himself. God, therefore, exists.

At first sight the argument may fail to carry conviction. It may appear a hazardous proceeding to argue from the existence of a desire to that of an object which will satisfy it. Are not, it has been urged, the most deeply felt and long cherished desires often frustrated? No wish, however ardent, carries with it a pledge of its fulfilment.[4] Yet it is hardly needful to say that this is not the meaning of the argument. Indeed, it is surprising that those who offer this reply should not have realized that they must have misapprehended its purport, and that thinkers of repute could not have employed so childish a sophism. We believe that, rightly understood, the proof will appear conclusive.

By way of preliminary it will be well to explain somewhat more fully the meaning of our assertion that all men desire perfect happiness. We do not signify that every man must have framed, however crudely, some idea of such a lot, and that he desires it for himself: that he must at some time or other have elicited the wish that he may arrive at perfect bliss. The desire of which we speak is not an act of the will -- though, of course, we may form such acts -- but a fundamental tendency of that faculty, belonging to its nature, and determining the direction of its activities. Every natural substance displays certain tendencies proper to its nature. The impulse in virtue of which a plant shoots upward and produces fruit and seed after its kind, furnishes a case in point. Such, too, are the chemical affinities of mineral substances. Such, again, are the instincts of animals by which they are enabled to accomodate themselves to their enviroment, and which prescribe in rigorous detail their way of life with a view to the preservation of the species. The human will is no exception to the rule: it possesses its own specific tendency. And in virtue of this tendency, as we contend, man is ever seeking, sometimes blindly, sometimes consciously, for perfect beatitude.

The sense of the term 'beatitude' also calls for a word or two of explanation before we begin to deal with the argument itself. It is here employed to express the state in which the will has found entire repose in the possession of good. It no longer strives for any further object: its appetencies are completely satisfied: it quiesces in the enjoyment of its final end.

It may readily be shewn that man does in fact desire beatitude, and, further, that the beatitude for which he craves can only be found in the possession of a universal good, which in some way contains within itself the value of all lesser goods of whatever kind. In every action to which our will impels us we aim at some good. Either we wish to secure something which attracts us, or we seek to free ourselves from something which we view as evil. In both cases, the object of desire is apprehended as a good to be obtained. Our judgment may, of course, be erroneous. There is good which is truly such (*bonum verum*), and good which is merely apparent (*bonum apparens*). And only too often the object after which we are striving is an apparent, and not a real, good. Besides, the term 'good' is used in various significations. A thing may be good because it is conformable to man's rational nature. In this case it is morally good (*bonum honestum*). Or it may be good simply in the sense that it is pleasurable (*bonum delectabile*). Certainly the pleasurable is a good; but it is one of quite another kind from moral goodness. Again, a thing may be regarded as good, not in virtue of any quality which it possesses in itself, but because it is a means to the acquiring of something which is either morally or pleasurably good. This is the goodness of utility (*bonum utile*). But though the aspect under which an object of desire is viewed as good, is different in different cases, and our judgment regarding it may be gravely at fault, it remains true that it is desired as being good: nor can the will desire anything save for this reason. In other words, the object of the will is good *as such*: it is not this or that particular kind of good, but good in its universality. Whatever the mind can apprehend as good, that the will can desire. Now every faculty involves a relation to its appropriate object in all its manifestations. The intellect tends to lay hold of the real in all its forms: the eye to exercise its power of vision on all coloured things. It follows that the will being of its nature an appetitive faculty, involves a longing for all good: and that this inborn craving, if it is to obtain full and perfect satisfaction, must find it -- not indeed in the

145

possession of every particular good thing, which would be impossible --
but in the possession of a supreme and universal good, in which all
particular goods are equivalently, or more than equivalently, contained.

We may reach the same conclusion in another way. The aim of every
voluntary act, as experience shews us, is some good. This is so, even
where the act is known by the doer to be in itself evil. The man who out
of hatred desires to injure another, and of set purpose inflicts a grievous
wrong upon him, does so because his malignant temper clamours for
satisfaction, and its satisfaction appears to him as a good. The suicide,
who purposes taking his own life, and believes that thereby he will lose
even existence itself, does not view the result as an evil to be avoided. To
him the sufferings which he is now enduring appear intolerable; and he
holds that their cessation must be a good, even though it be purchased at
the price of annihilation. Yet, although the will -- the mainspring of our
actions -- compels us to be ever striving after the good, experience makes
it no less certain that no particular good can bring full satisfaction to that
faculty. No sooner have we secured what we wish, than some other
desirable object presents itself to the mind, and we long to obtain it. The
will is restless till we have made it our own. Yet the moment our ambition
is realized, the same process begins afresh. Such is the law of the will's
activity, as we experience it. What is involved in this cannot be doubtful.
The will, it is manifest, craves for *all* good. And each time that it urges us
to seek this or that particular good, and yet remains unsatisfied when it
has attained it, it proclaims, implicitly indeed, but in no uncertain tones,
that only perfect goodness -- that which includes within itself the value of
all particular goods -- can bring it full satisfaction.

It may be urged, and at first sight with some plausibility, that most men
have no conscious desire for a complete and all-inclusive good. The goal
of their efforts, as they themselves would maintain, is not good in its
completeness, but something more limited and more practical. They
desire wealth, or fame, or advancement in their profession: or they have
formed an attachment, and are eager that their affection should be
returned. Give them this, they will say, and they will ask no more: they do
not ambition anything so chimerical as supreme and perfect goodness. It

is not to be denied that great numbers of men are so minded. They are persuaded that some particular good thing will satisfy them, and they devote all their energies to its pursuit, making it the final end of their life. This, however, only shews that many men misinterpret the promptings of nature. They wish for happiness: this is inevitable. But they are utterly mistaken in imagining that happiness will be found, if they do but gratify the most vehement of their present desires. As we have already pointed out, the expected happiness always eludes their grasp. Yet for the sake of argument let it be supposed -- an extravagant supposition -- that some man were to find full and absolute contentment in the enjoyment of a temporal good. If this were so, we contend that we should have before us a case in which human nature had undergone degradation and perversion. For in such a man the soul's infinite cravings would be replaced by a single poor desire: its limitless capacities cabined and confined within the narrow sphere of the visible and temporal. This would be no normal example of our nature: it would be as futile to adduce such a case as a basis of argument regarding the soul as it would be to take a hunchbacked contortionist as the type and model of man's physical powers.

It must, however, be shewn that the voice of nature is not deceptive: that this imperious craving of the human heart for a state of perfect happiness -- a craving which holds such sway over us that every voluntary action which we perform is due in the last resort to its influence -- affords a proof that such a state is really attainable, and that there exists an object the possession of which will confer this supreme boon upon us.

To establish this conclusion we appeal to the patent fact that there is no such thing as a natural tendency for which a corresponding satisfaction is not to be found. An induction of the widest range bears witness to this truth. It holds good through the whole realm of nature and admits of no exception. "Wherever we find a natural power," writes Professor Flint, "we find also a real and appropriate field for its display. The existence of any instinctive craving or constitutional tendency is itself a guarantee of the existence of due satisfaction for it."[5] Aristotle long since gave concise expression to the same principle in the well-known formula:

"Nature does nothing in vain."[6] This truth may indeed be regarded as but another aspect of that finality, which, as we have seen, is exhibited throughout the whole system of the universe. If throughout the realm of nature means are everywhere adapted to ends, it stands to reason that wherever any natural type is characterized by some constitutional craving, that craving will not be left unsatisfied. The fact of lactation, to which we have already referred, may serve us as an illustration. The young of the mammalia, when they come into the world, stand in urgent need of food of a very special kind. It must of necessity be liquid, highly nutritive, and most easy to digest. Nature has not left them unprovided for: but has established in the mother the wonderful process of lactation exactly meeting the requirements of the newly-born offspring. It will, we think, be readily admitted that the principle here illustrated is of universal validity, and that wherever any specific type displays a constitutional need, the existence of this craving affords proof that a satisfaction may be found.

As applied to the particular case with which we are concerned, the argument is of exceptional weight. It is impossible to represent the desire for good as an acquired characteristic of the will. It is the primary law of its activity. The impulse to the good is the fundamental characteristic which makes the will what it is. Without it the will would be something totally different. It would not in fact be the will at all. To suppose that this craving lacks a corresponding object is to suppose a wholly irrational element in nature. It may perhaps be urged that the appeal to the law, which prescribes that every natural craving shall find its due satisfaction, is invalid when applied to the desire for perfect happiness: that the case of the lower animals makes it certain that this is so, even though it may be hard to say why the law shall fail in this instance. The brute creation, like ourselves, seeks for full and complete satisfaction. A desire for the good is the explanation of their activities as it is of ours. Yet no philosopher concludes from this that they are destined for beatitude, and will eventually find some perfect good beyond which nothing will remain for them to seek. To this it may be replied that the parity between man and the lower animals in this regard is only apparent. The brute, it is true, experiences a craving for this or that object -- it may be for food for its stomach, for provision for its young, for a way of escape from some danger which it scents, and so on. But its desires are limited by the narrow horizon of the particular: for it knows no other good except that of the sensitive-appetite. Destitute of intelligence, it possesses no tendency which embraces in its range the good in all its universality. Nothing can be plainer than the difference between brutes and man when they have respectively attained some object which they have sought. The lower animal is perfectly satisfied. For the time, at least, it desires no more. Man, on the contrary, never reaches this state. Whatever he may have obtained, he knows that it is but a partial and incomplete satisfaction of his desire. He is not yet content; he still craves for something else. Is it possible to imagine that, whereas there is full and ample provision for the lower creatures, so that every craving which nature has implanted in them finds its appropriate satisfaction, for man it should be otherwise: that the tendency which determines the whole activity of the will should be doomed to ultimate frustration: that the very faculty by which man is raised above the brutes, should be the one to which final satisfaction is denied?

Moreover, just in so far as man emancipates himself from purely material cares, and gives scope to the higher elements of his complex nature, his longing for the good takes definite shape as a craving for the infinite. We recognize that no accumulated stores of knowledge, however extensive, could stay our quest for truth, no acts of virtue satisfy our aspirations for the Good. Even were life long enough to allow us to make our own the whole of man's heritage of knowledge, we should still be as far from satisfaction as ever. Were we to secure every good of soul and of body which imagination can picture, if these goods were finite, we should still desire something else. And this longing for the infinite is not, as we are well aware, a disease of the mind, a mere morbid symptom, which the wise man will dismiss as soon as possible. It is the natural prompting of the heart, which amid much that is sordid and base, by this at least testifies that our nature is noble. Were the True and the Good a mere dream, a figment of the phantasy, then man's plain duty would be to refuse to admit the deception, firmly to deny such imaginings any place in his mind, and to aim at nothing save what lay within his powers. Yet who is there who does not see that were he to do this he would be eradicating from his nature the noblest element which it possesses? Here our own heart seems of its own accord to affirm the truth of the principle we have just sought to establish, and to assure us that there is a Supreme Truth and a Supreme Good to which we may attain.

God then exists. For only if God exists is there a Being who possesses in Himself all the goodness which in diverse forms we find dispersed in creatures. If all finite things are the handiwork of a self-existent Creator, then whatever there is in the universe of perfection, whether moral or physical, is already contained in an immeasurably higher manner in the Source from which it sprang. In this case, and only in this case, the longing of the human heart is not doomed to frustration: for though its desires are infinite, there exists an Infinite Object, which will satisfy them When the soul reaches God, it will have found the goal for which it has been striving throughout its whole course -- the last end, the possession of which constitutes beatitude.

It may perhaps seem to some that the argument which we have employed will compel us to admit that all men reach beatitude. We have maintained that the existence of the desire is sufficient evidence that there exists a corresponding satisfaction. Now the desire is found in all men. Does not our reasoning, then, logically involve the conclusion that in all it must be satisfied: that every man, whatever be his character, must in due time attain perfect happiness? If so, the result is strangely at variance with the usual belief of theists. These commonly hold that life is a probation, and that man's attainment of his final end depends upon the manner in which he has conducted himself during the span allotted to him: that while many reach beatitude, many are finally excluded from it. We might, strictly speaking, neglect this objection, since it does not affect the value of the argument for God's existence. But it may be well to point out that it admits of an answer. Our argument deals with human nature as such: and establishes that since the nature of man involves this desire, an appropriate satisfaction for it must be found. It does not shew that in the individual that desire may not be frustrated. Man is endowed with free will: and the individual may so use, or rather misuse, his free will as to fail of attaining his final end.

There is, however, one conclusion regarding individuals which we may legitimately draw. Although it does not follow that all will attain beatitude, it does follow that beatitude must be within the reach of all. Beatitude is the last end of man viewed as a species -- of every member of the class. If this be so, it cannot be a good barred to all except a favourably circumstanced few, but must be attainable by all without exception, whether rich or poor, learned or unlearned, civilized or barbarian. Our conclusion that it is to be found in the possession of God satisfies this condition. Every human being who reaches the age of reason, may, if he will, regulate his life by the law of God: and those who so do will not forfeit the happiness for which they were created. On the other hand, those who deny God's existence, and who consequently regard temporal felicity in one or other of its forms as the sole aim of life, must perforce admit that the greater number of men are deprived of all possibility of attaining the end proposed to them. Most men are compelled to earn their bread in the sweat of their brow: their days are spent in hard monotonous toil. And even as regards the privileged few whose lot would appear to be brighter, disappointment, bereavement, disease, and at last the inevitable summons of death render void their struggle after happiness. A theory which makes man's last end practically unattainable is not one which the mind can readily accept.

In conclusion, we may call attention to the fact that this argument from the desire of happiness corresponds in a certain manner to the proof of God's existence as the First Cause. Just as a necessity of the intellect drives us to trace the series of efficient causes back to a primal source from which they spring, so in a similar fashion are we compelled to follow up the series of final causes, till we discover the ultimate reason of every choice. God, as we have seen, is alike the supreme efficient cause and the supreme final cause. From Him all came: to Him all tends: He is the Alpha and Omega of all being.

3. *Argument from universal consent.* The present argument may be said to be independent of any special system of thought. It has been employed by those whose philosophical positions are widely different. It rests simply on the principle that man's intellect is fundamentally trustworthy: that, though frequently misled in this or that particular case through accidental causes, yet the instrument itself is sound: that, of its own nature, it leads, not to error, but to truth. It follows from this, that if the human race, taken as a whole, agrees in regarding a given conclusion as certain, it is impossible to suppose that that conclusion is false. Could a general conviction of this kind be mistaken, it would argue that something is amiss with the faculty itself: that it is idle for man to search for truth, since the very organ of truth is fallacious. Pure scepticism would be the sole logical attitude. In point of fact, man cannot use his intellect without recognizing its trustworthiness. It is its own sufficient guarantee. When we judge, we do not judge blindly: we see that our judgment is true. This being premised, we urge that there is a veritable consensus among men that God exists. All races, civilized and uncivilized alike, are at one in holding that the facts of nature and the voice of conscience compel us to affirm this as certain truth. We do not, of course, mean that none are found to deny it. There is no proposition which some will not be found to question. The pragmatist denies the necessity even of the principle of contradiction. But we contend that those who admit the existence of God form so overwhelming a majority, that agnostics and atheists do not affect the moral unanimity of the race. If, then, the judgment of all mankind cannot be mistaken, we have here yet another valid proof of the existence of God.

It is unnecessary now to argue the point that there is no race without religion. In the last century the evolutionary school laboured much to shew that man in his natural state had none. It was from time to time confidently asserted that tribes had been discovered who possessed no notion of the supernatural. Closer investigation shewed that the travellers who brought these reports were insufficiently informed. The question, writes a competent authority,[7] "has now gone to the limbo of dead controversies. Writers approaching the subject from such different points of view as Professor Tylor, Max Müller, Ratzel, de Quatrefages, Tiele, Waitz, Gerland, Peschel, all agree that there are no races, however rude, which are destitute of all idea of religion." For the present argument, however, it is not sufficient to shew the universality of belief in a supernatural order of some kind or other. A mere cult of superhuman powers or of disembodied spirits does not involve belief in God. And we are contending that a true belief in God, the supreme self-existent Being, is found in all races.

Regarding the mode in which the different branches of the race first acquired the idea of God, we offer no opinion. We must not be understood as affirming that they reached it by process of reason. We know so little of the centuries which preceded all recorded history that such an assumption would be hazardous. Some theists hold that the primitive revelation mentioned in the book of Genesis was never completely forgotten by any race, though often distorted and overlaid with much legendary matter. But even those who believe that the knowledge of God's existence comes in the first instance through a direct revelation, admit that its preservation must be attributed to the fact that man's reason saw in the world around him and in the moral law within such unmistakable proofs of the same truth, that it was impossible that it should ever lapse altogether from his memory and be lost.

It is important to observe that an idea of God does not cease to deserve that name because it is inadequate. It is not necessary that He should be known as Creator, as omnipotent, or as omniscient. It suffices that the notion under which He is conceived should be applicable to Him alone. A conception which simply represents Him as the Supreme Being, personal and intelligent, to whom man owes honour and reverence, is a true idea of God, even though those who entertain it should have extremely imperfect and erroneous ideas regarding the divine attributes. Plato and Aristotle held the eternity of matter: yet no one disputes that they had reached an elevated conception of God. So too, savages may possess a true idea of Him, even though they have no notion of the infinity of His power or of the universality of His providence. It is necessary to call attention to this point, since certain authors, on the ground that the idea of the Supreme Being entertained by some primitive peoples is highly inadequate, draw the wholly illegitimate conclusion that they have no idea of God at all. The eminent anthropologist, Howitt, after establishing that certain tribes of Australia believe in a being who is creative, everlasting and benevolent, says: "In this being, although supernatural, there is no trace of a divine nature." A. Lang justly remarks: "Howitt was exigeant in his ideas of what 'a divine nature' ought to be."[8]

Again, the conception of God may be, in some regards, positively unworthy. Many, not merely of the cults practised by savages, but of the great historical religions such as those of Greece and Rome, have been polytheistic. Many have involved practices at which the conscience revolts, such as human sacrifice. Nearly all offer us fantastic mythologies, in which imagination has run riot. Yet none of these things invalidate the force of the argument; for notwithstanding the irrational element, we invariably find that the religion recognizes a supreme deity, the ruler of gods and men. Moreover, while belief in a supreme deity is common to all, there is no agreement in the respective mythologies, nor in regard to those features which are contrary to the moral law. The former of these is due to the play of human fancy: the latter reflects the low moral standard of a people at some period of its history. It is the central doctrine alone which is imposed by reason itself. Indeed, a careful consideration of the data not infrequently proves that the less worthy elements of a religion are later accretions, and were not found in its earlier stages. To this point we shall return.

In a work such as this it is necessary to present the evidence in a very succinct form. But even so, the argument is conclusive. So far as civilized races are concerned, a brief reference will serve, since the facts are not in dispute. Egypt, Assyria, Greece, Rome, India, Persia and China furnish the great examples of pagan civilizations. In all of them civilization and religion were so closely bound together that apart from religion civilization could hardly have come into existence. Religion, which was the bond of national life, was likewise the inspirer of all advance in the arts and sciences. But the point on which we desire chiefly to insist, is that in every case there was clear recognition of a supreme deity. Such was Marduk to the Babylonians: Zeus among the Greeks: Jupiter with the Romans. In the Vedic religion Varuna has the foremost place: and in the Iranian, the same deity under the name Ahuramazda is the sole god. The early Chinese writings represent Shang Ti as supreme. In Egypt the chief deity differed in the different nomes, the people of each district assigning the first place to their local god. It might, perhaps, seem that if we can thus make good our contention for the civilized part of mankind, we have established our conclusion: since it is civilized man, and not the savage, in whom we obtain the truest insight into human nature. The latter, it has been argued, affords an example of that nature arrested in its normal development and subjected to a long process of deformation: so that the information derived from this source is less trustworthy than that gained from the races who have gone forward on the path of progress. This view contains a measure of truth. There are undoubtedly savages who have sunk into deep degradation. Yet in general it seems to be the case that these peoples have simply stood still on the path of culture, and that they represent with a fair degree of accuracy the infancy of the race. Hence there is good ground for supposing that their beliefs should yield valuable data regarding the religion which is natural to man. Here, however, great caution is needed to distinguish those two aspects of belief in the supernatural which we have already mentioned -- the religious and the mythical. "There are two currents," writes A. Lang, "the religious and the mythical, flowing together through religion. The former current, religious, even among very low savages, is pure from the magical, ghost-propitiating habit. The latter current, mythological, is full of magic, mummery and scandalous legend. Sometimes the latter stream quite pollutes the former, sometimes they flow side by side, perfectly distinguishable, as in Aztec ethical piety, compared with the bloody Aztec ritualism."[9] Our argument, we need not say, is based entirely on the religious belief of primitive peoples, and not on the gross superstitions which are its too frequent accompaniment. Many recent writers ignore its existence, and represent the religion of savages as consisting of these superstitions. But such a view is completely at variance with attested facts. The superstitious rites are more prominent, and come more quickly under the observation of travellers. But a closer enquiry invariably proves the existence of religious belief properly so called, and yields additional proof that the idea of God is, as we are contending, universal to the race. The results of recent investigation are summed up by the writer of the article *Creation* in Hastings' *Encyclopaedia of Religion and Ethics* as follows:[10] "Increasing research into the mental habits of the least advanced races of mankind now living tends to demonstrate that side by side with the most foolish, tedious, and often repulsive myths, there is almost invariably a high if vague conception of a good Being who is the Maker of all things, the undying Guardian of the moral life of man."

Where uncivilized races are in question, our minds turn naturally to Africa. Regarding the peoples of this continent no witness can be better qualified to speak than Bishop Le Roy, C.S.S. His long residence among the natives, his close familiarity with their thought, and, further, his position as Superior of a religious order whose members are stationed in many different districts and thus come in contact with a great number of tribes, give to his judgments an altogether exceptional authority. In his work, *La Religion des Primitifs*, he does not hesitate to affirm in the most emphatic manner that the recognition of God is absolutely universal among the Bantu-speaking peoples: and that the denial of this fact so confidently made by anthropologists of the evolutionary school is attributable to the misleading reports of travellers incompetent to penetrate the native mind.[11] The error, he admits, was not wholly unnatural, inasmuch as though the natives speak of God, recognize Him as Ruler of all things, and hold Him in reverence, they offer Him no worship. Their family and tribal cultus is paid to the ghosts of departed ancestors. How sharp, however, is the distinction which they draw between God and the other supernatural beings whom they acknowledge, appears clearly from two features in their belief. In the first place, God is wholly beyond the reach of those magical incantations by which they endeavour to influence the spirit world. And, secondly, there can be no such thing as a fetish of God. Fetishism, which holds a prominent place among Bantu customs, may be said to consist in localizing a spirit in a material object with the result that its powers are at the disposal of the person possessing that object. To think that God could be connected with a fetish would be regarded by a native as the height of folly. Furthermore, although the name by which God is known varies from tribe to tribe, none imagines that there is a plurality of gods. Polytheism, such as exists in India, is unknown. Indeed, these names are themselves very instructive as to the manner in which God is conceived. They fall into four classes derived from roots which signify respectively 'to make,' 'life,' 'power,' ' the heavens.' With all this, it is true, the bishop admits, that in the native mind the idea of God lies so to speak in the background: it plays little active part in his life. Yet in view of the facts which we have cited, it can hardly be questioned that among the Bantu peoples of Africa religion is in no way identical with superstition. They possess a true belief in God.

The Pygmies of North Central Africa seem to claim a special mention, since as regards material civilization they are as backward as any race which exists. Bishop Le Roy was in personal contact with this strange people alike on the eastern and western sides of the continent. They make no attempt to cultivate the soil, but live on what they can pick up in the forest. They have no permanent settlements. They construct for themselves only the most temporary habitations. It surely is a very remarkable fact that this most primitive race have a clear knowledge of a supreme being, unique, the maker of all things, the lord of life and death, the guardian of morality, who rewards and punishes in the life to come.

The evidence forthcoming from Australia is no less striking than that which Africa supplies. The Australian aborigines are in a stage of culture as rudimentary as that of the Pygmies themselves. The tribes of the south-east of the continent have not emerged from the stone-age. If, as the evolutionary anthropologists allege, the idea of God is not a primary conclusion of the reason, but a creation of fancy and of very gradual growth, it might be confidently expected that here no such belief would be found. That such was the case was boldly stated by Huxley. Yet, as the knowledge of these natives advanced, it appeared that no greater mistake could be made. Many of these tribes, and notably those south-eastern peoples whom we have mentioned, possess a belief in a self-existing supreme being, known by them under various names, Baiame, Bungil,

Daramulun, etc., etc. Lang has given currency to the term 'All-Father' to designate this being. In view of the attributes assigned to him, it is impossible to doubt that we have here a true, if somewhat crude, belief in God.[12] He is, as might be expected, somewhat differently represented in the various tribes. But we find him regarded as self-existent, as the father and benefactor of man, the creator of all things useful to them, as the rewarder of the just in the future life, and, at least in one case, as consigning the unjust to a region of fire.[13] Moreover, the moral code of the tribe is held to have been imposed by him. It is noteworthy that this knowledge regarding both the nature of the All-Father and the ethical standard which he imposes, is only communicated at the initiation-ceremonies by which the full privileges of manhood are conferred on the youths: it is not shared by women and the uninitiated. These are only acquainted with the tribal myths regarding him, often ludicrous and trivial, about which no secrecy is observed. Howitt, even after a prolonged residence among the natives, knew nothing of the esoteric teaching, until he was admitted to the rites of initiation. This fact well illustrates how difficult it is to gain a knowledge of the more intimate beliefs of savage races, and should serve as a useful reminder that the statements of travellers that some tribe which they have visited, is destitute of all religion, should be received with great caution.[14] It is further to be observed that comparatively little worship is paid to the All-Father. Prayer and sacrifice, though not wholly wanting, are rarely offered to him. He cannot be swayed by gifts, whereas other spirits of a lower order are bribable. The inevitable result has been that the cult paid to these spirits is far more conspicuous, and has often led the unwary stranger to imagine that belief in these beings constitutes the sum of Australian religion. Most striking, again, is the case of the Andamanese islanders. These, says Sir Richard Temple, are "an aboriginal people uncontaminated by outside influences, whose religious ideas are of native growth and exhibit the phenomena of a truly untutored philosophy."[15] They are a race "as low in civilization as almost any known upon earth." Superstitions regarding evil spirits and the names of dead ancestors abound among them. Yet together with these beliefs and much puerile mythology, they acknowledge a god, Pulugu. "He was never born, and is immortal. By him were all things created, except the powers of evil. He knows even the thoughts of the heart. He is angered by *yubda* = sin or wrongdoing. . . . He is judge of souls."[16]

From many quarters there is testimony to the same effect. The Malagasy of Madagascar, whose practical recognition of the supernatural order consists in ancestor-worship and sorcery, nevertheless "believe in a god, whom they call Zanahary 'creator of all things'; but this god being essentially good and, consequently, incapable of doing evil, is more or less neglected."[17] Of the inhabitants of the Malay archipelago we are told: "In general it may be said that the pagan Indonesians recognize the existence of real gods, and that the supreme god is the creator, more or less directly, of the world, and the preserver of it, and punishes the transgressors of his laws."[18] The early missionaries to the Eskimos of Greenland found traces of the belief amongst them.[19] And the Jesuits who in the seventeenth century evangelized the Red Indian tribes of Canada witness that, notwithstanding their extreme barbarism, they acknowledged and invoked the Maker of all things.[20]

It will, we think, be granted that we have ample ground for our contention that the belief in God is morally universal: that it is no outcome of a developed civilization, but common to all, whatever their stage of culture: and that if this belief be false, there must be something radically amiss with the faculty of reason itself.

It will be well to notice here an objection sometimes urged as destructive of the value of this argument. In view of what has been said, it will be seen to be devoid of all force. Principal Caird employs it in his *Introduction to the Philosophy of Religion*; we cite his words. " It is," he writes, "only by thinning down the idea of God to an abstraction which would embrace under a common head the rudest fetishism and the spiritual theism of Christianity, that a *consensus gentium* can be alleged on behalf of the fundamental idea of religion. But of what worth as a criterion of certitude is an intuition which leaves out of the idea of God to which it certifies all that can interest the intelligence or elevate the character of the worshipper."[21] It is unnecessary to point out that the objection rests on a complete misconception of the nature of the argument. It is not grounded on the mere belief in the supernatural, including those gross superstitions which too often replace the worship of God; but on the universal recognition of a supreme being, so conceived as to furnish a genuine, even if inadequate, notion of God.

The theory of the evolutionary school calls for somewhat ampler consideration. Its adherents seek to shew that religion arose from some superstition entertained by man in his savage state: that his beliefs passed through various stages as he progressed in culture and little by little dropped those elements which were patently irrational: and that thus at last he reached the spiritual monotheism characteristic of Christianity. The conclusion which it is intended should be drawn, is that religion is in all its forms destitute of solid ground: and that those who to-day dismiss it altogether are on a higher level of culture than those who still retain a belief in a Creator. The defenders of the theory are not at one as to the primary germ of all religion. The view which has met with widest acceptance is that of Tylor. He maintained that the first beginnings of religion are to be found in the belief in spirits -- first in man's own spirit, and then in ghosts of the departed and in countless spirits of nature conceived after this model. Sir James Frazer sees the starting-point in magic. Man, he holds, first sought to influence the powers of nature by imitative magic: and then, finding that he failed to win the results for which he looked, he was led to conclude that these powers were in the hands of one stronger than himself, who could not be controlled by magic, but must be moved by supplication and sacrifice. M. Durkheim considers that the religious sense originated in certain emotions which arise spontaneously in bodies of men as bodies, totemism being the form in which that sense first finds expression.

The theory led naturally to a close investigation of the beliefs of uncivilized peoples, both on the part of those who believed that the whole process of development might be found going on before our eyes, and by those who held that the facts, if fully known, would prove that religion had a very different source from that suggested. The facts thus accumulated have furnished certain definite results: and they are by no means favourable to the theory.

It is essential to the validity of the evolutionary hypothesis that the successive stages of religious development should bear a direct proportion to the progress of civilization: that where culture is very low, there religious beliefs should be likewise on a low level, and that the grosser elements should be gradually eliminated as culture advances. Now, as we have already shewn, this is most emphatically not the case. Tribes which are at the very bottom of the ladder of civilization -- which, like the Pygmies, possess a more rudimentary culture than any prehistoric race which has left its relics for us fo study -- are found to possess an idea of God purer than that entertained by races far more advanced in social and material progress. Moreover, those superstitious beliefs and practices in which the evolutionary anthropologists see the source and origin of all religion are much less developed and hold a much less important place in the more primitive folk than among those who have raised themselves to a slightly higher level. Nor are these things peculiar to one part of the world only -- to Africa or to Australia, to the Malay archipelago or to Melanesia. They are of general occurrence wherever savage races are found. Furthermore, there is ample evidence that these superstitions, more particularly animism, fetishism, and magic, so far from affording a road to religion, tend to stifle, and eventually to extinguish it. The supreme being, it is felt, does not need our gifts, and is too exalted to be controlled by us. Moreover, he is good; he is not on the watch to injure us. But it is otherwise with the spirits which surround us. They are in large measure malevolent: and though powerful, they may be swayed by our rites. Little by little the worship of spirits and the practice of magic usurp the place of the worship of God. He passes into the background. So far is it from being true that these things lead to religion, that it is safe to say that the more there is of animism or of magic in any race the less there will be of religion.

Nothing can shew more clearly how refractory to the evolutionary theory are the facts which we have mentioned than the manner in which the evidence is burked by anthropologists of this school. They ignore the information about the supreme beings acknowledged by primitive peoples and decline to take account of such unwelcome data. Lang calls attention to this highly unscientific method in various of his writings[22] and the Austrian ethnologist, Father W. Schmidt, denounced it roundly in the pages of his learned periodical *Anthropos*. But their protests fell on deaf ears.

So far, indeed, is it from being the case that religion progresses *pari passu* with civilization, that, on the contrary, the advance of civilization seems invariably to be accompanied by religious decadence. In the very early stages God's supreme dominion and man's obligations to Him are more clearly recognized. Gradually these truths become obscured, and alien elements are taken up such as nature-worship or the cult of ancestors, which are wholly incompatible with purity of religious belief. Under these influences superstition invades the province of religion, and a primitive monotheism may lapse into polytheism. This is true not only of uncivilized peoples. It holds good generally. Indian religion affords a case in point. There is no question but that the Vedic religion was far purer and more elevated than the pantheistic Brahmanism of to-day. Or to take another instance, the development of Greek and Roman mythology lowered the religious level of these peoples. Spiritual decadence is, however, perfectly compatible with advance along the line of speculative reflection. The intellectual progress of a people secures for them a more accurate realization of the notions involved in religious thought. This process is conspicuously visible in the classical peoples of antiquity. The rapid decay of religion and the progressive deterioration of morals were no bar to philosophical speculation *de natura deorum*. If the testimony of history is to be trusted, the religion of a people does not assume a purer and more elevated character with the passage of the years. Its tendency is downwards not upwards. And to this law the ancient Hebrew religion and Christianity appear to be the sole exceptions.

The evolutionary theory is open to objection on yet another head. Animism, as we have seen, supposes that the cult of spirits led to polytheism, and that among the gods thus worshipped one was advanced to the foremost place -- a step which paved the way to monotheism. It has been pointed out with great force that ghosts and gods are utterly distinct: that the two notions have nothing in common: and that no possible reason, logical or psychological, can be assigned for the transformation of one into the other. A people might believe in ghosts, might fear them or try to control them: yet it does not appear why they should endow them with a totally new set of attributes and regard them as, *e.g.*, all-seeing, moral and benevolent -- the qualities almost universally assigned to a deity -- and place them in an entirely new category of being as divine. The conclusion at which the animistic theory artives is not contained in any of its premisses. We are asked to believe that the transition took place; but the process is purely arbitrary. And this criticism is all the more pertinent, when it is observed that the gods of primitive peoples are not conceived as spirits. The idea of the Deity as a 'spirit' is of late occurrence, and is foreign to the mind of early races. The Homeric gods are not spirits: they are conceived anthropomorphically. The same is true of the supreme beings of savages. Their nature is not accurately determined; but they, too, are conceived man-wise. Indeed, most of the Australian tribes, of whose beliefs we have knowledge, teach that their supreme being (Baiame, Bunjil, etc.) never died. A being who never died is not a ghost. [23]

It is manifest that the evolutionary theory fails to perform its promise of explaining the origin of the belief in God as an outcome of primitive superstition. We may justly claim that our original conclusion holds good, viz., that inasmuch as that belief is entertained with moral unanimity by all peoples in whatever degree of civilization, all alike acknowledging that the world they see around them must be the work of a personal and intelligent cause, it follows that the belief is true.

The conclusion receives further confirmation from the fact that no system of world-philosophy which rules out belief in God has ever succeeded in maintaining a permanent hold on any people. Buddhism used at one time to be cited as an exception. It is now recognized that it cannot be reckoned as such. In fact, the history of the Buddhist movement affords a conspicuous instance in favour of our contention. In India, the teaching of Sakya-muni spread widely. But it disappeared altogether to make way for modern Hinduism. No persecution apparently effected the change. The Buddhist creed proved incapable of holding its own.[24] In China, where the system still flourishes, it has become to all intents a mere polytheism. The adherent of Buddhism acknowledges a pantheon of divinities, amongst whom the Buddha himself takes rank.

In estimating the force of our argument, due weight should also be given to the fact that, were not the voice of reason so emphatic, man's natural inclinations would lead him rather to deny God's existence than to believe in it. Man craves for liberty of action: and his native pride makes him quick to resent the authority of a superior. The motives must be strong indeed which lead him to admit as perfectly certain the existence of One who is his absolute Master, who has imposed upon him an urgent moral law, and who will punish him if he should violate it. Only a cogent reason could induce him to bow down in worship. The evolutionary anthropologists suppose that he took the step of inventing God of his own accord. They shew no reason why he was bound to do so. It is for them merely another step along the road of superstition. It may safely be said that, were the case as they represent it, that step, human nature being what it is, would not and could not have been taken.

NOTES

{1} *Second Sermon on Human Nature. Works*, II., p. 26 (ed. 1835). The italics are ours.

{2} Cited in Lactantius, *Inst. Div..*, VI., c. viii.; cf. Meyer, *Inst. Juris Natur.*, I., n. 251.

{3} Spencer and Gillen, *The Northern Tribes of Central Australia*, p. 504. A later investigator, Mr. Howitt, arrived at very different conclusions. He shews that the moral doctrine is inculcated in connection with the initiation ceremonies, and that these ceremonies have a religious sanction. He was in a better position to form a judgment than were Spencer and Gillen, as he was himself initiated, whereas they were not. See A. Lang, *The Making of Religion*, p. 180.

{4} Mr. McTaggart writes: "I can see no contradiction whatever in the statement that a desire is real, but remains ungratified. The statement is often true. Many people had a real desire that the Pretender should be victorious in 1745, but they were disappointed. . . . If the reality of any desire is compatible with its non-fulfilment, then we can never argue from the reality of any desire to its fulfilment" (*Some Dogmas of Religion*, § 47).

{5} *Agnosticism*, p. 165.

{6} *De Anima*, III., c. ix., § 6. It is of interest to note that Sir Isaac Newton bases upon this principle the first two of his Rules of Philosophizing: and that it is by an appeal to these two rules that he reaches his conclusion that the force which the earth exerts upon the moon is the same force of gravity by which bodies are drawn to the earth's surface.

{7} F. B. Jevons, *Introd. to the History of Religion*, p. 7.

{8} Hastings' *Encyclopaedia of Religion and Ethics*, art. *God (Primitive and Savage)*, Vol. VI., p. 245.

{9} *Making of Religion* (2nd ed.), p. 183.

{10} Mr. J. Strachan.

{11} *Op. cit.*, p. 171. He quotes to precisely the same effect two English authors, whom he regards as of quite exceptional competence, Mr. R. H. Nassau, Fetishism in W. Africa, and J. L. Wilson, Western Africa.

{12} In the article Australia in Hastings' *Encyclopaedia of Religion and Ethics*, Mr. N. W. Thomas calls attention to the difference of opinion among anthropologists as to the position occupied in the aboriginal view of the universe by these beings. "Some authors have denied that the term 'god' can be applied to them, while others have maintained that they are eternal, omniscient, all-powerful creators. Probably the truth lies nearer the latter than the former view" (op. cit., II., p. 245).

{13} Lang, *Magic and Religion*, p. 73.

{14} On the secret religious tradition of savage peoples and the difficulty of discovering it, see also *The Life of a South African Tribe*, by H. H. Junod, c.ii., pp. 389 if.; also, *The Ila-speaking Peoples of Rhodesia*, by E. W. Smith and R. Murray Dale, c. ii., pp. 197 ff.

{15} Art. *Andamans* in Hastings' *Encyclopaedia of R. and E.*

{16} *Making of Religion* (ed. 2), p. 195.

{17} Hastings' *Encycl.*, VIII., p. 203.

{18} *Ibid.* p. 307.

{19} *Making of Religion*, p. 183.

{20} P. Ragueneau, S.J. (1648), cited apud Hastings' *Encycl.*, art. *Hurons.*

{21} P. 54

{22} *Magic and Religion*, pp. 53, 57; art. *God* in Hastings' *Encycl. of R. and A.*, etc.

{23} *Making of Religion*, c. xi.

{24} Cf. art. *Buddhism*, by Prof. Rhys Davids, in *Encycl. Britannica* (11th ed.), IV., p. 748.

Chapter VI. The Ontological Argument.

1. St. Anselm's Argument.

2. Descartes' Use of the Argument.

3. Modern Restatements.

1. *St. Anselm's argument.* The proofs of the existence of God which we have hitherto considered have all been *a posteriori* -- proofs in which the reasoning has been from the effect to the cause. The so-called 'ontological proof' of which we shall treat in this chapter, follows the opposite, *a priori*, method. Just as in geometry we argue *a priori* from the nature or essence of the figure, as expressed in its definition, to its various properties, so certain thinkers have sought to argue from the nature of God to the fact of His existence. God, it must be remembered, exists necessarily. To exist belongs to His very essence. In this He differs from all finite things. Their existence is contingent. Their natures may be expressed in concepts, whether they exist or not: and the concepts throw no light on the question of their existence. But, if we could arrive at a knowledge of the Divine essence, we could not represent it thus apart from its real existence. Existence is not something extraneous to its nature as such, but enters into the nature as a necessary constituent. And this it is which has led men to believe that it is possible to argue from the concept of God's nature to His actual existence, precisely as we argue from essence to property.

Those who made this attempt failed to realize that though God's nature demands existence, yet our human intellect is incapable of knowing the Divine essence as it is. We are on a lower plane of being, and our powers are proportional to our nature. Of natures which are above us we have but a meagre and inadequate knowledge, reached through abstraction and discursive reason. We know something *about* them, but cannot really be said to know them. Hence Aristotle made his well-known comparison of the human intellect to the eyes of bats, saying that as bats are blinded by the daylight, but see in the dusk, so man has but a dim and imperfect cognition of the things which in themselves are such as to evoke the clearest knowledge: and that he knows best those sensible objects, which by reason of their material nature are incapable of being apprehended otherwise than obscurely.[1]

Yet though the proof, as we shall see, is invalid, two thinkers of great eminence -- St. Anselm, who first propounded the argument, and, subsequently, Descartes -- have not only regarded it as sound reasoning, but as the most secure of all the demonstrations of God's existence: while Leibniz, a name of hardly less authority, also eventually gave it his adhesion. It thus possesses great historical interest, and cannot be passed over in silence. Something also must be said of the claim made by certain recent writers belonging to the idealist school to hold the existence of God on the basis of the ontological proof in a somewhat altered form. It will, however, appear that their argument has but little resemblance to the proof which enjoys a prescriptive title to the name. And it is to be regretted that they should suggest the existence of a connection which has no warranty of fact.

Eadmer, Anselm's biographer, tells us how the conviction forced itself upon him that there must be some simple yet cogent argument, shewing alike that God exists, and that He is the supremely perfect Being in whom all perfections are found: how this thought beset him night and day, so as to allow him no rest: and how suddenly, one night, as he stood in his stall in choir for the recitation of the night-office, the light came, and the form which the proof should take flashed into his mind.[2]

The argument is developed in the first chapters of the work to which Anselm gave the name *Proslogium seu Alloquium de Dei Existentia*.[3] It may be thus summarized. The term God signifies that than which nothing greater can be conceived. Even the fool, when he says in his heart *There is no God* (Ps. xiii. i), has an idea corresponding to the word 'God': and his idea is what we have said, viz., that of a nature than which nothing greater can be conceived. But a nature which is of this kind is a necessarily existing nature. For were it to exist only in the mind, we could conceive something greater, viz., a nature so great as not merely to exist in the mind, but to be exigent of real existence as well. God, therefore, exists.

The argument is invalid. A nature conceived as that than which nothing greater can be thought of, must, it is true, be conceived as necessarily existing, *if it exists at all*. But the point at issue is: Is there such a nature? May it not be that it is a mere figment of the mind? If so, although when we conceive it, we conceive it as self-existent, it will not really exist outside our imagination.

Many critics have seen no more in the proof than a patent sophism, and have marvelled that any person of intelligence could have been deluded into regarding it as a valid argument. Such was the attitude of Anselm's contemporary, the monk Gaunilo of Marmoutier. He urged that in this way he could prove the existence of a fabled Lost Island, which was supplied with all riches and all conceivable delights. "Let it be granted," he argued, "that the idea of that island is of a land which excels all others, and you must own that my fabulous region exists: for otherwise the idea of some really existing land would excel it." And to this day it is often thought sufficient to dismiss the reasoning in some such short and easy way. Yet reflection might well have suggested that one of the profoundest intellects of his age was not likely to have been misled by a childish fallacy: that there was probably something deeper in the argument than appears at first sight. That this was so, in fact, is shewn by Anselm's reply to his critic. He there states definitely that his argument holds only of the infinitely perfect being, and that to apply it to anything finite is to have wholly misunderstood its significance. [4] This throws new light upon the saint's meaning. It is, in fact, evident that a being possessed of infinite perfection must be self-existent. If He receives existence from another, He is dependent on that other, and not infinite at all. In other words, self-existence is part of the essential nature of the infinitely perfect. Now let it be assumed that there is nothing contradictory in an infinitely perfect nature: that no impossibility is involved in the idea: that it is capable of actual existence. It follows of necessity that it exists. Here, though not in other cases, *possibility implies existence*. In all other cases, if we say that a nature is possible, we signify that there is no internal contradiction involved, and that consequently, given an adequate efficient cause, the nature might be realized. But here, as we have seen, there is no question of dependence on an efficient cause. The nature is its own sufficient reason. If it be possible, it exists actually. It would be a contradiction in terms for such a nature to be a *mere possible* -- to be capable of existence and yet not to exist actually: for self-existence belongs to its essence. Anselm's real error lies in the assumption that an infinite nature involves nothing contradictory: that its possibility is not open to question. It is true that we detect nothing in the idea which suggests intrinsic repugnance. But it is one thing to be able to affirm of some essence which we can fully apprehend, that we can see its possibility: it is another to have to content ourselves with saying, as regards a nature obscurely and imperfectly known, that we do not detect its impossibility. The latter is our case as regards the infinite. Our concept of the infinite is negative. It gives us no insight into the essential nature of the one infinite Being, but simply asserts *absence of limits*. Indeed, that the possibility of an infinite nature is not immediately self-evident appears from the fact that at the present day certain philosophical writers are prepared to maintain the thesis of a finite God. The position, it is true, leads to all manner of contradictions, and is incapable of reasonable defence. But the mere conception of a 'finite God' is not a manifest absurdity, as it would be were the notion of the infinite evident *a priori*. The possibility of an infinite being must be established by proof. And this is done by shewing *a posteriori* that a First Cause exists: and then that He must needs be infinitely perfect. Since the infinite exists, we know that such a being is possible. *Ab esse ad posse valet illatio.*

It follows from this that the argument fails for the reason which we first gave. Inasmuch as our notion of the infinite does not assure us of its internal possibility, we can draw no conclusion save that an infinite nature must be conceived as existing necessarily, if it exists at all. We cannot prove that it does exist: for we lack the power to frame an idea of the essential nature of the infinite.

It is not too much to say that few of Anselm's recent critics have understood his argument. They think it sufficient to adopt an illustration employed by Kant, and to say that we cannot prove the existence of a hundred dollars from the idea of them, no matter how good the dollars are supposed to be. Of this imaginary refutation of the ontological proof Professor Sorley well says: "It really misses the point of that proof which was an effort to discriminate between the idea of God and all other ideas." And he adds, no less truly: "Gaunilo's objection comes nearer to the point than Kant's does. Anselm had argued that existence must belong to one idea, though to one only, namely, the idea of that than which nothing greater can be conceived. To say, as Kant does, that the idea of a hundred dollars does not involve their existence, is quite irrelevant, for we can easily conceive greater things than a hundred dollars: and, in a tolerable coinage, any one hundred dollars is not better than any other. On the other hand, Gaunilo's idea of a perfect island was at least the idea of something perfect or complete of its kind. Nothing greater of its kind could be conceived. We can, however, conceive something of a greater kind -- perfect of its kind, and of a kind more perfect."[5] In past days there have not been wanting those who saw clearly where the true difficulty lay. Scotus, and, long afterwards, Leibniz, both put their finger upon the weak spot, and pointed out that the argument was inconclusive because the mind cannot affirm with certainty that an infinite nature is possible.[6]

It has become, one might say, fashionable among modern writers to say that the ontological argument is really an abortive attempt on St. Anselm's part to express a truth which he only obscurely realized: that the actual argument, as he gave it, is of minor moment: its true significance lies in the truth after which he was groping. This they proceed to indicate in one fashion or another according to their individual predilection. Two of these arbitrary interpretations will be mentioned in the last section of this chapter. Here we may at least insist on the fact that there is no shadow of doubt regarding Anselm's meaning. He meant exactly what he said, and nothing else. We have, as we have seen, his exposition of the argument in the *Proslogium*, and his reply to criticisms in the *Liber Apologeticus*: while Eadmer's biography throws further light on his intention. We could hardly ask for better documentation. He believed that just as in the real order existence is of the essence of God, so it must be in the order of thought. He forgot, as we have said, the important truth pointed out long since by Aristotle that the range of our cognitive powers is narrowly restricted, that the supersensuous world is known to us only by discursive reasoning based on sensible data, and that for this reason it is impossible for us to know the Supreme Being in aught but an imperfect way.

2. *Descartes' use of the argument.* Descartes' formulation of the argument is not materially different from that of Anselm. It will be well, however, to see how it takes its place in his system. According to him, the concept of God is an innate idea. He denied, as is well known, what appears to be so evident, that through sense-perception we possess direct cognition of the external world, and held that the direct object of knowledge is always internal and spiritual: that we have no immediate knowledge of anything except the ideas within the soul. These ideas he distinguishes into 'adventitious' and 'innate.' Adventitious ideas include all particular perceptions: these appear to inform us of the existence of a material world outside us; yet it would be rash to accept their testimony on this point without further guarantee. As innate we must reckon our universal ideas, and all 'common notions,' *i.e.*, axiomatic truths. These cannot come from without: no particular impression can be the cause of an universal idea. Are, then, these innate ideas capable of giving us valid knowledge? And if so, what can we gather from them? He is enabled to answer this question by the application of his criterion of truth, viz., clearness of conception. If the innate ideas be tested by this criterion, it appears that they convey perfectly valid knowledge, but in reference only to possible existence, not to real. The note of possible existence is attached to every nature thus intellectually conceived: any one of them could be actualized in a real external order of things. Yet there is among them one which differs from the rest -- the idea of God. This contains the note, not of possible, but of real existence. It is the idea possibility may be involved in such a nature. That this is not so must be demonstrated. Descartes' contention that the idea is not gathered from created things, but forms part of the soul's initial endowment, seems to lend some colour to his

conclusion that the idea cannot be a figment of our own minds, but must needs represent objective reality. But, as we need hardly point out, his whole theory of innate ideas is baseless. The idea of God, the perfect Being, stands in no need of recourse to any such hypothesis. We reach it without difficulty by considering the finite perfections of the created world, and then forming a negative idea, in which perfection is conceived without any limit.

The importance attached to the argument in the Cartesian philosophy led Leibniz to give his attention to it. He recognized that if a self-existent being be possible, it follows that such a being exists: that in this case to conceive the essence as possessing potential, though not actual, existence would involve a contradiction, since such a nature is *ex hypothesi* its own sufficient reason. He saw, moreover, that the defenders of the argument had failed to make good this possibility. Yet he gives it as his judgment that the possibility should be assumed till the contrary was demonstrated: that it is for the opponents to prove the impossibility of a self-existent being: and that till this is done, the argument retains a high degree of value. Practically, however, this is not the case. The objective possibility of an infinitely perfect being is less evident to the mind than is the existence of God. Those who deny the latter are not likely to make their own refutation easy by admitting the possibility of an infinite being.

Kant criticizes the ontological proof at length in the *Critique of Pure Reason*. It is frequently assumed that his refutation was decisive; but in point of fact his arguments are wide of the mark. He throughout treats the notion of the infinite nature as though it were on a par with other natures, and could be represented either with or without existence. He fails to meet the fundamental contention of those who defend the proof, viz., that the nature of the infinite is inconceivable apart from real existence: and that, therefore, in this case, and in this case alone, we can establish the existence from the concept of the nature. The arguments on which he relies are two: (1) that if we deny the existence of a being, no question of repugnance is possible, for all notes are sublated: none are left between which repugnance can arise: and (2) that real existence is extrinsic to the essence of any being, and that consequently it is impossible to argue from the concept of the essence to real existence. The first of these arguments is invalid, if the possibility of a self-existent nature has been admitted. For, as we have seen, in the case of this nature possibility and actuality are inseparable. Hence the denial of existence is repugnant to what has been already admitted. Now Kant does not question the possibility of the self-existent being. Indeed, in admitting that He is a legitimate subject of predication he equivalently concedes the possibility. Of the self-contradictory nothing can be said. The second argument is valid against finite natures, but of no force whatever against that particular nature with which the dispute is concerned. Hence, although Kant dismisses Leibniz's considerations as valueless, there can be no question that the latter's criticism shewed a truer appreciation of the argument, and is of far higher worth.

3. *Modern restatements.* We have adverted above (§ 1) to the claim made by certain modern writers to explain what St. Anselm was really seeking to express by the ontological proof. Before we leave the subject, it seems advisable to notice two of these restatements. Little more will be needed than a bare account of the explanations offered: for it will appear at once that there is no connection whatever between the original reasoning and the alleged interpretation. The writers in question attribute to Anselm some thought which for themselves is of considerable importance, and maintain that this must have been in his mind when he framed his argument; but in no instance is there the smallest ground for the assertion. Such a proceeding presents certain attractions which sufficiently explain it. In the first place, it seems to solve the problem how a great intellect was led into a patent fallacy. And it must be remembered in this connection that most of those who offer these solutions see no more in the ontological argument than did Kant, and consequently hold it to involve a manifest paralogism, most perplexing in a thinker of acknowledged eminence. And, secondly, a certain support is won for their own view, if it be the case that the minds of two such men as Anselm and Descartes were travelling, even though unconsciously, in the same direction.

The first of these interpretations to which we shall call attention is propounded by Lotze in his *Microcosmus*. After declaring that Kant's refutation of the argument has shewn once and for all that as a logical proof it is wholly valueless, he proceeds:

"Anselm, in his more free and spontaneous reflection, has here and there touched the thought that the greatest which we can think, if we think it as only thought, is less than the same greatest if we think it as existent. It is not possible that from this reflection either anyone should develop a logically cogent proof, but the way in which it is put seems to reveal another fundamental thought which is seeking for expression. . . . It is an immediate certainty that what is greatest, most beautiful, most worthy, is not a mere thought, but must be a reality, because it would be intolerable to believe of our ideal that it is an idea produced by the action of thought but having no existence, no power, and no validity in the world of reality. . . . Many other attempts may be made to exhibit the internal necessity of this conviction as logically demonstrable; but all of them must fail. On the contrary, the certainty of this claim belongs to those inner experiences to which as to the given object of its labour, the mediating, inferring, and limiting activity of cognition refers."[8]

Professor Pringle Pattison's view is substantially identical[9]: and Professor Sorley, likewise, regards "the demand that our highest ideal, the best and most perfect being which we can conceive, shall not be severed from reality" as one of the two motives which underlie the argument.[10]

Nothing of this kind was in Anselm's mind. And to offer this as the true meaning of the argument is simply misleading. Such an attitude is only comprehensible in those who, by denying the value of the ordinary proofs for God's existence, have kicked away the ladder which supported them, and are reduced to a blind affirmation unsupported by valid reasoning. Anselm was not in this case. In his *Monologium* he had given what he held to be an absolutely solid demonstration of the existence of God. His long and painful effort for an *a priori* proof was no struggle to justify his belief in his ideal. It was, as Eadmer tells us, a search for a short and compendious demonstration of a conclusion already incontrovertibly established by valid but somewhat lengthy reasoning.

Of greater importance than the foregoing is the interpretation offered by idealist thinkers whose system is more or less closely related to that of Hegel. According to them, the truth which lies at the base of the ontological argument is, not that the idea of God as such involves His existence, but that every judgment of the intellect is found in the last resort to presuppose an ultimate Truth -- the ground of all reality -- which is God. We shall have to deal at some length with this system of philosophy in a later chapter (chap. xv.). Here it must be sufficient to say that its defenders hold thought and being to be identical. There are not, they contend, two distinct orders -- an order of being and an order of thought -- but a single order of experience, which may be viewed under either one of these two aspects. Furthermore, truth does not lie in the correspondence of thought with things, but in the coherence of our judgments into a consistent whole. Our particular judgments are partial and inadequate: and taken in their singularity, are found inconsistent with other aspects of reality. Perfect truth can only be realized in a judgment which is adequate to reality in its entirety. Hence all thought points on to an ultimate Truth: the conditioned points to the Absolute: and this is God. To many Hegelians, however, as we shall see, the Absolute is not a Person at all: and though they may still speak of the argument as a proof of God's existence, the term God is employed in a sense peculiar to their system, and the argument has, in fact, no bearing on God's existence at all. Others, at the cost of inconsistency, maintain that the Absolute is a conscious Thinker, whose experience is prior to our own, and embraces in its range that of all limited individualities such as ourselves. To this class belong the majority of English idealists. In illustration of this interpretation of the argument we cite a passage from Professor Edward Caird. He condemns the proof as used by Anselm and Descartes, and then adds:

"But it is quite a different thing, if we regard that argument as pointing to the ultimate unity of thought and Being, which is at once the presupposition and end of all knowledge. Taken in this sense, the argument is but one example of the principle that abstract and imperfect conceptions of reality give rise to contradictions, and so force us to put them in relation to the other conceptions which complement and complete them. For pure thought cannot be conceived as dwelling in itself, but only as relating itself to existence, to a world and in time and space; and it is only (1) through the opposition between itself and such a world, and (2) through the transcendence of that opposition, that it can come to full consciousness of itself. In the language of theology, the Ontological argument expresses the doctrine that God as a spirit is necessarily self-revealing in and to the world."[11]

Our estimate of this explanation will appear when we come to discuss the system which it succinctly summarizes. It does not seem necessary to point out that there is no vestige of a connection between St. Anselm's thought and this piece of Hegelian metaphysics.

NOTES

{1} Aristotle, *Metaph.*, II., c. i., 993b10; cf. *supra*.

{2} Eadmer, *Vita Anselmi*, c. iii., n. 26; Migne, *P.L.*, 158, 63.

{3} Migne, *P.L.*, 158, 227.

{4} *Liber Apologeticus contra Gaunilonem*, c. 3; Migne, *P.L.*, 158, 252.

{5} W. R. Sorley, *Moral Values and the Idea of God*, p. 311-313.

{6} Scotus, in *I.Sent.*, dist. 2., q. 2., n. 32; Leibniz, *De la démonstration Cartésienne de l'existence de Dieu*.

{7} *Principia*, I., nn. 13, 14; *Méditations*, n. *Réponses aux premières objections* (ed. Cousin, Vol. I, 389). Descartes employs other proofs of God's existence; but he seems to have regarded this as the most important: vide *Raisons qui prouvent, etc.* (ed. Cousin, I, 460). He gives it only the second place in the *Meditations*; but there were special reasons for this order.

{8} *Microcosmus* (Eng. trans.), II., pp. 670, 671.

{9} *Idea of God*, p. 240.

{10} *Moral Values and the Idea of God*, p. 315.

{11} *The Philosophy of Kant*, p. 645; cf. also John Caird, *Introduction to the Philosophy of Religion*, p. 144 seqq.

Chapter VII. Kant's Criticism and his Alternative Argument.

1. Kant's Criticism and its Fruits.

2. His Criticism of the Cosmological Argument.

3. His Criticism of the Teleological Argument.

4. His Alternative Proof from the Practical Reason.

1. *Kant's criticism and its Fruits.* Kant, it is well known, challenged the validity of the traditional proofs of God's existence. In his *Critique of Pure Reason* he examines the cosmological and the teleological arguments, and declares that they are both vitiated by a latent fallacy. In each case, he says, the reasoning of the ontological argument is surreptitiously introduced into the proof, so that the value of the conclusion stands or falls with that method of demonstration. That argument, however, he has already weighed in the balance and found wanting: it follows that these two famous proofs of God's existence are alike worthless. The mind, moreover, he contends, must recognize its incapacity to reach this conclusion by any demonstration of the speculative reason: for there neither are, nor can be, any other lines of proof save the three just mentioned. Either we argue from the peculiar constitution of the world of sense: or we argue from the nature of finite being as such, abstracting from any special laws of physical nature: or, lastly, we abstract from all experience, and base our reasoning on *a priori* conceptions alone. In the first case we have the teleological proof: in the second, the cosmological: while the third alternative gives us the ontological argument employed by St. Anselm and Descartes. Beyond these no other proofs by way of the speculative reason are possible. It is unnecessary to point out that this assertion that there is but one proof based on physical laws, and but one based on the nature of finite being, is a mere assumption, and altogether erroneous. Kant further undertakes to shew how it comes about that the human intellect in virtue of its very constitution is driven by a native tendency to the illusion of a personal first cause, and is thus disposed to

buttress up its figment by fallacious arguments. What, however, he takes away with one hand, he seeks to restore with the other. He maintains that though the speculative reason cannot provide us with a proof of God's existence, the practical reason will supply the deficiency.

It may be of interest here to give a summary account of his views regarding the alleged tendency of the reason to posit a personal first cause irrespectively of any real grounds for belief in its existence. Some leading features of the Kantian system have been already explained (chap. ii., § 5). It will he remembered that he held that things as we know them -- phenomena -- are not objective realities, but are the work of our own mind operating on and organizing the internal subjective sensations which are its sole data. The realities to which those sensations are ultimately due -- the noumena -- we cannot know. Space and time, in which things are known to us, are forms of sensibility. Our conceptions of things, whether as substances or accidents, and all our judgments regarding them, are determined by the categories of the understanding. Reason likewise has its laws: and these laws determine for us the whole process of our ratiocination. In argument, the mind is not, as we fondly imagine, taking each step in obedience to the assured claims of truth and in conformity with a real world of which it is representative. It travels along a road prescribed by its internal constitution. Its characteristic operation is the arrangement of our cognitions in a systematic unity. In virtue of this natural tendency we are irresistibly led to view all phenomena in reference to the total of reality -- this total, however, being a mere ideal and having no objective validity. Further, we come to regard this ideal total as the common ground or cause of all things, and hence as containing in itself all perfection. In this manner we reach the idea of God. But "we have not," he says, "the slightest ground to admit the existence of an object corresponding to this idea . . . . The idea of this Being is essentially nothing more than a demand upon reason that it shall regulate the connection which it and its subordinate faculties introduce into the phenomena of the world by principles of systematic unity, and consequently that it shall regard all phenomena as originating from one all-embracing Being, as the supreme and all-sufficient cause."[1]

It is not to be denied that ever since Kant's time an impression has prevailed widely that the old proofs are no longer defensible. Possibly the mere fact that an eminent thinker had ventured to call in question such seemingly irrefutable arguments seemed by itself almost equivalent to a disproof. But another reason also, extrinsic it is true to the merits of the criticism, but none the less effective, operated in favour of this result. During the last century, rationalism, in the form either of naturalism or of idealism, had become strongly entrenched in the great centres of learning. It was only natural that thinkers who had discarded belief in a personal God should applaud Kant's conclusion, even if they might hesitate to affirm that his criticism of the proofs was in all respects sound. Thus it came about that those who admitted the value of the traditional arguments were regarded as out of date. Often the validity of Kant's objections is simply taken for granted, and the proofs of God's existence dismissed without more ado.[2] Even some of the apologists of revealed religion, eager not to be behind the fashion, discard them as untenable. In *Lux Mundi* (1889), a book written by men of real academical distinction in view of the intellectual difficulties against faith then commonly felt, and intended to provide a reasoned defence of Christianity, the author of the essay on "The Christian Doctrine of God," says that in his opinion "there can be no proofs in the strict sense of the word of the existence of God. . . . Neither conscience nor the speculative reason can demonstrate God's existence" (p. 103)[3]: and proceeds to base his defence of the doctrine on the fact that belief in God is spontaneous and instinctive, and that it is confirmed alike by the experience of life and by the conclusions, so far as they will go -- which is not far -- of the speculative reason. Such an answer, it is plain, is no adequate reply to the rationalist attack. If philosophy can do no more for us than this on the most vital of all issues which fall within its scope, it is hard to avoid the conclusion that the popular idea which sees in metaphysics, once reckoned as the supreme science, nothing but profitless disputation leading to no practical result, is amply justified. Such, however, has never been the attitude of Scholastic thinkers. They have consistently denied that Kant detected a flaw in any one of the great traditional proofs of God's existence. On the contrary, they maintain that his analysis of these arguments is sophistical through and through, and destitute of all real value: and that the argument from the practical reason which he proposed as a sufficient substitute for those which he discarded, is itself quite incompetent to sustain the test of a critical examination. In the subsequent sections of the present chapter we shall endeavour to make good these contentions.

2. *Criticism of the cosmological argument.* Kant bases his attack on the cosmological proof chiefly, as we have already noted, on the ground that when analysed, it is found to reach its conclusion by the concealed employment of the ontological argument. It professes to argue from existing contingent beings to the existence of a necessary being, who is God. As a matter of fact, he maintains, it arrives at the existence of necessary being, not from the contingent existences which are its alleged ground, but purely from our ideal conception of the absolutely perfect being. He has other charges also against the proof. These, however, may for the moment be deferred. Our immediate task is to examine his first and principal gravamen.

The conclusion, Kant reminds us, is reached by establishing the two propositions: 'Contingent being involves the existence of necessary being': and, 'Necessary being is supreme perfection, *i.e.*, God (*Ens necessarium est Ens realissimum*).' From these two premises it is claimed that we have demonstrated God's existence. Yet so far, he assures us, is this from being the case that the second of the two propositions is worthless for our purpose, having no bearing on the existential world unless the validity of the ontological argument be presupposed. This he proceeds to shew as follows, The proposition, Necessary being is Supreme Perfection, is equivalent as logic teaches us to its converse. This converse would by the rules of logic take the form, Some supremely perfect beings are necessary beings. But as there can be but one supremely perfect being, we may state it as, Supreme Perfection is necessary being. This is neither more nor less than the ontological fallacy which has slipped in unobserved. The conclusion, which seemed at first sight to be based on experience, is really determined *a priori* by our conceptions, the notion of perfect being being conceived as necessarily involving its own existence in the real order.

The fallacy of this criticism is patent. In the cosmological argument the proposition, 'Necessary being is supreme perfection,' is concerned with *an existing reality*. We have already proved that a necessary being exists. We are now concerned to discover the nature of that being. Its necessity enables us to conclude to certain other of its attributes: and in this way we realize that this being of whose existence we are certain is in fact the living God, the source of all reality. In the ontological argument it is otherwise. The proposition, The perfect being is necessary, does not deal with an object whose existence is known. We are concerned solely with the concept of perfect being: and since we have only a vague and indeterminate notion of supreme perfection, we are not even aware whether such a concept is possible of realization in the objective order. We are not, in fact, justified in stating that supreme perfection is necessary, but only that supreme perfection, if it exists, is necessary.

It may well excite our wonder that Kant should have fallen into so manifest a sophism. But his discussion of the argument shews us how the error arose. He tells us that the *a posteriori* argument from experience only enables us to conclude to the existence of a necessary being of some kind or another, but is incompetent to shew us what particular thing possesses this attribute of necessity. "Experience," he says, "merely aids reason in making one step -- to the existence of a necessary being. What the properties of this being are cannot be learned from experience. . . . Experience is utterly insufficient to demonstrate the existence of this attribute [of necessity] in any determinate existence or thing."[4] He fails to see that there is no need for us to look to experience to shew us a determinate thing which is necessary: that just as reason is able to take the step which leads it from the existence of contingent being to the existence of necessary being, so it can go on to shew that necessary being cannot be limited, but must be being in the fullness of its perfection. Thus he comes to give a wholly erroneous account of the manner in which we reach the minor premiss, Necessary being is supreme perfection. "When we propose to ourselves an aim of this character," he says, "we must abandon the sphere of experience and rise to that of pure conceptions, which we examine with the purpose of discovering whether any one of them contains the conditions of the possibility of an absolutely necessary being." We find these conditions in our conception of *Ens realissimum*, Supreme Perfection. Moreover, not merely is Supreme Perfection conceived as having the attribute of necessity; but among all our conceptions it is the sole nature which has this attribute. Hence we are justified in identifying it with the *Ens necessarium*, whose existence we have proved, and saying, Necessary being is Supreme Perfection. But here, he contends, is the fallacy. We have no right to make this identification: for we have no ground for regarding our concept of Supreme Perfection as something which belongs to the real order. It is a mere concept: and when we treat it as something which belongs to the real order, and identify it with *Ens necessarium*, we are simply employing the illegitimate method of the ontological argument.

This account of the way in which the minor premiss is obtained is clearly quite inaccurate. Conceiving it thus, it is easy to understand how Kant came to regard it as invalid. But his criticism is throughout based on the strangest of misapprehensions.

Though this is Kant's principal accusation against the cosmological argument, it is not, as we have already said, his only one. Indeed, he goes so far as to say that it "contains a perfect nest of dialectical assumptions, which transcendental criticism does not find it difficult to expose and to dissipate": and he proceeds to enumerate four of the alleged assumptions. These we shall consider seriatim.

(1) In the first place, he urges that the category of causality belongs solely to the world of phenomena, and that we have no right to treat it as valid also for that world of noumenal realities to which God is held to belong. Causality is a mere 'form' imposed by the intellect. In virtue of our mental constitution we conceive every phenomenon as related to some previous one as its effect; but this does not justify us in believing that the relation holds good outside our minds, and in viewing God as the first cause of the world. The objection finds clear expression in the following passage:

"If the Supreme Being forms a link in the chain of empirical conditions, it must be a member of the empirical series, and like the lower members which it precedes, have its origin in some higher member of the series. If, on the other hand, we disengage it from the chain, and cogitate it as an intelligible being apart from the series of natural causes -- how shall reason bridge the abyss that separates the latter from the former? All laws respecting the regress from effects to causes, all synthetical additions to our knowledge relate solely to possible experience and the objects of the sensuous world, and apart from them are without significance" (*op. cit.* p. 382).

This objection rests entirely on Kant's theory regarding the data and forms of knowledge. That theory we reject as radically unsound. We have already argued at length (chap. ii.) that causality is no subjective contribution of our own without objective validity, but that it is a fact of the objective order: and that the principle of causality is a metaphysical truth of supreme certainty. The whole elaborate edifice of Kant's theory is, we contend, built on the gratuitous assumption made by Descartes, and accepted by Locke and Hume, that we are conscious of nothing but our own internal states.[5]

(2) As his next objection Kant urges that we have no justification for asserting the impossibility of an infinite series. The principles of reason, he holds, do not permit us to affirm the repugnance of such a series even as regards the world of experience. Much less, then, is it allowable as regards noumenal realities.

The objection is valid according to the principles of the Kantian philosophy. If there were a law of our mentality compelling us to regard every phenomenon as proceeding from a previous phenomenon, it would follow that the empirical series must be infinite *a parte ante*. We have already treated the question from the point of view of a metaphysic more conformable to reality. It was shewn that although there is room for difference of opinion regarding the possibility or impossibility of a series of causes whose sole function is to bring the subsequent cause into existence, this is not so as regards the causes whose actual operation is needed *hic et nunc* for the realization of the effect. An infinite series of these is intrinsically repugnant: and it is with these causes that the cosmological argument is concerned.

(3) In the third place we are told that the idea of necessity as applied to the First Cause is illegitimate and meaningless. The First Cause is, by hypothesis, unconditioned. But necessity is conceived as resulting from the fulfilment of requisite conditions. This, in fact, is the meaning of necessity, and apart from this no significance attaches to the notion.

To this we reply that Kant fails to distinguish between dependent entities and the independent, self-existent Being. Without doubt the necessity proper to dependent beings arises from the fulfilment of the conditions requisite for their realization: and we cannot conceive it save in this manner. But the self-existent First Cause is not a dependent being. It is not possible for us to form a *positive* concept of the necessity proper to such a Being, any more than of His infinity. Yet we gain a valid and significant idea of it when we conceive it as freedom from all conditions, just as we form a significant idea of infinity as being that which has no limits, and of eternity as that which has neither beginning nor end.

(4) Kant's fourth objection is that because we find no internal contradiction in the idea of a sum-total of reality, we conclude that this is capable of objective existence as an individual thing. We have, he maintains, no right to make this transition, unless we have first shewn the practicability of the objective synthesis. And yet, even did we do so, it would avail us little: for the synthesis thus vindicated would have reference solely to the world of phenomenal experience and not to reality.

The answer here is simple. We do not conclude the objective possibility of a Being, who sums up in Himself all reality, on the ground that we can detect no logical contradiction in the concept of the sum-total of perfection. We conclude to the possibility because we have shewn that such a Being exists. We demonstrate *a posteriori* that necessary being is, and by considering what attributes must pertain to a necessary being, we are able to conclude that this existing entity is the sum of all reality. Nor do we view this entity as the congeries of natural perfections, but as of an altogether higher order. In Him as in their sole source must be gathered up all that this world displays in such various forms and such diverse harmonies of goodness, beauty and truth. Yet created perfections, though of a lower order, nevertheless afford a sure basis for our argument. For they are objectively real: they are no phenomenal construction of our own minds.

It would seem, then, that "the nest of dialectical assumptions" was of Kant's own making. The traditional proof *a contingentia* is free from fallacy. But on the other hand, each one of his five objections is radically sophistical.

3. *Criticism of the teleological argument*. Of the teleological argument Kant speaks in terms of high regard. He says:

"It is the oldest [argument], the clearest, and that most in conformity with the common reason of humanity. . . . It would be utterly hopeless to attempt to rob this argument of the authority it has always enjoyed. The mind unceasingly elevated by these considerations which, although empirical, are so remarkably powerful, and continually adding to their force, will not suffer itself to be depressed by the doubts suggested by subtle speculation: it tears itself out of this state of uncertainty, the moment it casts a look upon the wondrous forms of nature, and the majesty of the universe, and rises from height to height, from condition to condition, till it has elevated itself to the supreme and unconditioned Author of all" (*op. cit.* p. 383).

On what ground, then, does he attempt to achieve the task which he declares to be a hopeless endeavour -- to rob this argument of its authority? The proof, he tells us, is based on the fact that there are in the world manifest signs of an arrangement full of purposes, and that "this arrangement is foreign to the things existing in the world -- it belongs to them as a contingent attribute." Things do not tend to these ends in virtue of their own nature: the arrangement must be imposed upon them from without by an intelligent cause. Now this reasoning carries us, he urges, no further than to an *architect of the universe*, whose efforts are limited by the materials in which he works. It will not take us to a *creator*: and consequently is no proof of the existence of God. Moreover, even as it is, we get no determinate idea of this architect of the world. We see that he must be 'very great' and 'very wise.' But such predicates as these merely indicate the relation which his greatness and wisdom bears to ours: they do not give us any definite knowledge regarding him. We have not any sufficient ground for judging that any attribute is absolutely his. Though wiser and greater than us, he may not be, absolutely speaking, wise or great. We cannot pronounce finally whether he is one or several, good or evil. Our knowledge is indeterminate. How then do we reach our conclusion? We fall back, Kant avers, on the cosmological proof. From this order and conformity to external aims, we infer the contingency of the world. The contingency of the world enables us to reason to necessary being: and then by the invalid ontological process we conclude that God exists. Only thus does our concept become determinate. For no other concept than that of the plenitude of reality, which contains all possible perfection, can he regarded as such.

Both these criticisms are unsound. It is, doubtless, true that the proof from final causes does not establish that the Cause who organized the world stands to it in the relation of Creator. It is unreasonable to demand that it should do so. To prove that God did not form the world out of preexisting matter, but created it, is a subsequent step to demonstrating His existence. The denial of a divine attribute may logically lead to the denial of God; but the questions involved are distinct: and a proof of God's existence is not bound to indude a proof of His attributes. It may, indeed, be urged that the teleological argument does not even shew that the architect of nature is self-existent: and that without this it cannot he said to shew that he is, in fact, God. Many theists admit that the objection as so stated is not without force. They grant that to be rigidly complete the teleological proof must be supplemented by the cosmological argument. That argument they hold, of course, to be absolutely free from any connection with the ontological proof. They point out, however, that practically, the teleological demonstration, even as considered separately, is decisive of the issue of theism. No one who admits the existence of an intelligent Author of Nature will have the smallest doubt that he has proved the existence of God. We have shewn reason in chap. iv. for thinking that even this concession is unnecessary. The teleological argument, as we pointed out, carries us not simply to an architect of nature, but to a First Source of order. Such a First Source must necessarily be self-existent.

The second objection, that the proof gives us no determinate knowledge regarding the Author of Nature is equally fallacious. Here, just as above, we must demand to keep the full treatment of the Divine attributes for later consideration. We are not bound, when establishing the existence of God, simultaneously to demonstrate the infinity of all His attributes. But we know that His wisdom and His power must be proportionate to the effects on which the teleological argument is based: that they are such as could devise and could realize the marvellous scheme of things which the created world offers to our contemplation -- surely a perfectly definite idea. The unity of the order displayed throughout the universe affords a weighty argument that He is One. But the formal proof that He is infinite in all His attributes, and the full discussion of His unity, are logically posterior to the question proposed to us.[6]

4. *Proof of God's existence from the practical reason.* While Kant denied the capacity of the speculative reason to establish God's existence, he believed that in the practical reason he had found a secure basis for holding this truth. Man's highest good (*summum bonum*), he tells us, consists, not in virtue alone, but in virtue united to happiness. For happiness is a good: and though virtue is a higher good than happiness, yet goodness wants something to its completeness if happiness be not joined to it. It is our duty to be ever aiming at the *summum bonum*, though the motive of our actions must be the moral law itself, and not the desire of the highest good. Here, however, we are faced by a difficulty. The causal series which constitute the world of experience do not operate in favour of virtue: they are altogether indifferent to it. Happiness does not result from a virtuous life, but from a knowledge of physical law combined with power to employ it for our advantage. The only manner

in which it is possible to suppose a connection between virtue and happiness is to postulate the existence of a Supreme Cause distinct from nature and able to effect a union between the two. Such a cause we signify by the name, God. Hence we are justified in affirming the existence of God as the holy and omnipotent Author of the world.

Is this an act of intellectual cognition? Emphatically no, Kant replies. The speculative reason leads us to a very different issue, shewing us that our idea of God arises from a dialectical illusion. Our belief in God is a moral conviction based upon our practical needs. It is a 'postulate.' The act is not an act of knowledge, but of faith. This employment of the term 'faith' merits attention: for it involves a radical change in its significance. The word in its accepted meaning denotes an intellectual assent given to truths which we know to have been revealed by God -- an assent which is grounded on an assured certainty of God's existence, and of the fact of revelation. With Kant it is used to signify a blind adhesion, in default of knowledge, to the 'postulate' of God's existence. Strictly speaking, as a matter of speculation, the postulate is still an hypothesis; but in view of our practical needs it becomes a legitimate object for an act of 'faith.' Yet this act must not be employed as a basis for any theoretic conclusions as to the nature of God: our speculative knowledge is not thereby enlarged.[7]

Kant's reason for thus refusing to allow the fact of God's existence revealed by the practical reason to be employed as a basis for the extension of our speculative knowledge, was that he held 'synthetical' propositions to be possible only in regard of objects which are capable of presentation to the senses.[8] God, it is manifest, cannot be sensibly experienced.

The reasoning here is marred by a fatal flaw. There is in Kant's system no ground whatever for his contention that happiness must be connected with virtue. This is a legitimate conclusion, when we already know that God exists, and that He has imposed upon us the obligation of the moral law. In that case it follows that the Supreme Lawgiver will not have left His law without its due sanctions. But if we have no assurance of God's existence, and do not regard the moral law as a divinely imposed obligation, there is no reason whatever to suppose that virtue will secure happiness for those who practise it. Yet Kant assumes that it is so, and builds his conviction of God's existence on this assumption. He does not postulate God's existence as that of the law-giver who will avenge wrong-doing and reward the just. He consistently maintains that the moral law makes no appeal to any higher lawgiver than reason itself. He concludes to God's existence, only because he holds it evident that the *summum bonum* must include happiness. This, however, on his principles, is a gratuitous assumption. Happiness and unhappiness, as he conceives them, belong to the phenomenal order, being dependent on physical law. We have no ground for holding that they possess any noumenal counterpart. Moral excellence is noumenal. It may, so far as we know, be wholly unrelated to happiness. It would seem that, on Kantian principles, where moral obligation is concerned, the phenomenal facts of happiness and unhappiness should be wholly disregarded as being altogether outside the question.

But even were Kant's reasoning as valid as it is invalid, how lame and impotent is the conclusion to which he brings us! We desire to know not merely God's existence, but much else about Him. Does He concern Himself with us, or is He wholly occupied in His own essential bliss? Does He exercise an immediate and direct providence in regard of each several individual or not? And many other questions are there which it vitally concerns us to know. Kant replies that we must be content to be utterly ignorant of these things: that we can know nothing but the bare fact that He is: and that even this is not properly knowledge, but a conviction based on a practical need. Such a theory is, as has well been said, the union of practical dogmatism with complete speculative agnosticism.

NOTES

{1} *Critique of Pure Reason*, Pt. II., Div. ii., Book 2, c. iii., § 7 (Meiklejohn's trans., p. 420).

{2} Cf. J. Ward, *Realm of Ends* (1911). "Can we then prove the existence of God? Attempts innumerable to prove this have been made -- as of course we know -- all of them reducible to one or other of the three forms called respectively the ontological, the cosmological and the teleological argument. The fatal defects of all these have, it is almost universally conceded, been clearly exposed once for all by Kant."

{3} Mr. Aubrey Moore. It would seem as if he had hardly troubled even to acquaint himself with the arguments which he so lightly sets aside. For he writes: "The so called proof *a contingentia* (which underlies H. Spencer's argument for the Unknowable) is an appeal to that very consciousness of dependence which some people consider a weakness and a thing to educate themselves out of." It is difficult to attach any reasonable meaning to such a statement.

{4} *Op. cit.*, p. 373.

{5} The objection that it is impossible to argue from the chain of contingent causes and effects to a cause which, being necessary, is of a different order, is still urged by some writers. Thus Principal Caird says: "You cannot in a syllogistic demonstration put more into the conclusion than the premises contain. . . All that from a finite or contingent effect you can infer is a finite or contingent cause, or at most an endless series of such causes. But if, because the mind cannot rest in this false infinity, you try to stop the indefinite regress, and assert at any point of it a cause which is not an effect, which is its own cause, or which is unconditioned and infinite, the conclusion in this case is purely arbitrary." *Introd. to Phil. of Religion*, p. 129. It would seem as though he had failed to see that not the contingent substances themselves, but the analytic proposition "Contingent being involves the existence of necessary being" provided the premises of the syllogism. The same objection is found in Edw.

Caird's *Phil of Kant* (1877), p. 646, and in Illingworth's *Personality Human and Divine*, p. 93.

{6} In the *Critique of Judgment* Kant calls the teleological argument in question on a new ground. He contends that the necessity which we feel of attributing finality to nature is purely subjective. We cannot study nature unless we view it as a unity. And we effect this end by conceiving it as a system such as a mind would have established; but it is quite conceivable that the order of nature may be due to purely mechanical principles without finality of any kind. This objection has its true origin in Kant's doctrine of the Categories. That teaching leaves, in fact, no room whatever for finality in nature: and Kant is thus logically compelled to suppose that the principle of finality is a sort of working hypothesis devoid of objective value.

{7} *Critique of Practical Reason*, Pt. I., Bk. 2, c. ii., § 5 - § 7 (Abbott's trans., pp. 223-234).

{8} Cf. the citation given on p. 225. On the significance of the term 'synthetical proposition' in the Kantian philosophy see pp. 48, 49.

Part II. Nature and Attributes of God

Chapter VIII. Agnostic Difficulties and the Principle of their Solution.

1. Agnostic Difficulties.

2. The Analogical Knowledge of God.

3. Solution of the Difficulties.

4. Modernism and Agnosticism.

1. *Agnostic difficulties.* Before commencing our discussion of the attributes of God it is necessary first to consider whether anything save the mere fact of His existence is not by the very nature of the case beyond the reach of our faculties. Kant is not by any means alone in maintaining this. Other thinkers also confidently assert that the attempt to attain to any positive knowledge regarding the Divine Being can bear no fruit except to entangle the mind in a series of contradictions, inasmuch as the conditions under which we exercise the faculty of reason put such knowledge altogether out of our reach. They assure us that the traditional theistic teaching according to which man, unaided by revelation and relying on reason alone, can establish that God is infinite, immutable, omnipresent, all-wise, and all-good, is grounded on palpable fallacies: that although in order to account for the world of experience we are compelled to postulate an unknown ground of being, reason will carry us no further than this. No attribute can be affirmed of this ultimate ground except that it is unknown and unknowable.

The chief exponent of this view is H. Spencer. In his *First Principles* he undertakes to determine the boundaries between religion and science. To science he assigns the sphere of the knowable, to religion that of the unknowable -- an impenetrable background, which science must suppose to exist, but concerning which it can predicate nothing. With this division he claims that the two contending parties -- for he holds the normal relation of religion and science to be one of antagonism -- should be content. Such a partition, it is needless to say, is radically opposed to theism. To the theist God is no unknown ground of being. He is not merely the First Efficient Cause of the world, but its ultimate Final Cause. Beatitude, the end towards which all human activity should be directed, and to the attainment of which all knowledge is but a means, lies in the possession of God. If, then, we are essentially incapable of knowing anything whatever about the Source of all being, and must resign ourselves to remain ignorant, whether it be spirit or matter, personal or impersonal, we are left without an end in life. Whither the theory leads is plain to see in Spencer's own pages. Notwithstanding his protestation that his doctrine contains the essential element of every religious creed, viz., the belief in an inscrutable something behind phenomena, and that he is by no means to be accounted a materialist, he does, in fact, explain all things in terms of matter and motion, and treats this explanation as ultimate. His system of philosophy is a materialist system.

The arguments by which he supports his agnostic conclusions are taken from the works of Sir W. Hamilton and Mansel, two writers who certainly had no intention of furthering the cause of religious agnosticism. They had both drawn a very different inference, viz., that the incapacity of human reason to frame a valid natural theology renders revelation all the more necessary to man. Spencer accepted their arguments, but employed them against natural and revealed religion alike. This train of thought, it should be noted, originated with Kant, some of whose views Hamilton had adopted, though differing widely from him in his general philosophical position.

In this chapter we are not concerned with the whole series of Spencer's arguments on behalf of agnosticism. Some of them will find their natural place in one or other of the chapters which follow. There is, however, a fundamental difficulty which calls for consideration at once. It is asserted that the so-called attributes of God are all of them perfections known to us from the world of experience and involving limitations proper to finite beings alone. If the theist will but scrutinize them, he will soon recognize that they are incompatible with the infinity which he is constrained to affirm of God: and that reason thus compels him to the admission that he knows nothing regarding God's nature. He attributes to Him intelligence, will, causality. Do not all of these of their very nature imply the determination of a substance by accidents? Is it, then, seriously contended that the Divine nature is a composite structure composed of diverse elements!

Kant raises this difficulty in his *Prolegomena to Every Future System of Metaphysics*, §§ 57, 58. Reason, he says, leads us to hold the existence of a Supreme Being, the ground of all reality: and this may be done, provided we confine ourselves to the "deistic conception, . . . which, however, only represents a thing containing all reality, without our being able to determine a single one of its qualities, because for this an instance would have to be borrowed from the sense-world, in which case I should always have to do with an object of sense, and not with something completely heterogeneous, which cannot be an object of sense." We are compelled, he admits, to judge that the world is related to the Supreme Being as a watch is to its maker or a ship to its builder, thus viewing it "as though it were the work of a supreme understanding and will." But we must not imagine that we thus arrive at any knowledge of the nature of the Supreme Being. We certainly cannot attribute reason and will to Him: for "I have no conception whatever of any understanding but of one like my own, namely of one to which intuitions must be given through the senses": and the same difficulty holds good as regards a will. All that our judgment implies is that the Supreme Being is in some way the source of the reason inherent in the world of experience. Here," he says, "only the form of reason everywhere met with in the world is considered, and to the Supreme Being so far as it is the ground of this form of reason in the world, Reason is attributed." In other words, we may judge that there is in the Supreme Being *something* in virtue of which He adapts means to ends, very much as our intelligence enables us to employ for various purposes the materials which nature provides. But what that *something* is we cannot tell. We have no ground for holding it to be intelligence: for intelligence, in the only form in which it is known to us, supposes conditions which belong essentially to the sense-world.

Mansel raises difficulties of a similar character. There is, he points out, no attribute which seems more certainly to belong to God than that He is the First Cause of finite being. Yet even the notion of causality involves limitations which we cannot possibly admit to be found in Him. For reason compels us to hold that God is the Absolute Being, viz., that He is no way conditioned by or related to anything outside Himself. Now a cause, Mansel contends, is essentially related to its effect.[1]

"These three conceptions," he writes, "the Cause, the Absolute, the Infinite, all equally indispensable, do they not imply contradiction to each other, when viewed in conjunction, as attributes of one and the same Being? A cause cannot, as such, be absolute: the Absolute cannot, as such, be a cause. The cause, as such, exists only in relation to its effect: the cause is a cause of the effect; the effect is an effect of the cause.[2] On the other hand, the conception of the Absolute implies a possible existence out of all relation. We attempt to escape from this apparent contradiction by introducing the idea of succession in time. The Absolute exists first by itself and afterwards becomes a cause. But here we are checked by the third conception, that of the Infinite. How can the Infinite become that which it was not from the first? If causation is a possible mode of existence, that which exists without causing is not infinite: that which becomes a cause has passed beyond its former limits."

He proceeds to point out that reason declares the divine nature, in virtue of its supreme perfection, to be simple to the entire exclusion of composition in any form. But if this be admitted, we are prohibited from supposing a plurality of attributes in God, or even the distinction between the thinking mind and its thought, which intelligence supposes.

"Not only is the Absolute, as conceived, incapable of a necessary relation to anything else; but it is also incapable of containing, by the constitution of its own nature, an essential relation within itself; as a whole, for instance, composed of parts, or as a substance consisting of attributes, or as a conscious subject in antithesis to an object. For if there is in the Absolute any principle of unity, distinct from the accumulation of parts or attributes, this principle alone is the true absolute. If, on the other hand, there is no such principle, then there is no absolute at all, but only a bundle of relatives. The almost unanimous voice of philosophy, in pronouncing that the absolute is both one and simple, must be accepted as the voice of reason also, so far as reason has any voice in the matter."[3]

It must not be supposed that these objections are altogether new and that the philosophers of the eighteenth and nineteenth centuries discovered difficulties for which theism was wholly unprepared. The agnostic controversy had in fact been fought out long before and by champions of the first rank. The famous Jewish doctor, Moses Maimonides, raised precisely the same issue in the twelfth century in his treatise, *Moreh Nebukim (Ductor Dubitantium)*.[4] This work was written in Arabic, but even before the author's death was translated into Hebrew for the benefit of his coreligionists, and soon became known in Latin versions to Catholic theologians. Its primary and professed object was to reconcile the conclusions of Aristotelian philosophy with the teaching of the Law; but it had also a controversial purpose. In contending that a knowledge of the Divine nature is wholly beyond the scope of human reason, Maimonides sought to undermine the basis of Christian theology. His objections are substantially the same as those which we have been considering. He, too, appeals to God's essential simplicity and to the impossibility of the Divine substance being conditioned by relations. His conclusion is that the attributes which we affirm of God are most frequently to be understood metaphorically. When we say 'God is intelligent,' we signify no more than that God acts *as though* He were intelligent: just as when we speak of God as being angry, we understand the word metaphorically and not literally. In other cases the terms applied to Him are to be taken as signifying a causal relation. God may be called intelligent or good as signifying that He is the cause of goodness and intelligence in creatures. Lastly, they can be understood negatively. We say God is intelligent to indicate that He is not inanimate matter or possessed of merely sensitive life like the animals. It is manifest that these conclusions hardly differ from those of Kant. It is to be regretted that neither Kant himself nor his English successors were acquainted with St. Thomas Aquinas's reply to the Jewish doctor. The greatest of the Scholastic thinkers was perfectly alive to the importance of the issue, and deals with it in more than one of his works.[5] He gives, it may safely be said, a full and final solution of the arguments advanced in the *Ductor Dubitantium*.

2. *The analogical knowledge of God.* St. Thomas bases his refutation on the certain principle that no cause can confer any perfection which it does not in some manner possess. The perfection is the result of the cause's action. And an agent must possess a perfection before its action can be of such a kind as to confer it. As a thing is, so does it act. If, then, it be admitted that God is the cause of created perfections, we must of necessity admit that in some way these perfections must be found in Him. It does not follow that the mode in which God possesses them is identical with that in which a creature enjoys them: it may be very different.[6] The artist could not carve the statue unless the form which he is giving to fhe marble were to be found in him. But its mode of existence in his mind differs from that which it has when realized in stone. In him it has a nobler and more spiritual manner of being: for it is not limited by material conditions. So, too, in regard to the creature and the Creator. The perfections of the creature are not merely referable to God in the sense that He has power to produce them, but the same perfections are actually in some way intrinsic to Him. Here, however, a distinction must be drawn. Among created perfections some there are, which involve in their concept no imperfection at all, as, *e.g.*, life, intelligence, existence. These are termed 'pure' perfections. The mode in which they are found in creatures may be an imperfect mode. Indeed, it must be so, for it is necessarily finite and limited. But the perfection expressed by the definition in each case, as distinguished from the particular manner of its realization, connotes no imperfection. These perfections may be affirmed of God in strict and literal truth. The perfection is really found in Him, though in a far higher manner than in

creatures. To use Scholastic terms which we have already explained, it is in Him both *formally* and *eminently*.[7] There are other endowments of the creature which in their very notion involve imperfection. Such are all those which imply material conditions. The faculties of sense, and all forms of physical beauty, will serve as illustrations. These are termed 'mixed' perfections, and these, it is manifest, are not found in their proper nature (*formaliter*) in God, though whatever there is in them of goodness belongs to Him in some sublimer way. Terms denoting such perfections as these can only be predicated of God metaphorically. Thus when He is declared to be 'merciful' and 'just,' the attributes signified are understood to be predicated of Him in their literal sense. But when God is spoken of as 'angry' with sinners, the term is employed metaphorically, and simply denotes that His action is comparable to that to which a just judge may be moved by a righteous indignation with crime.[8]

The agnostic objections, which we considered in the previous section, were one and all based on the supposition that inasmuch as our knowledge is derived from our experience of creatures, our concept of any perfection found in them necessarily includes the imperfect mode in which the creature possesses it: and that, consequently, if we predicate it of God we are implicitly attributing this mode to Him also. Thus Kant, as we have seen, urges that we cannot say that God is intelligent without thereby implying that He gathers information from the perceptions of sense. Mansel takes it for granted that the divine attributes must denote accidental determinations distinct one from another: and that since in efficient causality as we know it, not merely is the effect related to the cause, but the cause to the effect, we must necessarily imply the same when we say that God is the First Cause. Yet this is not the case. When we attribute to God a perfection which is found in the created world, we understand that in Him it has none of the limitations which adhere to it as it belongs to the creature. In other words, we employ the word not univocally, but *analogously*. Already in a previous chapter (chap. iii., § 4) we have explained these expressions. A term is univocal if its signification is precisely the same in regard of all the subjects of which it is predicated. The senses of an analogous term, on the other hand, are not absolutely identical. They are similar: there is a proportional resemblance between them. If the attribute 'intelligent' were, indeed, univocal, it could not be predicated of God in any literal sense. For in the form in which we are familiar with intelligence, its activity is accidental: whereas in the Infinite a distinction between substance and accident is inconceivable. Every term which is predicated both of the finite and the Infinite, of creatures and of God, is analogous. And this being so, there is absolutely no ground for assuming that the limitations which condition the perfection as it is found in the creature, adhere to it in the Divine Being: or that the multiplicity and variety of the attributes predicated are incompatible with the simplicity of the Godhead. It will indeed appear that the Divine attributes, many though they be, all signify one and the same Supreme Perfection, in whom there is no distinction; but that by reason of the infinitude of that Perfection the human mind can only represent it under a diversity of aspects and by means of concepts differing one from another.

That the terms signifying those 'pure' perfections, which seen first in the creature are then attributed to God, are all analogous, is easily shewn. We have pointed out (chap. iii., § 4) that the transcendentals themselves -- Truth, Goodness and Unity -- are analogous and not univocal: that since they are not restricted to any one of those divisions of being which we term the Categories, and in consequence do not connote the limitations which such a division involves, there is no reason why they should not be found in Infinite Being itself, existing in a different mode, but the same as regards their essential character. God is said to be One and True and Good, without it being in any way implied that His Being is limited, or qualified by accidents. This is equally the case as regards His intelligence, His will, His life, His causality, etc., etc. Intelligence is not, like sense-perception, a knowledge restricted in its scope to certain particular aspects of reality, and essentially proportioned to these limited aspects. It embraces all being in its range. It is the power to know being as such. It is related to being in so far as it is true. In man it may be hedged in by limitations. But intelligence as such connotes no limitation: it is a knowledge no less appropriate to an Infinite than a finite nature. The same is true of will. Will is related to being in so far as good. It is the propension of a rational agent towards being apprehended by the intellect as good. Life is implied in intelligence and in volition. There are modes of life which are finite: but life as such, *i.e.*, being in so far as endowed with the power of immanent action, does not involve finiteness. Efficient causality is the origination of being: final causality the purpose and end of being. All these terms, then, are, in the nature of things, analogous. And the same will be seen to be true as regards all other such attributes. We say that God is all-beautiful. Beauty is goodness, the contemplation of which brings delight to the mind. The moral virtues which we predicate of God (justice, mercy, etc., etc.) are the goodness of the Divine will in its various aspects.

Infinity, immutability, immensity, eternity, are attributes of an altogether different class. Here we are not concerned with something which is found, though in but a limited degree, in creatures also. These are perfections proper to God alone: and there is no call that the terms should be analogous. In the sections in which they are severally discussed it will appear clearly that they none of them involve any distinction in God. Here it is sufficient to note that infinity is simply the mode of being proper to God, just as finiteness is proper to creatures. It is not something additional to and distinct from that being. The other three are direct deductions from infinity, and are, in fact, but aspects under which infinite Being is apprehended in relation to creatures.

To understand the sense in which the same term may be employed of God and of the creature, it will be necessary to examine with some care the notion of analogy.

There are, as St. Thomas points out, two kinds of analogy, distinguished the one from the other by important differences. They are designated *analogy of attribution* and *analogy of proportion*[9] respectively.

We have analogy of attribution when a term is employed in a secondary sense (or senses) to denote things because of some relation which they bear to the reality which it signifies in its primary sense. Thus the term 'healthy' primarily signifies a quality proper only to a living body. But it is likewise used of food, of medicines, of the complexion, etc., etc., by reason of their respective relations to the health of the body. For food may be such as to promote health, medicine such as to restore it, a complexion such as to manifest it. These are, therefore, denominated healthy by attribution. The healthy body is known as the 'prime analogate': the things which receive the name in virtue of their relation to this are the 'secondary analogates.' It is characteristic of this species of analogy that the quality or 'form' properly signified by the term is found in the primary analogate alone. Secondary analogates receive the name by extrinsic denomination. Otherwise it would not be predicated of them by 'attribution.' Analogy of proportion arises when two different things display distinct but similar relations. Thus we speak of a man as being 'a pillar of the state' by analogy of this kind, because the relation which the man bears to his country is similar to the relation of a pillar to the building which it supports. So, too, we speak of a landscape as 'smiling,' when the beauty and fertility of a district makes Nature seem kindly and attractive in the same way that a smiling face will do, where persons are concerned. These are mere metaphors. But analogy of proportion may be *real* as well as *metaphorical*. It is real when the quality designated by the term is intrinsic to both analogates. Thus, we speak of 'sex' in regard both of animals and plants. The thing signified in the two cases is very different. But proportionally they are the same. There is a true analogy between sex in a vertebrate and sex in a dicotyledonous plant. So, too, we speak of the soul of a man, and the soul of a dog. It is only by analogy of proportion that the same term is employed of the indestructible spirit of man and the perishable vital principle of the brute. But, again, the analogy is real, not metaphorical.

When we affirm of God some perfection which is found in creatures, we do so by this second kind of analogy -- analogy of proportion. If the perfection is a 'mixed' perfection, including in its concept some imperfection, then we can only employ the analogy of metaphor. In this way we say that God is 'angry' with the wicked, that he 'lends an attentive ear' to the prayers of the just. The term employed denotes something which is intrinsic only to men. It is applied to God metaphorically because of a certain similarity of relations. But it is otherwise as regards 'pure' perfections. In this case the analogous term is predicated in a real not a metaphorical sense. When we say that God *lives*, that He created the world by *intelligence* and *will*, that He is *just* and *merciful*, we are well aware that in Him life, intelligence, will, etc., are something different to what they are in ourselves. Nevertheless, in each such case we hold that He veritably possesses the perfection signified. Although God's intelligence differs from our own, we are not wholly ignorant of its character: we know it as having the same relation to the Divine nature which our intelligence has to our nature. Kant saw correctly that our concepts of God must be analogical, and his explanation of the analogy here employed is in its general lines accurate.[10] But since he erroneously held that we neither have nor can have any knowledge whatever of God, he concludes that the fourth term of our proportion must likewise remain wholly unknown to us. In this he was mistaken. The mind has the power to form concepts which are truly, though of course inadequately, representative of God. This is best seen in the most fundamental of such concepts, that of self-existent Being. We derive the concept of 'being' or 'thing,' in the first place, from created objects. We apprehend the objects of sense in a confused way as 'things.' But we recognize that this concept is absolutely universal: that there can be nothing to which it does not apply. The perfection expressed is one which is present everywhere -- in qualities, relations, etc., as well as in substances. Yet a substance is a 'thing' in a very different sense from that in which an accident is so termed: and a quality again in a different sense from a relation. Thus we realize that the term is analogous, not univocal. It expresses a perfection which is found in different degrees, between which there is only a proportional resemblance. It has not always, like the univocal term, exactly the same meaning. Its precise signification only appears when it is actually predicated of a particular subject.

But if the term 'being' is analogous, it is applicable, not merely to contingent created being, but to self-existent being: and, as thus understood, is truly representative of its object, God. God, then, is not a mere name, for which the mind has no corresponding idea, and to which in consequence it attaches, as Mansel contends, a number of notions which are mutually repugnant. Our power of forming analogous concepts gives us ideas which are truly applicable to Him. Reason compels us to admit the existence of a First Cause, the originating principle of the contingent beings which experience manifests: and the mind conceives that supreme source as self-existent being. The whole series of our deductions regarding the perfections of God is ultimately based on concepts of this character.

Kant was wholly mistaken when he declared that we have no means of forming any idea whatever of the unknown x which is to the Supreme Being what our intellect is to us. Analogy enables us to conceive a perfection related to the Divine nature as reason is related to human nature. There is, of course, between the two an immeasurable difference. The one is finite: the other infinite. The one, a mere faculty sometimes producing an act, sometimes not so: the other is identical, not merely with the Divine Being Itself, but with its own activity and its own act. We cannot express the two by a concept which, like our specific and generic notions, is identical in its reference to all its subjects. But the concept of intelligence is analogous, and as such is referable, in different but proportionate applications, to both.

In the same manner the terms, beauty, goodness, justice, unity, causality, etc., are none of them, any more than intelligence or will, univocal. Not one of these expresses a generic or specific nature, as do, *e.g.*, such terms as colour, extension, corporeity. We cannot by means of abstraction form concepts of them such that whenever and wherever they are predicated, they always mean the same. It is only when they are actually predicated of a particular subject that we know the particular kind of goodness or beauty, etc., that is signified. Hence all these terms can be applied in their proper sense not merely to creatures, but to God as well.

It may, perhaps, be said that if there he a similarity of relations between human nature and its attributes on the one hand and the divine nature and its attributes on the other, a way is open to us to attain a full and perfect knowledge of God and to solve the riddles not merely of human, but of the divine being. So, indeed, it is contended by some. Thus, Principal Caird, when engaged in denying the possibility of mysteries, in the sense of truths revealed by God but impenetrable to human reason, enquires whether such truths may not be made known by analogies, and replies: "If a representation is a true representation, it must belong to the same order as the thing represented. The relation between them is a thinkable relation, and one which, though immature individual intelligence may not apprehend it, thought or intelligence in general is capable of apprehending."[11] Such reasoning would appear to view analogy after the fashion of a sum in proportion, in which, if the data are sufficient, we can readily arrive at an absolutely accurate knowledge of the unknown term. The resemblance of relations in an analogy is not of this kind. There is, for instance, a true proportional analogy between the perceptions of sense and the conceptions of reason in regard of their respective objects. But a knowledge of only one of these relations would not enable its possessor to attain a full and adequate idea of the other. How much more is this the case where one of the two relations involves an infinite nature. Do those who thus argue really believe that the human intellect is capable of forming an adequate mental representation of infinite being? The fallacy is patent.[12]

From a very different point of view it has been objected that in contending for a real, though analogical, knowledge of God, Scholasticism is inconsistent with itself. St. Thomas is express in asserting that while we can know God's existence, we cannot know *what* He is. We can know *quia est* (**hoti esti**) but not *quid sit* (**ti esti**). And the same teaching is common to the Schoolmen generally. How, then, can it be maintained consistently that we are able by analogy to acquire a very considerable measure of knowledge regarding God's nature? This difficulty has been recently urged by some modernist writers in defence of their own position. Yet the inconsistency is only apparent. In the terminology of St. Thomas, on the one hand, knowledge of the essence of a thing (*quid res sit*) requires far more than the analogical knowledge which we have described, and, on the other, knowledge *quia est* may include a good deal besides the bare fact of existence. We know *quid res sit* when our mind can form a concept accurately representing its constitutive principle, the form which makes the thing what it is. Such is the knowledge we have, *e.g.*, of a mathematical figure, when we are able to give its definition. This, manifestly, is impossible in regard of God. We cannot form a concept expressing His essential nature as it is in itself. We represent Him by a series of concepts, which either remove from Him some limitation proper to creatures, *e.g.*, infinite, immutable, or else signify some perfection, which we know as found in finite creatures, and which, inasmuch as it is analogous and not confined to its finite mode of realization, is attributable to God. These, however, give us only an imperfect and confused knowledge of Him.{13} But when our knowledge of anything, though real as far as it goes, is thus obscure, and falls short of an apprehension of that essential nature which makes it what it is, it is still classed by the Schoolmen, following the Aristotelian terminology, as knowledge *quia est*.

In this connection St. Thomas cites with approval the teaching of the pseudo-Dionysius to the effect that those perfections which are common to God and creatures are predicable of Him in three ways, termed respectively the way of *affirmation*, the way of *negation*, and the way of *eminence*.{14} The way of affirmation is exemplified when, *e.g.*, we say that God is just and wise and merciful. In such predications we have regard to the perfections signified by the terms wisdom, justice and mercy. But as we have explained at length, these attributes are not in God after the manner in which our minds are constrained to conceive them: for we can only conceive them as they are found in creatures, viz., as accidental forms distinct one from another. In God there can be nothing of this kind. His plenitude of being can receive no accidental determination: nor can there be in Him any composition of diverse elements, but only the one simple and supreme perfection which is Himself. From this point of view it may be said that God does not possess wisdom or mercy or justice. This is the way of negation. But these negations do not arise from any deficiency in God. They do not imply that He is devoid of these perfections, but on the contrary, that He possesses them in a mode which exceeds our power of comprehension. This brings us to the way of eminence: and we say that God is superlatively wise, superlatively just, etc., etc. He is, in the words of the Areopagite, 'the affirmation of all things, the negation of all things, that which is above all affirmation and all negation.'{15}

3. *Solution of the difficulties.* In the analogical character of our knowledge of God lies the solution of the agnostic arguments enumerated at the beginning of this chapter. This is manifest as regards Kant's contention that we cannot attribute reason or will to God, inasmuch as both intelligence and appetition, as we know them, are dependent for their exercise on sensible data. We shall shew that it is no less true of the other objections there mentioned. It will be convenient to treat first the difficulty urged by Mansel that a plurality of attributes is altogether inconsistent with the simplicity which the consentient voice of theistic philosophers declares to be a characteristic of the Divine nature.

In accordance with the doctrine of analogy we reply that the perfections which in creatures are found as distinct determinations, as, *e.g.*, justice and mercy, or even as separate faculties, as, *e.g.*, intellect and will, exist in God as one simple Reality, infinite perfection, containing within itself, but in a higher manner which our minds cannot conceive, all those aspects of goodness which in creatures are found distinct from one another. That supreme and simple Reality is the Divine essence. The limited powers of the human intellect on the one hand, and on the other the infinitude of the object under consideration, compel us to represent it by a number of different concepts drawn from those created perfections of which it is the source. These we call divine attributes. They are justly affirmed of God, and, notwithstanding their plurality, do not in any way, if rightly understood, imply any distinction in the Godhead.

Yet here a new problem awaits us. If the divine attributes are but one and the same reality, have they not one and all the same signification. When we speak of justice and mercy in a man, we speak of different things. But in God the thing is ever the same. How, then, can we avoid the conclusion that the divine attributes are synonymous one with another:

that we may say with equal truth, God pardons by His justice and punishes by His mercy, as that He pardons through mercy, and punishes through His justice? Yet to admit this would be to own that those terms which designate the divine attributes are not analogous in their reference to God and creatures, but equivocal.

The objection overlooks the fact that speech is immediately significative, not of things as they are in themselves, but as mentally conceived. The word denotes the thing, not the concept; but it denotes the thing as known by the mind. Now, since we do not know God directly, but only through the effects which He produces in the created world, we form concepts of Him viewed as the source of this or that created perfection. We conceive Him as merciful, as just, as wise, etc., thereby signifying that the plenitude of the Divine substance contains, in the mode proper to it, the perfections expressed by these terms. In Him, it is true, these perfections coalesce: they are one with the Divine substance and one with each other: but the terms are not interchangeable. Our minds can form no single concept to express that all-embracing unity of being: our only resource is to form partial concepts, each of which exhibits some aspect of the Divine fullness.

On this point the Scholastic logic provided, as usual, a clear and precise terminology. Between the divine attributes there is, it was said, 'a conceptual distinction grounded on the reality (*distinctio rationis cum fundamento in re*).'[16] The attributes, that is, are not distinct determinations in God, as are justice and mercy in man: the distinction is the work of the mind. But it is grounded on the reality, because the fullness of the Divine being contains all that is involved in these terms.[17]

We may now direct our attention to the difficulties connected with causation. It was asserted that the notion of causality is wholly incompatible with the concepts of the Infinite and the Absolute. We touched upon the question of the causality of the Infinite, when, in our discussion of the proof of God's existence from movement, we were dealing with the notion of the *motor immobilis*. Little will be needed now beyond a recapitulation of what was there said. We pointed out that the causes with which our experience makes us familiar are such as can only exercise causality in virtue of a change in themselves. Until this change takes place they remain causes in potency only. To pass from potency to act they must receive a new accidental determination which we term 'action,' and which constitutes them as 'agents.' Moreover, so far as the physical order is concerned, all causation involves corporeal action. But the term cause is analogous, as the term being is analogous. As being is predicated alike of those finite essences which are called out of nothingness, and of the self-existent essence which is in act from all eternity, so, too, the term cause is applicable, not merely to causes which are to begin with causes in potency and only subsequently causes in act, but to that Cause which needs no ulterior determination, but is a cause in the full sense of the term, a cause in act, from all eternity. God is the *motor immobilis*; in Him causation involves no change. He does not cause by external corporeal activity: nor does He need any internal change in order to produce His effects.

It may, indeed, be urged that if the cause be such *ab eterno*, the effect likewise must take place through all time, and be without beginning and without end. The conclusion, however, is fallacious, and is due to the error of conceiving eternity as an endless succession of time. Eternity, as we shall shew, is outside time and above time. But the discussion of this difficulty is reserved for the chapter on Creation (chap. xiv., § 3), as it can hardly be treated satisfactorily until the notion of eternity has been fully considered. For similar reasons we defer two other difficulties closely connected with our subject. It is urged that the idea of finite being, external to and distinct from infinite being, is self-contradictory: that to admit the existence of anything else is ipso facto to own that the Infinite is not infinite. And, further, it is contended that if God be a cause in act by virtue of His essence, there is no room in Him for the exercise of free-will: for wherever free-will makes a choice there must arise an internal act, which might have been other than it is. These two points will be dealt with in the chapters on the Divine essence (chap. ix., § 3) and the Divine will (chap. xii., § 3) respectively.

But is the idea of God as the First Cause compatible with the notion of Him as the Absolute? Is it the case that if we regard Him as the Creator, we necessarily admit that He is related to, and consequently determined by, the created universe, and for that reason cannot be the Absolute?

To deal with this question we must distinguish between two kinds of relation -- 'real relations' (*relationes reales*), in which the connection between one thing and another belongs to them as existing realities: and 'conceptual relations' (*relationes rationis*), in which we mentally regard things as connected, though there is no corresponding objective relation. Thus there is a real relation between the moon and the tides, between a number of men who are marching in step with each other, between the sculptor and the statue. But there is only a conceptual relation between the subject and predicate of a proposition: for in the real world subject and predicate are one and the same thing, conceived by us under diverse aspects. Similarly there is but a conceptual relation between a word and the thing which it signifies. The mind establishes a connection between the thing and a particular sound which is to serve as its sign; but the two are not objectively connected. A real relation confers on the substance which acquires it a new and real determination in the world of things. Order or harmony is a principal perfection of the beings which form this created universe. And in so far as anything is 'ordered to' another, it is thereby perfected. The connection with another entity is an increment of its being- -- an accidental perfection added to its substantial reality. Hence it is altogether impossible that God should be related to the creatures which He has made, by a real relation. He is not, so to speak, a part of a wider whole, which embraces both Himself and finite things, and whose constituents are perfected by their reciprocal relations. Creatures, it is true, are related to Him -- they are 'ordered to' Him as effects to their Cause -- but He is in no sense 'ordered to' them. We must, however, shew that such a condition is possible. In the immense majority of instances, relations, whether real or conceptual, are what is termed 'mutual': that is, the relation is either real in both of the related objects or conceptual in both of them. But cases occur in which a relation is real on one side and conceptual on the other. These are termed 'non-mutual.' An example is furnished by the relation between a material object and the mental concept representing it. The object is the exemplar cause of the concept, the 'measure' in conformity with which it is formed. The intellect confronted with the data which sense-perception offers, forms within itself, by its own immanent activity, the concept of which the object is the exemplar.[18] This being so, it is manifest that the concept is related to the object by a real relation. It really depends on it. But the object is not in any sense 'referred to' the concept. It belongs to an entirely distinct order of being -- to the world of real things and not to the world of ideas. The existence of an idea representing it does not affect it in any way: it confers on it no new determination. Mentally, it is true, we view the object in relation to the concept just as we view the concept in relation to the thing which it represents: for in the mind every relation involves a pair of correlatives. But objectively the relation is non-mutual. It is no less evident how the case stands as regards God and the created universe. An effect is necessarily related to its cause, the world to the Creator. But when the cause lies wholly outside the system of things to which the effect belongs, and therefore gains no perfection from its production, then the cause is not objectively related to the effect. The relation on the side of the Creator is conceptual, not real.[19]

It should, however, be noted that where efficient causality is in question, it is only in regard of the First Cause, the *motor immobilis*, that a non-mutual relation can arise. Every other efficient cause acquires a new perfection by acting. The new activity is an increment of its being -- a realization of what has been a mere potency. But in God, as will be explained later, there are no unrealized potencies. He works His effects without internal change.

We have finally to notice the difficulty that, if we attribute intelligence to God, we are driven to admit that there is in Him the internal relation between the thinking subject and the object thought. This distinction, it is urged, is inseparable from the action of intelligence. Yet to admit it is inconsistent alike with the Divine simplicity and with our notion of God as the Absolute.

The solution to this difficulty is similar to that of those which we have been considering. The term intelligence, as indeed we have already pointed out, is analogous. If we treat it as univocal, and argue as though the divine intellect must resemble our own, we shall inevitably involve ourselves in fallacious conclusions. When, in the chapter dealing with the Divine intellect, we come to consider what is really involved in the notion of the intelligence proper to an infinitely perfect Being, we shall see that in God the distinction between subject and object vanishes. In Him the intellect, its act, and its object coalesce in one single perfection embracing elements which in us are necessarily distinct: and this perfection is identical with the divine Essence.

Personality affords another instance of a perfection predicated analogously of God and of man. The traditional definition of 'person' first given by Boethius declares the term to signify 'a concrete individual whose essential nature is rational' (*substantia individua rationalis naturae*) [20] Two notes are thus assigned as primary, viz., the incommunicability of the individual, and rationality. Two derivative characteristics, however, seem also to enter into our conception of personality. A being possessed of reason is an *end* in a way which irrational things are not: and, further, on this account it is rightly said to exist *for itself*. It is manifest that the notion of personality as thus explained is verified in God, though in a manner altogether transcending what is found in creatures. He is infinite intelligence: He is an end and exists for Himself in a supreme degree: and in Him there must be found the incommunicability of the individual, even though our human reason does not permit us to determine whether the oneness of the divine nature involves that there should be only one individual in the Godhead.

In this age the personality of God has not been allowed to go unquestioned. A personal God is incompatible with pantheism. Hence, thinkers of the Hegelian school urge various difficulties against the doctrine of divine personality. These, for the most part, owe such speciousness as they possess to the mistaken supposition that the limitations proper to human personality must be present in all personality as such. Thus it is argued that the consciousness of self which characterizes personality necessarily involves the consciousness of an other than self, and that hence personality and infinity are mutually exclusive.[21] It is doubtless true that we ourselves only come to realize our personality in so far as we become conscious of something extraneous to ourselves. This is due to the nature of the human intelligence, which at first is blank like a *tabula rasa*, and derives its knowledge from without. The Divine Mind contemplating its own infinite perfections can need no non-ego to reveal to it its own personality. It may further be noted that consciousness of a non-ego does not *constitute* personality. A newly-born infant, even though it should have no such consciousness, is a person. Again, it is said of those who argue for personality in God: "The Deity, which they want, is of course finite, a person much like themselves, with thoughts and feelings limited and mutable in the process of time."[22] Such a travesty is only rendered possible by the failure to recognize that the principle of analogy renders it conceivable that the Divine Nature should have all the perfections which belong to personality, so that the relations between God and His creatures may be in the fullest sense what are termed personal relations, and that He should nevertheless be immutable and infinite.

4. *Modernism and agnosticism.* The system of thought called modernism was an attempt to accept the postulates of Kantian philosophy without going the full length of religious agnosticism. The modernist writers, while admitting the agnostic premises, claimed to have transcended the conclusion to which they lead, and to have found a basis for professing many of the truths concerning God which had hitherto been regarded as the results of rational demonstration. The scope of the system was by no means purely philosophical. It was, in fact, a complete reconstruction of religion, as regards thought and practice alike. Here, however, we are only concerned with it in its relation to Natural Theology. We have no occasion to touch on it in its other aspects except quite incidentally.

It was fundamental with the modernists that our cognitive faculties cannot reach extra-mental reality, but that their sole object is phenomena: and, further, that metaphysical principles like the principle of causality are not, as they seem, the expression of objective and necessary truth, but are due to "certain inborn categories of the human mind." It follows immediately from this that Natural Theology in the traditional sense is out of the question: that the proofs of the existence of God and the arguments which establish His attributes are entirely futile. "We recognize," say the authors of the *Programme of Modernism*, "that the arguments for the existence of God, drawn by scholastic metaphysic from change and movement, from the finite and contingent nature of things, from the degrees of perfection, and from the design and purpose of the world, have lost all value nowadays. The conceptions on which these arguments rest have now, owing to the post-Kantian criticism both of abstract and empirical sciences and of philosophical language, lost that character of absoluteness which they possessed for the medieval Aristotelians. Since the mere conventionality of every abstract representation of reality has been demonstrated, it is clear, not only that such arguments fall to pieces, but that it is idle to construct others of the same class."{23}

On what grounds, then, did the modernists believe in God, and affirm of Him those attributes without which we should not be conceiving a personal Divine Being, but simply the Unknowable of Spencer. They could not, having rejected philosophical proofs, appeal to the testimony of positive revelation: for they accepted the opinion, regarded by certain recent thinkers as an axiomatic truth, that every principle, speculative or practical, to which the mind yields an absolute assent, must be in its origin autonomous and autochthonous. "We find ourselves," the work just cited informs us, "in harmony with one of the fundamental tendencies of contemporary philosophy, and which is even considered the very condition of the possibility of a philosophy -- the immanental tendency. According to this principle, nothing can enter into and get hold of man's spirit that does not spring from it and in some way correspond to its need of self-expansion. For it there is no fixed truth, no unalterable precept, that is not in some way self-imposed and innate" (p. 109). They believed, however, that in this very doctrine of Immanence they had found a solution to the problem. Man feels within himself, it was asserted, a need for the divine. There arises within him a feeling -- a stirring of the heart -- impelling him to grope blindly after its connatural object, and he finds that object in God. "Not only our animal and race appetites and instincts, but also our spiritual craving for the divine precede any explicit knowledge on our part of the objects to which they are directed, It is solely by groping and trying that we discover what satisfies and explains them."[24] Religion is a vital activity of human nature, and is thus its own adequate justification: it needs no proof to establish the validity of its conclusions. "It may here be assumed," writes the author from whom we have just quoted, "that the divine which is immanent in man's spirit does naturally and inevitably at a certain stage of his mental and moral progress reveal itself to him, however dimly, as a *vita nuova*, a new sort of life, the life of religion, with its needs and its cravings for self-adjustment to realities lying beyond the bourne of time and place: that reflecting on this need man seeks to explain it to himself by various conceptions and beliefs."[25] In virtue of this internal experience men recognize the existence of God, and further are led to form a certain mental representation of His nature. These conceptions they embody in dogmatic formulas. And in so far as such formulas correspond, not merely to the experience of the individual, but to that of society as a whole, they have a valid claim on our acceptance.[26] It is thus, and not by reasoned demonstration nor by revelation communicated *ab extra* that man comes to a knowledge of God.

The attitude of modernism to Natural Theology is now clear. Its adherents followed Schleiermacher in denying all distinction between natural and supernatural religion. They admitted but one way of attaining knowledge of God -- the way of experience. This from different points of view might be regarded either as natural or as supernatural. Ordinarily, indeed, they spoke of it as 'revelation.' Yet, since they held it to be the result of the normal operation of our faculties, they might with better reason have styled it Natural Theology. But they desired to give this meaning to the word 'revelation,' that they might thus lend colour to their view that the revelations made by the prophets and by the Founder of Christianity Himself were, in fact, knowledge obtained in this fashion, differing only in degree, not in kind, from the knowledge of God common to every member of the race.[27]

But in what sense, it may be asked, can we reckon these conclusions as knowledge? Are our conceptions of God true in the sense that they correspond with objective reality? If this is not what is meant, then to call them true is a mere juggling with words. But this the modernist does not claim. Our conceptions of God, Sabatier maintains, are purely symbolical. They cannot be otherwise: for the categories of the understanding are only applicable in the phenomenal world of space and time. They express, not objective reality, but the relation in which the thinking subject feels himself to stand towards God. The ideas which we form of God, the attributes which we predicate of Him, are all metaphorical.[28] On this point Tyrrell is equally clear. Speaking of 'revelation' he says: "In what sense are religious revelations divinely authorized? What sort of truth is guaranteed to them by 'the seal of the spirit'? In accordance with what has been already said, we must answer -- a truth which is directly practical, preferential, approximative, and only indirectly speculative. What is immediately approved, as it were, experimentally, is a way of living, feeling and acting, with reference to the other world."[29] Our 'knowledge' of God, in other words, has a pragmatist value; but it has no claim to be regarded as true in the sense that it is really representative of Him.

Modernism, it is manifest, fails altogether to make good its claim to transcend the agnostic conclusions of Spencer. The 'symbols' which it offers us, avail us nothing, for we have no means of discovering what they symbolize, or, indeed, whether, far from being true symbols, they are not mere fancies, only of value because, as things stand, they are found to assist us in some measure towards the harmonious ordering of life. Of God, as He is, they can tell us absolutely nothing. If the modernist teaching be true, then we cannot even tell whether the supreme object, of which, they tell us, the soul is dimly conscious and towards which it blindly struggles, be personal or impersonal. Indeed, so far as we know, the word 'personal' may have no meaning as applied to the sphere to which that ultimate being belongs. That term is a coin from out our own mint, and may not be current in other regions. The utmost we can say is that it is well for us to act as though there were a personal God. The same holds good as regards other attributes such as intelligence, will, omnipotence, justice, mercy. They serve to direct our action; but we should be deceiving ourselves if we supposed that we have any grounds for holding that our conceptions are representative of reality and help us to know God as He is. We are, after all, left with Spencer's conclusion and no other: that besides the world of phenomena there exists an inscrutable Beyond.

NOTES

{1} *Limits of Religious Thought* (4th edit.), p. 31; cited by Spencer, *First Principles*, § 13.

{2} Cf. E. Caird, *Philosophy of Kant*, p. 648. "To argue positively from the contingency of this world to the existence of a necessary being, which is external to it, and related to it only as cause to effect, is to reduce the necessary being to another contingent. For if this world is determined only as an effect, and is conditioned by its cause, the necessary being is at the same time determined only as a cause, and is conditioned by its effect."

{3} *Op. cit.*, p. 33.

{4} Moses ben Maimon, born at Cordova, 1135, died at Cairo, 1204. He was the greatest of the medieval Jewish thinkers. He also attained eminence in the science of medicine, and was physician to the Sultan of Egypt. It is said that Richard Coeur-de-lion, when in Palestine, offered him a similar position at his court. His treatment of the Divine attributes is contained in Pt. I., cc. lv. - lviii. of his work. A full discussion of the agnosticism of Maimonides may be found in P. Chossat's article *Agnosticisme* in d' Alès' *Dictionnaire apologétique de la foi Catholique*.

{5} *Summa Theol.*, I., q. 13; *Contra Gent.*, I., cc. xxxi. - xxxiv.; *De Pot.*, q. 7, art. 4 -- 7, etc.

{6} Cf. *De Pot.*, q. 7, art. 5. "Cum omne agens agat in quantum actu est, et per consequens agat aliqualiter simile, oportet formam facti aliquo modo esse in agente: diversimode tamen. . . . Quando vero effectus non adaequat virtutem agentis, forma non est secundum eandem rationem in agente et facto, sed in agente eminentius."

{7} *Supra.*

{8} *De Pot.*, q. 7, art. 5, ad 2.

{9} St. Thomas terms them *analogia proportionis* and analogia *proportionalitatis* respectively. The employment of names so similar could only be productive of confusion. Hence the term *analogia attributionis* has been commonly used in place of *analogia proportionis*. The expression *analogia attributionis* does not actually occur in St. Thomas, but is founded on the terminology which he employs in *Opusc. 27 De Principiis Naturae.* 'Proportionalitas' is the word by which he designates the parity of two numerical proportions, *e.g.*, 5 : 7 :: 15 : 21. We have no English word for this except proportion.' In *De Veritate*, q. 2, art. ii, he somewhat unduly restricts the sense of *analogia attributionis*, and is in consequence led to deny that it is ever applicable to the case of God and creatures. This opinion he elsewhere abandons (*In Boeth. de Trin.*, q. 1, a. 2, ad 3).

{10} After stating that we are 'obliged to regard the world as though it were the work of a supreme understanding and will,' he says in the next section: "Such a cognition as this is one according to analogy, which does not signify an imperfect resemblance of two things, as the word is commonly taken to mean, but a perfect resemblance of two relations between totally dissimilar things." Kant here makes the conditions of an analogy somewhat too strict. It is not necessary that the resemblance between the relations should be perfect. It is sufficient that there should be a real, even though in some respects, an imperfect resemblance. In the same way the things in question need not be 'totally' dissimilar.

{11} Caird, *Philosophy of Religion*, p. 73.

{12} The real ground why Principal Caird holds it impossible that there can be any truth inscrutable to the human intelligence lies, of course, far deeper than this. According to his philosophy there is no essential difference between the divine and the human intelligence. There is one universal reason which emerges in different personalities, but ultimately is the same. "The real presupposition of all knowledge, or the thought which is the *prius* of all things, is not the individual's consciousness of himself as an individual, but a thought or self-consciousness which is beyond all individual selves, which is the unity of all individual selves and their objects, of all thinkers and all objects of thought. . . We might even say that, strictly speaking, it is not we that think but the universal reason that thinks in us " (p. 149). The doctrine is a form of Hegelian pantheism, though Dr. Caird, at the cost of inconsistency, rejects the pantheistic conclusion.

{13} "Haec omnia, ens, bonum, perfectum, substantia, sapiens, justus et similia, quae proprie de Deo dicuntur, communia sunt creaturis: quod si velimus ea concipere, ut propria sunt Deo, id facere non possumus nisi sub confusione quadam, ut cum dicimus Deum esse summe sapientem, aut ens complectens omnem perfectionem, vel quid simile. Plerumque autem id facimus adjuncta negatione illius imperfectionis quam tale praedicatum solet in creaturis habere, ut aliquo modo explicemus id quod confuse apprehendimus de tali perfectione prout in Deo est." Suarez, *Metaph.*, Disp. 30, sect. 12.

{14} *De Pot.*, q. 7, art. 5, ad 2; cf. Dionysius Areop. *De Div. Nom.*, c. ii., § 3; c. vii., § 3, etc.

{15} *De Div. Nom.*, c. ii., § 4. **hê pantôn thesis, hê pantôn aphairesis, to huper pasan kai thesin kai aphairesin**.

{16} It is sometimes termed *distinctio rationis cum fundamento imperfecto*. A conceptual distinction is said to have *fundamentum perfectum* when one of the forms thus distinguished can be realized apart from the other. Thus the distinction between genus and differentia is a conceptual distinction. Yet the generic nature is found without this or that particular differentia. Animality is found without the rationality which is its differentiating note in man. Between these two therc is a *distinctio rationis cum fundamento perfecto*.

{17} Scotus refused to admit the distinction of the attributes to be due to the operation of our own minds, which can only express the Divine plenitude after this fashion. He held that there must be an objective distinction between them viewed as forms; though they were certainly not to be regarded as distinct realities to the prejudice of the Divine simplicity. Unless such a distinction were admitted he did not see how the reality of our predications could be defended. It was replied that if the distinction was antecedent to the operation of the intellect, it must inevitably be between different realities, and thus be inconsistent with the simplicity of God's essence.

{18} Note that the intellect, not the material object, is the efficient cause of the concept. The intellect, employing the data of sense, produces the concept in itself. See Maher, *Psychology*, c. xiv.

{19} "Quandoque vero relatio in uno extremorum est res naturae, et in altero est res rationis tantum: et hoc contingit quandocunque duo extrema non sunt unius ordinis: sicut sensus et scientia referuntur ad sensibile et scibile: quae quidem in quantum sunt res quaedam in esse naturali existentes, sunt extra ordinem esse sensibilis et intelligibilis. Et ideo in scientia quidem et sensu est relatio realis secundum quod ordinantur ad sciendum vel sentiendum res. Sed res ipsae in se consideratae sunt extra ordinem hujusmodi. Unde in eis non est aliqua relatio realiter ad scientiam et sensum, sed secundum rationem tantum. . . . *Cum igitur Deus sit extra ordinem totum creaturae*, et omnes creaturae ordinentur ad ipsum et non e converso: manifestum est quod creaturae realiter referuntur ad ipsum Deum: sed in Deo non est aliqua realis relatio ejus ad creaturas, sed secundum rationem tantum." *Summa Theol.*, I., q. 12, art. 7.

{20} In this definition the term *substantia* represents the Greek **hupostasis** not **ousia**. Hence *substantia individua* seems to be correctly rendered 'a concrete individual.' Rufinus had previously, and more correctly translated **hupostasis** by *subsistentia* -- a word, which he seems to have coined for the purpose from *subsistere*. (Cf. *e.g. Hist. Eccl.*, I. 29, P.L. 21, col. 499.)

{21} McTaggart, *Some Dogmas*, etc., § 167.

{22} Bradley, *Appearance and Reality*, p. 532.

{23} *Programme of Modernism* (Engl. trans., 1908), p. 118.

{24} G. Tyrrell, rhrough Scyila and Charybdis, p. 172.

{25} *Op. cit.*, p. 205.

{26} A. Sabatier, *Esquisse d'une philosophie de la religion*, pp. 55, 56. M. Sabatier was a liberal Protestant. But his work was a potent factor in the formation of modernism, and is recognized as affording a convenient summary of the system.

{27} Tyrrell, *op. cit.*, p. 208.

{28} *Esquisse*, etc., pp. 390-400.

{29} *Scylla and Charybdis*, p. 210; cf. Mansel, *op. cit.*, p. 84.

Chapter IX. The Divine Essence.

1. Import of the Enquiry.

2. Essence and Existence in God.

3. The Analogy of Being in God and in Creatures.

4. The Metaphysical Essence of God.

1. *Import of the enquiry.* We have seen in the foregoing chapter that there is no real ground for the agnostic's assertion that we are incapable of attaining any knowledge of God and that we can say no more about Him than that He is 'unknown and unknowable.' But we saw likewise that our knowledge of God's perfections is restricted in its scope: that we know them only by an inferential process from the finite perfections of creatures, and in such a manner as our human faculties permit: that by the very nature of the case our knowledge must be analogical, not intuitive. With this proviso we are free to pursue our consideration of the Divine attributes.

In the present chapter we propose to treat of the Divine essence. This calls for a brief preliminary exposition of the notion of essence in its ordinary application to the finite substances of experience, prescinding from its reference to God. To some of our readers this will probably be familiar ground. But there may well be others to whom, without this, the subsequent discussion would lose nearly all its meaning.

In the Aristotelian terminology, as is well known, the essence denotes the *nature* of the thing -- that in virtue of which the thing is *what it is*. The significance of the notion is, perhaps, best grasped when essence is set in opposition to existence. Each individual thing, which the universe offers to our consideration, possesses existence: it is. But it is, after all, only one thing among many. It is not the whole of reality. In other words, the measure of existence which it possesses is limited. And if we ask what it is which determines the existence proper to each thing -- what are the confines of its reality, there is but one possible answer. Its limits are defined by the essence or nature. Or to put the same truth somewhat differently: the existence of a thing is its *being*: the essence is that which *determines* this being. To know the existence of a thing is to know that it *is*: to know its essence is to know *what* it is.

Here we may usefully call attention to the twofold use of the noun-substantive *Being* in English. We employ it both as a concrete and as an abstract term. We call the concrete substances which possess existence beings. But the word is also used to signify the existence in virtue of which they *are*. We speak of the being of a thing, just as we speak of its life. Thus employed it is an abstract noun. In Latin there is no difficulty. Being in the concrete is *ens*: while to signify existence, the verb-noun *esse* is used. It is plain that some care is needed to avoid confusion arising from this ambiguity.

The term Essence is employed in two senses. It may denote the nature as it is in the real order: or it may denote it as it is conceptually represented in our minds. In the former case it is called the physical essence: in the latter, the conceptual -- or by a misnomer, the metaphysical -- essence.[1] This distinction must be carefully observed. It may be illustrated from the case of material substances. The Aristotelian doctrine of matter and form is concerned with the physical essence of things. The nature of every material substance, it is argued, demands two constitutive principles, a form which, inhering in a material substratum, determines it to a certain type, and the substratum which is receptive of the form. In this sense we may say that a man's essence consists of two parts -- his body and his soul. The various theories regarding the ultimate constitution of matter are so many attempts to determine the physical essence of substances. On the other hand, the metaphysical essence is, as we have said, the conceptual representation of the nature. It is characteristic of our intellect that all its concepts are universal. Sense perceives singulars: and from the sense data the intellect abstracts concepts common to a class. Hence the metaphysical essence is the concept expressing the specific type. It represents the individual physical essence, but does so inadequately, since it contains only those notes which are common to the species to which it belongs. Moreover, inasmuch as in this universe natural substances are ordered in a hierarchy of classes, we form the concept of the specific nature by adding the differentia of the species to the concept expressing the type common to a wider class. Thus the metaphysical essence is composed of genus and differentia. Man is conceived as a 'rational animal': and the parts of his essence, as thus understood, are not body and soul, but 'animality' and 'rationality.'

The essence, whether we are speaking of the real or of the conceptual order, is rightly assigned when it gives us: (1) the fundamental constituents of the object: (2) those from which its other characteristics are derived: (3) those which distinguish it from all other things. It follows from this that the metaphysical essence is truly conceived when the concepts of genus and differentia really represent the fundamental characteristics of a given nature -- those from which the other characteristics may be deduced. It is wrongly conceived when the nature is known by its secondary and derivative properties. Thus, we should be wrong in defining man as a 'tool-using animal,' or as 'an animal capable of laughter': for though these are distinctive properties of human nature, they are secondary not primary. Both of them flow from man's rationality.

It is evident from what has been said in the last chapter how limited must be our knowledge of God's physical essence. His nature as it is, is hidden from our view. Such knowledge as we have is indirect, derived from the contemplation of creatures. Moreover, whereas in creatures we can distinguish between what is primary and what is secondary, between the soul and its faculties, the body and its resultant qualities, there can be no question of priority or posteriority in God. In Him there Th no composition, no distinction of attributes, save in our inadequate representation of His infinite Being. There is, however, one fundamental aspect in which His essence is known to us, viz., in its relation to existence. This will be our subject in the following section. We shall shew that, whereas in creatures, of whatever kind they may be, whether material or purely spiritual, there is a necessary duality, the essence and the existence being distinct principles, which combine to constitute the finite thing, in God there is no duality, no composition of any kind: His essence is His existence. Later in the chapter we shall treat of God's 'metaphysical' essence. It will appear that this also is a question of considerable moment in Natural Theology.

2. *Essence and existence in God.* The identity of essence and existence in God, and the diversity of these principles in finite things, are of primary importance in the metaphysical system of St. Thomas. For in this he finds one of the ultimate differences between Uncreated and created being. Apart from this, his whole teaching, both as regards God and as regards finite being in its relation to the Infinite, becomes obscured. It is true that the Scholastic doctors are not unanimous on this question. Some of them maintain that it is impossible to regard the essence and the existence of created things as principles really different the one from the other. But the arguments advanced by St. Thomas are in our opinion conclusive. And the issue is of so fundamental a character in Natural Theology that it is impossible to leave it unconsidered. Our treatment, however, will be brief, as the full discussion of the subject belongs to the more general science of metaj)hysics. Of the various proofs given by St. Thomas it will be sufficient to employ one.

For the purpose of our argument it will be necessary by way of preliminary to explain in some detail the distinction between *potentiality* and act, concepts which play so large a part in the Aristotelian and Scholastic philosophies. Not only here, but in many subsequent passages, we shall have to employ the conception of *Actus purus* in reference to God. In this case, as in the preceding section, we feel that no apology is needed for treating a point on which many readers are perhaps already sufficiently informed.

A *potentiality* is the capacity for the realization of some perfection. The realized perfection is termed the *actus* or *act*. Thus, an oak-tree is potentially any one of the thousand things which may be made out of it -- a floor, a cart, tables, chairs, etc., etc. It is not any one of these things *actually*. But it may become them. It has in it a capacity, a *potentiality*, in their regard. This potentiality is not nothing: it is something real. Were it not present in the wood, we should try in vain to make these things out of it. We cannot make chairs and tables out of water, or ropes out of sand, for the simple reason that these materials are destitute of any potentiality for the objects in question. Potentiality is, in fact, midway between nonentity and being. It is more than mere nothingness; but it is less than the achieved *actual* thing. The distinction between these two is of widest application. The human mind, for instance, has definite potentialities, the whole purpose of education being to realize these potentialities along right lines -- to reduce potentiality to act. But whether we are dealing with the material or the spiritual, the actuality is always strictly limited by the potentiality. We can only confer a perfection, where there is a capacity: and only in the degree which that potentiality admits. The artist may conceive an ideal of beauty; but he must realize that ideal in concrete matter. And, however great his skill, he cannot accomplish more than the matter -- and, indeed, the particular matter at his disposal -- will allow. So, too, as regards intellectual development. Human cognition takes its rise from sense: and even the greatest triumphs of the intellect have been, and must be, won by discursive reason based on data derived from sensible perception. But if there be intelligences which gain knowledge in some higher manner than by sense-perception and discursive reason, their achievements will be greater because their potentiality is not so restricted.

The sense of the word *act* as used in this connection should be very carefully observed. By 'act' we mean, in ordinary parlance, the operation by which a potentiality is realized. But here it is employed to signify the result of the operation -- the complement of the potentiality, the realized *actuality*. The Schoolman was able to employ different words for these two senses. When he desired to speak of actuality he used the term *actus* as the equivalent of Aristotelian **entelecheia, energeia**: the operation he designated *actio. Actus* is therefore synonymous with perfection. Our English terminology lacks the philosophical precision of the Latin. It was this all-important distinction of potentiality and act which enabled Aristotle to refute the fallacy by which Parmenides had sought to prove that change is impossible. The Eleatic philosopher had argued that whatever is, is Being: and that what is already Being cannot become: for becoming is merely the way towards Being. 'Becoming' is, therefore, an illusion: change is impossible. Aristotle replied that besides actual Being, there is potential Being; and every material thing while it is actually one form of Being, is potentially many other things: that change is no illusion, but the transition by which potentiality passes into act.

It is essential to our argument to observe that a potentiality and its corresponding act are distinct realities. This is involved in the notions themselves. If by potentiality we signify that which is capable of perfection, and by *actus* the perfection which realizes this possibility, it is manifest that the one cannot be identical with the other. In many cases, indeed, the two are separable, since the potentiality can exist without the act. But even where this is not so -- and we shall see that this is no exceptional case -- the two cannot be the same. They combine as two distinct principles constituting a composite entity.

In saying that potentiality and act are necessarily distinct the one from the other, it must be borne in mind that we are only speaking of the act which corresponds to a particular potentiality, and is complementary to it. That which is itself an act perfecting a potentiality may also stand in the relation of potentiality to an act of a different order. Thus the human soul is the *actus* perfecting the material substratum in which it inheres, and making it a human body. But when the soul exerts its power to think, the thought, while it lasts, is a new *actus* perfecting the spiritual soul. Yet here, too, our principle is applicable. The thought is not identical with the soul which it actuates. Otherwise the latter could not be found without the former.

There is another important conclusion regarding the metaphysics -- of potentiality and act, to which we must advert. It is this. A limited perfection -- -- and every perfection which falls within our experience is limited -- owes its limitation to the element of potentiality also present in the same subject: whereas potentiality, as such, needs no limiting principle extrinsic to itself. The latter part of this assertion need cause no difficulty.

A potentiality, as such, is a mere capacity for the reception of this or that perfection. But capacity, viewed as such, is simply a principle of limit determining the character and measure of the perfection received. It is plain that what is of its own nature a principle of limit, does not stand in need of an extrinsic principle to limit it. Were anyone to maintain this, he would have to demand an infinite series of limiting principles.

The case is different as regards perfection or 'act.' In perfection, viewed as such, the notion of limit has no place. Absolute perfection is nothing less than the Infinite. It follows as a consequence from the very notion of perfection, that if perfection is limited -- if it is not absolute perfection, but perfection of this or that definite and restricted nature -- the limiting principle must be extrinsic to the principle of *actus*. Perfection cannot be its own limit: for in so far as it is limited it is a denial of perfection. This point is well put by Professor Flint in an argument which, though employed in a different connection, expresses the very truth for which we are contending. "The limited," he writes, "always implies a limiting. It cannot be limited by itself: does not suffice for itself: supposes something beyond itself. The absolutely finite must be limited by something or nothing. If by nothing, it must be really infinite."[2]

There are two ways in which potentiality may thus give limits to act. We have already seen that an act is limited by the potentiality to which it corresponds and which it perfects. Thus form is limited by the matter in which it inheres. The sculptor's ideal, as it exists in his mind, belongs to the spiritual order and is not fettered by conditions of time and space. But when it is embodied in matter, it is tied down, so to speak, to this particular fragment of marble or bronze. This is one way in which potentiality effects the limitation of act. But act is also limited, in so far as it is itself a potentiality as regards an act of a higher order. For here, also, we are not concerned with *actus purus*, absolute and therefore infinite perfection, but with an entity capable of further perfectibility, and consequently one which is limited. But every limited entity involves of necessity principles both of perfection and limit, -- of act and potentiality.[3]

These preliminary considerations have inevitably been somewhat tedious. But their vital importance will appear now that we are in a position to apply them to the subject under consideration. Existence is an *actus* -- it is the perfection in virtue of which natures are not mere objects of thought, but are actualized in the order of reality. We may, if we will, conceive God as having before His mind an indefinite number of possible worlds. To one of these He gave existence: and the natures, spiritual and material, belonging to the order of things which He chose, became *actual*. They were endowed with the perfection of existence. The question now arises: What is the principle which limits the perfection, which acts as the potentiality in regard of this act? Every one of these natures is finite: it is a nature of this or that kind. Even Divine power cannot create a second Infinite. What is it which serves as the potentiality limiting the perfection of existence, where a pure spirit is concerned? There is only one answer possible. The existence is limited by the nature or essence. The essence itself furnishes the confines which determine the measure of actuality. The created essence is a veritable potentiality as regards the *actus* of existence.

We do not, of course, mean that the essence exists previously to its reception of existence. This would be a contradiction in terms. Neither essence nor existence can subsist alone and apart from the other. Created essence can only possess being in virtue of the gift of existence: created existence is inconceivable except in so far as it effects the realization of some finite nature. Essence and existence are but principles of finite being: they are not subsisting entities. But we contend that in the very nature of things every finite subsisting entity is composite: for these two principles must combine to constitute it. It may indeed be asked how it is possible to confer perfection on an, as yet, non-existent potentiality. But the question only needs to be asked for the answer to suggest itself. Created agents can only operate where an existing potentiality offers itself to them. God stands in need of no preexisting subject-matter. Creative power produces simultaneously the potentiality and its actuation.

The bearing of this on the nature of God is evident. In God, as we have already shewn, there can be no composition. For the composition of diverse elements postulates the action of an efficient cause: and God is uncaused.[4] In Him there are not two principles -- existence and an essence determining and confining the scope of His reality. He is absolute and subsistent existence, hedged in and restricted by no limits -- the very plenitude of all being. His uncreated existence is His nature. All finite beings are composed of potentiality and act, from the most elementary material substances to the highest of spirits. The potentiality is greatest in the lower grades of the great hierarchy of creation. Each ascending stage shews us more and more of actuality. In pure spirits the potentiality involved by matter is wholly absent: their essence is simple, not composite. But in every created substance, of however sublime a degree, the act of existence is limited by the potentiality of essence. God alone is actuality unmixed with any potentiality, Perfection which knows no limit: He is, in the expressive terminology of the Schoolmen, *Actus Purus.*

It is of the utmost importance to grasp the infinite difference here involved between God and creatures. That difference is sometimes overlooked. Thus Professor A. Russel Wallace, arguing for the existence of pure spirits, writes: "Angels and archangels ... have . . . long been banished from our belief. . . . Yet the grand law of 'continuity,' the last outcome of modern science . . . cannot surely fail to be true beyond the narrow sphere of our vision, and leave such an infinite chasm between man and the great Mind of the universe."[5] The Scholastic metaphysician has never lost sight of the existence of spiritual entities -- pure forms. But on the other hand, he has never imagined that they can bridge the gulf between God and man. The highest imaginable of pure forms is a creature. And no law of continuity will enable us to bridge the unfathomable chasm which separates the Infinite from the finite.

Our discussion of the Divine Essence has not taught us what it is, in the sense of enabling us to conceive, as they are, its infinite perfections. We have already shewn that this is intrinsically impossible. But it has, as we said at the commencement of the chapter, made known to us a fundamental aspect of that essence -- one which distinguishes it from every finite nature, viz., its identity with its own existence.

3. *The analogy of being in God and in creatures.* The conclusions reached in the last section enable us to arrive at a more accurate notion of the term 'being' as used of God and of finite substances respectively, than has hitherto been possible, and thereby to dispose of an important difficulty. Being (*ens*) as applied to a finite substance signifies a nature considered as possessing (or capable of possessing) actuality (*esse*). The mind distinguishes between the nature and the existence, viewing the object as a nature which has received existence. We apply this conception, representative of the objects of experience, to God. But as used of God it has a signification only proportionally the same as it has in regard of creatures. For the Divine nature, as we have seen, does not *receive* actuality: it is actuality. The being of God and the being of creatures are wholly incommensurable: they are on different planes. Here lies the solution of the objection frequently urged as admitting of no answer, and as fatal to any system of thought which maintains that God and creatures are distinct. To affirm at the same time the existence both of an Infinite Being and of finite beings external to and distinct from the Infinite, is, we are assured, a contradiction in terms. If necessary being is infinite, then there is nothing external to it: if finite beings exist as distinct from necessary being, it follows that necessary being is not infinite.[6] Yet the difficulty, insurmountable as it seems at first sight, disappears in the light of the doctrine of the analogy of being. God as subsistent actuality is infinite. He is the abyss of all reality, and can receive no addition. Created beings are, it is true, real. But however wonderful their created perfection, they can add nothing to the perfection or reality which there is in God. They contain nothing which is not found in an infinitely higher manner in Him. In Infinite Being and finite being, we have not got two things which can be added up, so that, taken together, they make more reality than is found in the Infinite alone. The perfections of finite being can no more add to God's perfections, than a thousand, or a million, superficies could add to the bulk of a solid body. To use a Scholastic phrase, the creation of the finite resulted in a greater number of real things (*plura entia*), but not of more reality (*plus entitatis*) Were God to create a thousand universes there would be no addition to perfection, any more than to goodness or

to truth. Finite perfection, finite goodness, finite truth are but the reflection on an infinitely lower plane, of what is already God's.

The difficulty which we have been considering is, then, based on a fallacy -- the fallacy of regarding 'being' as a univocal term. It will be found that the writers who urge it, sometimes almost contemptuously so confident are they that no reply is possible, one and all assume that the term can have but one signification, and that God and man are beings in the same sense. But even in its reference to the created order the word is analogous. It is used of all the categories alike. Yet it has not identically the same meaning as applied to substantial and accidental being, *e.g.*, to the thinker, to his thought, to his position in space. This alone might have suggested that there must be a fundamental difference in its application to the self-existent Being and to contingent beings.

If being be treated as univocal it is practically impossible to escape a pantheistic conclusion. In that case God does not contain all reality unless creatures form a part of Him: for their being is on a par with His. We are driven to conclude that creatures are a manifestation of God. This was in fact the root error of Spinoza and of many another defender of pantheism. The only other alternative would be the fanciful doctrine of pluralism, which rejecting creation maintains the independent existence of many thinking subjects, among whom the Supreme Spirit holds position of *primus inter pares*. But this theory, though enjoying some vogue at present, is too extravagant to win any permanent hold upon thought. Pantheism, on the other hand, is a form of error which has at all periods misled many of the greatest intellects.

In view of what has been said, it is hardly necessary to utter a warning against any confusion between being, viewed as a universal term, applicable to all things (*ens communissimum*), and being in its particularized reference to God (*esse subsistens*).[7] The former has the least content of all concepts which we can form. It is applicable to everything -- to the self-existent and to the contingent, to substance and the nine categories of accidents, to the real and the possible. Taken in abstraction, apart from any particular subject, it signifies no more than what is capable of existence. On the other hand, being when predicated of God denotes the fullness of all reality -- in the expressive words of St. John Damascene, 'the illimitable ocean of being.'[8] Yet the two have been confused. This was, in fact, one of the errors contained in the works of Rosmini, and condemned by the Church in 1887. Rosmini's philosophy was a form of ontologism, the doctrine which teaches that the human mind possesses a direct and immediate cognition of God, and is not dependent for its knowledge of Him upon the testimony of His works. This immediate cognition Rosmini held to lie in the indeterminate abstract concept of Being, of which all other concepts may be regarded as determinations. It is manifest that from such premises pantheism would follow as a logical consequence.

4. *The metaphysical essence of God.* We now turn to the question of God's metaphysical essence. We have pointed out already that though the Divine attributes are in fact one simple Reality devoid of any distinction, the human mind is compelled to conceive them separately: for our knowledge of them is derived from created perfections distinct one from another. It is further to be observed that, as found in creatures, certain of these perfections stand in a definite order of relative subordination. Thus, *e.g.,* in man, the exercise of external activity is dependent on will : will, in its turn, is directed by the intellect: while the faculties of will and intelligence both flow from man's possession of a spiritual soul. As a consequence of this our minds necessarily conceive the Divine nature on similar lines: certain attributes are viewed as dependent on others. Even though we know that in God there is no distinction between substantial nature, will and intellect, we cannot help representing them as holding the same order of relative subordination in which they are found in ourselves. This manner of viewing them, though due to the limitations of our minds, has a basis in objective reality. Reason forbids us to reverse the order. We cannot conceive God's volition as acting prior to His thought. Is there, then, among the Divine attributes one which *for our minds* stands to the others in the relation in which the metaphysical essence of a creature stands to its derivative properties -- one which (1) is absolutely fundamental, from which (2) the other attributes may be deduced, and

which (3) affords in its own right a basis of distinction between Him and creatures? If so, then in Natural Theology -- the science of God -- this attribute must be regarded as the metaphysical essence.

It will not improbably be asked what interest or importance attaches to this question. The answer is to be found in the claim which we have just made for Natural Theology, that it is a science. A science, as has already been explained (c. i., § I), is an organized body of truth regarding some object of thought. A few isolated facts, a few unconnected conclusions, do not constitute a science. A body of knowledge only merits that name when it is an organized whole. The form of the organization will vary very widely in accordance with the nature of the science. But in every case it largely consists in the accurate discrimination between the primary and derivative characteristics of the object. We endeavour to obtain an accurate definition of the object, the definition being nothing else than a statement of its primary characteristics -- in other words, its essence -- and to establish the connection between the derivative properties and those embodied in the definition. This Natural Theology does for us as regards God: and it is for this reason that we enquire which of the Divine attributes is to be reckoned as the essence.

We find what we are seeking in the concept of God as *Subsistent Being*, understanding by that term, as we have already explained, existence subsisting independently of any potentiality -- absolute and, consequently, unconfined Reality. God in the scholastic phrase is *ipsum Esse, Esse in se subsistens*. This is the concept which gives us the metaphysical essence of God.

Our conclusion is easily established. The notion of Being manifestly does not stand in a relation of dependence to any other attribute whatever. It is ultimate and fundamental. Moreover, this attribute distinguishes God from all other beings. In all else the essence and existence are really distinct, the one from the other. In God alone, the uncaused, are they identified. And lastly, from this attribute all His other attributes may be derived by logical consequence. This point will be treated in the chapter which follows.

There has been a certain variety of opinion among Scholastic writers on this subject: and it may be well in conclusion to notice briefly one or two other views which have been maintained, and to indicate our reasons for dissenting from them. (1) Some of the Nominalist school taught that the Divine attributes as a collective whole were to be regarded as God's essence. Here they confused the physical and metaphysical essence. It is manifest that among the Divine attributes, *as we conceive them*, some are derivative. Hence it is out of the question that the full collection of the positive attributes can be the metaphysical essence of God. (2) The Scotists held God's infinity to be His essential attribute. But infinity is more naturally regarded as a property affecting the essence and the positive attributes than as itself constituting the essence. (3) Much more, it would seem, can be said for the view taken by a certain number of Thomists, that God's essence is to be found in His attribute of supreme and self-existent Intelligence.[9] It is urged on behalf of this opinion that the metaphysical essence of God must express that which constitutes His essential perfection. But God's essential perfection -- His highest attribute -- lies in His supreme intellectuality. The argument, though specious, rests on a misunderstanding of the term Existence as employed in regard of creatures and of God respectively. As applied to creatures it signifies simply that they are not mere possibles, but are actually realized. Like *Ens communissimum* it prescinds from the degree of perfection which they contain, and hence denotes that only which is common to all actual things. The notion of intelligence clearly expresses a higher degree of perfection than existence thus understood. Intelligence is the highest grade of substantial perfection. But as employed in regard of God, existence, as we have seen, has a very different significance. Being or existence predicated of Him signifies the fullness of all Reality, embracing in its scope all perfection. (4) Very many hold the primary attribute of God to be His 'aseity' defining him as *Ens a se -- the self-existent Being.* This definition is adopted both by Father Hontheim and Father Boedder. The objection to regarding this attribute as God's metaphysical essence is that it does not really express what we conceive as an internal constitutive principle of the Divine nature. The real significance of the notion *Ens a se* is to deny that God is, like creatures, caused by another. He is conceived as self-existent in the sense of 'unoriginated.' Undoubtedly this is the first aspect under which we conceive God, as we reason from the existence of contingent things to that of a necessary Being. But it still remains for us to ask what is the internal constitutive, in virtue of which He is unoriginated and needs no cause. And to reply to this question we must fall back on our concept of Him as subsistent existence -- as the Being whose existence is his nature.

NOTES

{1} The term metaphysical essence, though the one commonly employed, is difficult to justify. We are here concerned with the nature as conceived, and not, as in metaphysics, with the nature in its aspect as real being, possessed of the attributes which belong to it as thus considered.

{2} *Agnosticism*, p. 554.

{3} It is a mere deduction from the principles which we have just explained, that if we are concerned, not with absolute perfection, but with perfection of a particular kind, and if that perfection be not limited by reception into a potentiality, it will be infinite in its kind. A form, as we have just seen, is limited by the matter in which it inheres. The type is reproducible indefinitely, because the perfection is limited to the matter which it perfects. Were it, however, realizable, not as a perfection embodied in matter, but as a 'pure form,' there would be no limiting principle in its composition. It would itself contain all the perfection compatible with such a type: in other words, it would be infinite in its kind. But if infinite, then unique. If there are two individuals of the same type, it follows necessarily that they are both of them limited expressions of the perfection in question, and that neither is exhaustive of the perfection exhibited in that type. Hence corporeal natures, such as man, are realized in many individuals of the same specific type. But in the case of a purely spiritual nature such multiplication is intrinsically impossible.

{4} *Supra.*

{5} Cited in J. Ward, *Realm of Ends*, p. 187.

{6} Cf., *e.g.*, J. Caird, *Fundamental Ideas of Christianity* I., p. 88. [The so-called cosmological argument] "starts from the assumed reality of the finite world as finite, and infers from it the reality of an infinite cause or creator. But an infinite confronted by a finite to which equal reality is ascribed -- an infinite with a finite world outside of it -- is a contradiction in terms."

{7} Kant employs the term *ens realissimum*. This is philosophically less accurate; but it serves equally to guard against the confusion of which we speak.

{8} St. Thomas. *Summa Theol.*, I., q. 4, art. 2, ad 3.

{9} Intelligere divinum, non radicale sed actuale, sub ratlone ultimae actualitatis per se subsistentis constituit metaphysice divinam naturam: unde Dei descriptio erit haec, ens summe et actualissime intelligens." Billuart, *Theologia*, Tract. de Deo, Dissert. ii., art. 1. Vol. I., p. 94 (ed. 1827).

Chapter X. Attributes relating to the Divine Nature.

1. Division and Deduction of the Divine Attributes.

2. Unity and Simplicity.

3. Truth and Goodness.

4. Infinity and Immutability.

5. Eternity.

6. Immensity.

1. *Division and deduction of the Divine attributes.* By the Divine attributes are signified those perfections which, to employ Scholastic terminology, exist formally and necessarily in God. We are not here concerned with terms predicated metaphorically in His regard, but with such as can be affirmed of Him in their strict and literal sense. We have already explained at some length that in Him these perfections are realized in a manner infinitely higher than that in which they are found in finite things, and that in consequence our minds can form no adequate representation of the mode of existence which they have in the Godhead. We merely know that in the Infinite Being they are not so many distinct determinations, but that they are one Supreme Substance in Whom are no accidents and no distinctions. The limitations of our faculty of knowledge impose on us this piecemeal knowledge of the absolutely simple. Perfections, which in the Infinite coalesce into unity, in finite things are distinct and demand to be known through different concepts. And such finite realities are all that our experience shews us. Nevertheless, we are justified in affirming of God certain perfections which the created world displays: for the terms by which they are designated signify the perfection without connoting whether it is limited or not.

Terms which are predicated of God consequently on His free actions, *e.g.*, Creator, Conserver, are not reckoned among the Divine attributes. It is in view of this distinction that we say that the attributes denote perfections which exist *necessarily* in God.

In this section we shall briefly enumerate the principal attributes, distinguishing them into the classes into which they naturally fall, and shall then proceed to shew how they may, one and all, be deduced from the notion of Subsistent Being, which, as we argued in the last chapter, must be regarded as being for our intelligence the essence of God[1] -- the primary constitutive of the Divine nature, from which all God's other necessary attributes may be deduced, just as within the limits of the Aristotelian categories the properties are derivable from the specific essence.

The main division of the attributes will be into those which relate to God's nature and those which relate to His actions. Unity and Simplicity, Goodness, Truth, Life, are properties predicable of the nature of God. And with these we may reckon certain other perfections, the concepts of which we reach by the exclusion of those limits which characterize finite things. Thus we say of God that He is infinite, eternal, immense. The first of these declares that there are no bounds to His essence -- that it embraces the fullness of all being: eternity affirms that lie is not measured by time: immensity, that spatial restrictions have no application, no meaning, in His regard.

The attributes relating to the Divine action are, in the first place, those which concern His immanent operations. We predicate of Him both intellect and will: and each of these activities gives rise to certain further denominations. In virtue of His intelligence we term God omniscient: in virtue of His will we attribute to Him love of the Good, and those moral virtues which are compatible with infinite perfection, *e.g.*, justice and mercy. To this division belongs, secondly, the Divine omnipotence -- God's power of producing as effects external to Himself whatever is not repugnant and self-contradictory.

We shall now establish that the attributes which we have just enumerated are all deducible from the notion of God as Subsistent Being: that when we have demonstrated the existence of the Supreme Substance, and proved that this Substance is Absolute Being, Actus Furus, the Reality in which existence and essence are identified, the mind is not brought to a standstill, but is able to shew how this Being is to be conceived. It is important to call attention to this point for more than one reason. Thereby we make good our contention that Natural Theology is in the strictest sense a science. Moreover, we here refute once and for all the assertion so frequently heard that the traditional Natural Theology is radically anthropomorphic in its conception of God: that it merely attributes to the Divine Being those qualities magnified to infinity which it regards as appropriate to an earthly ruler. It is true that the criticism is generally made by those who have not been at the pains to make themselves acquainted with the Scholastic philosophy, a fact which renders it of little real weight. But no reply can be more final than to establish that the Divine attributes are reached not by any *a posteriori* proof, but by *a priori* demonstration from the notion of Subsistent Being itself.

We have already (chap. iii., § 4) pointed out that goodness, unity and truth are attributes predicable of all being, as such. Every existing nature -- every `thing` -- is good, is one, and is true.[2] As existing in act it possesses some measure, however small that may be, of perfection, and is to that extent, at least, good; it is an undivided whole, and therefore one; it is capable of being the object of intellectual knowledge, and thus is true. Now if these attributes denominate all beings, they are applicable in a supreme degree to God. He is Being in a fuller sense than any finite entity: for He is self-existent Being -- Being which cannot not be: they are only contingent beings. Their hold upon reality -- their distance, so to speak, from nonentity -- is infinitely less than His. There is a similar difference in their right to the attributes of which we are now speaking. God is the sum of all perfection -- Supreme Goodness. He is One, with a unity which involves, further, absolute simplicity: for in Him there neither is nor can be any distinction of parts. He is the Truth. All things are intelligible in some measure: and the higher their plane of being -- the further removed from material conditions -- the greater degree of intelligibility. We speak here of intelligibility objectively considered. To certain intelligences an object may be incomprehensible, not through lack of intelligibility on its part, but because it surpasses the range of their capacity. It is thus, as we have already pointed out (chap. vi., § 1), with our minds in regard of God. To us it is easier to understand the concrete things of this world than God: since for all the data of our knowledge we are dependent on sense-perception. Just because God is so far above us, we cannot comprehend Him. Though He is supremely intelligible, we contemplate Him `as in a glass, darkly,' under analogies drawn from created things. Only the Divine intelligence can comprehend God.

Again, the perfection of Subsistent Being is not narrowed to the measure of some particular type. If, as Being, it is the sufficient reason of its own existence, then it must needs contain all the perfection designated by that name: it must be Being in the full and unrestricted sense of the term. In other words, it must be infinite. Infinity is no mere negation, as when, e.g., we say that God is invisible. The grammatical form of the word is negative: for we have no other means of conceiving or expressing infinity, than to negate those limits which are a necessary condition of all such being as falls within our experience. But the thing signified is positive -- perfection without end. Further, the Infinite is, of necessity, immutable. Were He susceptible of change, He would not be infinite. And immutability carries with it eternity. That which is immutable cannot be the subject of the continuous change which is implied in temporal existence. Moreover, since God as Subsistent Being is the source of all that is, the cause which sustains it in existence, it follows that He possesses the attribute of immensity. Nothing can come into being, or remain in being, unless His action, and therefore He Himself, is present to it. Subsistent Being is, in the nature of things, immaterial. Matter, as distinct from form, is mere potency, destitute of actuality of any kind.[3] In that Being which is *Actus Purus* there is no potentiality. In Him, consequently, matter can have no place. But immateriality, as we shall shew later (chap. xi., § i), involves the presence of intelligence, and, therefore, also of will, together with the other attributes which these activities imply.

Again, the powers of action proper to an agent are proportional to the perfection which it possesses. As it is, so does it act: for actuality is the source of action. We are accustomed to say that none can give what he has not got. But the converse of this is likewise true, viz., that the possession of any perfection involves a corresponding activity. Since then God is infinite being, it follows that His power extends to all possible modes of finite being: that He is omnipotent. The impossible -- that which is self-contradictory -- is not being at all. We do not claim for omnipotence the power to give existence to nonentity.

In the pages which follow we shall treat of these attributes severally: in this chapter of those which relate to God's nature, and subsequently of those which concern His operations. But it seemed desirable by way of preliminary to shew how Natural Theology frames its idea of God. Not merely is that idea not anthropomorphic, but each element which enters into it is reached by a strict deduction from the notion of Subsistent Being, each stage of the reasoning being a proposition in metaphysics based on those self-evident first principles which the mind cannot question without involving itself in universal scepticism.

2. *Unity and Simplicity.* (i) An entity, as we have seen in the preceding section, is termed one as being undivided: and unity is a transcendental attribute, predicable of whatever has the right to be termed a 'thing,' simply because, where there is division, there we have not *a* thing, but *things.* In so far as anything is *a thing,* it is undivided. Thus, if we are concerned with a composite whole, formed of parts, so long as the parts are separate one from another, it is many things, not *a* thing. It is only *a* thing when the parts coalesce into the whole, and it is undivided.

Division, however, is of more than one kind, and corresponding distinctions must be drawn in the use of the word unity.

By *logical division* a generic nature is distinguished (in the conceptual order) into a number of species by the addition of differentiae: and, similarly, a species is divided by the addition of individualizing notes. On the other hand, *real division* is the separation of a concrete object into distinct parts.

When we affirm that God is one, it is with the first of these that we are concerned. We assert that the Divine nature is such that it is not, and cannot be, multiplied in distinct individuals. It will be noted that we do not merely deny that it is actually so multiplied, but, further, that any multiplication is possible. A thing might be unique of its kind, and yet be such that a plurality would involve no intrinsic impossibility. The mediaeval philosophers used to instance the sun as a case in point. The sun, they not unnaturally believed, was sole in its own class: there was no other individual substance of a similar kind. Yet no impossibility is involved in the notion of two or even of more suns. In saying that God is one, we signify that where the self-existent nature is in question, the supposition of a plurality is intrinsically repugnant. That nature is of necessity singular. To the unity which results from the denial of real division we shall return later in the section.

One of the many arguments by which God's unity may be shewn has been given by anticipation in the henological proof of God's existence. It will be sufficient here to recall in the briefest manner the lines of that demonstration. We argued that the perfection of 'being,' common to all existing things, postulates a common cause: that in so far as, notwithstanding their diversity, they are *at one* in the possession of this perfection, they owe it to a single source since unity cannot spring from diversity. That single source, we pointed out, could only be uncaused self-existent Being, in other words, God, Who is thus shewn to be One. Were it supposed that there were two gods, we should be driven to admit that they were not self-existent, but derived the perfection of 'being,' common to both of them, from one higher than they.[4]

The following two arguments are independent of the henological proof. They are both based on the notion of God as *Actus Purus*, Being not confined by the limits of any potentiality, Subsistent Existence.

God's nature is identical with His existence. And where essence and existence are one and the same, plurality is wholly impossible. For existence is of necessity proper to the individual. Two beings cannot be realized by the same existence. Where existence and essence are distinct factors, the same type can be repeated in a number of separate individuals each possessing its own existence. But if there be a nature where there is no distinction, but where the essence is the existence, that essence must necessarily be sole. To suppose that there could be another individual of the same nature would be to suppose two Beings existing in virtue of the same existence. There can, therefore, be but One God.[5]

The other proof derived from the notion of *Actus Purus* is based on God's infinity. This undoubtedly is the argument which most people find the easiest to grasp. Inasmuch as the Divine existence is unmixed with any potentiality, it follows, as we saw, that it is the plenitude of all being (chap. ix., § 2). But this is precisely what we signify by the term infinite. Now it is plain that there can be but one infinite. If *per impossibile* we suppose two such Beings, they must necessarily be distinct the one from the other: the one must possess some reality in which the other is lacking. in other words, one, at least, of the two is not infinite at all: the supposition of two infinites is self-contradictory. God, therefore, being the fullness of being must be One.[6]

Not merely is the doctrine of the divine unity thus manifestly demonstrated, but it satisfies the almost instinctive demand of our rational nature to refer all reality to a single principle. That demand, as we have already noted, is exploited by modern pantheism, when it styles itself monism and, most fallaciously, reproaches creationism with being dualistic. It is indeed strange, therefore, to find even this doctrine, that unity is one of the essential attributes of the Divine nature, called in question by Professor Pringle-Pattison. When engaged in arguing on behalf of a creation *ab aeterno*, he asserts that: "in the world of reality there is no possibility of a start with a mere One" and gives as his reason that: "if we start *reflectively* with a One, we find that it inevitably involves a Many, for it is only as the unity of a multiplicity that you know it as one."[7] The mere One, he tells us is an 'abstraction of reflective analysis.' In other words, the one and the many are correlatives: neither can be found apart from the other. God is not One as regarded in Himself, but only as viewed in relation to a multitude in which He ranks as a unit. The difficulty thus raised rests upon a failure to determine accurately the notions of the One and the manifold. Multitude or plurality is constituted by units of which one is not the other: and as such it is defined. In the *real order* unity is prior to multiplicity: and no shadow of a reason can be given why the One should not exist before the many, why God should not have existed in 'undividedness' before He called created things into being. The two are opposites: they are in no sense correlatives. It is true that in the *order of thought* multitude is in a sense prior. This is so because our concepts are gathered from the data furnished by the senses: and the senses make us aware of the manifold before we form our clear-cut concept of unity as the undivided. But when we ask whether God is One, our whole concern is with the real order, not with the logical formation of concepts. Furthermore, the conclusion to which the view we are criticizing brings us, viz., that God may be reckoned as a unit together with others, and so may take part in forming a given manifold, is a patent absurdity.

(2) Unity may, as we have said, relate not to *logical* but to *real* division. It may bespeak, not the absence of others who share the same nature, but the undividedness of the individual entity. In this reference, a being which has a diversity of parts, and is thus capable of division, is said to be one with the *unity of composition*. A being wholly incapable of division, because there is in it no distinction of parts, has the *unity of simplicity*. Man is one. He is an undivided whole, but has many constituent parts. Substantially, he consists of body and soul. And his body has many members distinct from one another. Even in his soul there is accidental composition. His thoughts and volitions are not the soul itself: they come and go, while the soul remains. No creature is wholly immune from composition. In a pure spirit essence and existence are distinct principles. God alone is absolutely simple.

Since the world of our experience consists entirely of corporeal things formed of many parts, we find it especially difficult to realize this one of the divine attributes. Moreover, in our universe that which is most simple is least perfect. An increasing complexity characterizes what is more perfect. The amoeba, for instance, is conspicuously simple, and man more complex in his constitution than any other living creature. It is easy, however, to see that there is a simplicity due to imperfection, and a simplicity which betokens perfection. Material beings are perfected by a complex provision of endowments destined for various ends. Lacking these they are simple with the simplicity of imperfection. But supreme actuality needs no accidents, no variety of powers and faculties. God's being and God's activity are one sole and simple perfection, which is Himself.

Besides the proof drawn from God's nature as Pure Actuality, St. Thomas offers us various demonstrations of His absolute simplicity.[8] One of these may here be given. In a composite entity the component parts are prior to the whole. Even though they should not have existed previously to this conjunction, they possess a natural priority to the whole which arises from their union. The latter results from them, and is thus secondary in this regard. Now God is the first Being, all other things deriving their being from Him: He is not the result of anything else. It follows that it is absurd to suppose that in Him there can be any composition. His simplicity must be absolute.

Not merely is God's simplicity such as to rule out all composition in the real order; but it excludes likewise the possibility of metaphysical composition. Metaphysical composition belongs to the conceptual order, arising from the distinction of genus and differentia in the specific nature. Thus the nature of man, as conceived by us, is formed by the union of the elements 'animal' and 'rationality.' The metaphysical essence of other beings is always conceived under this form. But the Divine nature affords no ground for any such distinction. The reason is manifest. The genus denotes the limits within which the specific perfection is realized: the differentia gives us this perfection. The two stand to each other in the relation of potentiality and act. This relation, it is true, is conceptual. But since the genus, as we have just pointed out, is indicative of real limits, it is not merely a potentiality in the conceptual order but involves potentiality in the real order. It is wholly incompatible with the infinite perfection which is God's. The same conclusion may be reached also by another proof. Whenever different natures can be classed together in a genus, each of them possesses some perfection proper to itself: the differentia of one is not found in another. But God is the sum of all perfections. Hence it is impossible that the distinction between genus and differentia should be found in the Divine nature.

It is a consequence of His absolute simplicity that of God we can predicate all His attributes in their abstract form. We can say not merely, 'God is wise'; but 'God is wisdom.' The point is of sufficient importance to call for notice. An abstract term and the corresponding concrete word differ in logical value, inasmuch as the abstract term regards the attribute signified in isolation. We cannot say of any man that he is wisdom. He may possess wisdom; but wisdom is but a part of him -- one of many attributes that are his. On the other hand, the concrete word signifies the attribute as inherent in a subject. Though it gives explicit expression to only one quality alone, it does not view it in isolation and exclude the rest. It denominates the subject as a whole, and can therefore be predicated of it. We say of a man that he is wise. In God not only are the attributes, one and all, identical with that supremely simple reality which is the Divine Essence; but, even as conceived, each one of them implies the others. There can be no such thing as perfect conceptual distinction between them, as, as, *e.g.*, there is between two such concepts as animal and rational, of which one can be realized without the other. No one of the divine attributes can exist apart from the rest. Each attribute is the entire Divine Nature viewed under some one special aspect. Thus the mind, considering what is involved in the notion of infinite wisdom, finds that it implicitly involves the presence of all the Divine perfections. Hence, when we employ such expressions as 'God is wisdom,' 'God is justice,' we do not, as might seem, forego accuracy for the sake of emphasis. Such predications are logically correct.

We do not, of course, mean that the use of concrete terms in regard of God is erroneous. Our mental representations, and in consequence our modes of speech, take their form from the world of our experience. Within that world all that possesses subsistence is concrete. Hence only concrete terms convey that the object they denote is a subsistent reality. As, therefore, we are justified in employing abstract terms of God in order to express His simplicity, so we are justified in making use of concrete terms to convey His subsistence.{9} 3. *Truth and Goodness.* (1) Truth, in the primary sense of the word, is proper to the intellect: it is an attribute not of things but of thoughts. A judgment is true when it affirms of some subject a form which belongs to it in its objective reality, or denies of it some form which, objectively, is not found in it. Truth is, in fact, the relation of conformity which the intellectual act bears to its object. As applied to things, its sense is secondary and derivative. Things are termed true because they are capable of being objects of intellectual knowledge: in other words, because the mind can attain this relation of conformity in this regard. We have already pointed out (§ I) that, as thus understood, truth belongs to objects in very various degrees: that things do not all stand on the same plane of intelligibility. The reason is not far to seek. A thing possesses intelligibility in the same degree in which it possesses being or actuality.{10} Potentiality as such is not knowable; for in so far as it is potential it is not being at all, but a mere capacity for being. We only know potentiality in virtue of the act of which it is capable. It is for this reason that matter lacks all intelligibility.{11} Matter is pure potentiality. Since then the intelligibility of a being is in direct ratio to its actuality, it follows that the Divine Nature is supremely intelligible. God is subsistent actuality, and in Him there is no potentiality of any kind. He is, therefore, infinitely true: He is the Truth.

Things are called true in another sense, which calls for mention, since in this sense also the term has a special applicability to God. A thing which is the work of an intelligent agent is termed true in so far as it corresponds with the idea which he desires to realize. A house which an architect has built, is true, if it agrees with his plan a statue is true if in conformity with the artist's concept. Just as our act of knowledge is styled true if it corresponds with the object which is its standard and measure, so the object itself is spoken of as true if it conforms to the mental concept which is its norm. All created things are the handiwork of the Divine artist: and are called true because they agree with God's idea of the nature to be realized. In this sense Truth in a thing is its conformity with the divine idea. Does truth belong to God Himself in this sense? Yes: in God truth, as thus considered, is found in an infinite degree. For the divine essence is not merely similar to the thought of it in God's mind; but in God, as Pure Actuality, the two are one and the same. In place of conformity we have absolute identity.[12]

(2) Goodness is the relation in which being stands to the will as an object of desire or complacency. Just as truth is the relation which being, as knowable, bears to the intellect, so goodness is the relation which, as desirable or lovable, it bears to the other rational faculty, the will. It is the nature of the will to approve whatever is perfect: and in so far as an object possesses perfection does it command the approval of the will -- in other words, attract its love. Goodness is simply perfection considered in relation to the will. Beings are also termed good in another sense, viz., not in virtue of their intrinsic excellence, but because they answer to the need of some other entity, thus tending to perfect it. They are thus good in relation to it. In the former sense goodness is styled *absolute goodness*: in the latter *respective goodness*. God, it may readily be shewn, both possesses supreme absolute goodness, and is the supreme respective good of all creatures which are capable of deriving their happiness from so high a source. All things that exist possess some degree of perfection. Existence itself, apart from anything else, gives to them actuality and thereby perfection in some measure. But things are only termed good in the full sense of the word, when they possess the full measure of actuality appropriate to the species. For a natural substance to merit to be styled good of its kind it must have, besides its substantial perfection, the full equipment of accidental qualities appropriate to it. Anything less than this is only called goodness in a restricted sense. Further, the higher that any nature stands in the scale of being, and the ampler, thus, its measure of perfection, so much the greater is its goodness, and its claim on the rational will for approval and love.

God as Subsistent Being contains within Himself the plenitude of perfection. Whatever perfection is found in finite creatures, whatever perfection could be found in other universes than this, were it to please Him to call them into existence, must be derived from Him, who is the sum of all Reality, Pure Act. There is, and can be, no actuality which is not in the Divine nature. Nor is it possible, as in creatures, that any element proper to the full perfection of that nature should be absent. It follows that God is the supreme absolute Good, and merits to be loved supremely for His own sake.

Moreover, to every rational creature God is the supreme respective good. The beatitude of a being endowed with intelligence can only be found in the attainment of ultimate truth, and in the joy and delight which results from its possession. Till that goal is reached, the craving of man's highest faculty must remain unsatisfied: something is still lacking to it. The intelligence cannot rest till it has found the source of all reality and all truth. Even if direct and immediate knowledge of this object were beyond us by reason of the limitations of our nature, yet such knowledge of this Being as we could possess would be the highest happiness open to man. But this fountain-head of truth is none other than God. God then is the supreme respective good of man, and of every other nature, which like man is capable of knowing Him.

It is otherwise with the lower creatures. These cannot find their good in God. Their condition does not allow them to ascend so high. Even the most perfect among them has no knowledge but what sensation may afford. A being so constituted cannot attain to God, for He is out of the reach of the senses. But they receive their respective goods from His hand. No creature can possess aught save as His gift.

The term Goodness is often used with special reference to moral goodness the goodness of a will which acts in conformity with the law of right. In this sense also God is supreme Goodness. His will is the norm of all sanctity. It seems, however, more convenient to keep the discussion of this point for the chapter in which we treat expressly of the Divine Will.{13}

4. *Infinity and Immutability.* (1) It will not be necessary for us to offer proofs here of God's infinity. We have had frequent occasion to lay stress on the fact that as *Actus Purus*, He contains within Himself all perfection - - all reality. This is to be infinite. Something must, however, be said about the notion of infinity with a view to removing possible misconceptions.

The term signifies the *unlimited*. Now it will hardly be denied that our minds tend to connect the notion of limit -- at least of appropriate limit -- with that of perfection. It is claimed as one of the outstanding marks of the aesthetic genius of the Greeks that they had so just a sense of limit and of form. The unlimited may readily appear to us to imply simply the indeterminate and imperfect. Indeed, as what is individual must be strictly determinate, we may find a difficulty in reconciling the notions of infinity and individuality.

St. Thomas treats this subject with his customary insight.[14] In material things, he reminds us, the material and the formal element reciprocally exercise a limiting effect on each other, but in profoundly different ways. Matter limits form as the potentiality into which it is received. Form, on the other hand, limits matter, inasmuch as it confers upon it a determinate actualization, whereas, until so determined, it is capable of being actualized in a great variety of ways. Apart from the limit thus imposed by form, matter has the imperfection of indeterminateness, Hence the notion of infinity -- absence of limit -- envisaged in its relation to matter, implies imperfection, which demands the limiting operation of form to remove it. It is for this reason that the aesthetic faculty, which finds its principal object in the material world, is in so large a measure a sense of the due limit to be assigned.

But in relation to form the effect of a limiting principle is very different. Form is a principle of perfection. And limit attached to it is a restriction on that perfection. The statue, as conceived in the mind of the artist, has, viewed precisely as form, a higher degree of perfection than it possesses as embodied in matter, as we have already had occasion to point out.[15] When embodied in matter it is confined to a given block of stone, and is further limited by the various potentialities of that particular subject-matter. Where form is concerned, the notion of infinity does not imply indeterminateness, but rather free scope for the completest realization of the perfection. When, therefore, we affirm that God is infinite, the attribute in no sense connotes any indefiniteness. It asserts that He possesses in the fullest possible measure whatever falls under the notion of the Real: that there can be no addition to His perfection, for perfection is all summed up in Him.

A source of no little confusion in our idea of the infinite as a divine attribute is found in the fact that we are apt to have before our minds the idea of an infinite number, and to regard this as furnishing a serviceable analogy. This notion shews us infinity as imperfection, not as perfection. An infinite number is indeterminate. It signifies a multitude so vast that it exceeds any number which may be assigned. But it does not, and cannot signify, a multitude such that in it the full perfection of number has attained realization, in such wise that no addition to it is possible. Addition is always possible, where number is concerned. Number is capable of infinite increase precisely as matter is capable of division *ad infinitum*. Such a notion can only mislead us, if regarded as illustrating the infinity of God.

(2) By change is signified the passage from one state of being to another. In asserting God's immutability we deny that God is capable of any such transition, whether in the order of physical reality or in the order of thought and volition. This truth is sometimes expressed by saying that God is both *physically* and *morally immutable*. Here we need only concern ourselves with physical immutability, since God's moral immutability will best be treated later. Our conclusion results immediately both from God's infinite perfection and from His simplicity. Any change in God must suppose either the acquisition of a new perfection or the loss of one previously possessed. But infinite perfection excludes the possibility of either alternative. The infinitely perfect Being cannot acquire a new perfection, for He already possesses all: and He cannot lose a perfection, for in infinite perfection there can he no liability to loss. Again, change is only possible where there is composition of diverse parts. There can be no change unless there are two constituent elements, of which one is permanent, while the other admits of removal. But such composition of parts is wholly incompatible with the Divine simplicity.

5. *Eternity.* Eternity is the attribute which declares the nature of God's duration. We ourselves have experience of only one form of duration,

that which is measured by time. If then we are to attain to such a knowledge of eternity as is open to us, it can only be by considering the notion of time, and removing from it all that involves imperfection and limitation. In this way we may arrive at the idea of a duration compatible with the immutability of the Uncreated.

Time is defined as *a numerical reckoning of the succession involved in motion.*[16] The material world in which we live presents on all sides the phenomenon of motion -- of successive change. Since change takes place continuously, it is divisible into equal parts, succeeding one another. This succession, as numerically reckoned, is time. Time, therefore, is an external reality, not, as Kant fancied, an *a priori* form of our sensibility, nor yet as Einstein claims, a measure purely relative to the conditions of the individual observer. Yet the mind plays its part in it. It adopts some one series of motions, and employs these as a standard for the reckoning of the rest. The revolution of the earth on its axis, and its orbit round the sun, provide mankind with such a standard.

All material things, and man amongst them, exist in time. Their corporeal element renders them liable both to accidental and substantial change. Not merely do they come into being and pass out of being in time; but in virtue of their material constitution their substantial existence itself is successive. Temporal duration has change as its necessary condition. And where there is no liability to change, duration demands another standard of measurement.

God is immutable. In Him there neither is nor can be any change. Not merely is there no beginning and no end of His existence; but no new state can arise either in the order of being or in the order of thought and volition. The very possibility of succession is excluded. Such is the duration which is termed eternal. It will be seen that the notion of eternity goes much further than the mere absence of beginning and end. This alone would not confer eternity. We have seen that it cannot be proved impossible that creation should have had no beginning. Yet even if God had created the world *ab aeterno*, and should conserve it for ever, its existence would be temporal not eternal. Eternity demands absolute changelessness. Nor, again, must we allow ourselves to conceive the divine changelessness merely as an existence which persists unmodified through past, present and future. As soon as we admit the distinction of periods, we have reintroduced the notion of time: for we admit that God's substantial existence is divided into successive parts. In God there is no past, and no future: all is present. This was well expressed by Boethius when he said: 'Our Now, running on, as it were, makes time: the divine Now endures, and makes eternity.'[17] The notion of a stationary Now is, of course, beyond the range of human imagination. We cannot form any mental representation of such a state. But reflection on the necessary conditions of the Divine existence shew us that such must be the 'duration' of God.

The same philosopher whom we have just mentioned gave to eternity a definition accepted by later writers. "It is," he said, "life without end possessed perfectly, and as a simultaneous whole."[18] The terms of the definition are carefully chosen. It is called 'life' rather than mere existence, because in God existence and operation are identical. It is said to be 'possessed perfectly,' because its tenure is absolutely secure: it is independent of all conditions. And, lastly, it is 'possessed as a simultaneous whole,' because it is not realized in successive stages after the manner of temporal things, but exists from the first in its full actualization, in a manner to which our experience affords no parallel.

It follows from what has been said that the now of eternity is exclusive of all temporal differences. In regard of one another temporal things occur in a succession. God beholds them simultaneously. He does not, like ourselves, need to await the occurrence of events, or to register them in memory. The whole course of events, in all its parts, lies open at once to His gaze. Things which in regard of the time series are past, and those which as yet are future, are seen by Him as present occurrences. Just as an instant is indivisible, and has neither past nor future, so too is eternity indivisible. Only, an instant is indivisible by reason of its imperfection: eternity, because in its supreme perfection it is inclusive of all the parts of time. The Eternal is outside the time-series: and the limitations proper to things which possess the defective mode of existence which we style temporal, have no bearing upon Him. We have, as has just been said, no power to imagine such a mode of being. Yet to aid the mind to grasp the conclusion to which reason has brought it, St. Thomas provides us with one or two apt illustrations. In a circle, he reminds us, the points on the circumference are of necessity separate. If the circle is revolving, one such point follows another, but never overtakes it. Yet they are all equidistant from the centre. The relation of the Eternal to the temporal may not inaptly be compared to that of the centre to the several points of the circumference.[19] Or again, somewhat similarly, when men are walking along a road, those who have started first do not see those who are behind. But if someone is watching the scene from a neighbouring height, he looks simultaneously upon those who precede and those who follow. He is outside the series: and his relation to every part of it is one and the same.[20] Doubtless these are but imperfect analogies. Yet they help us to realize a truth which is difficult to grasp, because so remote from anything which can fall within our experience.

If, then, there is no succession -- no before or after -- in God, can it be said that He has duration? Can there be duration without succession? The answer to this question appears, when we consider what duration is. It is simply persistence in being. But if this be so, God's duration is more truly such than any which can belong to the things of time. Their being is ever changing. It is realized successively: and the existence of this moment is not the existence of the last. But God's being knows no change. Its permanence is absolute. Hence He alone has duration in the fullest sense of the word.

But God's duration is not something other than Himself. Time, as predicated of some subject, involves a relation to something external. We estimate a thing's duration by days and years. They constitute a measure by which its span is reckoned. It is not so with God. His duration is His own existence -- that subsistent existence which is God Himself. This attribute, like God's other attributes, is objectively identical with the Divine Essence. As mentally distinguished from it, it gives expression to God's changeless stability, in so far as that changeless stability may be viewed as measuring the duration of God in a manner analogous to that in which the time sequence is the measure of the duration of temporal things.

Besides eternity and time there is another mode of duration termed by the Schoolmen *aeviternal*. This calls for mention here, as its consideration will assist us to gain more precise notions on a confessedly difficult subject. 'Aeviternal' duration is that which is proper to a created spirit. The substantial being of a spirit does not admit of change. Substantial change is only possible in corporeal substances compounded of matter and form. In these the material principle is essentially mutable: its changes may even be such that a new formal principle replaces the previous one, and a new substantial existence supervenes. In a pure spirit such transformations are impossible. It is true that God might annihilate a spirit by ceasing to exercise His conserving activity in its regard. But in this case its destruction would come from without: it would not arise from internal liability to change. It follows from this that in regard of its substantial being a spirit does not admit of succession. Its duration does not consist in a series of states. Yet a spirit is not immutable. It admits of accidental changes: for it is capable of thoughts and volitions, and passes from one of these to another. These permit us to distinguish 'before' and 'after' in the existence of spirit. But it is manifest that 'aeviternal' duration is essentially different from time. Temporal duration consists in continuous change. Aevum is in itself changeless, though connected with changes in the accidental determinations of the subject: and, further, these changes are not continuous but discrete.

In virtue of these accidental changes the time-measure may be applied to a pure spirit. We may say that so much time has passed between this and that activity on the part of an angel. Yet it should be remembered that in so speaking we are applying to the spirit a measure which belongs to ourselves, not to it. Properly speaking, time does not run for these beings.[21] They exist *during* time: they do not, like ourselves, exist in time.

Yet though *aevum* differs fundamentally from time, it differs even more radically from eternity. God, as we saw, in His changeless Now, coexists with all parts of time, however remote the one from the other. All that has ever happened, or ever will happen, lies before Him, not as past and future, but in its reality as present. Duration such as this belongs solely to Subsistent Being, changeless Himself, from Whom the changing time-series receives all the being which it possesses. No finite being has part in it. 'Aeviternal' existence is not inclusive of past and future. For a spirit the past is past, and the future has not come. To coexist with a temporal event, that event must be awaited. Only the Infinite transcends the differences of time.

6. *Immensity.* Immensity is the attribute signifying that spatial limits and restrictions can have no application in regard of God: and, further, that He is present everywhere, in all things and in all places throughout space, nor can any thing or any place come into being in which He is not present. Some writers draw a somewhat rigid distinction between the two parts of the notion, confining the word immensity to the first alone. The latter they signify by the term *omnipresence*. There can, however, be no doubt that, as ordinarily understood, immensity is a complex notion and includes both the elements mentioned.

The significance of the denial of all spatial limits will probably be better understood if we here give a brief explanation of what space properly is, and of the different ways in which substances can be in space.

Our notion of space, like our notion of time, is concerned with an objective reality, but with that reality as conceived under a special aspect considered in abstraction from every other. The reality to which it corresponds is the extension of all actually existing bodies. This it views in abstraction from the particular substances in which it inheres, considering it as contained between any surfaces which the mind may assign. It regards it purely in its dimensional aspect. The concept of space is the concept of extension thus abstractly represented, with its relations of length, area and volume: these are consequent upon dimension as such. Thus, though space is not identical with real extension, if there were no extended bodies, there would be no concept of space. That concept only corresponds to a real object, so far as extended bodies actually exist, *i.e.,* to the limits of the created universe.

We are, inevitably, led to imagine the parts of space as so much emptiness -- sheer nonentity -- filled successively with this or that body. Many, probably, look on this as a picture of what space really is. Yet it is evident that here we have a chimera of the imagination. What is absolute nothingness cannot be measured in terms of length and breadth and depth, or we should have to admit that nonentity could have accidents in the category of quantity. Nor can nonentity be filled with actual reality. This representation of space is formed by picturing the abstract notion as something which possesses existence in the real order. This, too, is the basis of that other creation of our imagination which represents space as existing before creation -- a vast vacuity stretching to infinity in all directions, waiting for God to fill it with the works of His hands. The Schoolmen speak of this as *spatium imaginarium*, 'imaginary space,' distinguishing it not merely from real space, but also from possible space: for it is evident that the Creator might, if He would, add to space by giving yet further extension to the universe.

There are two ways in which things can be in space, proper respectively to corporeal and spiritual substance. A corporeal substance, by reason of its extension, occupies space in such a manner that its different parts correspond to different portions of space. Half the space only contains half the substance. This is said to be in space circumscriptively (*circumscriptive*). Circumscriptive presence is peculiar to material things: for these alone have extension, and, in consequence, parts which are distinguishable from one another.

Spiritual substance is not extended. A spirit has no spatial distribution. Wherever it is, it is there in its entirety. An example is furnished by the human soul. A soul is in the body; but no one imagines that it is spread out within its tenement of clay so that half the body contains but a moiety of the soul. It is present whole and entire in each portion of the body which it animates. It is said to be in the body definitely (*definitive*), the term signifying that the body defines the limits within which the soul exists and acts.

Now granted that there exist spiritual beings which are independent of body, such substances do not belong to the spatial order. One place is not nearer to them than is another. For 'near' and 'far' imply relations of distance, and these beings have no dimensional relations at all. Yet since the immaterial is higher than the material, it would seem to follow that they can act on corporeal substance. If, then, one of them should exert such an activity, it must for the time be, in a manner, in space. Where it acts, there it must be. Furthermore, since their power is not infinite, there must be a limit to the extent of their local action. No finite spirit can possess power to act in every part of space which God has created or may yet create. It is, so to speak, localized within limits fixed by the measure of its efficient powers. Hence in this case it also is in space 'definitely.'

It is manifest that in neither of these ways can God's presence be subject to spatial restriction. Since in Him there is no distinction of parts, there can be no question of such limits as circumscriptive presence entails. And since His power is infinite, a presence defined by the measure of His efficiency is equally repugnant.

It remains, however, to establish that He is actually omnipresent: that not merely does space, however extended, offer no bar to His presence, but that He must, of necessity, be present everywhere.

Whatever exists is the immediate subject of divine action. Every finite thing demands the continuous exercise of God's power in its regard. He gives it being, and were He to cease to do so, it would immediately cease to be. No creature can act on God's behalf in the matter. Being is a result beyond the power of any finite agent: God alone can confer this gift. But of God, as of every other agent, it is true that where He acts, there He must be. Indeed, this holds good in an even fuller sense of God than of finite agents; for God's action and His essence are not distinct realities, but identical the one with the other: God's action is Himself.

God, therefore, is present in everything that exists, whether substance or accident. Nor can anything come into being in which He is not. He is omnipresent.

It may, perhaps, be urged that man effects results beyond the place where he is immediately present by the employment of instrumental causes. Yet the difficulty thus raised is but trivial. That we do this is due to the limitations of our nature. Our mode of being, as we have just seen, is such that spatial distance often prevents any immediate contact with the object of action. But instrumental agency is simply a mode in which we give a further extension to the narrow range of our body's activity. We are truly present by means of the instrument which we use. Such artificial extension of his powers is proper to the finite agent: it can have no meaning where the Infinite is concerned. God needs no instrumental aids.

The argument will have rendered it clear that this attribute belongs to God alone, and is shared by no creature. Immensity, like eternity, is the exclusive prerogative of the Self-existent.

NOTES

{1} We have followed here what seems the most convenient terminology. There is some diversity of usage on the point among Scholastic writers.

{2} The attributes of truth, unity and goodness are predicable of 'things' *properly so called* -- entities. Only the individual singular substance is in the primary sense of the word an *ens*: the term is applied to accidents as secondary analogates. It is also to be noted that only the complete nature, *e.g.*, a tree, a bird, is rightly called an *ens*: a mere fragment, *e.g.*, a table, a chair, a feather, is but a fragment of the true 'thing.' It is by a somewhat extreme extension of the principle of analogy that *ens* and the other transcendentals are predicated of such objects. Further, by an inevitable misapplication we use the word `thing' of any object of thought, even of such as are not entities at all. Thus we call a disease, *e.g.*, a cancer, a thing, whereas it is merely a disordered condition in part of a 'thing' -- the human body. Cf. St. Thomas in *Metaph.* IV., lect. i.

{3} Arist. *Met.* VII., 1029a, 24. **hôste to eschaton kath hauto oute ti oute poson oute allo outhen esti.**

{4} St. Thomas Aq., *Contra Gentiles* I., c. xlii., n. 16.

{5} *Ibid.,* n. 14. "Esse proprium cujuslibet rei est tantum unum. Sed Deus est Esse suum. Impossibile est igitur esse nisi unum Deum."

{6} *Summa Theol.* I., q. xi., art. 3, c.

{7} *Idea of God,* p. 312.

{8} Cf. *Summa Theol.* I., q. 3, art. 7; *Con. Gent.* I., cc. xvi., xviii., xix.

{9} *Summa Theol.* I., q. 13, art. i, ad 2.

{10} Aristotle, *Metaph.* II., c. i., 993b, 31. **hekaston hôs hechei tou einai houto kai tês alêtheias.** Cf. St. Thomas *in loc.,* lectio ii.

{11} *Supra,* c. ii., § 3.

{12} *Summa Theol.* I., q. 16, art. 5.

{13} *Infra,* c. xii, § 5.

{14} *Summa Theol.* I., q. 7, art. 1. Considerandum est igitur quod infinitum dicitur aliquid ex eo quod non est finitum. Finitur autem quodammodo et materia per formam et forma per materiam. Materia quidem per formam, in quantum materia antequam recipiat formam, est in potentia ad multas formas: sed cum recipit unam, terminatur per illam. Form a vero finitur per materiam, in quantum forma in se considerata communis est ad multa: sed per hoc quod recipitur in materiam, fit forma determinate hujus rei. Materia autem perficitur per formam per quam finitur: et ideo infinitum secundum quod attribuitur materiae habet rationam imperfecti: est enim quasi materia non habens formam. Forma autem non perficitur per materiam, sed magis per eam ejus amplitudo contrahitur: unde infinitum secundum quod se tenet cx parte formae non determinatae per materiam, habet rationem perfecti."

{15} *Supra*, c ix., §2.

{16} *Numerus motus secundum prius et posterius.* The definition is Aristotle's, *Phys.*, IV., C. xi., §§ 5, 12. **arithmos kinêseôs kata to proteron kai husteron.**

{17} Boethius, *De Trin.*, c. iv. (Migne, P.L. 64, 1253). "Nostrum Nunc quasi currens tempus facit . . . : divinum vero Nunc permanens . . . aeternitatem facit."

{18} *De Consolatione Phil.*, V., Prosa 6 (Migne, P.L. 63, 858). 'Interminabilis vitae tota simul, et perfecta possessio.'

{19} *Con. Gent.*, I., c. lxvi., n. 6.

{20} *Summa Theol.*, I., q. 14, art. 13, ad 3.

{21} *Summa Theol.*, I., q. 10, art. 5, ad 3. "Quod dicimus angelum esse vel fuisse, vel futurum esse differt secundum acceptionem intellectus nostri, qui accipit esse angeli per comparationem ad diversas partes temporis."

Chapter XI. The Divine Intelligence.

1.   The Divine Intelligence.

2.   Its Primary and Its Secondary Objects.

3.   The Divine Foreknowledge.

4.   Physical premotion and *Scientia Media.*

1. *The Divine intelligence.* From the consideration of the attributes which relate to God's being, we now pass to those which regard His action. His intellect and will are principles of immanent action: and these will be treated in the present and following chapters respectively. Another chapter will be devoted to the Divine omnipotence -- the principle of God's external or transitive activity.

The distinction to which we have just adverted between immanent and transitive action calls for a word of explanation: it is of considerable importance in this part of our treatise. Immanent action is such as is not productive of an external effect, but takes place wholly within the agent itself. Such are, *e.g.,* the vital activities of perception, thought and will. Transitive action is that which produces an external result, *e.g.,* to paint, to carve, to teach, etc. In the creature immanent action is an accident; in the Creator it is identical with the Divine Essence. Transitive action, in the strict sense of the term, cannot be attributed to God. For as we shall shew later (chap. xiii., §1), it differs from immanent action in this point among others, that it is necessarily an accident. God's action in creation is said to be *virtually transitive*: since, though not accidental, it is like transitive action, productive of an external effect.[1]

That God possesses intelligence follows immediately from the principle already established (chap. viii., § 2) that every pure perfection found in creatures is found likewise in God, though in a higher manner of being. Such perfections, we saw, are predicated of God as belonging to Him in their true nature (*formaliter*), and not merely in a metaphorical sense. It is manifest that intelligence is to be reckoned in this class, since it involves no imperfection. But it may be well also to shew that the attribute of intelligence follows logically from our definition of God as Subsistent Being, *Actus Purus*. Knowledge, like being, is an ultimate fact not admitting of explanation. But we recognize that an essential condition of knowledge is the power on the part of the knowing subject so to transcend the limits of its own being that natures other than its own are realized within it, not indeed in the order of objective reality, but in the order of cognition. It thus receives into itself the natures or 'forms' of other things: and it becomes conscious of them in so far as it is thus 'informed.' Thus the human intellect is blank and empty till it has produced a concept. Whatever it knows, it knows through a concept: and a concept is simply the intellectual expression of some 'form.' For the mind, though of itself bare of thought -- a *tabula rasa* -- possesses an active spiritual power. This power operating on the data of sense thence abstracts a multitude of conceptual forms. These are the raw material of all our knowledge. The greater the range of the intellect as regards the representation of alien forms, the greater its power of knowledge. To say this, however, is to say that the power of knowing depends on immateriality. Matter is the principle of limitation. A purely material object is incapable of assimilating any form beyond its own. And just in so far as anything transcends the conditions of matter, it is receptive of other forms. A sense-faculty does this in a very limited degree. It is receptive of forms of a particular kind only: the eye, of colour: the ear, of sound: and so on. The intellect, because spiritual, has a far more perfect capacity of knowledge. It knows realities which are beyond the reach of sense, such as substance, cause, goodness. God's immateriality is of an infinitely higher order than that of the human soul: for His perfection is free from limit of any kind. The actuality of the creature is limited by its essence: and its cognitive power is of necessity proportional to its essence. But the cognitive power of the *Actus Purus* must be infinite, reaching to the furthest bounds of reality. There can be no conceivable object to which the Divine intelligence does not extend.

Our human intellect displays many features which involve finitude and potentiality. All these elements of imperfection must be stripped away from the notion of intelligence as it is applied to God. They do not belong to the notion as such: they are merely the mode in which intelligence is realized in man. It is not unnecessary to give this caution. For it is contended by some adherents of the prevalent idealism that it is impossible there should be any reality which is of its nature beyond the scope of human reason.[2] To those who do not adequately distinguish between God and man, and hold that the human mind is fundamentally identical with the Divine, such a conclusion is no more than natural. But when we have given a little consideration to the limitations of human knowledge, we shall be disposed to take a more sober view of what we are. The narrowness of our bounds will convince us that the Infinite Reason must bear a relation to our own not unlike that which the light of the sun bears to that of a wax-taper.

Man starts life in complete ignorance, with a mere capacity for knowledge. As he grows he learns to use his powers, and little by little he stores his mind. His whole life is a transition from potentiality to actuality in this regard. But even though he spares no efforts to acquire knowledge, and though he inherits the labours of past generations, these achievements are of small extent. He gathers his knowledge by intermittent acts, in their nature mere accidental determinations of his rational faculty. Moreover, so restricted are his powers, that he can only know the object of his consideration by means of a multitude of diverse concepts, each representing some single aspect of the reality. These he refers to the thing in question in a series of propositions of which they form the predicates: and thus he laboriously pieces together, so to speak, the concrete individual object. Again, his intellectual knowledge is by means of universal ideas: particulars he must discern by sense-perception. And he is forced to pursue his way with many a stumble along the difficult track of discursive reason, arguing from effect to cause or from cause to effect.

Not one of these limitations is compatible with the infinite perfection of the Divine mind, to which our reason bears but an analogical resemblance. In God there can be no transition from ignorance to actual knowledge. He enjoys full omniscience. His intellect is not, like ours, a faculty distinct from the nature to which it belongs. It is identical with His substance. God's thought is His essence. Nor does the Divine mind operate by successive and accidental acts. In Him there is no change, no passage from quiescence to action, nor from one phase of activity to another. His intellect is one unchanging, all-embracing thought.

But, it will be asked, does not knowledge involve necessarily a relation between the subject and object of thought, and are we not here faced with a grave difficulty in regard to the Divine simplicity. For this relation postulates a distinction. Subject and object cannot be identified. Were they so, the relation would disappear, and with it also would disappear the act of thought. The objection is often produced as though it were a modern weapon, entirely destructive of old-fashioned theism.[3] It is, in fact, ancient and out of date. It was urged long since by the Neoplatonist Plotinus. Mansel, as he himself informs us, drew it from his works. Such apparent force as the argument possesses is derived altogether from the limitations of human knowledge, and disappears when once it is seen that these limitations do not and cannot belong to the supreme intelligence. The human mind is only in act in so far as it has formed a concept within itself. When the mind conceives, it knows the object of its thought, and simultaneously knows itself as the thinking subject actuated by the concept.[4] Until it thus passes into act by conceiving, it is not conscious of itself. It is impossible that it should be so, for the simple reason that apart from a concept it is not knowable. Until it conceives, it is a mere potentiality, not yet actuated in the order of thought at all. What has no actuality is not an object of knowledge. Only in so far as the mind is *in act* in the conceptual order is it actually knowable: otherwise it is only potentially so. We might as well expect matter to be knowable apart from any form, as the human intellect to be known apart from the presence of a concept. But it is far otherwise as regards God. The Divine mind is eternally active. It needs not the presence of a concept to bring it from a state of potentiality to act. It is itself essentially knowable. Thus it is at one and the same time the knower and the known. Indeed, so little is it true that thought essentially demands a distinction between the subject and object, that even in ourselves, given the presence of a concept, the mind is immediately conscious of itself. As regards its *self-knowledge*, there is no distinction between subject and object. It is because our intellect, except in so far as it is determined by some object other than itself, is a mere potentiality, that we are misled into thinking that a distinction between knower and known is essential to thought. Nor does God's knowledge of creatures involve such a distinction. For, as we shall shew in the coming section, God in knowing Himself knows all things else.[5]

2. *Primary and secondary objects of the Divine intelligence.* The various powers of man's complex being have each of them a primary, or as it is often called, a 'formal' object. Where his cognitive faculties are in question the term signifies some special aspect of reality which falls within the scope of the faculty in its own right; while in so far as the faculty is able to take cognizance of anything else, it does so in virtue of this primary object. This is the actuating principle of the faculty, which latter can only operate when moved to activity by its appropriate stimulus. Thus, the primary object of the sense of sight is colour. It is true that vision is not restricted to colour as such. It perceives extended surface, and estimates distance. Yet these are secondary objects: they fall under the sense simply as manifested through colour. In like manner the human intellect has its primary or formal object. This consists in the types or forms realized in the material substances around us. Senses perceive these things: and intellect expresses their nature in universal concepts derived from the data of sense. Thus, as we have already explained (chap. ii., § 3), we obtain, *e.g.*, the notions of substance and cause, and all those universal concepts employed in the various branches of mathematics. Whatever else the mind conceives must be expressed by it in concepts formed on the lines of this sensible experience: since the primary object of a faculty determines the mode in which it shall exercise its activity. Thus, discursive reason brings us to a knowledge of God. But when we seek to express the Divine attributes, we can only do so through concepts significative of accidental forms: though we are perfectly aware that this is an altogether imperfect way of conceiving them.

What, then, is the primary object of the Divine intellect -- the reality in regard to which it exercises its connatural activity, while all else is known by reason of the knowledge of this? There can be but one answer to this question. The primary object is, as we have seen, the actuating principle of the faculty. Were, then, anything else but God Himself the formal object of the Divine intelligence, we should be driven to admit that God's knowledge -- and His knowledge is identical with Himself -- is the effect of a cause. That which stands in this relation to the Divine Mind can only be the Divine Essence Itself. We mean here, of course, the physical essence, the sum of all perfection and reality. It is, further, to be noted that in speaking of this as the actuating principle of God's intellect, and as standing in a certain relation to it, we are employing modes of speech appropriate only to created intelligences. For, since the Divine Essence is one with the Divine Mind, it cannot, strictly speaking, be said to actuate it. No exercise of causality is here involved. God's intelligence needs no actuation: it is itself pure act. In God, intellect, essence and the act of thought are one and the same. Nor, again, does the Divine reality need to be translated into the order of thought that it may be known. Just as God's nature is self-existent in the real order, so is it self-existent in the cognitive order. Or rather in God, and in Him alone, the order of thought and the order of being are not separate and parallel. They are one.

In view of this conclusion it is a mere concession to human modes of thought to declare that God's knowledge of His essence is 'comprehensive.' By comprehensive knowledge is signified knowledge which includes and exhausts the whole cognoscibility of the object known -- which leaves nothing in it unknown. Thus to possess comprehensive knowledge of a created substance, it would be necessary to know every principle of its constitution, both in regard of form and matter, every accident which qualifies it, every relation which connects it with other beings: so that it has become a commonplace to say that for the human intellect comprehensive knowledge, even of the humblest natural substance, is an impossibility. Yet the infinite mind must possess comprehensive knowledge even of an infinite object. Such, then, is God's knowledge of Himself. Or to reach the same conclusion in another manner. Knowledge is comprehensive where knowledge and being are identical. In God this is the case. Only because we are compelled to distinguish in God, those aspects which, though in Him they are one, are in the world of our experience different, do we view God's knowledge and His being as though they were distinct from one another.

God's uncreated Being is the exemplar cause of all created being. Whatever perfection there is in creatures is a far-off representation of the perfection of God. As we descend the stages in which finite things are ordered, we see how that perfection is reflected in ways ever more and more limited. Yet, however lowly the creature, within its narrow confines it possesses *reality*. And what is real is so simply as being the shadow in some measure of Him who is Himself Absolute Reality. God, in knowing His own essence, knows the myriad forms in which that essence may be imitated. Did He not do so, His knowledge of Himself would not be comprehensive: a cause is not fully known unless the full measure of its causality is understood. Hence we say that while the Divine Essence is the sole primary object of God's intelligence, the secondary object comprises all possible creatures. The universe of which we ourselves form a part is but one of an infinite number of the ways in which creative power might have called finite being into actuality. When we treat of God's free-will and of creation, it will appear how utterly erroneous and how inconsistent with the infinity of God is the opinion which sees in the universe as it is a necessary complement, if we may use the expression, of God: which declares that God cannot exist without the world. All possible orders of creation are objects of the Divine mind, and every least part of every such order. God contemplates them, not in successive thought, but in one single and eternal intuition in which He knows His essence and all that it contains.

From among the infinity of alternatives thus presented, God by a free choice has decreed that certain things should be actually realized, and should thus constitute what we term the created order. In His essence as thus determined by His free act He beholds the whole course of actual events from the first instant of creation onwards, not merely the necessary sequences of natural causes, but also the free acts of created personalities. For even those free acts which violate His law could not be, did they not receive their being in accordance with His will. Yet when we say that God's knowledge of the real order has its explanation in His essence as determined by His creative decree, a word of caution is necessary. We are compelled to speak in terms derived from our own activities, as though His free act were something additional to His essence, an internal change from the potential to the actual, a determination of the hitherto indeterminate. This, plainly enough, it is not. God's free act involves no internal change. This point will be more fully discussed later. Here we are only concerned to point out that God in one changeless act of knowledge knows, not only all possibles, but the whole course of real events -- a series which had indeed a beginning, but which will have no end.

What we have just said will have pointed to an essential difference between Divine and human knowledge of the real order. Human knowledge is related to things as an effect to its cause. Things are the measure of thought. The judgments of our intellect are true, when they are in conformity with things. Those which fail of this conformity have no title to any place in the mind, and are cast away. It is otherwise as regards Divine Knowledge. Things are not the cause of God's thought, but its effect. God is the great artificer: and as He designs, so the created order takes shape. His thought is the measure: and things are what they are, because they must be in conformity with God's design. Things stand, so to speak, midway between God's mind and ours. They are dependent on God's thought, and our thought is dependent on them.[6]

3. *The Divine Foreknowledge.* A problem of special difficulty is presented by the question of God's knowledge of our future free actions. Indeed, the idea of such knowledge is so perplexing to the human mind that many non-Catholic writers have declared the problem insoluble, and have maintained that we must needs either give up man's freedom or else admit that God does not possess a foreknowledge of the free choices of the human will. In previous centuries this generally led to a denial of human freedom. More recently there have been found thinkers who have

adopted the other alternative, and have maintained that in this regard, at least, the Divine knowledge is limited. Scholastic philosophers are at one in asserting alike human freedom and Divine prescience. Yet, as will appear, there is a profound divergence of opinion among them, when it comes to the question how that prescience is to be explained.

The fact that God possesses such a foreknowledge can be demonstrated in various ways. Our first argument may be drawn from the Divine infinity. God, as we have shewn, is infinite alike in the real and in the cognitive order. From this alone it follows of necessity that He cannot become aware of anything not already known to Him. To admit that His mind could learn a truth of which it was previously ignorant, would be to allow that there is potentiality in the Divine intellect: that it is not infinite, not *Actus purus*. Hence whatever be our explanation of that foreknowledge, and even if we should be unable to provide an explanation, the reality of God's prescience must be granted.

Again: God, it will be admitted, knows these truths, when they actually come to pass. Even those who deny that a free act is knowable before the elective choice is made, do not dispute that God knows it as soon as it takes place. But God's knowledge, as we have seen, is eternal. For Him there is no flow of time. To us who belong to that flow, whose existence is realized part after part, each event which has already happened stands in a different relation according to its place in the time-series: while future happenings have, as yet, no actuality, and are only knowable in so far as they are determined in their causes. But to God, Who is outside the time-series, the relation borne by every such event is always the same. He sees the whole course of time as a present reality. Events which to us are future, He beholds now. Thus the very conditions of God's existence demand His foreknowledge of the whole future. Indeed, it is hardly accurate to speak of foreknowledge or of prescience in this connection: for these terms are not applicable from the point of view of eternity. God knows the future: He does not foreknow it. The difficulty which we experience in regard to this truth is due to our inability to imagine any other mode of being than a temporal one. But as soon as reason has convinced us that in God's existence there can be neither before nor after, we must recognize that His knowledge of the future must be as His knowledge of the present.

Another argument may be derived from God's government of the world. Although this proof may not possess the apodictic certainty of the two which we have just given, yet its grounds are so weighty that it can hardly fail to recommend itself to the rational judgment. God, as we have seen, is the Author of nature. All the beings which constitute the great whole, and all the events which take place within it, are due to Him as their First Cause. But His government of the universe is directed to a definite end. Apart from an end to be obtained an efficient cause does not operate. To suppose that it could be so -- that an efficient cause would act without an end in view -- would be to suppose that an event could happen without a sufficient reason. This conclusion, based on *a priori* grounds, is borne out by experience. Finality is the law of the universe. The divine order, doubtless, is of an intricacy which is ever eluding us. Yet new marvels of harmonious correspondence are ever revealing themselves. All conspires to bring home to us that each smallest detail in God's disposition of things is directed by a purpose. Moreover, within the sphere of the divine government there appears a twofold order -- a physical order and a moral order. And none who accepts the theistic standpoint can doubt that of these the less important is subordinated to the more important: that the two do not, as a first appearance might suggest, form two independent systems, each pursuing its course in independence of, and often in antagonism to, the other; but that the physical order is relative to the moral order: and that the end, in view of which the whole vast process is carried on, is the discipline, and through discipline, the perfecting of human souls.

But if this be so -- if the world is a place where God realizes in all its details an immense scheme of providential wisdom, in which the principal part is the training of free agents, He must know how such an agent will act when called on to choose between two courses. Were it otherwise -- were He ignorant what the issue will be, His providence would not be, as reason and experience seem to assure us, a process of supreme wisdom, carried on in view of a definite end. He who does not know how subordinate agencies will act, cannot shape his means, save in a halting and imperfect way, to the attainment of his purpose. We must either admit that God knows the future free acts of his creatures, or admit that His providence is marred by frequent failure and often at fault: that He who is infinite alike in wisdom and power, often adopts the wrong means for the achievement of His purposes: and that in the attainment of His ends He is at the mercy of His creatures. Such a conclusion the intellect instinctively rejects.

Martineau has employed this argument in his *Study of Religion*. His words may well find place here. "It can hardly be denied," he writes, "that the idea of Divine foreknowledge is involved in both the sources to which we have referred our apprehension of God. If we know Him as *intending Cause*, if we see in the universe an organized system of ends beyond ends, He comes before our thought as a prospective Mind, whose agency at every present moment has regard to an anticipated future; and to suppose that future invisible is to suppose the present impossible. And if, again, we know Him as *Supreme authority of Right*, if we see in our own conscience the reflection of his Will, we thereby place ourselves under a discipline of progressive character, and the human race under a moral education, by which all life and history are turned into a probationary scheme of government. Such a scene ceases, by the very light that shews it, to he a blind jumble of accidents, and becomes a *Drama*, in which the end is preconceived from the beginning, and each act, as it passes, brings up the conditions and the persons needful to lead on to the consummation. He without whom there would be no future but His own, cannot create a future of which He has not first the idea. It is not without reason, therefore, that prescience has been assumed by theologians as part of the conception of a perfect Being."[7]

Is then Divine foreknowledge compatible with real freedom in human action? Some authors deny that the two are capable of reconciliation. Martineau, in the passage from which we have quoted, thinks it needful to distinguish. If the foreknowledge extends to individual acts of the will, there is, he holds, no possible escape from determinism. Hence the prescience which he demands has regard, not to individual volitions, but to the full number of possible choices which may be made, so that whichever course the will may take, God is able without fail to work out His ultimate purpose. "An infinite Mind, with prevision thus extended beyond all that is to all that can be, is lifted above surprise and disappointment, and able to provide for all events and combinations. . . . Is this a *limitation* of God's foresight, that He cannot read all volitions that are to be? Yes: but it is a *self-limitation*, just like His abstinence from causing them."[8] Another recent writer, Prof. J. Ward, goes so far as to say that from the standpoint of theism "the necessitarian position appears to he axiomatic. . . . The absolute omniscience and omnipotence of God are regarded as beyond question: and from these follow as a corollary the absolute and eternal decrees."[9] Bishop Gore, in a work designed to reconcile the claims of reason with a belief in revelation, refuses to meet the challenge. "To me," he writes, "it seems that belief in divine foreknowledge is incompatible, according to any standard of thinking possible to us in our present state with belief in human freedom": and he resigns the belief in God's foreknowledge of our future free acts.[10] We have seen that there is no such contradiction as is imagined, that the idea that God's prescience is incompatible with freedom on man's part is due to the failure to understand the difference between eternity and time: and that when this is once understood the alleged incompatibility disappears.

In the light thus thrown on the Divine foreknowledge it is of interest to consider the familiar objection that what God foresees must necessarily take place: and that, this being so, it is impossible that man's actions should he free, necessity and freedom being mutually exclusive. St. Thomas, dealing with this difficulty, points out that a free action, so soon as it is actually realized, becomes, in virtue of the principle of contradiction, necessary. It cannot both be and not be. Since, then, it has actually occurred, it cannot be otherwise. Thus it is open to a man to walk or sit still. But granted that he has chosen to walk, it is impossible that he should be sitting still. Now the Divine knowledge, as we have seen, regards things in their actual occurrence as present happenings, since there is for God no such thing as future time. But when we say that if God foresees a thing it must necessarily take place, we are considering the thing, not in relation to its physical causes, but as an object of the Divine knowledge. The necessity, then, which we affirm of it, belongs to it under that aspect -- not in virtue of the manner of its causation, but in so far as it is viewed as an actual occurrence. This, as is manifest, is in no way incompatible with contingency in regard of its immediate physical cause. The objection as stated is fallacious because it fails to distinguish two totally different aspects: and thus confuses the necessity which belongs to an event considered as an actual occurrence, with the very different necessity proper to the effects of causes which are determined to a single mode of action.

4. *Physical premotion and 'scientia media.'* Yet in affirming that a Divine knowledge of the future in its utmost detail is compatible with full elective freedom, we have not solved, nor even touched, the question how God knows what choice will be made. It is impossible that He should be dependent for His knowledge upon His creatures. Yet if it were granted that He knows the free choice because the creature makes it, we should be affirming such dependence. We should be allowing that the Divine mind acquires from the creature a knowledge which it does not otherwise possess. God's knowledge must be due to His own infinite perfection alone. The creature's choice may be a condition; but the source of the knowledge must be sought in God Himself. On this point all Scholastic thinkers are at one. But as regards the manner in which the knowledge is to be explained they are sharply divided. The question is hotly debated between the advocates of two rival theories -- the theory of physical premotion and the theory of *scientia media.*

The theory of physical premotion teaches that the source of God's foreknowledge is to be sought in the decree by which He has determined what the future choice of the will shall be, and in accordance with which He premoves the will to its act.

God's premotion, we are told by the defenders of this view, is always such as corresponds with the nature which receives it: and He premoves rational agents in such a way that they choose freely and not by constraint. In this manner, it is contended, the divine decree accounts for

God's foreknowledge of the future volition without destroying the freedom of the act.

Those thinkers, on the other hand, who find themselves unable to reconcile the notion of predetermination with that of freedom, hold that God, in virtue of His essential perfection, knows what choice each human will would make in any given circumstances in which it might be placed. Knowing thus what the agent would do in a particular set of conditions, He knows what it actually will do in virtue of His decision to bring about those conditions and not others. This Divine decree is the medium in which God knows our future free actions only because He possesses antecedently a knowledge of the conditional future. However we are to explain this latter knowledge, we are compelled, they consider, to admit its existence. Apart from this the foreknowledge of free actions is a sheer impossibility.

This Divine knowledge of the conditionally future action is termed *scientia media* or 'mediate knowledge,' an expression employed by way of contrast with two other Scholastic terms. If we consider God's knowledge in regard of its different objects, we may usefully distinguish His knowledge of mere 'possibles' from His knowledge of those things which at some time or other have been, or will be, realized. The former is called *scientia simplicis intelligentiae*: the latter *scienfia visionis*. An event, however, which would take place in certain given circumstances is something more than a mere possible, but is less than an event actually to be realized. Hence God's knowledge of free actions, viewed as conditionally future, is conveniently designated by the term 'mediate knowledge.'

The respective merits of these two theories were earnestly contested at the beginning of the seventeenth century between the theologians of the Dominican and Jesuit Orders, the former contending for physical premotion, the latter for *scientia media*. The debate was theological rather than philosophical, the actual point at issue being the mode in which Divine grace influences the will in the performance of the good act. Yet the Dominican teaching on efficacious grace necessarily involved the theory of physical premotion, as did the Jesuit teaching that of *scientia media.* The theological aspect of the question lies, of course, altogether outside our scope in the present work. Our defence of *scientia media* must be based on grounds of reason alone. It is summed up in the contention that unless this knowledge be admitted, we are forced to deny either the divine foreknowledge or human freedom. Only on this supposition can both be true.

Yet when such knowledge is attributed to God, care must be taken to avoid anthropomorphism. We are not to be understood as signifying that the Divine knowledge passed through successive stages corresponding to the terms *scientia media* and *scientia visionis*: that God first saw which alternative a man would in fact adopt in each several situation in which he might be placed, and that subsequently, having decreed to place him in such and such circumstances rather than in others, He beheld in virtue of this knowledge the actual course of future events. This would be to suppose that God's knowledge can pass from indefiniteness to definiteness, that it can be first incomplete and then complete. His knowledge of the future has been from all eternity the absolutely complete knowledge of the *scientia visionis*. The triple distinction which we have drawn expresses, not three stages in God's knowledge, but three modes in which by reason of our creaturely limitations, we are compelled to think of His knowledge. They are based upon the stages of knowledge in which man envisages the objects he himself calls into being. We attribute them to God because His infinite knowledge must in some manner equivalently contain them. When, *e.g.*, an artist paints a picture, it comes before his mind (1) as a mere possible which he might produce, if he so desired. This is followed by an act of will in virtue of which his idea passes to the stage of practical knowledge (*scientia practica*), and he contemplates the object (2) as about to exist in the future. Finally, after execution, he sees it (3) as a real thing. Here are three stages really distinct from each other. There is nothing like this in God's knowledge. From all eternity He contemplated by the *scientia visionis* the actual free choice which will in fact be made. Yet our supposition of a Divine knowledge antecedent to the decree to realize a particular course of events, though an unreal supposition, is representative of a veritable reality in the only way in which it lies in our power to represent it. The course of events proceeds precisely as if God at a given moment foresaw what decision my free-will would adopt, were He to abstain from any act of free-will on His own part. Divine knowledge, while eternally contemplating the future as actualized, nevertheless contains within itself all that could he found in the successive stages which analogy with human knowledge leads us to distinguish.

It may be frankly admitted that it is beyond our power to give any explanation how God can know the choice which a free agent would make, were he placed in given circumstances. Yet this inability on our part constitutes no objection to the theory: for it arises from the very nature of the case. Our knowledge of God, as we have frequently had occasion to urge, is restricted within narrow limits. We know Him as the first principle of created being, and can affirm of Him the perfections which this involves: beyond this our knowledge is negative. The Divine attributes, which do not belong to this class, merely deny in His regard the imperfections which attach to finite things. But no analysis of what is involved in God's relation to the world as its efficient, exemplar and final cause, will shew us the manner in which He knows the truths with which we are here concerned. We can deny of His knowledge all dependence on the creature: and we can reject any explanation which is inconsistent with the freedom of the secondary agent. But we can go no further. It is idle for us to seek to know the how of the Divine knowledge. The data for such an enquiry are absolutely lacking to us.

There is, however, one point which we must make good. We must shew that the conditionally future choice of a free agent has sufficient objective reality to be an object of knowledge. The problem here presented to us will be appreciated if it be remembered that knowledge is relative to being. Where there is no determinate being there can be no knowledge: for in this case there is no thing to be known. That which has no determinate being in itself nor yet in its cause is a *non ens* -- a nonentity. Now a future free volition, viewed as future, is as yet wholly indeterminate. The agent is at liberty to choose one course or the other: and not until he has done so will there be anything to be known -- a possible object of knowledge. It is, of course, otherwise where necessary agents are in question. Here the event, though not determined in itself, is determined in its causes. Hence within the sphere of physical science we possess valid knowledge regarding the future: since there we are dealing with agents which operate necessarily. Where free agents, however, are concerned, an intellect which is conditioned by the time-sequence can have no knowledge regarding their free choices till the choice is actually made. But, as we have shewn, God's mind is not fettered by the restrictions which the time-sequence imposes. His is the knowledge of eternity, not of time. The events which stand in such diverse relations to a knower, who is himself a member of the same series, have one and all the same relation to the Eternal. Each such choice lies before Him as fully determinate, as possessed of the reality which renders it an object of knowledge.

Our argument, it will be observed, has hitherto been restricted to the actual future. And in this reference the cognoscibility of the future choice has been fully vindicated. But we contend that the solution offered is valid not merely of the actual order of providence, but of all possible orders. God, in contemplating His Essence, beholds not merely the order of things which He has in fact established, but all those myriad orders to which He might have given actuality had He so desired. Each of these lies before Him in its entirety: and by a single act of intuition He knows every event which would take place in each, seeing them in the light of His eternity. In this manner, because the successive acts of every time-series are to the Divine Mind present occurrences, the conditionally future acts of every free agent -- the course which such an agent would adopt in any given circumstances -- are objects of knowledge for God.

We pointed out in chap. x. that some Scholastic writers find difficulty in accepting the notion of eternity which we have defended, and which we believe to be the only defensible one. They regard it as a veritable duration, holding that it has past, present and future, differing from time only in being a state without change. It is perfectly evident that those who take this view cannot appeal to God's eternity as the ground which renders future free actions possible objects of knowledge. They adopt another expedient, but one which in our judgment is philosophically unsound. They urge that it is possible to form two contradictory propositions regarding any possible alternative which we may conceive as presented to the choice of a secondary agent. If we suppose the agent placed in such and such circumstances, either he would adopt a given course or he would not. Both of these propositions cannot be true. One of them, the law of excluded middle assures us, must be so. To God alone is it known on which side of the alternative the truth lies. For His knowledge is infinite: and to infinite knowledge all truth is open, even though we are unable to fathom in the case of certain truths how this can be. Yet the argument here employed is fallacious. It is not the case that of two contradictory propositions relating to a free act considered as future, the one must be true and the other false. For the reasons which we have given, neither is true. Aristotle most rightly teaches that the only true proposition which can be framed regarding these acts is the disjunctive: the agent will either adopt this course or he will not.[11] Only, we hold, on the basis of the true doctrine of eternity can the possibility of God's knowledge of futuribles be defended.

We have declared our conviction that it is, in the nature of things, impossible that the human mind can throw any light on the manner in which God knows these truths. Yet it should be remarked that some of the defenders of *scientia media* have propounded theories on this point. The view of P. Luis Molina (1535-1600) on the subject claims a mention, even though we cannot admit its validity. For Molina was the first to treat at length of this aspect of the Divine knowledge, and to point out the necessity of holding that God knows, not only the free actions which will actually be realized, but those also which would take place, were the free agent placed in other circumstances: the very term *scientia media* was introduced by him. He held that God, in knowing His own essence, possesses so adequate and comprehensive a knowledge of the finite natures which He could create, and penetrates so completely their characters and dispositions, that He can see what course any one of them would adopt under any given set of conditions.[12] Were this the true account of the matter, it is difficult to see how the immediate agent could be really free. If a knowledge of the agent's nature, combined with that of the circumstances in which he is placed, granted only that it be sufficiently comprehensive, reveals to its possessor what course that agent will adopt, this can only be because the action is determined -- because given these conditions it must of necessity follow. But if this be so, the agent is not free in the sense that, after weighing the motives on either side, it is open to him to choose whether he will act or not, and, if he elect to act, to determine what his action shall be. It is only because of the incompleteness of our data, that we regard the action as contingent. Were all the facts of the case known to us, we should be able to foretell the future actions of a man in the same way as we foretell those of an inanimate agent.

Descartes, it may be noted, gives a similar explanation of the Divine prescience to that which we have just considered. "Before sending us into the world," he writes, "[God] has known exactly what would be the inclinations of our will. He Himself has planted them in us: He has also disposed all things externally to us that such and such objects should present themselves to our senses at such and such times, on occasion of which He has known that our free-will would determine us to this or that: and He has willed it thus; but for all that, His will has put no constraint upon us to act thus."{13} In one point, it will be observed, the account of Descartes differs from that of the Spanish theologian. The latter is careful to exclude all dependence from God: he points out that the Divine essence, and that alone, is the source of the Divine knowledge. Descartes would seem to imply that God gains His knowledge of future free actions from the contemplation of the finite essences which He is about to create.

We now pass to the consideration of the theory which seeks the explanation of God's foreknowledge in physical premotion. The premotion of the will, even in its free actions, seems to have been the teaching of the Thomist school from early times. Whether the doctrine is contained in the writings of St. Thomas himself has been disputed; it would, however, be beside our purpose to touch on this question.

It is contended on behalf of the Thomist view that it is a necessary deduction from assured principles of metaphysics. It is impossible, it is urged, for a secondary agent to perform an action of any kind unless determined to do so by a cause other than itself. Be the agent free or necessitated, the passage from potentiality to act must in the last resort be referable to the operation of the First Cause: and this conclusion is as true of the choice made by a human will as it is of the motion of purely material bodies. The one, as the other, takes place and can only take place in virtue of a divine premotion. Nor need this, they maintain, do away with liberty. Just as God in virtue of His infinity is the source of every sort of being, spiritual or corporeal, so too He is able to premove each to its connatural mode of action, be that free or necessitated. He predetermines both the act and the mode of its production. Only by reason of His decree can we say of a free creature that in certain contingencies it would act in such and such a way. Without a decree determining what its action shall be, it would not act at all. Its action would not be a conditionally future act, but a mere 'possible.' If these conclusions be admitted, the whole problem of Divine foreknowledge disappears. God knows our future actions, because they, like all else in the created order, are due to His decree. We do not need to have recourse to the plea that the how of the Divine knowledge is beyond the range of our understanding. God knows this, as He knows all things, in His essence, but in His essence as it includes the free decree by which He has fixed the order of His providence in regard to creatures.

At first sight it might seem that there is no room whatever in this system for any conditionally future event. Unless God has decreed that a free agent shall actually adopt a given course, its choice, it would appear, is wholly indeterminate, so that it is not more true to say that it would act in one way than that it would act in another. This is, in fact, the solution of a few of the Thomist writers. But the position was theologically difficult, in view of certain Scripture passages which seem to shew that God has full knowledge of what men would do, if placed in circumstances which in fact are never realized.[14] To solve this difficulty, the advocates of this view commonly maintain that, besides the decree which God has made determining the actual future, He has also made many decrees regarding the course which He would take in other orders of things, and that where such decrees exist, the conditional future becomes a possible subject of predication. The passages in question are to be explained in this way.

The Thomists contend that their doctrine is to be preferred, not merely on account of its intrinsic merits, but because of insuperable difficulties which beset *scientia media* on metaphysical grounds. That theory, they object, involves that the will can give itself a new actuality apart from the determining influence of the First Cause: that the First Cause is supposed to abdicate its office as the universal source of all being and all action, and the secondary cause to become a primary initiator of change. This, it is urged, is wholly incompatible with the axiomatic truth, *Quidquid movetur ab alio movetur.* It demands the metaphysical absurdity of a thing passing from potentiality to act of its own accord, and thus is a patent violation of the principle of sufficient reason.

Nor is this all. It is on both sides admitted that the Divine knowledge has no other source than the Divine essence. But, argue the Thomists, even if the free agent could, as is supposed, make its act of choice independently of a Divine predetermination to a particular alternative, the Divine essence could not in that case be a source of knowledge regarding the act. For if the essence be considered purely as it is in itself, *i.e.,* apart from its decrees concerning the created order, there is no reason why it should represent one alternative rather than another: *ex hypothesi* either might equally well have occurred. But if the theory of *scientia media* be accepted, there is nothing save the Divine essence as it is in itself which can come into consideration as a source of knowledge. The existence of a Divine decree is denied: and God cannot depend for His knowledge on the act itself or on anything belonging to the created order.

It is not to be denied that both of these are weighty objections. And we have endeavoured so to state them that their real force may be understood. Nevertheless, they do not seem to be conclusive. Our reply to the first can best be given in connection with our treatment of the Divine concurrence. It must, therefore, be deferred till we speak of that subject (chap. xvi., § 6). As regards the second, we may freely admit that we are wholly ignorant how the Divine essence can be a source of knowledge as regards the free act: and, further, that no enquiry on our part will throw light on the matter and enable us to read the riddle. At the same time, in view of the fact that we are dealing with the Infinite, who is Himself the source of the created agent and of all its powers, we have no right to declare that because our mind cannot solve the difficulty, it is therefore evident that we are asserting what is intrinsically impossible. We must take our stand upon that of which we have certain knowledge. It is certain that the future in all its detail is known to the Infinite Mind. It is certain, moreover, that our will is free. The doctrine of *scientia media* holds to both these truths, though it recognizes the inability of the human intellect to explain how the independence of the action can be reconciled with the independence of the Divine knowledge. To affirm that God knows our free acts in His predetermining decree does not solve the problem. It cuts the knot by a reply which amounts, as we maintain, to a direct contradiction. Predetermination and freedom are, as we shall shew, exclusive the one of the other. Moreover, the doctrine of predetermination is open to the gravest objections on another side: for it leads directly to conclusions which seem incompatible with the moral attributes of God.

Liberty, as commonly defined, is the power of the will, when two or more alternatives are presented to it, each of which may be viewed as good in some respect, to choose the one or the other as it may itself determine. Our choice may lie only between acting and abstaining from action. In this case we are said to have *libertas exercitii* -- freedom in the exercise of our powers. Or we may have the choice between action of various kinds. This is termed *libertas specificationis* -- freedom in the specification of the act.

It is of primary importance to notice that the will can only choose what the mind regards as good. 'Good' is the object of the will, as colour is of the eye, and sound of the ear. In so far as the mind pronounces an object to be good, the will tends instinctively towards it. One object there is, which the will must needs desire, if it acts at all in its regard, viz., full and complete happiness -- beatitude. Where this object -- the perfect good -- is concerned, it possesses merely a *libertas exercitii*: it need not desire it here and now. But it is not free to prefer something else to it: it does not enjoy *libertas specificationis* where it is concerned. But only in this one case is the will under this constraint. All other things which are viewed as good may he considered in some other aspect as unsuitable, even as repugnant: God Himself, Whom reason shews to be the supreme good, may be considered simply as the source of retributive justice, and may be held in aversion. Thus it is that in regard of every other object of desire save complete happiness the will is free to yield to some rival attraction and give its preference to what is, perhaps, intrinsically far inferior.

The ground of man's liberty is to be sought in his rational nature. The faculty of intellect enables us to recognize in what consists the goodness of any object, what it is that makes it in some particular respect suitable to our needs. It is through our intellect that we can compare its goodness in one regard with its unsuitableness in another, and having weighed the one against the other, can adopt it or reject it, as we determine. The animal, endowed with sense-faculties and sense-instincts alone, sees an attractive object, and forthwith pursues it. Its appetites can doubtless be modified by habit. The dog can be taught to wau patiently till his master gives the signal for it to take its food. But here there is no freedom, no elective choice to follow this or that motive. The action is ruled by habit, exactly as it would otherwise have been ruled by impulse. But man is free, because he knows that none of the goods which present themselves to him are the supreme and all-sufficing good, which alone imposes itself upon his choice and constrains his will to desire it. He sees, *e.g.*, that the service of his Creator is good in one respect and repellent in another: that his rational nature demands that God should be his first aim, and that on the other hand obedience to the moral law is painful to flesh and blood. His will determines the issue. In obedience to his elective choice the *judicium ultimo-practicum* declares that here and now the motive of duty or the motive of present gratification is to prevail.

It is characteristic of our present life that we should be able to elect what is morally evil because of some partial and inadequate good annexed to it.

Here lies the probation of man. Yet the power to choose evil is not essential to liberty. In the next life, as we trust, we shall be free, without the possibility of being misled by apparent good. We have argued above (chap. v.) that man's destiny is the possession of that all-sufficing good, which is God Himself. Just as in this life it is impossible for us to desire anything save for some goodness belonging to it, so those who possess Him who is Essential Goodness can desire nothing except in reference to Him. But the love of God as the ultimate aim of all action no more involves determinism in those actions than does the love of the good in general involve determinism in our present choices.

If physical premotion be admitted it is, to say the least, extremely hard to see where liberty comes in, and in what sense we can speak of a probation. God decides which course we shall adopt, and premoves us to its adoption. We could not, if we would, choose another alternative, for the simple reason that God does not supply us with the premotion necessary for it. Those who hold the theory contend that God so premoves us that we choose freely. But to this it is replied that the answer involves two altogether incompatible conceptions. For freedom implies, not merely that we approve the choice which we have made, but that, had we wished, we might have chosen otherwise: whereas, if the theory of premotion be true, we could not act otherwise. To say then that we are premoved by God and, as such, act freely, is to say that our action is at the same time free and not free.

It is of interest to observe that Cajetan, the greatest of St. Thomas's commentators, recognizes the difficulty involved in the doctrine that our actions must inevitably be as God has foreordained. He says that he sees no solution except to hold that the divine providence so foreordains the future that we can neither say that our actions are avoidable, not yet that they are unavoidable. These terms, he thinks, have no applicability: for the divine decree operates upon a higher plane, which is beyond the reach of our minds. But, he urges, whatever the solution may be, it is absolutely essential that in all our investigations our starting point should be that of which we are absolutely certain: and that is our own freedom.[15]

The other difficulty which the doctrine of premotion seems to involve, concerns moral evil. Evil, it is true, is nothing positive: it is a mere privation. The human will contracts moral evil when it adheres to something contrary to that due order which right reason requires. God permits evil: He allows the created will to violate right order by desiring objects which it is bound to avoid, by turning away from objects to which it ought to adhere. But in no sense is God the Author of evil. For since evil is simply a privation, the creature in virtue of its own defectibility can be a prime agent in its regard.[16] God simply concurs in the physical act, which is in itself morally indifferent. Yet if man fails to act in accordance with right order because God has denied him the premotion requisite for obedience, it seems to follow as a necessary conclusion that God is the author of sin. This conclusion, it is needless to say, is repudiated by the doctors who defend the doctrine; but only, as it would appear, at the price of inconsistency with their own principles.

It may be freely admitted that neither theory affords a complete solution of the problem. In both a difficulty remains. Yet surely it is more prudent to leave the difficulty, as does *scientia media*, in the mysterious region of the divine knowledge and of the activity of secondary causes, than to adopt a solution which seems to place in jeopardy both human freedom and the moral attributes of God.

NOTES

{1} "Duplex est actio. Una quae transit in exteriorem materiam: ut calefacere et secare. Alia quae manet in agente ut intelligere, sentire et velle. Quarum haec est differentia: quia prima actio non est perfectio agentis quod movet sed ipsius moti: secunda autem actio est perfectio agentis." *Summa Theol.*, I., q. 18, art. 3, ad 1. In the creature immanent action involves change. There is transition from quiescence to activity, or at least from one mode of activity to another. This, however, is not essential to the notion of immanent activity as such.

{2} Cf. *e.g.* J. Caird, "We know of no other reason than one, and what cannot be brought into coherence with that reason is to us equivalent to the absurd or self-contradictory. Of what is in itself knowable, though beyond our present knowledge, we can pronounce that it is not contrary to reason. But we cannot say the same of that which is above reason in the sense of absolutely transcending human intelligence, of that which can never be construed by human thought. What lies beyond reason in this sense is simply the irrational or nonsensical." *Philosophy of Religion*, p. 68.

{3} Cf. *e.g.* Pringle-Pattison, *Idea of God*, p. 312.

{4} "There is always a consciousness of objects other than self on which the reflex consciousness of self depends." Sorley. *Moral Values*, etc., p. 139.

{5} Essentia igitur Dei, qui est actus purus et perfectus, est simpliciter et secundum seipsam intelligibilis: unde Deus per suam essentiam non solum seipsum sed etiam omnia intelligit. . . . Sed quia connaturale est intellectui nostro, secundum statum praesentis vitae quod ad materialia et sensibilia respiciat, consequens est ut sic seipsam intelligat intellectus noster secundum quod fit actu per species." *Summa Theol.*, I., q. 87, art. 1.

{6} Cf. Augustine, *De Trin.*, XV., c. xiii."Universa autem creaturas suas et spirituales et corporales, non quia sunt, ideo novit, sed ideo sunt, quia novit. Non enim nescivit quae fuerat creaturus. Quia ergo scivit, creavit:

non quia creavit, scivit. Nec aliter ea scivit creata quam creanda: non enim ejus sapientiae aliquid accessit ab eis: sed illis existentibus sicut oportebat et quando oportebat mansit quod erat."

S. Thomas Aq., *De Verit.* Q. 1, art. 2, Sciendum quod res aliter comparatur ad intellectum practicum, aliter ad speculativum. Intellectus enim practicus causat res, unde est mensuratio rerum quae per ipsum fiunt: sed intellectus speculativus, quia accipit a rebus est quodammodo motus ab ipsis rebus: et ita res mensurant ipsum. Ex quo patet quod res naturales ex quibus intellectus noster scientiam accipit, mensurant intellectum nostrum: sed sunt mensuratae ab intellectu divino: in quo sunt omnia creata, sicut omnia artificiata in mente artificis."

{7} *Study of Religion*, vol. ii., p. 277.

{8} *Op. cit.*, p. 279.

{9} *Realm of Ends*, p. 308. Professor Ward would appear to be under the impression that the treatment of the subject by Jonathan Edwards, the eighteenth-century Calvinist, is adequately representative of the theistic standpoint. This argues a curious want of familiarity with the literature of theism.

{10} *Belief in God*, p. 126, cf. p. 142. It is true that Dr. Gore declines to pronounce definitely that Divine prescience is necessarily irreconcilable with human freedom. The two are incompatible "within the range of our present capacity for thinking." But the qualification thus made is destitute of value. If our intellect as at present conditioned judges the two to he inconsistent with each other, this can only be because it sees that this simultaneous admission involves a breach of the principle of contradiction. To allow that further light could lead to a reversal of such a judgment would be to call in question the veracity of the intellect, and to open the door to scepticism.

{11} *De Interpretatione*, c. ix. Truth, he urges, is relative to being (**homoiôs hoi logoi alêtheis hôsper ta pragmata**). So that, since there is no determinate fact, neither is there any determinate truth. Suarez in his treatise *De Scientia Futurorum Contingentium*, lib. i., c. ii., n. 12, declares this reasoning fallacious: "Respondetur, veritatem harum propositionum non esse sumendam ex causis secundum se, sed ex determinatione earum quam in aliquo instanti habebunt." Cf. c. viii., 11. 3. *Opera*, Vol. X., pp. 166, 183 (Venice 1741).

{12} "Deus per scientiam naturalem se ipsum comprehendit, et in se ipso omnia quae in ipso eminenter sunt, atque adeo liberum arbitrium cujuscumque creaturae quam per suam omnipotentiam potest condere. Ergo ante ullam liberam determinationem suae voluntatis, ex altitudine suae scientiae naturalis, qua infinite superat singula quae in ipso eminenter continet,pcnctrat quid liberuni arbitrium cuj uscuncjuc creatufic, data hypothesi quod velit illud creari, in hoc vel in illo ordine rerum cum his vel illis circumstantiis aut auxiliis, pro sua innata libertate sit facturum." *Concordia*, Q. 14, art. 13, disp. 49 (ed. 1876), p. 290.

{13} *Oeuvres* (ed. Cousin, 1825), c. ix., p. 374, cited by Martineau, *op. cit.*, p. 274.

{14} I. Sam., xxiii., 11-12; Matt., xi., 21-23.

{15} Cajetan, *in Summ. Theol.*, I., q. 22, art. 4, ix. "Optimum autem atque salubre consilium est in hac re inchoare ab his quae certo scimus, et experimur in nobis, scilicet quod omnia quae sub libero arbitrio nostro continentur, evitabilia a nobis sunt."

{16} "Peccare nihil aliud est quam deficere a bono quod convenit alicui secundum suam naturam. Unaquaeque autem creatura . . . potest per seipsam deficere a bono, sicut et per seipsam potest deficere in non esse, nisi divinitus conservaretur." S. Thomas Aq., *Summa Theol.*, I., q. 109, art. 2, ad 2.

Chapter XII. God's Will and His Beatitude.

1. The Divine Will.

2. Its Primary and Secondary Objects.

3. The Freedom of God's Will.

4. Apparent Frustrations of God's Will.

5. The Moral Attributes of God -- His Justice, His Mercy.

6. The Divine Beatitude.

1. *The Divine will.* We distinguished in the foregoing chapter two forms of immanent action in God -- knowledge and will. It is with the latter of these that we are now concerned. The treatment of the subject will be aided, if we first consider in general what the will is, and what its relation to the intellect. It is from our own nature that we must learn this. By will we signify in man an appetitive tendency towards a good presented to us by the intellect. We may define it as a rational appetency for the known good. Experience shews us that every living thing, alike in the vegetable and the animal kingdom, tends towards that which is in conformity with its nature, striving after it if it lacks it, and reposing in it with satisfaction if it possesses it. But this is to tend towards the good. For that is good in regard of any particular thing, which is in harmony with its nature (or with some particular part of it): that is evil which is discordant with the nature and detrimental to it. Thus plants by a provision of nature draw their appropriate nourishment from the soil to the exclusion of its other constituents, and throw out shoots in such a manner as to secure the most favourable conditions for their growth. Animals, in virtue of their inborn instincts, perform a vast number of actions directed to their own good and to the good of the species. Precisely the same principle is exemplified in man. But man's nature is complex, and his appetencies are various. We have sensitive appetites like the brute animals. An experience

is *felt* as good: and the sense craves to prolong that experience or to repeat it. But we possess, further, a rational appetite, which comes into play when the intellect has pronounced an object to be good. This appetency of the rational nature is termed volition: and the faculty exercising it is the will. As we have seen in a previous chapter (chap. v., § 2), the goodness of an object may be of different kinds. It may be a true good conformable to the rational nature as such: or it may be something which, while in harmony with some part of our nature, is repugnant to it in so far as rational, and hence merely a *bonum apparens*. Again, our appetency or love for the object, itself admits of an important distinction. Reason recognizes, not merely what is good, as being beneficial in some way to us, but what, regarded in itself, possesses intrinsic perfection (chap. x., §3). Hence our will may tend to an object for its own sake, simply because of its own proper excellence: or, on the other hand, our love for it may be self-regarding, tending to it because in some way it brings us advantage. The former is the love of complacency: the latter the love of desire. A man's love for his friend, so far as it is unselfish, is of the former kind: his love for his worldly goods or his pleasures, of the latter. But these distinctions, however vital, need not now detain us. The point which we desired to explain is the essential nature of the will, viz., that it is the appetitive tendency of the rational part of our nature to that which the intellect declares to be good.

Many modern psychologists refuse to reckon the will as appetitive. The appetites, they hold, are necessary, and therefore belong to a different order from the will. Hence they distinguish our mental activities into desire, will and intellect. This new division is, however, misleading, since it separates operations which are connected in the closest possible manner. The will tends necessarily and inevitably to that which the intellect pronounces to be good. It is beyond all question appetitive in its regard, desiring it because it is good. Its freedom of choice can be exercised only within the limits of that which the intellect views as good under one aspect or another. It is no less evident that, like every other appetitive faculty it does not merely tend towards the objects of desire in its absence, but quiesces with satisfaction in that object when attained.

The loving adhesion to the good as possessed is no less an activity of the will than is the antecedent appetency or the act of deliberate preference of one alternative over another.

It may now be readily established that will is one of God's attributes. Every nature tends towards its proper good: and if the nature in question is intelligent, the tendency likewise belongs to it as such. In other words, where there is intelligence there must also be will. Since, then, the divine nature is intelligent, will, too, belongs to God. Nor does this conclusion involve that anything is lacking to Him. The essential activity of the will is love of the good. If the good be absent, then love produces desire. If it be present, joy is the result. In God there can be no question of an absent good: for He is Himself infinite goodness. His will has its connatural activity in the blissful possession of that supreme good which is Himself.

Other arguments may be employed to the same effect. Will is one of the perfections of man; and is, moreover, a pure perfection involving no imperfection. In man, it is true, the object of the will is frequently merely a relative good: indeed, it may be something which has only the appearance of goodness, not the reality. But will as such is simply the love for that which the reason pronounces to be good. Here there is no imperfection whatever. It follows that will is found in God, existing in Him formally, and not, as would be the case, were it a mixed perfection, only eminently.

Further, God made the world with wisdom. The marks of His intelligence are everywhere visible -- a point on which we dwelt when dealing with the teleological argument. But the application of intelligence to the production of an external effect demands the directive activity of the will. The intellect alone, apart from the motive force of will -- the purely speculative intellect -- effects nothing.

Again, the universe in which we live is far from exhausting the possibilities of creation. God might have created an infinitude of beings other than those which in fact He has called into existence. He might have left this universe unrealized, and framed a wholly different order of things. If, then, He has created the world as we know it, it is because He chose so to do. But the act of choice necessarily supposes the attribute of will.

2. *The primary and the secondary objects of God's will.* We explained in the last chapter the difference between the primary and secondary objects of a faculty. We saw that in all those beings in which the faculties are so many distinct endowments, each faculty is directed to a particular aspect of reality which constitutes its connatural object, and which when present determines the faculty to activity. In God, it is true, there is no distinction between faculties, nor yet between faculty and essence. Yet we are compelled by the limitations of our own minds to contemplate His infinite perfection under different aspects and by partial views corresponding to the distinction of perfections in created things. This justifies us in asking what is the primary and what the secondary objects of His will. Since will is an appetitive tendency, it is plain that the primary object of will is that which is desired for its own sake and as the end: the secondary objects are those which are desired simply on account of the primary object, this being the end to which they are referred. This may be illustrated in our own case. We have said that the object of our will in its present state is good in general. The good is man's primary end: though men differ greatly in their judgment where good is to he found, many reckoning as good only that which will afford them pleasure. Things which are desired simply as conducive to the possession of some good are secondary objects. Yet were man to see clearly and beyond the possibility of error some supremely good thing, something containing within itself the fullness of good, his attitude towards the good would change. This thing alone would be the primary object of his will, and all else would be secondary. If he loved other things, he could do so only in virtue of their relation to the primary object.

It may readily be shewn that the primary object of God's will is the Divine essence. This, and only this, can God love for its own sake: whatever else He loves, is loved in reference to this. Only the infinite good can be the connatural object of an infinitely perfect will. For the perfection of the act of volition stands in direct relation to the object.

The object is the measure determining the perfection of the act. But God alone -- the Divine essence -- is the infinite good. Hence only in God does the Divine will find its primary object. Or to employ another mode of proof: the primary object stands to the will in the relation of motive to that which is moved -- of cause to effect. Were that object anything external to God, it would follow that God's will is caused. Yet this is wholly impossible, for God's will is Himself. It follows that the object of the Divine will can be none other than God Himself: and that His act of will is uncaused, because it is one and the same with the self-existent Essence which is its object.

When we first meet this doctrine, it is apt to suggest to us the idea of egoism. Yet we have only to reflect to see that such a notion has no place here. For what do we signify by egoism? We mean an undue esteem for our own merits and excellencies, the assigning of an undue prominence to our own interests, and the exploitation of others for our personal advantage. In God this is impossible. There can be no question of self-seeking with Him; for He possesses the infinity of good. There can be no exploiting of others; for whatever finite beings possess they possess from His liberality, nor could anything drawn from them add in any way to His beatitude. God's infinite love for Himself is not inordinate. It is strictly due -- no more than right reason demands -- for He is infinitely worthy of love. Even from our own case we know that love for self, or self-regard as it is commonly termed, where it does not exceed its legitimate bounds but is governed by reason, so far from being a fault, is a necessary condition of virtue. A well-ordered self-regard protects a man from acts that are unworthy of the nature which God has bestowed on him and of the gifts with which that nature has been enriched, and stimulates him to develop his powers to the highest perfection which is within his reach.

That the Divine will has also secondary objects is manifest. The created universe came into existence and is sustained in existence because God wills it. Were it not an object of God's will, it would lapse into nothingness. But here we are met with what seems a grave difficulty. We said that secondary objects are desired, not for their own sake, but in reference to the primary object. They are viewed as means: and means are desired by reason of their connection with the end. It follows necessarily that so far as God cares for any finite thing, it is because it is referred in some way to Himself as its end.[1] Is such a conclusion possible?

The difficulty is apparent only, not real. There is an essential difference between the motive which makes man desire the secondary objects of his will, and the reason why the Divine, will includes such objects in its range. If we desire secondary objects, it is with a view to the acquisition of some good which we do not possess. God who is the fullness of all being can acquire nothing. If He has secondary objects, it is that His goodness may thereby find an outlet, and flow forth upon them. He desires them, not that He may gain anything, but that He may bestow. His love for them depends, it is true, wholly and entirely on His love for Himself. Loving His own essence, the sum and source of all goodness, He desires that because of its supreme excellence it should spread abroad. Consummated perfection tends to communicate itself. Our own experience affords illustrations of this truth. Living creatures both in the animal and vegetable kingdoms, when they have reached the full perfection of their nature, crave to perpetuate it in other individuals. The rational agent, who by assiduous toil has attained some excellence, is not satisfied till he has imparted it to some disciple. God likewise sees in His own perfections a reason why He should call creatures into being. Their reflected goodness becomes an object of God's will, because of His love for that essential goodness which is Himself.[2]

Thus creatures exist for the sake of God; and, so far, are not the end of creation, but exist purely by reason of that which must in the nature of things be the end of God's action -- His own goodness. It is totally impossible that it should be otherwise. All things come from God: and all must tend to Him. This is a universal law of all being. Just as it is absolutely necessary that God should he the First Efficient Cause of all things, so it is no less necessary that He should be the ultimate Final Cause. Yet creatures are not 'means' in the sense in which we employ that term in reference to some end of our own. We seek for means, that we may gain something for ourselves: no advantage accrues to the means. But where God and creatures are concerned, the creature alone benefits.

All its perfections all it is and all it has -- come to it because it is an object of God's will.

Not all thinkers have realized this truth. Thus Kant teaches that God created the world, not for Himself, but for man -- to bring man to the absolute end of morality.[3] It is plain that such a position, however specious, involves conclusions which are incompatible with the reason of things.

We pointed out in the last chapter (§ 2) an essential difference between the relation borne by the Divine and human intellect respectively to objective reality. Things are related to human thought as cause to effect: to the Divine thought as effects to their cause. A similar difference holds good as regards the Divine love. We love things because of some goodness which is theirs already: their goodness is the motive which arouses love within us. But all the goodness which creatures possess belongs to them simply because they are objects of God's will. His love is the cause of their goodness. He does not love them in the first instance because they are good, but they are good because He loves them.[4]

3. *The Divine free-will.* When we attribute to God the power of free-will, we are not to be understood as implying that this freedom is absolutely universal, including even the act by which His will is directed to its primary object. His love for His own essence admits of no elective choice. It belongs to the essential perfections of the Godhead: and without it God could not be. To love the infinitely good is a perfection. If beings endowed with intelligence and will fail to love the sum of all good, this is only because there is something amiss with them. Their knowledge of Him is inadequate: and what they know they do not rightly esteem. In God there can be no question of these defects: hence His love for Himself is necessary. Moreover -- to treat the same point in a different manner -- if we make the supposition, however extravagant it be, that God could cease from His act of love towards Himself, it follows by way of consequence that during the intermission His will would not be actualized at all, but would be a mere faculty -- a potentiality. This conclusion is inevitable, for, as we have just seen, God's will for

secondary objects is wholly dependent on His will for His primary object. He loves creatures because of His love for His own essence. If, then, His love for His own essence were to pass into abeyance, His will would become, as we have said, a mere potentiality destitute of act. This, however, we need not say, is wholly impossible. It follows that God's love for His essence admits of no suspension, but belongs to the Divine Nature itself.

If, however, God's will is necessary as regards Himself, it is otherwise where creatures are concerned. He was free, we maintain, either to create or to abstain from creating. No physical necessity of His own nature, no reason grounded on the intrinsic fitness of things, demanded the existence of any finite being. And if He decreed to create, He was no less at liberty as regards the objects of the creative act. No constraint bound Him to confer existence on the special order of things which He actually realized. He chose it, because it seemed good to Him. The proof of this conclusion is decisive. Viewed as objects of God's will, creatures stand to His essence in the relation of means to an end. God wills the Divine goodness for its own sake and as the end: creatures He wills, not for their own sake, but by reason of their connection with that end. But where the desire for any object depends on the will for the end to which it is referred, the necessity or freedom of the will in its regard is determined by its relation to the end. If its connection with the end be such that without it the end is unobtainable, then the will for the latter carries with it of strict necessity a will for this particular means. But if our possession of the end is not thus narrowly conditioned, then the will remains perfectly free to desire or to abstain from desiring this means. Thus the desire for good health necessarily carries with it the will for a given remedy, if the disease only admits of cure in one way. But if there are various methods of healing the malady, the will is under no constraint to seek any particular medicine. Now the divine goodness does not depend on creatures. God gains nothing by the existence of creatures, and loses nothing by their non-existence. The outpouring of perfection upon created being adds nothing to the Divine infinity. It is not a necessary means without which the end cannot be secured. It follows that as regards creatures God's will is free. We said above that perfection tends to communicate itself, and attributed God's will to create to this tendency. But it was not thereby meant that God, being supremely perfect, could not do other than create. This would have been to make the infinitely perfect dependent on the finite for His perfection -- a contradiction in terms. We signified simply that where there is perfection, it accords with the fitness of things that that perfection should spread itself abroad. This is altogether different from asserting that perfection is strictly exigent of such expansion. Were this the case God would not be self-sufficing.

We may urge here, too, an argument employed already in the first section of this chapter. It is abundantly clear that the present universe is not exhaustive of God's powers. The created order, full of wonders though it be, does not represent in every possible way the inexhaustible treasures of the Divine Reality. Yet if God's act of will in regard of His own essence carried with it of necessity an act of will for that essence as represented on the plane of finite being, it would follow that the act of creation must include every possible representation of the supreme exemplar cause. There would be no exercise of choice on God's part. By a law of His being He would be constrained to bring about the realization of every possible form of created reality. Since it is manifest that nothing of this kind has taken place, it is certain that He has exercised a choice in regard to what He shall create, in other words, that His will is not necessitated but free.

There are, however, not wanting thinkers who reject our conclusion, and contend that freedom can have no place in the Divine nature. We find this paradox maintained by not a few of those whose philosophical standpoint has been determined by Hegelian influences. We are justified in speaking of it as a paradox, for we recognize in the freedom of the will the highest prerogative of rational nature. In this more than in anything else consists the dignity of man: and it is this which elevates us to a different order of being from the brutes. Our actions are our own -- the fruit of free self-determination. Yet we are asked to believe that this perfection is lacking to God. Before, however, we examine the arguments brought by those who hold this view, it will be convenient to notice the essential differences between God's free act and our own. Certain characteristics must of necessity belong to God's elective choice, which serve to bring home to us how far removed is the infinite mind from our limited powers.

(1) The divine act is eternal. It did not come into being, but always was. With us the free choice of the will follows upon a state in which the agent has not yet chosen what course he shall adopt. But it is impossible that for God there should be a period in which His decision was not made. Such a delay would only be explicable, if He were not fully cognizant of the circumstances which furnish the occasion for a decision, or if, knowing the circumstances, He could not resolve upon His course. Both these hypotheses are impossible. We have, it is true, no means of imagining how an act can be at one and the same time free and eternal. But we are compelled to admit that so it is. And the fact that it is so makes it less difficult to conceive the possibility of creation ab aeterno -- a point discussed at some length in chap. iii.

(2) God's free decree is in the nature of things irrevocable. With man it is otherwise. We resolve upon a course of action: and then in the light of fresh knowledge, or even upon a reconsideration of the same data, we decide otherwise. It is part of wisdom not to be so wedded to our decisions as to refuse to modify them when reason so demands. But this possibility of change is the result of our limitations. It is partly due to our ignorance, and partly to the very character of the human intellect. Our mind does not know things by a single act of thought, which penetrates simultaneously every aspect of the object under consideration, but in a series of distinct concepts, each representing only one aspect of reality. And thus it comes about that we are swayed now this way, now that, according to the different aspect which we view. But God from all eternity has known to the full every element of every problem -- all the circumstances of each conjuncture that will ever arise -- by that one act of thought which is Himself, and has in the light of that knowledge decreed the course of providence. No new contingency can arise which can afford

a reason why He should alter His design. His free act of will abides eternally unchanged.

(3) God's exercise of free-will is not, as is the case with us, a transition from potentiality to act. Though the volition is not a necessary accompaniment of His essence, its presence involves no change of any kind in the divine immutability. No reality would have been absent from God had He not made this free elective choice. The point with which we are here occupied is one of the most mysterious in the whole of Natural Theology. We are totally unable to conceive how an act of will can on the one hand be freely posited, and on the other involve no change in the agent. Our inability should not, however, cause us any great surprise. It must necessarily be just as impossible for us to grasp the mode of the Divine action as it is to grasp the mode of the Divine being. The finite cannot grasp the nature of the infinite. Yet there are certain considerations which may render the notion of such an act easier of realization. The capacity of free action may be viewed in two different ways, viz., as a power to be exercised in regard of different internal acts of the will, one of which may be realized in preference to others: or as a power to be exercised in regard of different external effects. If it be conceived in the former of these two ways, it cannot be reckoned as a pure perfection. The realization of the internal act presupposes a subject capable of ulterior actuation. Hence the very notion of such an elective choice involves limitation and potentiality in the nature of the agent. It is after this fashion that free-will belongs to us: and in this sense, as is clear, it cannot belong to God. But if, on the other hand, it be conceived as an elective power having regard, not to internal acts, but solely to external effects, then no imperfection is involved in the idea. As thus understood, it is rightly reckoned among the Divine attributes. To put what we have said in another way: free-will in man is a power of elective choice determining the *immanent* action of the will, while in God it is a power determining those external effects which are God's action viewed as *virtually transitive*. Here, in fact, even more perhaps than with the other divine attributes, it is necessary to bear in mind that our concept is

analogous, and that we must not imagine that the perfection signified belongs to God in the precise manner in which it belongs to us.

It should further be noted when considering the difference between divine and human free-will that human volitions are caused by the objects desired. The latter are truly called the will's 'motives': they move it to action. They give, moreover, to the acts of the will their specific character. The nature of the particular act is determined by the motive. Hence a plurality of distinct objects involves a plurality of acts. In God there is nothing of this. The divine volition is identical with the divine essence. The number of its objects does not necessitate a corresponding number of acts. It is but one: and it is not caused by its objects, but is their cause. These essential points of difference may make it less difficult for us to realize how it can be, that, while in us each act of choice involves a new determination of the faculty, the will of God, without internal modification of any kind, extends itself to such finite objects as He sees fit to include within its scope.

To the question in what precisely does God's free act consist, the Scholastic philosophers reply that it is in fact God's necessary will in so far as besides its necessary object, viz., the Divine essence, it extends to other objects which are not necessary, these being things outside God.

Now that we have examined, in the degree in which it is possible, the nature of the divine freedom, we may more conveniently consider the objections urged against the doctrine by certain recent writers.

It is contended by some that spiritual perfection lies in obedience to law as the embodiment of reason: that, on the other hand, free-will apart from law is, as a principle of action, simply irrational caprice: and that the higher the perfection of an agent, the more absolute is his adherence to law, and the more does will fall into the background. Hence in God, the supremely perfect, mere free-will will have no place, but His activity will be in all things rigorously determined by immutable law. [5]

The objection here raised derives any apparent force which it may possess from the fallacious identification of free-will with caprice. By caprice we signify a decision made without sufficient reason, or even in defiance of reason. It is perfectly true that man may abuse the gift of free-will by thus employing it. But it does not follow that a choice made in perfect independence of the constraint of any law is necessarily a capricious choice. There may be various alternatives open, and good reason may be assignable for each of them. The free adoption of one among the number is not caprice. It is the exercise of a high prerogative, in virtue of which an agent endowed with intelligence dominates his materials. Thus, the artist contemplating his picture sees that the figures which he intends to introduce, may be disposed in various manners. Each way which suggests itself, presents some special aspect of beauty and grace. His mind is not a piece of mechanism working along a fixed groove, and determined by blind necessity. He is master of his choices, and he chooses with freedom. He need not even select the most beautiful of the arrangements open to him. He chooses the particular beauty which he desires. It is a mere error to call such a choice caprice. Thus, too, God acts with full and absolute freedom in regard of creatures. Whatever He does is assuredly in accordance with supreme wisdom and supreme goodness. He cannot act in a way contrary to His own attributes. But of the infinitely various possibilities before Him, He chooses that which seems good to Him. No constraint either from His own nature or from creatures compels Him to this or that course. He is master. To suppose, as does the argument which we are criticizing, that free-will has no place in His actions, is, in fact, an error drawn from a philosophical system, which, as we shall see later, has no room for a personal God at all.

It has further been urged, from the same point of view, that freedom carries with it the power to choose amiss, and consequently is not a pure perfection at all: that though the acts of the rational will are undoubtedly more perfect than those of inanimate nature, this is not because they are free, but because they alone are exercised with a knowledge of the end and with a conscious assent on the part of the will itself. Liability to error can never be aught but an imperfection. Hence it is concluded, God's acts are rational but not free.[6]

The difficulty here raised rests on an erroneous theory regarding the nature of freedom. It may easily be shewn that the power to choose wrong instead of right is due to the special conditions under which man in his present state exercises the faculty of election, and is not essential to freedom as such. The capacity of self-determination, as we have already pointed out, does not extend to the end at which the will aims, but solely to the means by which that end is to be secured. Whatever we choose we choose with a view to the attainment of the Good. About this we have no choice. But we are free to seek the Good in various ways. Our power to choose wrong arises from the fact that in our present state we are able to choose, not merely that which is truly good, but that which is only apparently so. Were it given us to have a clear apprehension of the Infinite Good we should no longer be able to misuse liberty by choosing what withdraws us from that supreme object of desire, but we should retain full freedom in regard of the manifold ways of doing right. This, the Catholic Church teaches, is the condition of the Blessed in heaven, who see God. It is plain that the argument which seeks to deny God's freedom, on the score that He cannot choose amiss, is a mere sophism. The power to choose evil is no necessary constituent in true liberty. It is a sheer defect, marring the purity of its perfection.

Certain other objections by which it is sought to shew that God's action in the world is not free but necessary, still remain to be considered. But as they are not directed against freedom as such, but against the possibility of freedom in the creative act, it seems best to reserve them till the chapter which deals with Creation.

4. *The apparent frustrations of God's will.* It would appear at first sight, in view of the use made by man of his freedom, that the divine will is in no small measure frustrated and unrealized. The dictates of the moral law declare what is God's will for rational agents. And though men may and do fall into gross errors about its precepts, yet its fundamental principles are, as we have urged (chap. v., § I), not merely known to all, but recognized as being the commands of a supreme legislator. Nevertheless, man habitually violates it: and by this violation has brought about the scene of moral and social wreckage in which our lot is cast. It seems as though

God's purpose were everywhere defeated through man's rebellion. Yet the entire dependence of created being on God renders such a conclusion altogether impossible. The relation of God to finite agents is not comparable to that of an earthly ruler to his subjects. God has foreseen from all eternity what each of His free creatures would do, if placed in any given circumstances: and, further, the act thus foreseen only takes place in so far as He, the Prime Mover, wills to permit it. Where other causes are in question, frustration of the effects intended is always conceivable. But where God is concerned, as we pointed out in the last chapter (§ 3), we have no choice but to allow that all this apparent frustration has its place in a providential scheme: that God, when He created the present order of things, foresaw how the free agents which He was creating would refuse obedience; but that He willed to permit this and to make even their acts of rebellion subservient to the execution of His purposes. God, it is carefully to be noted, did not will the evil. He cannot will what is contrary to His own attributes: and moral evil is in direct opposition to His essential sanctity. But in the event of the created agent choosing wrong, He can use that very choice to bring about some good result. Thus the cruelty of the persecutors became the occasion of the heroic virtue of the martyrs. This latter God willed. But though He turned the former to good account, He did not will it. He willed -- a very different thing -- to permit it. We have seen that the last end of God's action is, of necessity, Himself: that contemplating the supreme excellence of the Divine nature, He desires that its perfections should be manifested in the created order. The ultimate reason of creation was that God's infinite perfection should be reproduced in the only manner in which this was possible. In this sense all things are created for God's glory. But He desires as a secondary end the good of the creature. Where free agents are concerned that end is beatitude: and, inasmuch as the attainment of beatitude demands their free cooperation, this secondary end may, through their own perversity, be forfeited. Yet even so, it is utterly impossible that the creature should not tend to that primary end for which all things are made. Only it subserves that end in a different way. It no longer contributes to God's glory by the perfections with which it is endowed, and the beatitude it enjoys. But by the punishment

which it has drawn upon itself -- the just retribution of its rejection of
God -- it manifests His justice and His hatred of evil.[7]

In connection with this subject an important distinction is drawn between
the *antecedent* and the *consequent* will of God. The distinction does not, of
course, imply a plurality of acts of volition. Viewed as men, God desires
the beatitude of all without exception in virtue of their nature as rational
creatures: and, by reason of this desire, gives to each the helps necessary
to this end. Here by a logical abstraction we are considering His will
antecedently to His prevision of their final state when their probation
reaches its term. Thus God's antecedent will is the will by which He
desires the beatitude of each one, abstraction being made from His
foreknowledge of the state in which the individual will be found at the
hour of death. Thus considered, God's will, it is evident, is often not
fulfilled. But this is due, not to the frustration of an absolute will of God,
but because this abstract consideration does not, in fact, give us God's
actual volition regarding the individual case. This must take account of
the man's state at the close of his probation. God's ultimate decree in
view of the man's merits or demerits -- His will viewed as consequent to
His foreknowledge of the man's final condition -- is termed His
consequent will. This is always realized.

5. *The moral attributes of God.* By the moral virtues we signify, when
speaking of man, certain stable dispositions inclining him to act in
accordance with the law of reason. Every such exercise of freedom
depends upon the will. When the other powers are employed in free
actions, they are directed by the will. Hence the office of the moral
virtues is either to dispose the will itself to the observance of the law of
reason, or to bring some appetite under control, and render it obedient to
the dictates of the rational will. The mere cultivation of the intellect, apart
from the will does not, as Socrates imagined, ensure virtuous conduct. It
gives an enhanced capacity for right action, by shewing us the better
course. But it does not guarantee that we shall adopt that course.
Knowledge is not virtue: and ignorance is not identical with vice. Moral
virtue is essentially an inclination which gives a right direction to acts
proceeding from the will.[8]

It is manifest that among the various perfections of which human nature is capable, these are the highest. It is the possession of these which gives a man the title to be termed a good man. Without them he may, indeed, deserve to be called good in this or that particular respect -- a good soldier, a good artist. But only if he has the moral virtues, does he merit to be called simply good. We naturally ask whether they are found in God. If He has them not, it is simply misleading to speak of Him as a good God: for as applied to a being possessed of intelligence and will, this is the meaning of the term. Yet certain modern thinkers would have us answer the question in the negative. To attribute moral virtue to God is, they hold, anthropomorphism.[9] We shall see that there is no justification for this view. It is true that for some human virtues there is no room in the Divine nature, since they are proper to beings of flesh and blood like ourselves. But others exist formally in Him, though after a manner not identical with, but analogous to our own. They are attributes of the Divine will, and hence call for treatment here. In us the moral virtues are of two kinds. Certain of them are concerned exclusively with the control of the passions. Concupiscence, anger, fear, hatred and the like, speedily reject the guidance of reason, and make man a slave to the strongest impulse, unless he arms himself with the virtues which render them pliant to the will. Only if he acquires temperance, chastity, patience, fortitude, meekness, etc., is he master in his own house. The passions, though they can be stimulated to activity, not only by sensible goods, but by those which are more spiritual, such as the desire of revenge, of honour, etc., etc., belong essentially to our sensitive nature. The irrational animal creation is endowed with the same appetites, though with different provision for their control. It is evident that those virtues whose sole office it is to hold in check the passionate part of nature have no place in God. But there are other virtues, which involve no necessary connection with the sensitive part of man, but are perfections of the will as such. Such, for instance, are the virtues of justice, liberality, obedience, and veracity. Some of these, it is true, connote imperfection as well as perfection. Thus obedience implies subordination to a superior. Others, however, are pure perfections, and as such must be found formally in God. In Him, as we have said, they exist in a different manner to that in which they are found in us. In man the different virtues are distinct from one another: the inclination to truthfuness is not identical with the inclination to justice. Each is a separate principle, limited to a narrow sphere of action, and effecting a certain particular good. In God all are one supreme perfection, the Divine will. When we predicate these virtues of Him, we do not thereby signify the presence in Him of limited principles of action, such as are found in our own souls. We are constrained so to speak, because His sole perfection includes within itself that which we only know as realized in ourselves through a multiplicity of distinct determinations. Again, man acquires perfection gradually by the performance of virtuous acts. With God it is not so. Being infinitely perfect He can gain no increase of goodness by any effect external to Himself. He would not have been less good, had He never called man into being, and thus provided Himself with objects upon whom His virtues might be displayed. God's infinite love for the supreme Good -- the act of love which is His will -- is in itself the fullness of moral perfection, essential sanctity. The virtues which we affirm of Him are but aspects of this love, in so far as it finds a secondary object in creatures -- they do not make it greater than it was.

Amongst the virtues which we attribute to God we propose to consider two in particular, viz., Justice and Mercy. It will appear how the essential character of both is found in Him, yet without anthropomorphism of any kind.

(1) Justice is the disposition of the will which leads us to render to each his due. But justice is of more than one kind. For our present purpose we must distinguish between two forms of this virtue. There is the justice which holds between those, of whom the one has been in some manner benefited by the other, and remains bound to render an equivalent. The relations between the two are those of creditor and debtor: there is a strict right on the one side, a strict obligation on the other. This is called *commutative justice*. The other kind which calls for mention is *distributive justice*. This is the justice of a ruler in regard to his subjects. The ruler practises this virtue when he apportions in accordance with reason and equity the benefits which it falls to him, as a ruler, to dispense. Reason, as

both Aristotle and St. Thomas remind us, demands that the apportionment, whether of privileges or other benefits, should have regard to the relative importance of the persons as members of the body politic: and this will be conditioned largely by the constitution of the particular state.[10] A bare equality all round would in most cases be unreasonable and therefore unjust. It belongs, too, to this justice to reward merit and to punish evil-doers. It is to be observed that distributive justice differs from commutative justice in this, that the ruler is not handing over to the subject that which by right is already his. He is not, strictly speaking, a debtor to the subject; his obligation is to the law of justice, not to the individual. In human affairs, it is true, the subject's claim is frequently of a mixed character, based partly on distributive, partly on commutative justice. But we are here concerned to indicate the distinctive character of the two notions. It is further to be considered that, though distributive justice primarily has regard to subjects, there is a sense in which the ruler exercises it even towards himself. He must assign to himself that which reason requires should pertain to the ruler.

We are now in a position to understand in what sense justice may be predicated of God. There can be no question of commutative justice. God cannot reap any benefit from creatures, or be under obligation to repay any of them for services rendered and value received. What the creature has -- his possessions, his faculties, even the very impulse which prompts him to serve God -- comes from the sole source of all good.

The justice of God is distributive justice -- the justice proper to the ruler. God bestows on each of His creatures that which reason demands. For His will of necessity accords with His wisdom: and the Divine wisdom is essential reason. A human ruler conforms his will to a law which is above him. God's will cannot fail of conformity to that law: for it is one with Himself.

When God bestows on each creature that which reason demands, justice appears in two relations. He renders to Himself what is due: and He renders to the creature what is due to it. It is due to Himself that finite being should manifest what His wisdom and His will have prescribed:

and it is due to the creature that it should possess those endowments without which the nature would be incomplete, the specific type imperfectly realized. Thus it is due to man that he should have the use of reason, and to the plant that it should bear fruit after its kind. God displays His justice when. He confers on each of His creatures its appropriate gifts. But this justice implies no debt on God's part towards the creature. These gifts are due to the creature because God owes it to Himself that the creature shall realize His purpose.{11}

Yet when we speak of the divine justice we refer more usually to the rewards and punishments, which the common voice of humanity declares await us in the next life. In this regard also we rightly affirm that God is just. Man is a free agent, subject to the moral law. A law involves the sanction of punishment: without such a sanction attached to it it would be incomplete and defective. Moreover, while the other beings of this material universe attain the end for which they were created by a mere exercise of physical activity, it is not so with man. No use of his physical forces will bring him to beatitude. If, then, he is to attain beatitude by his actions, it must be by their moral value, and by way of merit. Thus natural reason itself assures us that rewards and punishments await us according to our deserts. Revelation has much more to tell us on this head; but the doctrines of revelation fall outside our scope. Reason can hardly do more than convince us of the fact of rewards and punishments, and assure us that God's distribution of them will be supremely just. Two further points, however, seem to call for notice in this connection. First, it has sometimes been said that any doctrine of merit supposes that God is a debtor to His creatures. This, manifestly, is not so. There may be a true proportion between the action and its reward in virtue of which the reward is really merited, without indebtedness on God's side. He gives to human nature various powers, and He proposes a reward commensurate with the endowment which he has bestowed.{12} He owes it to His own wisdom that His plan should be accomplished, and that the creature should attain to beatitude by the means which He has prescribed for it. But to the creature itself He owes and can owe nothing. In the second place, it must not be overlooked that the infliction of punishment, even though the sentence be, as revelation tells us, final and irrevocable, would seem to follow by necessary consequence from God's nature as the sum and source of all goodness. It is the vindication of the claim of Absolute Goodness to be supremely loved. Even natural reason seems to demand that the definitive rejection of this claim -- a rejection by which the rational agent freely and deliberately repudiates the infinitely good and chooses evil -- should entail an enduring state of punishment.

(2) God's mercy is sometimes understood in a somewhat wide sense of His benevolence in general towards His creatures. This benevolence is mainfested towards all His works in the gifts which He bestows upon them according to their kind. God loves all that He has made. And, as we have already seen, His love is absolutely generous, since it is not aroused by the good which He finds in us; but, on the contrary, the good that is in us is the effect of His love. Usually, however, the attribute of mercy has the more restricted meaning which is the term's true sense. In men mercy is understood as the virtue which inclines the will to aid another in his misery. And in this sense, too, it is predicated of God. In ourselves our kinship with the sufferer as sharers in a common humanity results in a fellow-feeling, affecting the sensitive part of our nature. The mercy of God is, of course, purely spiritual.

Mercy properly so called is, it is important to observe, restricted in its application to man. Only a rational creature endowed with reflective self-consciousness is capable of misery. A being which cannot turn its thoughts inward upon itself and contemplate the measure of its joy or its sorrow, may be susceptible of pleasure and of pain, but it can know neither felicity nor misery. The question of animal-suffering, in which so many see a difficulty against the goodness of the Creator, will be discussed in the chapter dealing with the problem of evil. It does not belong to our present subject.

The light thrown by mere natural reason on God's mercy, is, just as is the case with His justice, scanty but still adequate. We can affirm *a priori* that He possesses the perfection. But its manifestation in great measure eludes us. Yet this is not wholly so. The data of experience suffice, if we will only weigh them well, to shew us that He is ever seeking to aid man in his misery. We are apt, indeed, to overlook the vital truth that there is but one evil which is such in the full sense of the term, and which really justifies us in calling a man miserable, viz., separation from the Supreme Good which is his last end. Temporal misfortunes are such only in a qualified sense: they are evil in a certain respect, but not absolutely. Only the man who is separated from the Supreme Good, and knows that he is on the road to that final separation which is the irremediable shipwreck of his whole being, is justly miserable. A mere consideration of human life as we know it, shews us that God endeavours to deliver man from this fate. He tolerates the flagrant violation of His laws and the open defiance of His authority, and even after years of such conduct providentially enables a man to rectify his life and once again make his peace with Him. Were He just only, and not also supremely merciful, this would not be. The sinner -- at least, the great sinner -- would have no ground to suppose a way of return open to him. We may find yet another proof of God's mercy in the trials which He sends us. Man is so prone to seek his happiness in the good things of this life, that if our path were made smooth and pleasant, there would be few indeed who would not forget God altogether, and thus forfeit their hope of eternal beatitude. God in His mercy sends to all without exception a measure of suffering, depriving life of much of its attractiveness, and constraining us to seek a more durable happiness than we can obtain here. Again, the common consent of mankind proclaims that God hears our prayers: that even for relief in our temporal sorrows we may appeal to Him: and that, because He is merciful, He will grant our requests so far as is compatible with our true good.

Even if we keep within the strict limits of Natural Religion, the considerations just advanced might well convince us that mercy is one of the attributes of God. Yet man could never have fathomed the measure of that mercy, had not God Himself made it known in the Christian revelation. The very purpose of that divine interposition in human history was to bring God's mercy to men. And if we abstract from the stupendous work of love by which God Himself came amongst men to deliver them from their misery, all our conclusions on this subject are but faint and far-off suggestions of the reality within our reach.

It only remains to point out that there is no opposition between mercy and justice. A judge whose office it is to deal with crimes committed against others cannot, it is true, consistently with justice remit the penalty. The satisfaction is not owing to him, but to a third party or to the state. But where the divine tribunal is in question, it is against God Himself that the offence has been committed. He is not bound to exact the penalty. If He remits it, He violates no principle of justice. Justice is opposed to that weak indulgence which is hurtful to the very person who is its object: it is not opposed to mercy. Mercy, says St. Thomas, is the complement of justice.[13]

6. *The beatitude of God.* By beatitude we understand the possession by an intellectual nature of its full and final good -- the good beyond which nothing remains to desire, and in which it enjoys delight without alloys. It is a state beyond the reach of irrational creatures. As we said in the foregoing section,, only the self-conscious intelligence can reflect on and be aware of its own condition; and without this awareness, just as there can be no misery, so there can be no true felicity. It is evident that the degrees of beatitude of which different beings are capable will vary greatly. The intensity of the happiness will be greater in proportion as the good possessed is ampler, the union between the experiencing subject and the good is more intimate, and the comprehension of the good by the intelligence is more complete. In God all of these are found in an infinite degree. The good which He enjoys is the abyss of all perfection, His own essence: the union is replaced by identity: and the comprehension of the intellect is absolute. It follows that the Divine life is an abiding state of infinite bliss.

The eternal act by which God contemplates the riches of the Divine essence is not to be conceived as a mere recognition of the happiness arising from His perfections. That act of contemplation is not simply awareness of beatitude: it is itself beatitude. God's essential beatitude lies in His knowledge of Himself, the fountain of all Reality, all Goodness.

The proof of this is easy. Beatitude is the condition towards which an intellectual nature tends as its ultimate perfection. But the ultimate perfection of an agent is found in the most perfect of its activities. We are speaking here, of course, of immanent activities, not of such as are transitive. The end to which a transitive operation is directed, is the perfection, not of the agent, but of the object on which it takes effect: and the ultimate perfection of an intelligent nature cannot consist in an action destined to perfect an external object. But immanent actions are the perfection of the agent as such. The perfection of an intelligent being must consist in an activity of this kind. The highest of all activities is that of the intellect. It is, therefore, in the operations of the intelligence that the Divine beatitude must lie. And if it be the case that God's felicity is found in the activity of the Divine thought, then the object of that thought must be the most perfect of all objects, the Supreme Good, His own essence.

It seems worthy of remark that the reasoning, which we have here employed, is the same as that by which the Schoolmen prove that man's beatitude is to be found in the knowledge of God. His beatitude, they argue, must of necessity consist in the highest of his activities. But his highest activity is attained when the noblest of his faculties is in exercise in regard of the noblest of objects. His noblest faculty is his mind: and the noblest object on which his mind can be employed is God.[14] The point is one which well merits our consideration. For it thus appears that our faculty of reason, limited and fallible as human reason is, gives us at least to this extent a resemblance to God, that we can find our beatitude in Him alone. Wherever there is intelligence, be it the infinite intelligence of the Creator, or the finite intelligence of the creature, full and final felicity can only be found in the possession of the Real, the True, and the Good -- in other words, of God.[15]

The objection may well suggest itself that beatitude should be referred to the will rather than to the intellect. Does not felicity consist in the joy which is ours when the will reposes in the object of love? Is it not this that we really mean when we speak of bliss? Undoubtedly, beatitude carries this joy with it. Were this joy not present, we should not possess beatitude. Alike for God and for man, the state of bliss includes love as well as knowledge. The only question at issue is which of these two is the constitutive principle of beatitude. And there can be no doubt that St. Thomas Aquinas is right in maintaining that the intellect, and not the will, is to be regarded as such. The beatitude of any nature consists in its possession of its last end. When this final good is won, ultimate perfection is reached. But the actual attainment of the last end is the work of the intellect. The joy of the will supposes that the prize has already been won: fruition is consequent on possession. Joy, then, is not so much the essence of beatitude as a property which necessarily derives from it. Yet since beatitude involves the activity alike of intellect and of will, comprising both knowledge and love in the highest degree, this seemed the more natural place in which to treat of it. It could not have been so suitably dealt with in the chapter on the Divine intellect.

God's bliss, it is evident, is immutable, infinite, eternal. It had no beginning, and will have no end. It admits of no increase: nor can anything arise to cloud it even for an instant. It abides ever the same, without change. Yet its changelessness is not the monotony of inaction, but the exercise of the highest activity.

It might, indeed, seem that since such is God's life, He must be ever absorbed within Himself, and can have no concern with aught that lies outside: that it is impossible to suppose that such a God could ever feel desire to call finite being into existence: and, even if we should imagine Him to create, that He could not occupy Himself with mundane events. So, in fact, has it been urged.[16] But, as we have already seen, this is very far from being the case. The very love which He bears to His own supreme perfection itself affords a ground why He should will to give existence to an order of created things in which that perfection should be exemplified in the manifold types of finite reality. And granted that He is thus led to exercise His freedom of will in creating, He must needs love each one of His creatures in proportion to the resemblance which they bear to His own goodness. Moreover, in virtue of His infinite wisdom, He will direct every least detail of earthly affairs, guiding all things towards the end which He has appointed.

NOTES

{1} The purpose of creation is discussed further below, c. xiv., § 6.

{2} "Res naturalis non solum habet naturalem inclinationem respectu proprii boni ut acquirat ipsum cum non habet, vel ut quiescat in illo cum habet: sed etiam ut proprium bonum in alia diffundat secundum quod possibile est. Unde videmus quod omne agens, in quantum est actu et perfectum, facit sibi simile. Unde et hoc pertinet ad rationem bonitatis, ut bonum quod quis habet, aliis communicet secundum quod possibile est. Et hoc praecipue pertinet ad bonitatem divinam, a qua per quandam similitudinem derivatur omnis perfectio. Unde si res naturales in quantum perfectae sunt, suum bonum aliis communicant, multo magis pertinet ad bonitatem divinam, ut bonum suum aliis per similitudinem communicet, secundum quod possibile est. Sic igitur vult et se et alia: sed se ut finem: alia vero ut ad finem: in quantum condecet divinam bonitatem, etiam alia ipsam participare." St. Thomas, *Summa Theol.*, I., q. 19, art. 2.

{3} *Critique of Judgment*, § 85.

{4} Thomas Aq., *Summa Theol.*, I., q. 20, art. 2; I. II., q. 110, art. 1.

{5} "When you say of a human being that he does anything simply because he wills it, you degrade his action below the movements of a weather-vane. . . . On the other hand, the more a human will is subjected to law, the less of caprice and the more of reason we find in its action, the higher and

{6} The objection is that urged by Anton Gunther, *Eurysthetis und Herakles* (1843), p. 517 (cited in *Kleutgen De Deo*, § 567, n. 6). On this writer and his philosophical system see the article in the *Catholic Encyclopedia.*

{7} "Cum igitur voluntas Dei sit universalis causa rerum, impossibile est quod divina voluntas suum effectum non consequatur. Unde quod recedere videtur a divina voluntate secundum unum ordinem relabitur in ipsum secundum alium: sicut peccator, qui quantum est in se recedit a divina voluntate peccando, incidit in ordinem divinae voluntatis, dum per ejus justitiam punitur." St. Thomas Aq., *Summa Theol.*, I., q. 19, art. 6.

{8} Subjectum vero habitus qui simpliciter dicitur virtus, non potest esse nisi voluntas vel aliqua potentia, secundum quod est mota a voluntate. Cujus ratio est, quia voluntas movet omnes alias potentias, quae aliqualiter sunt rationales ad suos actus. Et ideo quod homo bene agat, contingit ex hoc quod homo habet bonam voluntatem." *Summa Theol.* I. II., q. 56, art. 3.

{9} Cf., *e.g.*, Bradley, *Appearance and Reality*, p. 533. "The Absolute is not personal, nor is it moral, nor is it beautiful nor true." The evolutionary theory of the origin of human morals brings us to the same conclusion. Professor Romanes writes: "For anything we can tell to the contrary, the moral sense may have been given to or developed in man simply on account of its utility to the species -- just in the same way as teeth to the shark or poison to the snake . it may be quite as anthropomorphic a notion to attribute morality to God as it would be to attribute those capacities for sensuous enjoyment with which the Greeks endowed their divinities." *Thoughts on Religion*, p. 81.

{10} Aristotle, *Nic. Ethic.*, V., c. iii.; St. Thomas Aq., *Summa Theol.*, I. II., q. 61, art. 2,

{11} Debitum est Deo ut impleatur in rebus id quod ejus sapientia et voluntas habet, et quod ejus bonitatem manifestat. Et secundum hoc justitia Dei respicit decentiam ipsius secundum quam reddit sibi quod sibi debetur. Debitum etiam est alicui rei creatae, quod habeat id quod ad ipsam ordinatur: sicut homini quod habeat manus, et quod ei alia animalia serviant. Et sic etiam Deus operatur justitiam, quando dat unicuique quod ei debetur secundum rationem suae naturae et conditionis. Sed hoc debitum dependet a primo: quia hoc unicuique debetur quod est ordinatum ad ipsum secundum ordinem divinae sapientiae." St. Thomas, *Summa Theol.*, I., q. 21, art. 1, ad 3.

{12} According to the teaching of the Catholic Church the end actually proposed to us is a supernatural, not a natural end: hence, that we may be enabled to merit it, our nature is elevated by a supernatural endowment of grace. It would be beside our purpose to touch on this subject.

{13} Misericordia non tollit justitiam, sed est quaedam justitiae plenitudo." *Summa Theol.*, I., q. 21, art. 3, ad. 2. "We should," writes Mr. C. J. Webb, "scarcely call an unmerciful person just; and in speaking of a person as unjust, we should rather think of his hard treatment of those who do not deserve it, than of his comparative over-leniency to others: we should certainly think it strange to describe him on account of such over-leniency as a merciful man. The truest justice would seem to include mercy, and mercy in the highest sense would vindicate for itself the name of justice." *God and Personality*, p. 257.

{14} St. Thomas Aq., *Summa Theol.*, I. II., q. 3, art. 5.

{15} So far as Natural Theology is concerned, it would appear that the disproportion between the infinite divine essence and the finite powers of the creature is such that a direct and immediate knowledge of God is beyond the power of any created intellect: that the creature can rise no higher than to know about God by deductions from the created world: that a direct and immediate insight into the Divine essence is proper to God Himself alone. Revelation assures us that this natural incapacity will be transcended: and that the blessed will, in fact, possess that direct knowledge, and thus be made sharers in God's own beatitude.

{16} The account here given of the Divine life was derived by the Schoolmen from Aristotle. He reaches the conclusion that it can be nothing else than an activity of thought, in which the thought and the object of thought are identical (*Metaph.*, XII., c. ix.). He further declares that this existence is the best of possible existences, and necessarily accompanied by delight (c. vii.). Commenting on this Dr. Edw. Caird says that such a deity "cannot logically be conceived as going beyond itself to create the finite world of movement and change." *Evolution of Theology in the Greek Philosophers*, II., 241 (cited in Ward's *Realm of Ends*, p. 33).

Chapter XIII. The Divine Omnipotence.

1. The Attribute of Power.

2. The Scope of the Divine Onmipotence.

3. Divine Omnipotence Denied: 'A Finite God.'

4. Miracles.

1. *The attribute of power.* By God's power -- or as we generally call it, His omnipotence -- we understand the principle of His external activity. To this attribute we refer all that He effects externally to Himself.

God, as we have already seen, does not produce His effects by transitive action. Transitive action, though it proceeds from the agent, is consummated in the object of the activity. Undoubtedly we sometimes give the name of action to the preliminary changes by which the agent brings his powers from their normal condition of mere potentiality, and renders them in fact active. But until this process is complete, he is not yet, properly speaking, an agent: and the action cannot take place until he is so. Thus to take an example: when we impress a seal on wax, all our movements till the seal is actually communicating its shape to the sealing-wax are preliminary to the exercise of causality by which the shape is transmitted. They are necessary as conditions; they are not the action denoted by the verb 'to impress.' As Aristotle accurately points out, wherever transitive action takes place the action of the efficient cause is not something different from the actual change effected in the patient. The same change which as received into the subject is termed its *passio*, viewed as emanating from the agent is that agent's *actio*. *Actio est in passo* -- 'the action is in the patient' -- was the formula in which the Schoolmen summed up this most important doctrine.[1] It follows from this that such action can never be other than an accident. A determination which, emanating from the agent, is received by the patient, and thus is a perfection of both,[2] cannot be substantial being. Transitive action therefore can have no place in God. God's action is identical with His substantial essence: it is Himself. The Divine action, therefore, is necessarily immanent. Yet since God can, by His free-will, produce finite things external to Himself, we say of Him that His action is *virtually transitive*.

There has been some debate whether God's power is to be reckoned as an attribute distinct from intellect and will: and some authors have held that it is so. But there can be little doubt that this view is erroneous. Nor does it seem that it should be referred to His intellect, though the intellect exercises a directive function in its regard. God's power is an aspect of His will. We may distinguish between God's free-will as elective and as executive. His power is His executive will. That we are right in this identification seems evident from the fact that our own will possesses a capacity for direct executive action. It is able to move the body. How it is that the spiritual faculty initiates the impulse to which bodily motion is due, we are perfectly ignorant. The fact, however, is certain. And since every perfection belonging to a created will must necessarily be found in the Divine Will, we need not hesitate to regard God's power as pertaining to His will.

It is doubtless true that, except in regard to the initial impulse of motion, our executive powers are situated in physical organs. Our hands and feet are not moved immediately by the will; an apparatus of nerves and muscles transmits the will's commands, and acts instrumentally on its behalf. And *a fortiori* this is so where our activity is exercised on other bodies. But this is to be attributed, it would seem, not to any necessity of the case, but to the special conditions of human nature as such. Our nature is composite, partly spiritual and partly corporeal. And functions which in a purely spiritual nature would be exercised through spirit alone, in us become complex and demand the participation of both portions of our being.

The power of creatures is limited in various manners. If a creature does not possess a given perfection, it cannot communicate it. The natural generative force of a sparrow cannot result in an egg which will hatch into a bird of paradise. A man cannot carve a statue, unless he first conceive a form which he may transfer to the marble. And even if the agent possesses the perfection, the means for achieving the result may be lacking: the hand or eye may be insufficiently trained, or the external aids requisite to the work may be unobtainable. But there can be no limit to God's power. He possesses within Himself all perfection, for He is the fullness of being. Moreover, for that very reason, He is not dependent upon means. He may employ means, if He will; but He stands in no need of them. His power, like His intellect, is infinite: and for that reason is termed omnipotence. And being infinite, it follows that He can create; that by His will He can call into existence that which had no existence before.

2. *The scope of omnipotence.* The precise meaning of omnipotence calls for elucidation. For even those who affirm the absolute infinity of God's power, admit that there are things which He cannot do: *e.g.*, that He cannot bring it about that two and two make five, or that the past should not have happened. Difficulties have often been felt on this subject. And some have held that those who make this admission are inconsistent in maintaining the Divine omnipotence.

The object of active power, whether in God or in creatures, is *being which is causally produced.* Power, as we have already noted, is based on some perfection -- some mode of being -- possessed by the agent: and is directed to the communication in some manner of this perfection. It is impossible that power should have any other object than such being, just as it is impossible that hearing should perceive what is not sound, or that sight should perceive what is not coloured. It may, indeed, be asked whether we cannot employ power to destroy? But the reply is easy. We can only destroy by putting the thing in a new state of being. The direct object of our action is not destruction but the realization of the new condition, which involves the absence of the form whose removal we intend. If, *e.g.*, I break or deface a statue, the immediate result is the production in the marble of a new shape, of which it previously had but the potency. The actualization of this new shape involves the disappearance of the old. God, doubtless, can annihilate in the full sense of the word. But were He to do this, it would not be by the use of His active power, but by ceasing to use it. Created being only exists through the continuous conservation of God. Did He not conserve things in being, they could not endure for an instant. Annihilation denotes simply the withdrawal of the causal influx we term conservation.

Since then the object of active power is *being as causally produced*, it follows that omnipotence does not extend to what is not being, nor yet to what is incompatible with the necessary conditions of that which is due to efficient causation.[3] This does not involve limits to omnipotence. Infinite power can realize all things. The objects excluded from omnipotence are so because they are not things at all, but no-things, and hence are incapable of realization by reason of their own nonentity, not by reason of any lack of power in God. It may be well to illustrate each of these two sources of impossibility. Notions which contain contradictory elements are not being. Each element may signify something real: but since the other is contradictory in its regard, it removes the being thus signified. Thus God cannot create a material spirit. Spirit is being; but matter is the express denial of the form of being which spirit signifies. The notion is a non-ens. Similarly, God cannot bring it about that two straight lines should enclose a space. The terms are reciprocally exclusive. Two lines such as to enclose a space are *ipso facto* not straight lines. Lines which are straight and yet not straight are a chimera. So, too, it is impossible that the past should be made not to have happened. If it is past, it has happened. A thing which both has and has not happened is meaningless. Nor can God create a thing which lacks any of the conditions essential to being which is due to efficient causation. He cannot make a creature which will exist in such a way as not to need His conserving action. He cannot endow a creature with infinite power.

Again, it is no diminution of omnipotence that God cannot do those things which are inconsistent with infinite perfection, and only possible to a finite agent. We saw in the last chapter that He cannot change the free decrees which He has made, Yet it appeared that this is due to the infinitude of His wisdom, and not to any limitation in His perfections. Change of purpose in a free agent supposes the presence of a reason for the new resolve. To the infinite, however, who from all eternity has possessed the perfect intuition, of every aspect of truth, no such reason can arise. In other words, our power to change springs from our finite limitations -- from our imperfect knowledge and our faulty judgment. Under this head we may reckon all other 'mixed' perfections, which are found eminently, but not formally, in God. God's power is not limited, because, *e.g.*, He cannot exercise sense-perception but possesses His knowledge in a different and higher manner. We have touched on this point frequently in the course of the work, and there is no need to enlarge upon it here.

Somewhat more consideration must be given to the objection arising from the fact that God can do no evil. It has been urged that here, at least, there is a real restriction on His power, which renders the word omnipotence a misnomer. It is sometimes replied that the essence of sin lies in the adhesion of the will to something which withdraws us from our last end, God: that it is an act of the created will at variance with the law imposed by the Divine will; and, consequently, that in reference to God, the term can have no significance. God's will cannot be in opposition to itself. Yet this answer, though true, seems to evade the real point of the difficulty. What is really intended is that the moral law does not depend on God's mere decree: that to lie, to act unjustly, and the like, are wrong antecedently to any Divine command: and that because they are wrong, God cannot do them. This, it is argued, is a positive restriction of Divine power. Certainly, it is true that the moral law is not constituted solely by a Divine precept. Though some have so taught,[4] Scholastic philosophy maintains unhesitatingly that there are actions which are good or bad, as the case may be, in virtue of their own intrinsic nature, and independently of positive law. No positive law could make injustice right. To render to each his due is in accordance with reason: to do otherwise is to violate the order which reason demands. Similarly, to lie is of its own nature contrary to right reason. The purpose of speech is the manifestation of thought. To turn it to a contrary end is a perversion of its very nature. it is wholly impossible that such things can be the object of the Divine will. The primary object of God's love, as we explained above (chap. xii. § I), is His own infinite nature. That nature is the supreme exemplar of all harmony and order. Whatever God has made partakes in its degree of that order: and the more perfect, the higher in the scale of being, any nature is, the more marvellous is the harmonious order which it displays. God cannot will the disordered: for in so far as there is discord and disorder, there is unlikeness to the Divine essence, not likeness. He is supreme reason: and has stamped the reflection of His reason on all His works. He cannot approve that which is the antithesis of reason. Thus, man's nature being what it is, God could not have commanded that the passions should dominate the spiritual part of man, that hatred, anger, and concupiscence should be reckoned as right, and forgiveness of injuries, self-control and temperance should be punished as wrong.

It must not, however, be imagined from what we have said that God's hatred of sin is simply a disapprobation of the disordered, and that His love for the virtues of the just is a mere aesthetic approval of the perfect and the harmonious. It is far more than this. God is the last end of the creature. And the rational agent tends to God by the observance of the natural law. To disobey it is to refuse God as our end. It is to make our likes and our dislikes, and not God's will, the norm of our action. Sin is no aesthetic error, but the rejection of God. And on the other hand, the life of virtue is obedience inspired by love.

Yet God's inability to do evil places no restriction on His omnipotence. We have seen that when some property of finite creatures carries imperfection with it, God possesses all that there is in it of reality and perfection, but not the imperfection: and that this involves no limitation of His being. Such is the case here. Acts contrary to right reason involve imperfection of the gravest kind. God can do whatever is positive and perfect in such acts, but not what is imperfect. Our own power to do wrong is no perfection in us. It springs not from power, but from weakness -- from the blindness of the intellect and the infirmity of the will.

3. *The Divine omnipotence denied* -- 'A finite God.' Several recent philosophical writers have maintained that God is not infinite but finite:

that He is limited both in being and in power. The predicate 'Almighty,' it is said, is a relic of semi-civilized ages, in which men had not yet learned to conceive God in His ethical aspect as the God of Righteousness. We are bidden to remember 'how closely the associations of oriental monarchy have wound themselves round the God-idea,' and to trace the belief in His omnipotence to this source. The notion, we are assured, cannot be justified by the speculative reason. Since this opinion has obtained some vogue, it is necessary to discuss it and explain the grounds on which it is based. And this seems to be the most convenient place for doing so.

At many periods of human history the evil and the suffering of the world have given rise to dualist theories. The universe has been regarded as due, not to a single Creator, but to the operation of two opposite principles -- the one the source of all perfection and all order, the other the source of imperfection, privation and evil. Both Plato and Aristotle held that God's action had been limited by the pre-existent matter out of which He had formed the world; while the followers of Zoroaster, and later the Manichaeans, taught that over against God was set a hostile power, the spirit of evil, self-existent like Himself: and that the world was the theatre of a vast conflict between the two. Dualism as such is extinct. But the problem of evil is, undoubtedly, responsible in a measure for the somewhat similar doctrine of a finite God today. The theory first obtained a foothold in contemporary thought through the writings of William James.[5] He expressly declares that he cannot withstand the conclusion that the "sweat and tragedy of life" are not merely the conditions of spiritual growth in man, but that the very being of God Himself is thereby being perfected.

Yet so far as philosophical circles were concerned, the problem of evil played only a subsidiary part, and was by no means the main cause of the welcome accorded to James's suggestion of a finite God. The chief factor was the growing reaction against that idealist monism which for some decades had held a dominating position wherever the influence of Hegel was paramount. With this monism we shall deal at length in chapter xv. Here it must be enough to say that it rules out all individual personality, maintaining that we are not so many complete and distinct substances, but mere modes of that universal 'experience ' which constitutes the sole Real. Such a theory conflicts so sharply with the testimony of consciousness that a reaction was bound to follow. Hence James himself and other thinkers protested emphatically that, whatever philosophical speculation may say on the subject, individual personality is a fact which cannot be explained away. Now it is evident that if finite minds are real in the same sense that God is real -- in other words, *if there be no analogy of being* -- then God is not infinite: the Divine essence is limited by reality which is exclusive of God. It is idle to say that the existence of other minds brings enrichment, not limit, to God's being. Such an argument is its own refutation. A being susceptible of enrichment is not an infinite being. If God and finite minds mean more than God alone, as these writers hold, then God is limited. This is true, even if it be maintained that finite minds owe their existence to creation. But in point of fact this is not always admitted. One writer at least, Professor Howison (of the University of California), boldly maintains that minds are not due to efficient causation at all, but that, like God Himself, they are underived and self-existent: that God is *primus inter pares.* "The distinction between the soul and the God who recognizes it and redeems it, can never be truly stated as . . . a contrast between efficient cause and produced effect. . . . *No* mind can have an *efficient* relation to another mind."[6] He contends that "no being that arises out of efficient causation can be free": that even if we imagine it to be endowed with an inner principle of activity of its own "it is only apparently, not really, self-active. . . . It would be derived from the contriving thought of the maker, would be completely in subjection to that, must simply unfold and follow out the course implanted in it" (p. 332). It follows that we do not owe our being to any save ourselves. We simply *are.* God, however, does hold a certain supremacy -- the supremacy of the final cause of all. He is the "central guiding light in a realm of self-governing persons" (p. 61). Omnipotence, of course, disappears. The term, however, is retained, in accordance with that ancient practice by which the authors of revolutionary theories prefer to veil their full import by the employment of customary terminology. "Genuine omnipotence and omniscience," we are told, "are only to be realized in the control of *free* beings, and in inducing the divine image in them by moral influences instead of metaphysical and physical agencies: that is by final instead of efficient causation" (p. 64).

In view of what has been said in previous chapters a brief criticism of this theory will be sufficient here. We have already seen that self-subsistent being is of necessity infinite being: that if being is found hedged in by limits, the reason of the limit must be looked for in an external cause: that if it exists of itself and underived, it must exist in its plenitude -- not as restricted to this or that particular mode or type. In other words, for a finite nature to be the source of its own existence is, in the nature of things, a contradiction. A multitude of self-subsistent beings would be a multitude of infinites -- of Gods. Professor Howison is eager to deny that he supposes any such absurdity as this. But the absurdity is a necessary conclusion, which given his premises, must perforce follow.

Again: there is yet another metaphysical absurdity in the notion of a being which, though it has no efficient cause, has yet a final cause. What is self-subsistent, having no efficient cause outside itself, is thereby shown not to be dependent on any external causality. It exists of and for itself. To suppose that it needs a final cause external to itself is to suppose that it is not self-subsistent. If its actions need a final cause, so, of necessity, must its existence require one. And an external final cause can only determine a being to existence in so far as it moves an efficient cause to operate.

Furthermore, it is the merest unproved assertion that God cannot create a free being. To create at all, no matter what the object, demands, as will appear in the next chapter, infinite power. But, if it be once granted that God possesses infinite power, and employs it to call finite being into existence, there is no apparent reason why the created thing should not be a spirit; and if spiritual, free. Infinite power can effect whatever is not self-contradictory. No contradiction is contained in the notion of a created free being.

Other criticisms might be offered. But these will probably be sufficient. It has seemed worth while to call attention to this theory as one of the eccentricities of modern thought. It is little wonder that many able men hold philosophical speculation in little esteem, when it offers them systems so divorced from reality as this! What reasonable man will really believe for an instant that he is self-subsistent? He knows for certain that he is nothing of the kind. There was a time when men looked to metaphysics to vindicate the first principles without which no science of any kind is possible. Such is its true office. But this it will never accomplish until it is rescued from the chaos to which recent speculation has plunged it, and is brought back to the sure guidance of Aristotle and St. Thomas Aquinas.

The discussion of the problem of evil is reserved for our last chapter. It will there appear that neither the existence of physical nor of moral evil is irreconcilable with the goodness or with the omnipotence of God.

4. *Miracles.* Our treatment of the Divine omnipotence would be incomplete without some discussion of the possibility of the miraculous. Among the various questions with which Natural Theology deals, hardly one has been more debated during the last century than this. There is no reason here for surprise. Miracles are only intelligible if the creationist explanation of the world be true, and if the Creator takes a personal interest in the lives of men to the extent of interfering from time to time with physical law for moral ends. Neither pantheists, nor Kantians, nor materialists, have any room for the miraculous. Their respective systems exclude it altogether, and these important groups are reinforced by those who, though perhaps little interested in philosophical speculation, reject the idea of a direct Divine revelation. For the Creator's interference with physical law is usually held to have as one of its primary objects the authentication of a Divine message to mankind. To all of these the issue is vital. It is alleged that the occurrence of miracles can be established by adequate testimony. The opponents of the miraculous are thus called on to cope with the weightiest of all arguments -- the argument from facts. They meet it by contending that, even for the theist, the miraculous is open to fatal objections: and that for this reason theists no less than themselves are bound to reject the testimony offered, no matter what its apparent value. We maintain, on the contrary, that not merely are

miracles possible, but that no valid reason can be shown why God should not for wise and adequate ends intervene from time to time in human affairs by thus altering the normal course of nature.

A miracle may be defined as *a marvellous event, occurring within the sphere of sensible experience, which involves the suspension of some law of nature, and hence must be attributed to the direct action of God.* The definition demands that the event should be the object of sensible experience. A miracle is understood to be a sign -- to be a means employed by the Creator to compel the attention of His rational creatures to His immediate action. If it did not fall under our senses it would not serve this end. Catholic theology teaches that God does in fact suspend natural laws in cases where sensible perception is impossible, *e.g.*, in transubstantiation. These events it does not term miracles in the technical sense. The point at issue between theism and those who reject the miraculous is the possibility of a suspension of natural law. It will greatly assist us in forming a judgment on this subject if we consider first what is meant by a law of nature. It is manifest that before we can argue concerning the possibility of exceptions, we must know what laws of nature themselves are. A confusion of ideas on this subject would render the whole discussion futile. Yet there is little doubt that a good deal of confusion exists: and that some at least of the disputants have not taken the necessary preliminary step of clearing their ideas on this point.

A law of nature is *a uniform mode of activity which natural agents of the same type observe when placed in similar circumstances.* The agents of the material universe fall into definite classes -- species -- each of which is characterized by a series of properties possessed by every member of the class. Thus the specific properties of any given metal are everywhere the same. Pure lead, *e.g.*, has everywhere a specific gravity slightly more than 11,352 times that of water: it melts at 327.7 degrees c; it boils at a temperature between 1450 degrees and 1600 degrees. The same holds good as regards living things, whether of the vegetable or animal kingdom. Each type is marked by its own characteristics, its own way of acting. The oak will not produce the foliage of the acacia; nor will a sparrow's egg hatch into any other bird but a sparrow. We call these uniformities laws of nature. They are rightly termed necessary, though not all are necessary in quite the same measure. Under certain conditions some of them admit of modification. Both animals and plants occasionally produce individuals displaying some new and unexpected quality. Yet this does not show that the uniformity previously noted was not a law of nature, but merely that within the type lay concealed a certain potency of variation hitherto unobserved, which, given the requisite environment, would become apparent. What was conceived as rigidly necessary, was so only within certain limits. It is, further, to be noted that these properties are reckoned as generic or specific according as they are peculiar to a particular species or common to a wider class. There are some properties which are common to all material substances, *e.g.*, the laws of motion: others, to certain definite classes of greater or less extent. Hence a miracle may affect either a generic law or one peculiar to a species. The resuscitation of a dead body is an exception to a law common to all living substances. To walk on water would involve a change merely in a property of water, as such.

These properties are the original endowment of natural substances, conferred on them by the Creator. When He formed the various orders of being, animate and inanimate, He gave to each type its natural properties and its determined mode of acting. Man, in virtue of his reason, is rightly regarded as the lord of nature. But he exercises his dominion solely by employing substances in accordance with their respective laws. These prescribe the manner in which alone he may use them. These laws he is powerless to change in the least particular. In his regard they are necessary. But it does not follow that they are necessary where the Creator is concerned. He established them: and He can alter them. No consistent theist can doubt that it is within the divine competence to suspend the operation of any natural property, or to give to a substance some new property for the time being. He cannot, as we saw, make two lines enclose a space: for this would be a contradiction in terms. But no contradiction is involved if fire does not burn, or if water sustains a body heavier than itself. The substance remains what it was; only the operation of a particular property is suspended.

The difference between the meaning of the term 'law' as used to denote these fixed modes of physical activity and as used of some positive enactment, whether made by God or by some human authority, must be carefully observed.[7] The two senses are only connected by an analogy. In the latter case the efficient principle is the decree of the superior in so far as it is obligatory on the will of his subjects. The same single decree is operative in every instance: and if a dispensation is given, it is a dispensation from the binding force of this decree. But it is quite otherwise in regard of a law of nature. Here the efficient principle is not something common to all, but a physical property inherent in the individual. If a miracle occurs, it is this individual substance alone which undergoes change. The point deserves attention. For many, in dealing with this subject, speak as though some enactment were in question, and the suspension affected, not an individual substance, but a general decree. They seem to imply that a miracle involves two contrary acts of will on the part of the Creator -- one imposing the law on a class and including within its scope every individual of the species, the other granting an exception.

Not merely is miraculous action not impossible to God; but it may justly be said to be no less natural to Him than his action in accordance with the particular specific properties with which He has endowed substances. Indeed, there seems to be an antecedent probability of His adopting this course. We see, in fact, a valid reason for divine intervention in the ordinary course of nature. The physical order of the universe is not the only order which He has instituted. The moral order likewise owes its existence to Him. This, too, has fixed laws, though they are very different from the laws of which we have been speaking. The sphere of their operation is the free will of man: and the ultimate purpose of this order is that man by his observance of its laws should tend towards God as his last end. It is true that the ordinary course of nature suffices to make God's existence known to men. Yet they are terribly prone to forget Him altogether, and to live as though there were no God. More than this: the story of the past shews that even when they reflect on these subjects, the human mind tends, by a strange perversity, to misinterpret the testimony of created things. On the one hand it falls into pantheism and identifies the Creator with His works: and on the other it lapses into materialism, declaring that the universe with all its wonders is simply the chance collocation of atoms. In view of the issues at stake it is not wonderful that God, for the sake of the higher order, should make exceptions in the lower. For no way is better suited than miraculous intervention to compel His rational creatures to recognize His existence and His supremacy over that order of nature which seems to so many to be the All. In this way miracles become an effective means to save mankind from disastrous error. Those who deny the possibility of the miraculous usually argue as though the physical were the sole order. And they conclude that it is inconceivable that God should mar its harmony by an exception. The divine government of the world must be considered in its entirety. When that is done, it will appear that the miraculous may have its due place in the whole, and may afford a signal example alike of God's wisdom and His mercy.

All that we have said about the antecedent probability of the miraculous acquires double force if there is question of a divine revelation. Theism affirms that such a thing is possible. And though theism does not necessarily involve belief in a revelation, yet, historically considered, the two are seen generally to go together. Indeed, if it is incumbent on all men, of whatever degree of culture, to recognize God as their last end and to direct their lives to Him, it must be admitted that a revelation is morally necessary. In view of the wide prevalence of error, how shall the uneducated, or the half-educated, and those who are occupied from morning to night with the urgent duties of daily life, attain to certainty regarding the most essential truths, if speculative reason be man's only guide. But if a revelation be given, it must be authenticated: a dubious revelation is none at all. It must be marked with the Divine character, and that in such a way as shall be plain to see, even for those who are uncultivated and ignorant. Here it is that miracles have their true function. Precisely as exceptions to the laws of nature, they fulfil their natural and appropriate office as the seal which authenticates the communication, the sign-manual putting its authority beyond all doubt, and as such suited to the capacity of all alike, whatever their condition or degree. Viewed as instruments for this end miracles have their own special place in the divine plan: and so far from being discordant notes marring an otherwise perfect scheme, they enter as integral elements into the total harmony.

In the light of what has been said the customary objections against miracles present very little difficulty. Some mention, however, must be made of the more important. It is urged that they are inconsistent with the Divine wisdom: that it is inconceivable that it should be needful for God to correct errors in the order which He has established. "To suppose," says an eminent Protestant divine, "that He by continual interventions sets at nought that whole system of His universe which is the manifestation of His Divine Reason, in order to remedy continual defects, is to reduce cosmos to chaos."[8] It will be observed that such an argument is only of force if it be assumed that the order of nature is the only order which God has instituted, and that miracles are requisite because it fails to achieve the purpose intended by God. No theist has ever explained miracles thus. We have seen that the change in the physical order is employed, not for an end proper to that order, but for one which lies outside its scope, viz., to manifest the personal intervention of God by a striking and unmistakable sign, and more particularly to authenticate a Divine message. Such an argument Inerely evinces that the writer who makes use of it has failed even to understand the theist position.

A more specious objection, though equally invalid, is that proposed by Kant, viz., that if we admit the possibility of exceptions in physical law, we have no guarantee that God may not act in the same way in regard to moral law; but that alterations in the moral law are inconceivable, since, were such exceptions possible, all our assurance regarding right and wrong action would be taken from us, and the foundations of morality would thus be overthrown. We have in substance replied to this difficulty earlier in the chapter (§ 2), and there is no need for us to discuss the point afresh. The moral law does not take its origin from the positive decree of God. Actions are right and wrong in themselves -- because they are what they are. It is as impossible for God to make a wrong action right as to make a triangle which shall not have three angles. And the will which deliberately adheres to a wrong action is, apart from all question of a Divine precept enjoining the moral law, an evil will. It is altogether otherwise as regards physical laws. Here we are dealing with what is absolutely dependent on the divine choice. God was in no way bound to give to this or that substance that special mode of action: and having given it, He remains free to alter it.

An argument frequently employed by the spokesmen of that scientific materialism which was so widespread during the latter half of the nineteenth century was the alleged incompatibility of miracles with physical science. Physical science, it was urged, consists in the power to predict the action of natural agents. Its very basis is the absolute uniformity of nature. Unless this principle be accepted as valid always and everywhere, science is at an end. But to assert the possibility of miracles is to call in question the universality of this principle, and equivalently to deny the worth of science. Yet the progress of the human race is neither more nor less than the ever-advancing march of science. Even the theist should see that miracles are irreconcilable with that supreme wisdom which he believes God to possess. So argued that vigorous disputant, Huxley. And the argument is still often advanced as though it were conclusive. Yet it is thoroughly fallacious. Science does not consist precisely in prediction. Its conclusions would not be rendered less valuable, even if a miraculous exception should occur: nor would the principle of uniformity, as rightly understood, be thereby shaken. Science consists in the knowledge of the universal as distinguished from the particular. We reach scientific knowledge when we pass from an experience of particular instances to a knowledge of the type: when we are able to affirm that the oak *as such*, or that iron as such, has these or those properties. But this knowledge is valid, even if in certain individual cases God should bring about exceptions to the rule. Even though on a given occasion fire should have no effect on a human body, it remains no less true that fire as such burns.

Nor is the principle of uniformity affected. The same cause in similar circumstances produces the same result, because the connection between agent and patient is one of true causal efficiency, and not a mere time-relation of antecedent and consequent. The reason of the effect is to be sought in the respective natures of the agent and the patient. The result is that of which such an agent is connaturally productive when it operates on such material. It follows that natural agents act with absolute uniformity. Reason compels us to hold that the Divine omnipotence has power to impede that uniformity, and to make the agent operate in an unwonted manner. But in admitting God's power to do this we are not invalidating the principle of the uniformity of nature.

Such are the chief controversial arguments brought to show the impossibility of miracles. In themselves they are of but little weight. As we said above, the real reason for the rejection of the miraculous is to be sought, not in these objections, but in the philosophical presuppositions of the opponents. Miracles are only conceivable if we admit the existence of a personal God distinct from the world which He has made. If nature be the All -- if there be no God, or if the universe be, not the work of His hands, but the necessary expression of His being -- then miracles are out of the question. It only remains for us now to speak of another mode of attack, viz., the contention that, however wonderful an event may be, it can never be certain that it is a divine sign: it may always be attributed to some unknown law of nature. The difficulty, it must be said, is a strange one: for it denies to God what is within the power of man. Men can find ways to guarantee their works as genuinely theirs: no one maintains that it is impossible to do this. Yet we are asked to believe that the wisdom and omnipotence of God find the task too much for them: that God is unable to stamp a work as His in such a manner as shall give us real certainty regarding its authorship. Surely this is the mere extravagance of controversy. Indeed, it is not hard to show that many of the events which claim to be miraculous are such that it is wholly impossible to refer them to unknown laws of nature. Such, *e.g.*, is the instantaneous restoration of decayed tissue or of missing portions of bone. We know enough of the methods of nature's laboratory to be aware that the building up of flesh and bone, even when conditions are most favourable, takes place very gradually: that the cells are formed one by one out of materials furnished by the blood: that no medical skill can avail to make the process a rapid one. Bone is formed from the phosphate of lime which exists in the blood: and in case of a fracture this is slowly supplied to the broken ends to effect the consolidation. The amount of this salt contained in the blood at any one time is not more than twenty grains. If then a piece of bone is suddenly restored demanding far more phosphate of lime than the body contains, we have proof which admits of no question.[9] Even more clear, if possible, is the case of a raising from the dead. Here the essential condition of recovery is absent. For there can be no healing save through the instrumentality of the vital principle. Yet this, by reason of the havoc wrought in the body by natural sickness or by violence, has left it. If, then, some power does in fact restore the body, and further unites the soul to it again, that power can only be divine. In works which deal *ex professo* with miracles, the various criteria to be employed to distinguish true miracles from events, which may reasonably be attributed to the unexpected operation of created causes, meet with full discussion. To enter on this subject would carry us beyond our limits. It is sufficient for us to have shewn that God is able to work miracles, and to do so in such wise that it is evident beyond all possibility of doubt that the work proceeds from the divine omnipotence.

NOTES

{1} See the passage from *Physics*, III., c. iii., cited above, p. 89. cf. Farges, *Théorie de l'acte et de la puissance* (Paris, 1895), p. 85; De Régnon, *Métaphysique des causes*, 1. iii. a. 3, p. 191.

{2} [Actio] transiens perficit non solum agens emanando ex ipso, sed etiam perficit effectum causando ipsum. Joan. a S. Thoma. *Phil. Nat.* I., q. 14, art. 4.

{3} St. Thomas Aq., *Con. Gent.*, I., c. xxv., n. 8. "Quia potentiae activae objectum et effectus est *ens factum* (nulla autem potentia operationem habet ubi deficit ratio sui objecti, sicut visus non videt deficiente visibili in actu) oportet quod Deus dicatur non posse quidquid est contra rationem *entis* in quantum est ens, vel *facti entis* in quantum est factum."

{4} Leibniz attributes this opinion in its most uncompromising form to Samuel Rutherford (1600-1661), a well-known covenanting divine, at one time professor of divinity at St. Andrews. "Samuel Retorfort, professeur en théologie en Ecosse dit positivement que rien n'est injuste ou moralement mauvais par rapport à Dieu et avant sa défense: ainsi sans cette défense il serait indifférent d'assassiner ou de sauver un homme, d'aimer Dieu ou de le haïr, de le louer ou de le blasphémer." *Théodicée,* &secr; 176,

{5} Mill broached the view in his *Three Essays on Religion* (1874), p. 36, seqq. It was noticed as an interesting speculation, but found no support.

{6} *The Limits of Evolution and other Essays,* by G. H. Howison (London, 1905), p. 73.

{7} On this important distinction, cf. McTaggart, *Some Dogmas,* etc., § 189.

{8} Dr. C. D'Arcy, Archbishop of Dublin, in a paper read at the Leicester Church Congress, 1919: see the *Guardian* for October 16, 1919, p 1,048.

{9} On this subject see *Medical Proof of the Miraculous* by Dr. E. Le Bec (Eng. trans. 1922).

Part III. God in His Relation to the World.

Chapter XIV. Creation.

1.   The Idea of Creation.

2.   Proof of Creation.

3.   Creation and the Immutability of God.

4.   God's Freedom in Creation.

5.   The Exemplar Causality of God.

6.   The Purpose of Creation.

1. *The idea of creation.* By Creation is signified the act by which God freely produced as a reality other than Himself a universe which before this act had no existence in any form. The world, it is here asserted, is not as pantheists maintain, an aspect of God Himself: nor, as the materialists declare, self-existent. God gave it being as its efficient cause: and in doing this He called into existence a reality external to Himself. This externality of the world in regard of God must not, however, be understood as denying His omnipresence. God is immanent as well as transcendent. In treating of His immensity we have shewn that He is intimately present to all His creatures. But the creature is 'other' than God. Moreover, the universe had no existence previous to the creative act. God did not form it of pre-existing matter, for there was none such: nor did He draw it forth from His own substance, as was held by those ancient thinkers who professed one or other of the various emanationist theories.

Two definitions of creation employed by the Scholastic writers will serve to elucidate the idea. (1) *Creatio est productio rei secundum totam suam substantiam* -- the production of a thing in regard of its whole substance. Production, so far as our experience goes, is never production of the whole substance of a thing: in every case it supposes subject-matter. In other words we are familiar with change but not with creation. We have experience of substantial change, such as takes place when a living creature is generated, and matter thereby receives a new substantial form: and of accidental change, as when the sculptor gives to the marble the new shape which makes it a statue. But there is always a subject in which the production takes place. Creation, on the other hand, is a production of the whole substance without a subject of any kind. St. Thomas, when giving this definition, adds to it the words "nothing being presupposed whether created or uncreated," thus ruling out the notion of a subject in set terms.[1]

(2) *Creatio est productio rei ex nihilo sui et subjecti* -- the production of a thing from a previous nonexistence alike of itself and of any subject-matter. The former definition had reference to the *terminus ad quem* of creation; this one expresses the *terminus* a quo, and declares creation to be production out of nothing. In every real production the result is produced *ex nihilo sui* -- from a previous non-existence of itself. The form of the statue has no existence until the sculptor gives it being in the marble. Creation, however, is distinguished by this, that in its case even a subject-matter is wanting.

It might seem unnecessary to explain that the phrase 'production out of nothing' is not to be understood as signifying that 'nothing' in some way serves the Creator as a material cause, were it not that opponents of the doctrine still appear to attribute some such meaning to it.[2] Yet the Scholastics were careful to give the term its true explanation. The expression 'ex nihilo fieri,' says St. Thomas, may legitimately be taken in two senses. We may understand the phrase (1) as simply signifying the order of succession, exactly as it is permissible to say *Ex mane fit meridies*, though the relation of morning to midday is purely one of temporal succession. Or again (2) we may take it as signifying that though the world is produced, it is not produced out of anything. Thus we sometimes say of a man that he is sad about nothing, meaning that there is no reason for his sadness.[3]

It is not to be denied that the notion of a causality which extends to the whole substantial reality of a thing is something quite remote from our experience. We recognize without difficulty the fact of causal activity in the world. We see around us on all sides agents determining other things to new modes of being. But causation such as that which the doctrine of creation supposes has no parallel in our surroundings. This need not mean that the notion involves any repugnance. Indeed, a little reflection on the limits which hedge in the causality exercised by finite agents, will shew us that it could not be otherwise. Where the causality of finite beings is in question, the power exercised is necessarily finite. And for this very reason it is requisite that it should act upon a subject -- a material cause -- which possesses a potency in regard of the achieved result. For in this case the interval between the *terminus a quo* and the *terminus ad quem* of the action is finite and therefore not incompatible with a finite causal power. It is manifest that the interval between these two must be commensurate with the causal power exercised. In proportion as the *terminus a quo* is more remote from the result to be achieved, will more power be required to attain the *terminus ad quem* and realize this result. It follows that only an infinite power can produce the whole substantial reality of a thing without subject-matter of any kind: for the result in this case involves the transition from sheer nonentity to being, and the distance between these *termini* is infinite. On the other hand, finite causality demands, as we said, as an essential condition of its exercise a real potency, and in consequence a real material cause. And since our experience is limited to finite agents, it is plain that creative causality can have no parallel within the sphere of our immediate knowledge.

We may reach the same conclusion in another way. The action of a finite being is necessarily an accident.[4] But an action which is an accident demands a subject in which it can take effect: it is impossible that it should result in the production of a substance without subject-matter of any kind. This is evident. Transitive action, as we have seen (ch. xiii., § 1), is the effect viewed as proceeding from the agent. If, then, the action is accidental, that effect can only be a modification of a pre-existing subject. Now creation excludes the idea of such a subject. It is by definition *the production of a thing in regard of its whole substance*. It follows that creation is beyond the power of any finite agent, and is only conceivable where we are concerned with a being whose action is identical with his substance. [5]

We have thus shewn by two independent lines of reasoning that a finite cause is, as such, incapable of effecting the production of a substance in its totality, but requires of necessity subject-matter for its operation. It follows that physical agents -- and these alone fall within the range of our experience -- can never shew us anything which resembles creative action. For this reason the mind must always find the idea of creation a difficult one. Imagination has no means of representing such an event.

We have enlarged on this point for a special reason. For we are now in a position to ask ourselves the question: Is the idea of creation *ex nihilo* absurd? Is it one which, when analysed, the mind cannot entertain, but rejects as self-contradictory? It is evident that there is no such internal contradiction. The idea of a divine act productive of a substantial reality from a previous non-existence alike of itself and of any subject, consists of simple and intelligible elements, which are not repugnant to each other. The notion of causality as such does not exclude the idea of the production of substantial reality. And though the finite causality with which we are familiar does not admit of such an effect, we have seen that there is no reason to extend this impossibility to God. Our reasoning went far to shew, that since He is infinite, and since His activity is not accidental but is identical with His substance, the production of the complete. substance lies within His power. In the course of the chapter we shall examine the objections urged against the doctrine of creation on the ground of its alleged incompatibility with certain of the Divine attributes -- infinity, immutability, liberty. It will appear that in no case is such incompatibility capable of proof.

2. *Proof of creation*. To those who have studied the previous chapters, and have realized what is involved in the concept of self-existent being on the one hand, and of contingent being on the other, a set proof that God created all things other than Himself will hardly be necessary. The arguments of chap. iii., by which, from the contingent, mutable, multiple

things of experience we established the existence of the Necessary, the Uncaused, the Changeless, the One, will be seen to involve creation as an immediate corollary. If two such realities exist, there is no other possible explanation of the origin of the one whose reality is on the lower plane, than that it was produced *ex nihilo* by the Self-existent. Yet since it may be urged that our reasoning failed to touch explicitly on the subject of creation *ex nihilo*, it seems desirable to express the arguments in a form leading directly to that conclusion. It should be noted that we do not here enter into the question whether the world had a beginning or not. We are solely concerned to shew that it is due as regards the whole of its reality to an act of divine causation, apart from which it would have no being of any kind. This is equally true whether it had a temporal beginning or existed from all eternity.

It is manifest that necessary being, and necessary being alone, is the sufficient reason for its own existence. Necessary being possesses existence in its own right. Other things have in their own right no existence at all. They are not exigent of existence. If existence belonged to their essential nature, they could not be at one time mere unrealized possibles, and subsequently be determined to the possession of real existence; they would exist *ab aeterno*. But a nature which is not exigent of existence is of itself nothing. Whatever removes it from nonentity it has received from elsewhere. In other words, if it exists at all it has been produced *ex nihilo*: it owes its existence to creation.[6] Now the finite substances which form the universe are all contingent. Neither any one of them in particular, nor the whole collection of them, is necessary being. We treated this matter in chap. iii., and the arguments there employed have been immensely reinforced by the demonstration subsequently given that necessary, self-existent being must be infinite in perfection. There is no need for us to go over the same ground here, especially as in the next chapter, in which we deal with anti-creationist theories, a certain amount of repetition will be unavoidable. It will be sufficient to remind our readers that the universe of which we form part has no characteristic more fundamental than change. Change in its various forms -- substantive transformation, qualitative and quantitative modification, local motion -- meets us on every side. Nothing is exempt from it. And change is wholly incompatible with necessary being. In view of what has been already said on the matter, there is little need to labour the point. It is of the very essence of motion that the thing moved should pass through successive stages of actuation. Throughout its course it is in potency to some mode of being. But that being is not yet actualized. It is *becoming* something; but has not yet attained *being* in that regard. It is *in fieri*; but it can only possess the *esse* to which the *fieri* is directed, when the motion ceases. Motion stamps its subject as imperfect. On the other hand, necessary being is as such actual and perfect. It needs no process to actualize it. In so far as it is not actual, it is not necessary.[7]

We tend, it is true, to regard motion as something additional to mere being. It is looked on as involving an increment of perfection, as something which is an advance on any mere static condition, and we find it hard to grasp the truth that ultimate Perfection must of necessity be changeless. This erroneous view of motion is attributable to the fact that we regard it, not in its relation to the *terminus ad quem* towards which it is directed, but in its relation to the *terminus a quo*. It is natural that we should do so, so long as we allow mere sense-perception to rule our consideration rather than the rational intellect. For in the order of time the *terminus ad quem* is subsequent to the motion and does not appear to determine it in any way. Yet the true aspect under which to regard motion is, as we have already shown, as a passage to the *terminus ad quem*.[8] This is the end to which it is directed. It is what it is by reason of its relation to that end. Indeed, essentially it is a mere tendency towards that term. Save as tending to that term, the subject of motion would not move in that direction rather than another. It would be capable of moving in many directions, but would not actually move in any.

Another argument no less decisive may be drawn from the henologicai proof of God's existence. In that proof we urged that, unless we were prepared to reject the principle of sufficient reason, we must admit that when the same perfection is found in a number of different individuals, it is derived from a single source: that it is philosophically impossible to maintain that they possess it Independently, that unity cannot have its ultimate explanation in diversity. And we further argued that the ultimate source of the transcendental perfections, being, goodness, and truth -- perfections in the notion of which is involved no imperfection or limit -- could be none other than One in whom they are realized in an infinite degree, Himself at the same time subsistent being and subsistent goodness. It is hardly necessary to point out that creation follows by immediate consequence from this conclusion. For if finite things owe all the being which they possess to the causative activity of the Infinite Being, viz. God, so that, in so far as they are at all, they are effects produced by Him, it is plain that apart from this Divine activity they are nothing -- mere nonentity. They have been transferred from nothingness to being by Him. In other words, He created them *ex nihilo*. It may be asked perhaps whether we are not somewhat hasty in our assumption that the Infinite Being produces finite beings by efficient causality? May it not be that they arise by some kind of emanation? We have already excluded such a supposition. For finite things are limited. And we pointed out above that to suppose necessary being to be realized in limited modes is to postulate a cause which is capable of acting upon necessary being and bringing it into composition with a limitative principle. This, however, is out of the question. There can be no such thing as a cause capable of acting on necessary being.

These arguments give us apodictic proof that every finite substance is due to creation *ex nihilo*. Yet it is notorious that this conclusion is widely rejected. The philosophy prevalent in the universities is pantheism in one or other of its forms: while outside the seats of learning a more or less crude materialism has a wide vogue. 'Evolution' is held to be a sufficient explanation of all things. It is believed that the primaeval world-stuff somehow gave rise to living organisms, and ultimately issued in man -- the less producing the greater, and perfectionless matter raising itself without efficient agency of any sort to those miracles of beauty and of contrivance with which the world is filled. These opponent theories must be carefully weighed. But it will appear that they involve far more serious objections than any which can be urged against the creationist solution. This in itself constitutes an additional, if indirect, proof of our thesis. This examination of rival views we reserve for another chapter. For the present we must confine ourselves to the further elucidation of the doctrine of creation and to the removal of difficulties which have been urged against it.

3. *Creation and the immutability of God.* In considering whether creation is compatible with the attributes which reason compels us to ascribe to God, it might seem natural to begin with the attribute of infinity. The objection can scarcely fail to suggest itself that a being who creates a world external to and other than Himself, is by that alone shewn not to be Himself the Infinite: for the infinity of God supposes that His being is exhaustive of all reality. We have, however, already had occasion to treat this point, and have seen that it admits of a perfectly satisfactory solution (chap. ix., § 3). Finite things are real; but they cannot add to the reality of the Infinite.

We may pass on to the question whether the difficulties which arise in connection with the Divine immutability are surmountable. Here it is to be noted that we are concerned with creation viewed as an event occurring in time and not realized *ab aeterno*. Although we have stated that in our opinion it cannot be established by mere reason that God might not, had such been His good pleasure, have given being to the universe from all eternity, nevertheless we claim that reason can demonstrate that a temporal creation is within the scope of His omnipotence: that no impossibility is involved in the supposition that the universe once had no existence, and that it came into being at a certain moment, which, however remote, is separated from the present by a finite interval measurable in terms of time. This conclusion is of no little importance. Christian dogma affirms that the world is not infinite in duration: that it had a beginning. On the other hand, it is confidently maintained by a certain school of philosophical opinion that creation is involved in the very being of God: that it is no free act on His part, but one that is absolutely necessary. We shall treat of this view in the next section. Those who hold it seek, not unnaturally, to shew that the position for which we are contending is open to fatal objections and is incapable of a reasoned defence. It is urged (1) that what God regards as a good to be realized must be viewed by Him as such from all eternity, and in consequence must be realized eternally and immutably: that the theist doctrine of a long delay and of a subsequent change to creative activity is repugnant to reason. Thus Professor Ward writes: "Whatever the reason or motive for creation may have been -- and some reason or motive the theist must assume -- it seems 'absolutely inconceivable,' as von Hartmann puts it, 'that a conscious God should wait half an eternity without a good that ought to be.'"{9}

It is further contended (2) that an exercise of causal power, previously quiescent, is in itself a new perfection -- an increment in the being of the causal agent. Hence, to assert that God creates in time is to hold that He undergoes change and acquires perfection by creating. But God is perfect by nature, and immutable because perfect.{10}

It is worth noting that this question was an extremely vital one in the mediaeval schools. Aristotle had maintained the eternity of the world (*Phys.*, viii. 3; *De C. et M.* ii. i): and the Averroists of the thirteenth and fourteenth centuries defended his view, and urged it as a fatal objection to the Christian doctrine on the subject. They laid special stress on the reason last given, viz., that a new action is impossible apart from a passage from potentiality to act in the agent.{11} Their various arguments are examined in detail by St. Thomas: and he offers us a full and adequate solution of each of the difficulties urged.{12}

Before proceeding to the discussion of the points raised, it may be noted that the alternative offered by modern pantheism, so far from removing the difficulty, gravely increases it. We are told that creationism is impossible since it logically involves a single change in the Godhead, and we are bidden accept in its place a doctrine which requires us to hold that unintermittent change is a necessary condition of the Divine Being. For the thinkers to whom we refer affirm that the world, of which every part is in perpetual flux, is one with God. It may at least be said for creationism that, consistently or inconsistently, it declares that God is changeless, and that He creates the world without any change occurring in Himself. Pantheists, on the other hand, are held to the glaring contradiction of holding that change is an essential condition in the very being whom in controversy they own to be immutable.

The first of the two difficulties which we have mentioned arises, as is evident, from that fruitful source of fallacy, the representation of eternity as though it were simply time without commencement and without end. When von Hartmann asks how God can be supposed to have waited half an eternity before creating, he clearly regards eternity and time as durations of similar character. In view of our treatment of the Divine attribute of eternity there is no need to enlarge on this point. There was no time until God created the universe. Only when things came into being, whose existence is not actualized in all its parts simultaneously, but is ever advancing from potentiality to actuality in a continuous progression of successive and homogeneous parts, did time exist. God did not create the universe at a given point of time, but created time with the universe. The term 'waiting' has no significance as applied to eternity. Nor is it less meaningless to say that God could have created the universe before He actually did. For in what sense can the words 'before' and 'after' be understood, save in reference to an existing flow of time? It is doubtless possible to ask why time had any beginning at all -- why the universe was not created *ab aeterno*? To this subject we shall recur later in this chapter. Here it is sufficient to point out that the difficulty with which we are concerned, viz., that the long delay involved in the doctrine of a temporal creation is repugnant to the Divine wisdom, is based upon a sophism.[13] Moreover, the argument is open to exception on another count. It is urged that the theist must own that the same motives which induced God to create when He did, were present to the Divine mind from all eternity: and hence, since *ex hypothesi* they sufficed to move the Divine will at last, they must perforce have produced the same result from the very first. Here we find the objector assuming that God's will is conditioned in the same manner as that of the creature: that He is aware of certain objects of desire, which He does not possess, and which in some way will conduce to the perfection of His state: and that being guided in His volitions by right reason, He must needs allow His will to be swayed by these motives. On the principles of theism, which we claim to have established by adequate proof, such reasoning involves manifest errors. It assumes that God does not possess in Himself the plenitude of beatitude: that He may be in some way dependent on the existence of creatures for the attainment of some more perfect state: and, further, it supposes that the Divine action -- which is identical with the Divine essence -- is determined by creatures. Our discussion of the Divine will has shewn how radical are the misconceptions here. God, assuredly, creates for a purpose. Of that purpose we shall treat in a subsequent section of the present chapter. But there can be no question of a motive which rules the Divine activity, and has force to determine its exercise. Neither the Divine excellence nor the Divine beatitude can gain aught from creation. The creature, not God, is the gainer when God gives it being.

We have now to examine the second of the two difficulties mentioned, viz., that any fresh exercise of efficient causality is *ipso facto* a new actuality in the agent, and in consequence involves in him a change by which he acquires a greater perfection. This, as we saw, was the primary argument of the Averroist opponents of the faith. They maintained that it was impossible that a new action could take place without a transition from potency to act.

To this it is replied that God possesses in Himself *ab aeterno* all the perfection requisite to the actual exercise of causality. In Him there is no potency of any kind. In created agents the exercise of causality involves a passage from potency to act, because while nature gives them the power to act, the power needs a complement in order to its actual exercise. They are not actualized as causes save by such a complementary change. God needs no such complement to His actuality. It is true that, though He is fully constituted as a cause from all eternity, His effect does not proceed from Him eternally, but has a beginning in time. But this is because its realization depends on His free-will, and in consequence comes to pass as and when He decrees.[14]

What then, it may be asked, do we mean, when we speak of God's *act of creation*? We have already (chap. xiii., § 1) called attention to the two uses of the word action. It is, we saw, employed to signify (1) the process by which an agent passes from a condition of potential to one of actual causality -- the acquisition, in other words, of the complement to which we have just adverted. Thus the action of writing is often taken to mean the various bodily movements requisite before the letters actually take shape on the paper. It signifies (2) the effect in so far as it emanates from the agent, *e.g.*, the actual *fieri* of the script itself. The former of these two senses is, as we explained, philosophically inaccurate, since until all these motions are complete, the agent is not fully constituted as cause of the writing: and till he is so constituted, the real action of writing is impossible. Yet such a use of the term is inevitable. For we rightly conceive action as intermediate between cause and the abiding effect: and so far as the perceptions of sense are concerned, this preliminary process is what appears to hold this place.

When, therefore, we ask, what is the act of creation, our question may signify: What are we to conceive in God as being the immediate principle of His creative activity? or: What is the effect immediately issuing from God as actually creative? In the first sense, we say that inasmuch as God needs no complement to His causal power, the act of creation is the Divine essence, eternal and immutable, viewed in its relation to the new created order. In the latter sense, the act of creation is the created order itself, as newly existing, and in its relation to the Creator as dependent on Him for being. It is no process of *fieri*: for the creature does not pass by degrees from nonentity to being. Either it is not, or it is. The act of creation is simply the newly fashioned universe in its relation to God. As we have already explained (chap. viii., § 3), the relation of the creature to the Creator, and that of the Creator to the creature, are widely different. The former is a 'real' relation: the dependence of the creature on the Creator is a real determination of its being. The latter is 'conceptual' only. The Creator acquires no new determination when He creates: the Infinite does not become part of a wider whole embracing alike Himself and finite things, so that He is ordered in some way to them. But our mind views Him in connection with them, and therefore relates Him to them in thought, because they are related to Him.[15]

4. *God's freedom in creation.* We mentioned above the existence of a school whose adherents, while prepared to admit a doctrine of creation, deny that God was free not to create. The world, they maintain, is 'as necessary to God, as God is necessary to the world.' From this it follows that creation took place *ab aeterno.* The thinkers who adopt this position are those who, while accepting a large measure of Hegelian idealism, nevertheless claim to be theists and not pantheists, inasmuch as they hold the existence of a personal God, the Supreme Spirit, who is distinct from the finite personalities which owe their being to Him. In England this idea of creation has been defended in our own time by several writers of influence. We may mention among the number, Professor Pringle Pattison, Principal J. Caird and Dr. Rashdall. It calls, therefore, for our consideration.

A word must first be said about the Hegelian idealism from which it sprang. This system, though owing its origin to the speculations of Kant, was none the less in great measure a reaction against his theories. Hegel rejected *in toto* the distinction between noumena and phenomena. He denied the existence of a world of realities which we can never hope to know, and our judgments regarding which, so far as we can judge about them at all, must inevitably be conditioned by subjective categories of the understanding precisely as are our judgments regarding phenomena. There is, he contended, no noumenal reality outside the facts of experience. The universe which we know is the sole reality. It is thought and being at once: for being has no existence apart from thought. It is, moreover, self-existent and necessary. But the necessity which Hegel attributed to the universe differs widely from that which the creationist attributes to God. For, whereas the creationist views God as self-existent being, Hegel conceives the universe to exist in virtue of a logical necessity belonging to the order of thought. The supreme idea, he holds, involves its own reality. The question forthwith arises: Is there any room in such a system for God? To Kant God was a noumenal reality. Is the idea of God a pure figment of the imagination? It was answered, God is the supreme Idea which finds its self-realization in the universe. The universe is the Divine thought. We are thus justified in retaining the notion of

God as the source of all things. The answer may be understood in various senses: and, as we shall see in the next chapter, Hegel and his real followers were far from intending to signify a belief in a personal God. But a certain number of those who accept his general philosophical position are not prepared to go this length, and have sought to find room in it for religious belief, and even for the acceptance of a modified form of Christianity.

The world, these writers tell us, is the thought of God, the term and likewise the object of the immanent intellectual process which constitutes His life. It has and can have no being outside God: for being outside experience there is none. It is then in no sense an external embodiment of the Divine thought. It is that thought in its objective aspect. We finite spirits know the world because we are admitted to share in the Divine life, the Divine experience. Hence thought as realized in us offers the same experience as does the thought of God. Here lies the solution of the problem involved in the fact, otherwise so enigmatic, that the world presented to all finite minds is one and the same. Creation thus understood is necessarily *ab aeterno*. The Divine life is eternal, and consists in thought: and a thinking subject is impossible apart from an object distinct from itself. Moreover, when it is once realized that the universe is the thought of God, it is seen that God could not have created any other universe than that which we know. For the universe of experience is exhaustive of the Divine being. Or to speak accurately, it is identical with the Divine being. It is the complete and ultimate expression of God's essence.

This last point is of such importance that we quote Professor Pringle Pattison's own words. It is true, he tells us, both of God and of finite minds, that they "cannot be substantiated as static units apart from the process in which they live or which constitutes their life. In the case of the finite conscious being this is fairly obvious, for he plainly receives his filling from nature, and is reduced at once to a bare point or empty focus if we attempt to lift him as an independent unitary existence, out of the universal life from which he draws his spiritual sustenance. But it is apt not to be so obvious in the case of God. And yet in this ultimate reference it is equally essential to be clear on the point, if we are not to involve ourselves in meaningless speculation. . . . Even a theory like Hegel's, which insists so strongly on the idea of creation as an eternal act or an eternal process, seems repeatedly by its form of statement to suggest just that prior existence of the bare universal, which it is the essence of the theory to deny."[16] In other words: God, if viewed apart from the universe, has no being save a logical one. Where thought is concerned, we inevitably distinguish subject from object. But we should greatly err if we regarded this subject as possessed of independent reality apart from the thoughts which we view as his. As such he is merely a focal point to which we logically refer the 'experience' in question. So it is as regards God. God is constituted by His thought.

"The only real creation," the same author assures us, "is that of minds." [17] Yet it is manifest that on the principles of this philosophy it is difficult to defend the creation even of minds as subsistent entities external to God. If we are to be thoroughly consistent, they too must resolve themselves into divine experience without subsistent reality of their own. Hence we are not surprised when what is given us with one hand is promptly taken away by the other. "Creation," we are told, "if it is taken to mean anything akin to efficient causation, is totally unfitted to express any relation that can exist between spirits. Spirits cannot be regarded as things made, detached like products from their maker."[18]

It is clear that we have here reached an impasse. On the premises of this philosophy the existence of finite minds, which are not merely, like the other parts of the universe, terms of the Divine thought, but personalities to whom the Divine thought is communicated, and who thus share in the Divine life, is wholly inexplicable. It can be maintained only at the price of manifest inconsistency. And indeed no explanation is offered us: the two parts of the system are left unreconciled.

Apart from the general principles of their philosophical system, the thinkers who defend creation *ab aeterno*, lay stress on another consideration. God, they say, would not possess the fullness of life did He not call finite creatures into existence and enter into relation with them. "May we not say," writes Principal Caird, "that there is something in the very nature of God which would remain unrevealed and unrealized, but for His relation to the world, and especially to the finite spirits He has made in His own image."[19]

It will be convenient to defer our criticism of the Hegelian view of the world as experience until the next chapter. Here it must be sufficient to say that any system which fails adequately to distinguish between the real and the conceptual must needs be radically fallacious. We have to deal with two orders -- the order of objective existence and the representative order of thought -- which form the subject-matter of two totally distinct sciences, metaphysics and logic. A philosophy which denies this fundamental and evident fact, which identifies the science of being with the science of 'second intentions,' can only lead us into a quagmire of inconsistencies and contradictions. Of the demerits peculiar to the doctrine with which we are here dealing, we have already indicated that which seems to us the most notable, viz., that it can only maintain the existence of finite personalities at the cost of internal contradiction. On other grounds also it must be pronounced gravely at fault. We have seen that it declares the universe to be the complete expression of the Divine being, so that apart from the world God is a mere abstraction, a focal point. The position is intelligible in an avowed pantheist, but not so in those who attribute to God personality in a true and proper sense so that He merits the appellation of the Supreme Spirit. Once let this be granted, and it is manifest that God, apart from the world, is no mere abstraction, any more than a man is an abstraction apart from the thoughts which he has *hic et nunc* before his mind. The infinite intelligence must be aware, not of the existing order of things alone, but of innumerable things, persons, events, and even whole orders of being, which, though not actualized and never to be actualized, are nevertheless possible. If creation consisted simply in existence as the term of a Divine thought, all these would be created things. Yet, in fact, although the mind of God contemplates them, they lack the actuality which would place them among creatures. Even were it to be maintained that the universe is exhaustive of reality, so that God cannot contemplate entities as possible, which are not at some time or another actualized, since all such possibility is a fiction: yet the existing order of things is not realized in its entirety simultaneously. The world of to-day is not the world of the igneous or of the glacial ages. God, if He be a subsistent Person endowed with intelligence and will, most certainly foresaw from the beginning all that nature's laws would bring about. A limited degree of foresight belongs even to the finite spirit. The same perfection cannot be denied to God. Yet the theory which we are criticizing, if logically applied, demands that whatever is actually an object of Divine thought, enters thereby *ipso facto* into the actual created order: for creation is identical with the thought of God. It is plain that the theory is untenable. No argument for creation *ab aeterno* can be drawn from the fact that God's thought is eternally present to the Divine Mind.

The other argument which we mentioned, viz., that God acquires a fuller and richer existence by the creation of finite spirits, need not detain us. We have seen in previous chapters that God is of Himself in possession of infinite perfection and infinite beatitude. He can gain no 'intensification of life' through creation. The argument is, in fact, mere anthropomorphism. Man is imperfect and incomplete apart from society. It is rashly and unphilosophically assumed that what is true of man is also true of God.

5. *The exemplar causality of God.* We have hitherto considered God simply as the efficient cause of creatures. But this is far from being the sole aspect of His causality in our regard. Our dependence on Him for our being is more complete than is suggested by the relation between an efficient cause and its effect. He is likewise the exemplar cause, and as we have already indicated, the Ultimate final cause of all created things. In the present section we deal with His exemplar causality.

Whenever an agent possessed of intelligence exercises the causality proper to it as such, his action must be directed by an exemplar cause. For an agent of this kind is not, like mere natural agents, determined by nature to the production of a particular effect. He enjoys the power of self-determination, and decides by free election what the term of his activity shall be. So far as the actual exercise of causality is concerned, the principle of determination is the will. But the specific character of the result is determined by the intellect. And the intellect can only perform this office by the conception of a directive idea, in other words, an exemplar cause. If creation were no free act on God's part, but were an operation necessarily involved in His nature, as is held by the thinkers whose views were controverted in the last section, any discussion of exemplar causality would he idle: for no such directive idea would be required. But once admit that God in creating acts as a free agent, and it is evident that He too must direct His activity by exemplar causes. What has been said will throw light on the nature of the causality exercised by the idea. Though presenting characteristics peculiar to itself, it enters into the scheme of the four causes enumerated by Aristotle -- the efficient and the final, the formal and the material: it does not demand a separate place, and thereby render the Aristotelian enumeration incomplete. It is to be accounted primarily an efficient cause, as giving to the agent the ultimate determination in virtue of which he produces the effect, and also as directing the various stages of his activity. It must, however, further be reckoned as exercising a special kind of formal causality in regard of the effect. For the idea serves as the model or standard to which the work produced must conform. It is not merely an efficient principle, but a norm. It is an extrinsic type or specific character, to which corresponds the intrinsic type which we call the formal cause. It may be noted that Aristotle, when mentioning it, classes it with the formal cause. [20]

This question is one of those which first received adequate treatment in Christian philosophy. Neither Aristotle nor any other of the Greeks had any true idea of God's efficient causality in regard of the world. They were thus debarred from realizing the need of the exemplar cause. But the revealed doctrine of creation soon led Christian thinkers to the consideration of the exemplar ideas which directed the Divine action. Both Augustine and the Pseudo-Areopagite, as later the Schoolmen, recognized in the Platonic theory of ideas the suggestion of a profound truth. They saw, however, that the ideas were not, as Plato surmised, subsistent realities external to the Divine intellect, but within it. To say that God creates without such ideas is tantamount, says Augustine, to saying that His work is not directed by reason. [21]

It is manifest that the exemplar ideas of the creature present only a remote analogy with those of the Creator. Certain fundamental divergences must be carefully noted, if the doctrine here explained is not to he in open conflict with what we have said as to the Divine infinity and Divine simplicity. God, as we have often insisted, embraces in His essence the plenitude of reality: and other things are only in so far as in finite modes they imitate some aspect of that 'immense and unbounded ocean of being'[22] which is God. It follows from this that the exemplar ideas of God are drawn from His own essence Man draws his ideas from without. He contemplates nature, and finds in her perfections the material elements of those types which his intellect conceives and to which he subsequently gives external actualization. God, knowing His own essence, knows it not merely in itself but as imitable in countless types of finite reality. He sees how His infinite being contains the Possibility of innumerable created perfections Amongst these He sees material natures, graded by their respective forms into genera and species -- some inanimate and others endowed with vegetative or even animal life. Highest among them is man, whose vital principle is a soul capable of independent subsistence, and who thus forms a link between the material and the spiritual. And higher yet than man He sees the possibility of many kinds of immaterial essences. All alike by the mere fact of their existence reflect the perfection of Him, who alone in the full sense of the word is. But as the vast hierarchy of being ascends in its myriad types from the elementary forms of inanimate matter to the most exalted of created spirits, each successive stage represents, however inadequately, the inexhaustible perfections of the Godhead. Yet while the contents of the divine ideas are drawn from God's essence, the constitution of the exemplar cause as such must be attributed, as is evident, to the Divine intellect The very reason why we have been led to assert their existence is that creation is a free act on God's part and therefore directed by ideas present to the Divine mind. The presence in God's essence of perfections imitable by creatures will not suffice, unless the Divine intellect holds them as ideas and views them as models of dependent being. Moreover, the operation of the intellect is also necessary to organize the perfections into types. As they are found in God Himself they are not gathered into groups corresponding to the specific natures subsequently to be realized. They are in Him one infinite perfection, comprehensive of all being. To employ Scholastic terminology, the exemplar ideas are *fundamentaliter* in the Divine essence, but *formaliter*, *i.e.*, in their formal character in the Divine mind, as exemplars, The exemplar ideas of actual and possible creation are, it is evident, innumerable. Yet it is not to be imagined that they are, as with ourselves, so many separate acts. The act of the divine intelligence is, as we pointed out in chap. xi., one and one only, and its immediate object is the divine essence. But, since that act is infinite, it apprehends the divine essence in all the multiple aspects under which, it may be known. And inasmuch as its exemplar causality constitutes one of these aspects, it is apprehended in this manner. Thus it is that in the one act of the Divine Mind, God contemplates the exemplar ideas of all possible creatures. St. Thomas, in order to assist us to imagine how this can be, reminds us that in virtue of the hierarchical order of created natures, a knowledge of a higher nature gives knowledge also of the lower. If we consider the nature of man, we have but to abstract from his rationality, and we see what is involved in mere animality: and if from this we abstract the notion of sense-perception, we understand what is signified by vegetative life. Similarly, since the Divine essence contains all being, the mind which contemplates it and views it in its various proportions to possible creatures knows them all.

Yet if creatures can, in certain respects, be viewed as exhibiting, inadequately yet truly, some aspect of the Divine essence, there are points of such fundamental diversity between the subsistent being of God and the being of creatures that philosophy has often been at a loss to understand how the one can really be derived from the other. God is essentially Infinite and essentially One. How is it possible that, being such, He can he the sole origin of finiteness and multiplicity. It would seem, at first sight, as though the contemplation of His essence could in no sense manifest these among the conditions of dependent essences modelled on His own. If He does indeed draw ideas of possible reality from the contemplation of Himself, must not the ideas thus formed be in conformity with His essential characteristics? In view of these considerations can our theory of exemplar causality be maintained? Moreover, the objection seems to receive strong confirmation from the existence of evil in the created order. Can God draw from the treasures of His own essence the exemplar ideas of evil things.

The mind of Plato saw no other way to solve the difficulty than to accept the theory of uncreated matter, the source of finitude and multiplicity in the universe. Yet such an answer was worse than none: for nothing can be more repugnant to reason than the supposition of uncreated matter.

Here, too, it was reserved for Christian thinkers to deal successfully with the problem, and to shew that it admits of a satisfactory solution.

Finiteness, as they point out, is an essential condition of created being as such: and this for a twofold reason. On the one hand, the Infinite can be but One. Two infinites is a contradiction in terms. And on the other, since created being is drawn from nothing, it follows that its existence is dependent on the causal influx of the Creator -- that it is capable of annihilation. But such a condition cannot belong to a being which is infinite in perfection. Infinite perfection must include the note of perpetuity. If God, then, conceives the possibility of created beings, He must, in the nature of things, know such beings as finite. Nor is the note of finiteness repugnant to an idea derived from the Divine essence. For finiteness is nothing positive. It is merely the negation of ulterior perfection. An exemplar idea of finite being does not contain the representation of some reality which has no place in God. A finite being is simply the imitation of the Divine essence in a certain measure, and not beyond. In the finiteness of created being lies the explanation of the multiplicity of the exemplar ideas realized in creation. The very purpose of creation, as we shall explain more fully in the next. section, is to make known the Divine perfections. Since, then, the creature is of necessity finite and only capable of shewing forth some limited aspect of God's being, it is manifest that nothing can be more conformable to the end for which He creates, than that He should call into existence a multitude of diverse things. In this way, by means of multiplicity He displays the unfathomable abyss of perfection which is His essence to a degree which could not be attained through the limited essence of a single finite nature.

Nor does the existence of evil in the world compel us to regard anything as outside the exemplar causality of God. For the essence of evil lies in privation. Evil is the absence of something which is requisite to the perfection of some nature or some action. The thing is termed bad because it is incomplete or because in some way the perfection of right order is wanting to it. It lacks some integral part, or some quality or relation which should be present. So far as it possesses being it deserves to be called good; it is bad by reason of the privation which mars it. The crippled limb is not bad because it consists of bone and flesh and sinew, but because these are lacking in their due development or in their proportion to one another. Sickness is the want of vigour in this or that organ: or the absence of harmonious order in the constituents of the body. The same is true of the will, the seat of moral evil. The act of the will, viewed purely as an exercise of active power, and in regard of its reality, is good. It is evil, not in itself, but because in regard of this particular object it is contrary to the due order required by the moral law. But God is the exemplar cause of creatures in respect of what they have of being, not in regard of not-being. Privation, like limit, is not-being: and as such has no exemplar cause. There are, of course, other questions, and those most weighty, regarding the existence of evil, which claim our consideration. They do not, however, concern God's exemplar causality, but the wisdom and sanctity of the providence, which He exercises over the world. They will receive treatment in another chapter.

6. *The purpose of creation.* We have shewn, when dealing with the Divine will, that the ultimate purpose of creation is God's glory. Creation is the realization outside God of certain aspects of His infinitude -- the overflow, if we may so term it, of infinite perfection -- and has its final reason in that perfection itself. We argued at some length that in the last resort the Divine action can have no other reason than God. Every end is such because it is good: were it not good, it could not be an end. But God

is the Good: and other things are good, only in so far as they reproduce in some way the perfections of the supreme Good. Though we may say, and with truth, that the excellence of the work -- its wisdom, its beauty, its magnificence account for God's creation of the universe, and made it a fitting end for His action, yet that excellence is not something apart from Himself. The attributes which arouse our admiration are but the external manifestation of His perfections. The excellence of His perfections made it good that they should be communicated to created being. The true end of His action is to be found in Himself.

We must not, however, conclude, because God is the primary end of creation, that the creature is a mere means. It, too, is truly an end, though in an inferior degree. To see this, it is sufficient to reflect that God's glory is found in the perfection of the creature. The more fully the good of the creature is realized, the more adequately, in other words, it attains its ideal, so much the more fully is God's glory manifested. The good of the creature is not a thing indifferent in itself, which conduces somehow to the final end of creation. In it the final end is realized, since it is itself identical with the Divine glory. God, in desiring His glory and delighting in its realization, of necessity desires and delights in the good of the creature. But if this be so, the creature is itself an end. For a means is regarded as a good, simply inasmuch as it leads to the attainment of something other than itself. God seeks the good of the creature, not to obtain something else, but because in that good as such is found the end of His creative action. His glory and the creature's good are not distinct: they are two aspects of one and the same end. Of these the Divine glory is rightly reckoned as primary, since God, not the creature, is the final cause of all that is. But the two are not divergent. God, in desiring one, desires the other.[23] It appears from what we have said that creatures are truly the objects of God's love. To love anything is to desire its good, and to take pleasure in that good when it is attained. And this, as we have just seen, is true of God as regards creatures. Moreover, the greater the degree of perfection with which God endows a creature, the greater is the love of God for it, and the more does it deserve in comparison with other creatures to be an end of Divine action. Animate natures as more perfect than inanimate are rightly held to be of more value in God's sight. The latter fulfil an appropriate function when they become means to the perfection of the animate. Animals He esteems above plants. While man, who in virtue of his rational nature stands in an entirely different category from all other material beings, is the object of a love incomparably higher than they.

Some difficulty may perhaps be felt with regard to our assertion that the Divine glory as realized in creation is to be identified with the good of the creature, on the score that it would seem to follow from this, that every individual substance is bound to attain its specific perfection: whereas nature, as we well know, presents to our view a very different state of things. The objection is, however, to a large extent removed by the reflection that the material universe is a vast organized whole of which individual substances are the constituent parts. Though not an organism in the sense that other things are not complete substances in themselves but merely organic parts in a single all-embracing substance, the universe is a veritable cosmos, and not a mere collection of independent units. The constituent parts are subservient to the good of the whole. Man, by reason of his personality, is an end in himself. But other substances cannot be viewed in isolation, abstracted from the universe of which they are portions. The purpose of creation is not the manifestation of God's glory in the perfection of each individual substance as such, but in the perfection of the universe. He desires the perfection of the individual thing in so far as it is compatible with the perfection of the whole.[24] How that perfection is determined we shall consider when in a later chapter we come to discuss and to controvert the erroneous theory known as optimism.

It may, however, be contended that for the Christian philosopher at least a crucial difficulty yet remains in the doctrine of eternal punishment. We have admitted, it will be urged, that man's good is not subordinated to the *bonum universi*. Indeed, it will be argued later that the universe exists for man, and that its character was determined in reference to him.[25] If then God's glory and the creature's good are not two distinct objects of desire, but one: and if each human being is an end in himself, it would seem to follow that the Divine glory demands that not one member of the human race should fail of attaining the beatitude proper to man. Yet it is a fundamental doctrine of the Christian religion that God has made this dependent on man's right use of his freedom: and that, in consequence, the final condition of many is one, not of beatitude, but of eternal punishment. The difficulty is, however, less than at first sight would appear. Doubtless the very existence of moral evil in the world at all is a profound mystery. But since to man has been granted the power to choose freely between good and evil, it follows that he is able to thrust from him the perfection which should be his, and to choose by his own deliberate act a condition in essential opposition to his true ideal. Yet it is impossible that God should permit a creature to frustrate the primary end of creation. Since through man's own fault God's glory is not attained through his perfection, it is attained through his punishment. Another series of Divine attributes is manifested. God's majesty, His justice, His hatred for sin, are exhibited in the penalties inflicted upon the unrepentant sinner. The gift of freedom enables man to separate in his case the primary end of creation from the secondary. But by doing so, he only renders it yet more abundantly evident that the ultimate purpose for which creation exists is the manifestation of the fathomless perfections of the Godhead.

NOTES

{1} *Summa Theol.*, I., q. 65, art. 3. "Creatio autem est productio rei secundum suam totam substantiam, nullo praesupposito, quod sit vel increatum vel ab aliquo creatum."

{2} "We talk of creation out of nothing. But if the qualification 'out of nothing' has any meaning at all, it implies a certain lack of reality on the part of the creature." J. Ward, *Realm of Ends*, p. 39.

{3} *De tot.*, q. 3, art. i, ad 7; *Summa Theol.*, I., q. 45, art. 1, ad 3.

{4} The Statement that the action of a finite being is, of necessity, accidental, hardly calls for proof. It seems evident that, save in the Infinite Being who embraces in one simple actuality all the perfections found in the various modes of finite being, the mode which we term action must be other than the mode of substantial existence, and therefore accidental in its regard. A proof is, however, here given; but in view of its abstract character we have thought best to place it in a note. In finite entities action, like every other perfection, is the actuation of a potency. The potency which it actuates, is not, however, the substantial essence. That is, indeed, a potency, but a potency in regard of existence. The potency of action has regard to a perfection other than mere existence: to act is something over and above mere being. It follows that action presupposes the substance as already existing. It is the actuation of a potency belonging to an existing thing. But a secondary actuation in an existing substance is an accident. In the Infinite Being it is otherwise. Action is not the actuation of a potency, for in Him potency has no place: He is *Actus Purus*, and His action is identical with His substance.

{5} Tertia ratio est, quia cum omne accidens oporteat esse in subjecto, subjectum autem actionis sit recipiens actionem: illud solum, faciendo aliquid, recipientem materiam non requirit, cujus actio non est accidens, sed ipsa substantia sua, quod solius Dei est." St. Thomas Aquinas, *De Pot.*, q. 3, art. 4.

{6} "Un être qui n'est ni l'être necessaire, ni partie de l'être necessaire n'est *de lui même rien*: si donc il existe, il a été à la lettre *produit de rien*, donc créé. . . . Le principe ici formulié est evident, puisqu'il n'y a pas de milieu, entre être nécessairement, ou *être par soi*, et n'être pas nécessairement, ou *n'être rien de soi* ." H. Pinard in article *Création* in *Dict. apologétique de la foi Catholique*, edited by A. d'Alès (Paris, 1911), vol. 1., p. 726.

{7} Cf. Bradley, *Appearance and Reality*, p. 499. "Is the Absolute better or worse at one time than another? It is clear that we must answer in the negative, since progress and decay are alike incompatible with perfection. . . . Nothing perfect, nothing genuinely real can move."

{8} *Supra.*

{9} *Realm of Ends*, p. 233. The same objection is proposed and solved, *de Pot.*, q. 3, art. 17, obj. 13.

{10} Cf. Mansel, *op. cit.* p. 32, p. 205, where he notes that the difficulty is urged by Rothe, *Theologische Ethik*, § 40. The latter writer was a Lutheran divine of some eminence as a thinker: he sought to combine Hegelian philosophy with the acceptance of liberal protestantism.

{11} Thus the Dominican, Nicholas Eymeric (1320-1399), mentions among the Aristotelian errors prevalent at his time. "Item: quod nihil novi potest a Deo immediate procedere, quia nihil potest fieri sine dispositione praevia et motu praecedente. Deus autem immobilis perseverat." *Directorium Inquisitorum* (Paris, 1587), p. 238, n. 8, cited by Duplessis d' Argentré *Collectio Iudiciorum* (Paris, 1728), I., p. 205. The error was among those held by Siger of Brabant and condemned by the bishop of Paris, in 1277. Cf. Aristotle, *Physics*, viii., c. i., 251a2O.

{12} *Con. Gent.*, II., c. xxxiii.; *de Pot.*, q. 3, art. 17.

{13} Cf. *De Pot.*, l.c. " Consideraverunt [sequaces Aristotelis] primum agens ad similitudinem alicujus agentis quod suam actionem exercet in tempore, quamvis per voluntatem agat: quod tamen non est causa ipsius temporis, sed tempus praesupponit. Deus autem est causa ipsius temporis. Nam et ipsum tempus in universitate eorum quae a Deo facta sunt continetur. Unde cum de exitu universi esse a Deo loquimur, non est considerandum quod tunc et non prius fecerit."

{14} Cf. *De Pot.*, q. 3, art. 17, ad 6. "Sicut quod est a causa naturaliter agente, retinet similitudinem ejus prout habet formam similem formae agentis: ita quod est ab agente voluntario, retinet similitudinem ejus prout habet formam similem causae, secundum quod hoc producitur in effectu quod est in voluntatis dispositione, Ut patet de artificiato respectu artificis. Voluntas autem non disponit solum de forma effectus, sed de loco, duratione et omnibus conditionibus ejus. Unde oportet quod effectus voluntatis tunc sequatur quando voluntas disponit, non quando voluntas est."

{15} *De Pot.*, q. 3, art. 3.

{16} *Idea of God*, p. 309.

{17} *Op. cit.*, p. 308.

{18} p. 315.

{19} *Fundamental Ideas of Christianity*, I., p. 162. Similarly Prof. Pringle Pattison speaks of creation as involving for God "an intensification of life through realization of the life of others." (*Op. cit.* p. 308).

{20} *Met.*, IV., c. ii.

{21} *Lib. de lxxxiii qq.*, q. 46 (P.L. 40, col. 30).

{22} **pelagos ousias apeiron aoriston.** Greg. Naz., *Or* xlv. 3. (P.G. 36, col. 625).

{23} Au lieu d'un mouvement divergent de l'Absolu vers le contingent, nous ne constatons en Dieu qu'un seul mouvement toujours vers soi, mais à double effet. A ne considérer cette solution que pour sa valeur philosophique, on jugera sans doute qu'elle résout mieux que les autres les difficultés du problème. Elle paraît de plus s'appuyer sur une conception plus profonde de l'être nécessaire. Les autres avec leurs scrupules d'écarter de lui le repoche d'égoïsme, n'en jugent en somme qu'à mesure de notre humanité." H. Pinard, art. *Création* in *Dictionnaire de Théologie Catholique* (Vacant-Mangenot), III., col. 2169.

{24} Cf. *Summa Theol.*, I., q. 22, art. 2, ad 2. "Aliter de eo est qui habet curam alicujus particularis, et de provisore universali: quia provisor particularis excludit defectum ab eo quod ejus curae subditur, quantum potest: sed provisor universalis permittit aliquem defectum in aliquo particulari accidere ne impediatur bonum totius. Unde corruptiones et defectus in rebus naturalibus dicuntur esse contra naturam particularem: sed tamen sunt de intentione naturae universalis, in quantum defectus unius cedit in bonum alterius, vel etiam totius universi. . . . Cum igitur Deus sit universalis provisor totius entis, ad ipsius providentiam pertinet quosdam defectus esse in aliquibus particularibus rebus, ne impediatur bonum universi perfectum."

{25} *Infra*, c. xvii., § 1.

Chapter XV. Rival Theories Considered: -- (1) Pantheism, (2) Naturalism.

1. Pantheism and Creationism. Hegelian

2. Pantheism.

3. English Idealist Systems -- (a) Absolute Idealism; (b) Mitigated Idealism.

4. Naturalism.

1. *Pantheism and creationism.* We established in the preceding chapter that the true explanation of the existence of finite and contingent things must be sought in the creative act by which God, the Infinite and Necessary, called them out of nothingness by a free act of His will. Reason, we saw, leaves no room for any other conclusion: while every objection which is urged admits of a satisfactory answer. Yet the history of human thought shews plainly enough that the doctrine of creation *ex nihilo* has never been universally held: and its claim has never been more vigorously contested than at the present day. Three other solutions of the problem are possible -- pantheism, dualism, and materialism. The first of these theories denies that there is any substance except the Divine, and contends that the universe and all its constituents, including ourselves, are in some sort to he identified with God. Dualism asserts the existence of two self-existent beings -- God,the efficient cause of all perfection, and matter, the source of all limitation and imperfection, or according to some systems, a principle of evil, to which the origin of matter is to be attributed. Materialism dispenses with God altogether. Those who maintain it hold that the primary constituents of the universe -- -matter and its laws -- need no explanation other than themselves: they have always existed, and are the first cause and sufficient reason of all. From them the world has, by a natural process, evolved to its present state.

Dualism need not detain us: for no one now defends it. Reason cannot finally acquiesce in the idea that the source of all imperfection can possess in its own right the supreme perfection of self-existence. Indeed, there seems to be a manifest contradiction involved in the supposition that self-existence can be an attribute of two natures essentially contrary to one another. An identical property found in two distinct natures is proof of a common element. But here *ex hypothesi* the two natures are radically diverse -- the one the principle of actuality and perfection, the other of limit and imperfection. It may, indeed, be admitted that, faced with the physical and moral evil of the world, the human mind could hardly avoid entertaining at least for a time the hypothesis of two opposing principles. Even the greatest of Greek thinkers could not entirely emancipate themselves from it. Nor can it be said to be wholly extinct even now. The theory of a finite God, which we have examined and rejected (chap. xiii., § 3) is only intelligible on dualistic presuppositions.

As regards pantheism and materialism the case is far otherwise. These are perennial forms of human thought. Both systems have numerous adherents at the present time. Indeed, contemporary thought, outside the circles in which the influence of Christianity is still felt, accounts for the world, not in terms of creationism, but of pantheism or materialism. For, as we shall shew, the system now commonly termed naturalism, is, whatever its defenders may maintain, indistinguishable from materialism. The purpose of the present chapter is to estimate the worth of these two systems viewed as rivals to creationism. In this section we shall treat briefly of pantheism in general: and in the following one consider in more detail the special forms in which the doctrine is prevalent to-day.

It would be altogether beyond our scope to give even a cursory account of the various pantheist systems which have left their mark upon philosophical thought. Among the more important schools of antiquity, stoicism, which at one time -- in the second century of our era -- became the predominant philosophy of the Graeco-Roman world, was a system of undiluted pantheism. It taught the absolute identity of nature and God. The universal substance was, it held, simultaneously matter and spirit :

these being but two aspects of the same reality, and not, as might appear, different the one from the other. From this substance all things, even the soul, are formed. Neoplatonism, the last effort of pagan philosophy to hold its own against the advancing tide of Christian thought, hardly, perhaps, deserves the name of pantheism, since it gave to God an existence outside the world. But it held all things to proceed from God by emanation, and hence to be formed of the Divine substance. In the middle ages pantheism reappears in Scotus Erigena (fl. c. 800 a.d.): and somewhat later in certain thinkers influenced by the Arabian philosophers. Towards the end of the sixteenth century, Giordano Bruno (1548-1600) revived the memory of classical pantheism. But it was reserved for the genius of the Jew Spinoza (1632-1677) to reestablish in Western thought what had long been regarded as an outworn creed. More recently the writings of Hegel (1770-1831) gave to the system a vogue, which in this country at least it still retains. Moreover, it must not be overlooked that it is the fundamental principle of Indian philosophy, which during the last century exercised, and still exercises, an undoubted influence on many European thinkers.

This much may be said to be the common teaching of all forms of Western pantheism: that there is but one substance, God, and that God and nature are identical: that God has no being outside of nature.[1] All the particular things of nature are regarded either as parts of the all-inclusive unity, or as modes in which this infinite being finds expression. They are not substances, but 'adjectives' of the one Reality. By their multiplicity and their perpetual change they testify to the infinity of the Divine Whole. Though the Godhead is rational, as is manifested by the reason immanent in the ordered universe and by the conscious reason of man, yet it must not be regarded as individual or personal. These conceptions involve limit: and God is above all limit. Nor does he exercise free-will. The inviolable regularity of natural law faithfully expresses the inevitability of the Divine action. Moreover, as he is the unity of all differences in the physical order, so is he likewise in the moral order. He must not be regarded as possessing moral goodness in our sense of the term -- as being merciful, or just, or holy. For from him flow also those activities which we regard as the direct contrary of these attributes. In some way he transcends the difference between all opposites: so that the terminology of human ethics has no applicability in his regard.

We might fairly claim to have already put the truth of creationism beyond all question by arguments bearing in different ways upon the subject. But in the comparison between it and pantheism we prescind for the moment from proofs already given. We approach the subject purely from the point of view of the difficulties which face any theory that finds in a Supreme Being the source and the explanation of the present world order. Every such philosophy must undertake to explain how from the Perfect and Necessary Being, who is the origin of all, has come the evil and the contingency which are so patent in our experience.

And we aver without hesitation that so far from pantheism removing or even lessening these difficulties, the solution which it imposes is wholly repugnant to reason, while that offered by creationism is one, which the mind can accept without doing violence to itself.

The full treatment of the problem of evil in the light of creationism is reserved for another chapter. The essential point to be observed in this connection is that according to this system evil and imperfection are altogether external to God. Physical evil, admittedly, abounds in the world around us. Indeed, imperfection, suffering and death, enter as necessary elements into the present order. That order is all directed to the harmonious working of the universe as a whole, not to the perfection of each several substance taken in isolation. We have already pointed out that no objection can be raised to the doctrine of creation on the score that God has formed a world in which the good of the whole demands the sacrifice of this or that particular part viewed as a separate entity. Moral evil is, in the nature of the case, confined to rational agents alone: and is referable, not to God, but to the misuse by such agents of the gift of free-will. Pantheism, however, is very differently situated. It makes evil actually inherent in God. The disease, the corruption, the suffering, by which the perfection of particular things is destroyed, belong, on its principles, to God Himself. These things are modes of the Divine being: and what is predicated of them is, in fact, predicated of Him. The conclusion, it is plain, stands in direct contradiction with the perfection of the Absolute. And this becomes yet more patent, if moral evil is taken into consideration. To the pantheist all actions, good and bad alike, are God's actions, for He is the sole real agent. The foul and criminal deeds which dishonour human nature are God's work: the responsibility is His. The necessary deduction from such a thesis is, as we have already argued, that moral distinctions are purely relative and destitute of objective validity: that on the divine plane the difference between the two is transcended. A system which leads to such an issue is surely self-condemned as an explanation of the universe.

Nor is the contrast less trenchant when there is question of explaining the mutability which characterizes the world of our experience. Creationism affirms that in God there can be no change: that necessary being as such excludes change. Were necessary being to gain a new perfection, or to lose one which it possessed, it would to that extent be shewn not to be necessary. What is necessary must always exist: it cannot either be acquired *de novo*, or pass out of being. But necessary being, the creationist holds, is a sufficient reason for the existence of mutable being. It can give existence to beings other than itself, which, inasmuch as their existence is dependent, are contingent and finite, and consequently admit of change. They can acquire further perfections, or lose what they possess. Pantheism, on the other hand, is forced to hold that the changes of the universe take place in necessary being itself: that what comes into being, and consequently is proved not to be necessary, is nevertheless an element in necessary being. It is even maintained by certain of its defenders (e.g., Bergson) that change is of the very essence of necessary being, in other words, that the necessary is essentially contingent: that what *ex hypothesi* is its own sufficient reason and is unconditioned, can only come to be when in due course the requisite conditions are realized. A theory which involves so flagrant a contradiction has little indeed to recommend it to our acceptance.

2. *Hegelian pantheism.* We touched in the last chapter on the relation of
Hegel to Kant, and saw that the system of the former is in some respects
a reaction against that of his predecessor, inasmuch as he rejects the
distinction between phenomenal and noumenal reality. But in another
aspect the influence of the earlier philosopher on the later is decisive.
Hegel accepted Kant's theory of categories as the determining principles
of phenomena. And since with him knowledge and being are one, and the
phenomenal order is the only order, the categories become, not, as with
Kant, merely principles of knowledge, but at the same time, principles of
being. Further, he undertakes to shew that these categories possess
objective existence by virtue of a logical necessity: that they cannot not
be: that the world which is simply the categories as actualized, is real
because the laws of reason forbid that it should be otherwise.

The basis of this contention lies in his views regarding the supreme idea.
This he holds to be the idea of Absolute Self-consciousness. To assign
the first place to being is, he urges, a palpable error. For the supreme idea
must be the fullest of meaning: whereas those philosophers who have put
the idea of being first, have chosen that which contains the least meaning
of all. All other categories are but abstractions from the absolute idea:
they express some portion only of its fullness. It is, moreover, exigent of
realization. It passes by an inner necessity to actuality: and in its self-
realization it calls into being all that it contains. Thus the Absolute Self-
consciousness is, in truth, the sole fact, and may justly be termed God.
The world-process is nothing else but the self-realization of God: and in
the Whole we have the self-manifestation of the Divinity. The categories,
which we see exhibited in natural types, are the partial expression of
God's reality. As we have already said, they may be derived by abstraction
from the Absolute. These categories of nature form the lower stages of a
great ascent. Through them we pass by a strict logical necessity -- a
development of thought which is out of all relation to time -- from the
bare idea of being to the highest of all notions, that of self-conscious
spirit.

The pantheism which we have here summarized appears at first sight to
regard the world as spiritual through and through -- as being the

manifestation of the self-existent absolute spirit. Yet a more careful consideration will shew that this is far from being the case: and that Hegelian idealism, in its theory of the origin of finite being, involves us in the impossibilities of pure materialism. Here the account of the development by which the absolute is reached claims our attention. It has two divergent aspects irreconcilable the one with the other. On the one hand it is declared to be out of relation to time, and to be a matter of purely rational necessity. On the other, it is identified with the actual course of events occurring in the time-series. The history of the world, as Hegel conceives it, is an activity determined by its final cause. It is destined to issue in spirit, conscious of itself as the explanation of the whole process, the presupposition of every previous stage. This is the end-in-view which has governed the process from the beginning. What in nature is mere potentiality attains actualization, when spirit becomes conscious of itself as free. This result is differently mediated in different spheres. For man as a social being it is the work of the state. In the sphere of knowledge it is the work of philosophy. The final perfection thus reached is the development of the Absolute. The development takes place in time, but time is unessential to it. It is manifest, however, that here we have a difficulty which cannot be thus summarily dismissed. If the development is a matter of a timeless logical necessity, there can be no question of a real evolution, historically conditioned. The term of the process must be present from the first. A temporal evolution is no more possible than in the case of the conclusion of a mathematical theorem. There, too, we distinguish between principles and resultant conclusion; but the conclusion is not reached by a development in the physical order.

Indeed, as conceived by Hegel, the Absolute is not really comparable to a derivative conclusion. It is the principle of the whole: and the so-called principles of its development are mere abstractions from its reality. It is to this aspect that the system owes much of its speciousness. The less perfect is represented as having its explanation in the absolute and perfect: and the absolute is shewn us as the necessary presupposition of all things. Yet we see that when he applies his philosophy to the concrete facts the order is reversed. He gives us a time-development: and so far from the perfect accounting for the less perfect, the latter is found at each stage to be productive of the former, the processes of nature issuing at last in conscious spirit. But this is precisely the position of the materialist. The fundamental error of that system is that the less is conceived as the sufficient reason of the greater, potentiality as the sufficient reason of act. How near akin the two systems are was evidenced when not a few of the more eminent of Hegel's followers accepted materialism as the legitimate outcome of his system.

What then is to be said of the explanation of finite being offered by this philosophy? How, according to Hegel, is the Absolute related to the things of experience? In view of what we have already said, it is plain what the answer to this question must be. There has, it is true, been much discussion among Hegelians as to their master's personal views regarding God. With these we are not concerned. In his system there is no room for God at all. The Absolute is reached in man. It is attained by the development of personal self-consciousness: and it is in man that this is attained. In Hegelianism the term God is really an appellative of man as rational and self-conscious. There can be no other claimant. Indeed, as has often been pointed out, the principles of the system permit us to make our conclusion yet more precise. Man, it is asserted, reaches the perfection of self-consciousness in the knowledge of philosophy. But it has been reserved for the Hegelian philosophy to give to the human race the true knowledge of man's place in the scheme of things. It follows that the Hegelian philosopher, and he alone, is the realized Absolute. There can, then, be no question of creation. For the explanation of finite being anterior to man's appearance on earth we are thrown back on Hegel's deduction of the categories. We are told that the inorganic and organic kingdoms come into being in accordance with a rationally determined process. In them the categories of being take shape as reality, and follow each other in necessary sequence. But why, we ask, should they be at all? Destitute of a basis in an existing Absolute, the existence of the evolutionary process lacks an explanation. Real being, if finite and contingent, demands a real cause. The sequence, which Hegel claims to establish between the categories, will not account for the actuality of any one of them. Moreover, what can be more fantastic than to seek to describe the world process as the embodiment of a logical deduction? Even were it possible to schematize the varied types which nature displays, the concrete individuals and their respective happenings are not reducible to schemata. The created world undoubtedly bears marks of an organizing mind; but the course of its development does not present us with the successive steps of a chain of reasoning, in which first principles proceed inevitably to their conclusion. Much more is this the case in human history, where the operation of free-will puts even to-morrow beyond our calculation. Aristotle judged more correctly when he declared that the individual is only intelligible in virtue of the universal type which it embodies, and that viewed as individual and subject to contingency it is the proper object of sense-perception, not of intellect at all. To sum up, it may safely be said that the system of Hegel, whatever its ingenuity, is, philosophically, unsound from top to bottom, and viewed as an explanation of finite being, *i.e.*, as a rival to creationism, is wholly worthless.

3. *English idealist systems.* Hegelianism exerted little permanent influence in the country of its origin. Such success as it enjoyed was shortlived. It was otherwise in Great Britain. Here fortune smiled on it: and it reaped an ampler success than its intrinsic merits warranted. Its appearance occurred just at the time when the total inadequacy of the empiricism, which had prevailed since the days of Locke, was becoming generally recognized. Several able thinkers adopted it, and secured for it a firm foothold in the universities. They relinquished, it is true, as indefensible much that was characteristic of Hegel's own teaching. But fundamentally their systems are modifications in one form or another of the pantheistic idealism taught by him. It is not too much to say that for the last forty years the current of philosophical thought in this country has flowed in Hegelian channels. The English disciples of the founder of modern pantheism fall naturally into two groups, which we may conveniently distinguish as the defenders of absolute and mitigated idealism. We shall give a summary account of these two schools of thought, premising that a

considerable amount of variety of opinion is to be found among the individual exponents of either system.

(a) *Absolute idealism* lays it down as fundamental that there is but one order of reality -- an order which presents everywhere a twofold aspect, that of subject and object. Its essential character is to be 'experience': and it may be viewed alternatively as objects experienced or as the experience of a subject. The two aspects are inseparable. The subject is nothing without an object: if we endeavour so to conceive it, our idea is reached in virtue of an unreal and illegitimate abstraction. For the subject in experience is simply a term of a relation: and we cannot have one term of a relation without the other. Similarly, there can be no objects without an experiencing subject: for they too are what they are as related. As to the nature of this reality we should err if we said that it is purely mental. Such a statement would imply a distinction between the order of being and the order of knowing. Knowing and being are one. We must accept reality, in which both these aspects are present, as ultimate, when we have proved and purged it by the dialectic reason. It is idle to attempt to refer it to any order other than itself. Indeed, the very name idealism may mislead, in so far as it is taken to suggest some such theory as Berkeley's, according to which our experience, being limited to ideas alone, is not in contact with the real.

Moreover, reality is one. It is inconceivable that the world of experience should present ultimate differences. The fact that all parts of reality fall within experience shews that they are interrelated: and things which are related to each other constitute of necessity a single system -- a unity. This unity should be conceived after the analogy of a living organism. Where unity is less than this, it is not a veritable unity, but presupposes independent and separate entities brought into artificial connection by an external agent. Yet in regard of reality the idea of an external agent, such for instance as God, is out of the question. For the unity which forms the real order must itself include that ultimate reality which is the source of the manifold of experience, and which we term the Absolute or God. For the Absolute is not unrelated to the manifold; but, as we have just said, is its source. It is the One which the mind postulates as the explanation of the many. And again, the principle which gives unity to a manifold must of necessity be of it and not outside it.

This conclusion that reality is a single organism inclusive of the Absolute which is its ultimate Ground, is also established by an argument of different character. As soon as we philosophize on the data of experience, we find ourselves involved in insoluble contradictions. Those fundamental notions which meet us upon the very threshold of philosophical enquiry -- unity, multiplicity, identity, diversity, cause and effect, time and space, etc., etc. -- are seen to lead up to contradictory conclusions. We are driven to the conviction that our knowledge is of appearances only, and that human reason is debarred from knowing reality as it is. Yet on the other hand we are no less convinced that our knowledge is true. It is the very presupposition of our enquiry that our minds are capable of truth: and without this belief it would be idle to reason at all. The only means of reconciling these opposite convictions is to admit that ultimate truth can only be attained when the knowledge of the whole is reached. It is here as with the knowledge of an organ of a body. If we consider it apart from the whole organism of which it is a member, our conclusions, however carefully formed, are incomplete and erroneous. Only when we know it in relation to the whole of which it is part, do we arrive at the real truth regarding it. The same holds good of reality. Our best knowledge is provisional and partial: it is a stepping-stone only, and will require revision as we gain further and further experience. It is not truth, but truth mingled with error. For what is truth? The old explanation that truth lies in the correspondence of the notion with the reality is meaningless. If, as has been argued, there are not two orders -- knowing and being -- but only one, there can be no question of correspondence. Truth lies in the coherence of knowledge. When knowledge reaches its final term, and all its parts are integrated into a consistent whole, then we shall have truth in the full sense of the term. At present we can do no more than, at each successive advance into the real, bring into a coherent system the data which we possess. It is truth now -- provisionally so. But a higher truth lies behind it -- the truth of the Absolute. And we must anticipate that little by little our truth will be sublimated by approaching nearer and nearer to this ideal of entire and final truth -- an ideal never to be fully attained.

This explanation must not lead us to suppose that there is an Absolute Mind whose experience constitutes reality, so that we attain to truth in so far as we grow to share His experience, while our knowledge falls short of truth in so far as it is different from it. We have no ground for asserting the existence of any self-consciousness other than human. We are not set over against the Absolute: we are ourselves the Absolute as self-conscious. The experience which is reality becomes self-conscious experience in us. Hence minds should not be regarded as substance: they are 'adjectival' to reality, which is the only veritable substance. The status of independent and self-contained units which we are disposed to attribute to ourselves, is not really ours. Our independence is but relative: and we are not complete units. Indeed, it would be more in accordance with fact to speak of Mind than to employ the plural and speak of minds. The latter mode of expression inevitably suggests the false idea of independent agents.[2]

Nor again must we conceive that there is an objective reality prior to the activity of our minds and independent of it. This would involve the supposition of an experiencing subject other than conscious. Reality is what it is for our experience, and beyond our human experience it is not. Knowledge and reality advance *pan passu*. As our knowledge goes forward along some hitherto untrodden path, so does reality widen its area. Nor do we thus open the door to any arbitrary action on the part of thought. The advance takes place along definite lines. It is an evolution of reality in accordance with its inner nature.[3]

It is manifest how closely this system is related to Hegelianism proper. The deduction of the categories and the self-realization of the Absolute Idea have, it is true, been discarded. But the single order of reality, the identification of reality with the Absolute, the denial of a personal and conscious God, and the restriction of consciousness within the Absolute to the human mind -- all these are Hegelian. And these may be said to form the backbone of the system. The idealism which has won such a hold upon English speculation owes all its fundamental positions to the German philosopher.

Nor is it less evident that the term idealism is accurately applied. It is the case, as we have noted, that the adherents of the system frequently deny that reality is according to them purely mental, inasmuch as they hold that the mental is the real; but the denial cannot be taken too seriously. For they assert that the 'real' belongs to the same order as the discursive operation of the reason. It would need hardihood beyond the ordinary to maintain that the concepts, judgments, and deductive processes of reason have any other existence than one which is purely mental. It follows that the same is, in their view, true of the factual world. Indeed, the more consistent idealists are frank in acknowledging this. "The distinction between reality and the discursive movement of the intellect," writes Mr. Bosanquet, "appears to me to be for us a distinction *within the intellectual world*." [4] It is not our intention to enter upon a general discussion of idealism. We are only concerned with it as an explanation of finite being. But before we deal with it from this point of view, it seems worth while to call attention to a radical error which lies at the foundation of the system: and, further, to notice a rooted prejudice -- an idol of the schools -- which has infected all these thinkers, and which operates to their serious detriment in the pursuit of truth.

The error to which we refer is the position regarded by them as certain, that subject and object are inseparable the one from the other: that the intelligent subject is inconceivable without objects, and similarly the objects inconceivable without the thinking faculty for which they exist, and which is the principle of their coordination. It is, of course, true that the subject, viewed precisely as thinking, presupposes the presence of an object, and, conversely, the object considered as the term of a thought, presupposes a thinker. But in this form the statement is a barren tautology. The point at issue is other than this. We are concerned to know whether the thinking subject does not possess being other than that which consists in the mere relation involved in cognition -- whether thought is not an activity of a subject possessing existence in a real order, an order in regard of which thought is merely functional: and, further, whether the object does not likewise possess real existence utterly distinct from any ideal representation. It is not unknown for the idealist to assume the principle as though it were the tautology we have mentioned, and then to import into it the negative answer to this very different problem. Yet in many ways does it appear that the thinking subject is far more than a mere consciousness of objects. The fact of volition suffices to establish this. No one will dispute that it is the same subject which thinks and which wills. But to will is a wholly different activity from thought. In other words, the being of the subject does not consist in knowing: knowing is but one of its activities. The idealist confining his attention exclusively to the intellectual operation, and abstracting from all else, arrives at the conclusion that to know constitutes the whole essence of the subject. Yet reflection assures us that inasmuch as it possesses other modes of operation, it must *be* before it knows. Indeed, a sane psychology will go further. To think and to will are not the only functions of the soul: it is likewise the principle of life. A man may lapse into coma, so that reason and volition are both alike dormant. Yet this inaction on the part of thought and will is not the extinction of being. The soul continues to be, and continues to operate.

What has been said of the subject is to be said likewise of the objects of thought. No vestige of proof has ever been given that they are mental constructions belonging to the same order as the concepts of the discursive reason. The testimony of the sense-faculties is clamorous that through perception we have direct and immediate contact with external reality: while our intellect witnesses no less emphatically that our concepts and judgments are internal representations of these same realities on a totally different plane. It is sometimes said that things are ultimately constituted by their relations, and that since objects are essentially related to thought, it must be owned that they owe their being to thought. The argument is a pure fallacy. A thing is not constituted by its relations, for it cannot have relations unless it already is. It must possess substantial reality before it can receive an additional determination through its connection with something else. To speak of a thing as constituted by relations suggests that those who thus argue have never asked themselves what a relation is. Mr. Bradley rightly says: "Relations are unmeaning except within and on the basis of a substantial whole."[5] But we have further pointed out above (chap. viii., § 3), that where knowledge is concerned we are in presence of a non-mutual relation: that though our concepts are related to their objects as their exemplar cause, the objects are not related to them.

English idealists are, further, hampered by a prejudice from which none amongst them seems to be free, to the effect that no other philosophy is possible save one framed on monist principles. They mention creationist systems, not to refute them, but merely to dismiss them as 'precritical,' 'mediaeval,' 'having no place either in serious thinking or in genuine religion,' etc., etc. Thus Professor Pringle-Pattison, speaking of God viewed as an absolute Creator, writes: "This solitary ante-mundane figure is the residuum of a primitive and pictorial fashion of thinking, a magnified man, but rarified to bare mind."[6] This attitude is part and parcel of that strange but deeply-rooted conviction that the centuries during which intellectual life was most active in every urliversity of Western Europe, were dark ages, wholly barren in speculative thought: that they may safely be dismissed without the trouble of studying their productions or even asking what they were. It is needless to say that such a prejudice can only be detrimental to those who allow themselves to entertain it. One of the objects of the series of which the present work forms part, is to shew, however inadequately, that the philosophy of the Schoolmen was no 'residuum of a primitive and pictorial manner of thinking,' but a solidly constructed metaphysical system, grounding its solutions on a firm base of reasoning, a system consistent alike with itself and with the data of experience. It would be difficult to say as much of idealism. We have already seen that Mr. Bradley is driven to the conviction that our knowledge can only be of appearance and not of reality, because his endeavour to provide a metaphysic of the world leads him on every side into insoluble contradictions. No one who had any acquaintance with the Scholastic metaphysics, even though he might not adopt the system, could maintain that creationism is a wholly unphilosophical conception, having "no place in serious thinking." He would realize that, in view of the Scholastic philosophy, such statements approach to the ridiculous. In what measure, then, can idealism afford us an explanation of the finite and contingent things which form the universe? This is the question which lies before us in this chapter. And it is a question which furnishes a crucial test of the system's real value. For the very function of philosophy is to provide a rational explanation of the world known to us. If instead of explaining it, and thereby rendering our knowledge intelligible, it reaches conclusions utterly inconsistent with the data of experience, and involving the denial of evident facts, it is shewn to be a false philosophy, to be simply one more chapter in the tale of human error. Weighed in this balance, idealism breaks down utterly. It will suffice for our purpose to urge two points. They are salient ones.

It is certain that this planet had being before the race of man, or indeed any animal life whatever, existed upon it. The evidence for this is overwhelming, and the fact is undisputed. Yet idealism contends that the real order has no existence apart from the activity of conscious Mind: and that conscious Mind is realized in the human intellect alone. It is manifestly impossible to reconcile these two positions. The idealist, however little he may relish the necessity, is bound to reject the testimony of geology. His theory, in other words, is in the most palpable contradiction with facts. The only other alternative before him would be to assert that there could be an order of thought without a conscious thinker, an experience without an experiencing subject. This solution, however, notwithstanding the support which it finds in Hegel's own system, he rightly rejects. A thought without a thinker is a fiction which belongs of right only to that Wonderland where the smile remained after the cat had disappeared. We are surely not going too far when we claim that on this count alone the idealist explanation of the world must be rejected as false. Creationism contains no difficulty comparable to this.

The other point to which we call attention has reference, not to the world outside us, but to ourselves as substantial agents. Our own activity is part of our experience: we are our own objects. And there is no fact of experience of which we are so certain as that we are independent agents. When in face of a moral issue we exert our power of free choice, when we deliberately set aside inclination in order that we may follow what is right, we know beyond the possibility of doubt that we are not 'adjectival to reality' -- not mere qualifications of some substantial reality other than ourselves -- but that we are independent in our action, and therefore independent substances. This is a truth so immediately evident, that, if it be denied, this can only be for the sake of maintaining a thesis, not because of any real possibility of doubt. Creationism admits the fact, and shews us how the notion of substance is analogically applicable both to God and creatures. Idealism, as we have seen, finds itself driven to deny it. But by the very denial it convicts itself of being a false philosophy, and its arguments, however ingenious, of being mere sophistry.

Under yet another aspect the falsity of this theory is evident beyond the need of formal demonstration. We know perfectly well that our minds are not identical with that Spirit which is the source and origin of all things -- that we are not the Absolute. A theory which maintains that the Absolute finds its realization in ourselves, that the world in some fashion owes its being to the activity of our minds, stands self-condemned. No truth forces itself so insistently upon us, both in the physical and moral order, as our weakness and our incapacity. What measure of self-deception is requisite, we may well ask, for a man to delude himself into believing that he is identical with the Power from which the universe springs? It may safely be said that only the exigencies of controversy could lead anyone to defend such a paradox.

Mr. Bradley, it is true, assigns to the Absolute a life distinct from our own. Yet, if we except this one admission, the theory which he offers us is not more satisfactory than that of his fellow-idealists. According to him, in the Absolute all differences and distinctions must disappear. Its life must be a pure unity. Hence he is led to conclude that to it belong none of those predicates which express the highest perfections known to us in the world of our experience. It is not personal. It does not possess morality, nor goodness, nor beauty, nor will, nor truth. These, as known to us, are appearances, not reality. In the Absolute they disappear in an undifferentiated unity. It is true that Mr. Bradley claims that the life of the Absolute lies on a higher plane than these. But since these are perfections in the fullest sense, it follows inevitably that humanity which possesses them is nobler than the Absolute which possesses them not. The Absolute of Mr. Bradley is surely a miserable substitute for the God of creationism. Nor will the theory serve us as an explanation of the universe of finite being. It declares the world of our experience to be full of inconsistency and contradiction, and thereby to be shewn to belong to the sphere of mere appearance. Our knowledge, such as it is, is devoid, he tells us, of objective value. But, as we have already urged, a philosophy which, instead of providing a rational explanation of science, demands that we shall declare science to be objectively invalid, is not a philosophy which the mind can accept. The validity of our knowledge is far more certain than is the truth of any such speculative construction.

(b) Mitigated idealism. Certain mitigated forms of idealism have during the past half century enjoyed a considerable vogue in England. They seemed to offer a basis for a belief in a personal God and in independent human personalities; and, further, to assign to God a quasi-creative relation in regard to the world and to ourselves. The most conspicuous upholder of this line of thought was T. H. Green. His views were adopted by very many, who believed it thus possible to reconcile the acceptance of the prevailing philosophy with a retention of the dogmatic standards of Christianity. As a matter of fact, the advantages which the system appeared to offer were illusory. They were only secured by refusing to draw the conclusions which the principles of the system really involved.

Green's position may be briefly summarized. He maintained that the world of experience could not be other than an ideal construction. Things, he argued, are essentially constituted by relations: if we seek to remove from any object of experience the relations which enter into it, we shall find that nothing is left. But relations can exist for a mind only. It follows that the objects of experience are purely mental, and not, as we tend to imagine, extra-mental in nature. He proceeds to conclude from the unity of the world viewed as a system of relations, to the unity of the mind for which it exists. This mind, he contends, must be regarded as the Author and Sustainer of the universe. On it the universe depends for its existence. It is, in fact, God. Moreover, the knowledge which human minds have of the world is only explicable if we suppose a relation of the most intimate dependence between the human and the divine intellect. Not merely is all our knowledge a participation in that Divine idea which is the world, but the fact of knowledge itself -- the unity which the world possesses for us as knowers -- is only explicable if we suppose the Divine mind to be in some sort thinking in us and through us. Idealism, thus understood, it is urged, gives all that the religious consciousness demands: a personal God, Creator of the world and of all finite spirits, and independent human personalities, spiritual in nature and therefore endowed with freedom.

It is unnecessary for our purpose, and would take too long, to enter into a detailed criticism of Green's arguments. We may, however, note in passing that the two assertions that relations can exist only for a mind, and that the objects of experience are constituted by their relations -- both of them absolutely essential to the system -- are alike pure fallacies. The sole basis for the former statement lies in the fact that a relation, as such, is not cognizable by sense-perception, but only through an intellectual concept. Sense, *e.g.*, shews us two similar things; but it needs the abstractive power of the intellect for us to grasp the relation of similitude. But this is not to say that there is no such thing as a relation of similitude save in the mind. The relation is a real objective fact, and as such the mind knows it. Nor is the statement that things are constituted by relations better founded. As we have already pointed out, a thing must be before it can possess relations. A relation is a secondary determination qualifying something real. A relation suspended so to speak *in vacuo*, and without a real substance which it qualifies, is a wholly impossible conception.

Our concern, however, is not so much with Green's reasoning as with his claim so to defend idealism as to reconcile it with a belief in a personal God, and, in some sort, with creation. And we contend that the principles of his philosophy, if faithfully applied, give no ground for these beliefs, but that they are introduced at the price of inconsistency. The mind which Green supposes as the ground of the universe cannot logically be represented as a personal Deity. For in his system it is simply the universe under another aspect. The universe displays a manifold of relations: and a consciousness is therefore postulated as a principle of unification. But this consciousness is merely the focus of the manifold -- the necessary condition of its forming a world. Green himself tells us that just as the manifold of experience has no reality other than that which it has for the unifying principle, so we must not conceive the unifying principle as possessed of a nature other than that which it has as the consciousness of the world. It is plain that this does not give us a Creator -- a Person endowed with will and intelligence, who freely gives being to a world other than Himself. We are involved in pure pantheism, and it is a matter of choice whether we say that God constitutes nature or that nature constitutes God.

Moreover, the system leaves us in doubt regarding the relation of human minds to the universal consciousness. Are the former distinct from the latter? Green certainly wishes us so to conceive them; but he fails to make good his position. Logically, the theory seems to demand that the universal consciousness should be the constitutive principle of finite minds as it is of nature. There, seems no more reason for giving independent existence to one class of objects than to the other. In both a principle is needed which shall give unity to the manifold: and there does not appear any sufficient ground for a different answer in the two cases. Hence on this point the system is ambiguous, and it becomes difficult to distinguish the activity attributed to the human and divine mind respectively. It is evident that were the theory thoroughly consistent with itself, the finite minds would be eliminated, and we should be left with one sole thinking consciousness identical with world, the object of its thought.

In our last chapter we called attention (§ 4) to certain thinkers who defend an idealism offering even more points of contact with theistic belief than does the system of Green. They claim explicitly to be theists and not pantheists. Of these the best known is Prof. Pringle-Pattison. He rejects Green's theory as inadequate on the ground that according to it God is nothing save the mere consciousness which sustains the relations that constitute the universe.[7] For him the Absolute is "the infinite spirit," "the Power which cradles and encompasses all our lives."[8] This Absolute we must interpret by the highest categories within our reach: we must speak of God in terms of personality, morality and religion. Such language, he admits, possesses "only symbolical truth." Being ourselves finite, we cannot obtain any real comprehension of the Divine existence. "But both religion and the higher poetry -- just because they give up the pretence of an impossible exactitude -- carry us, I cannot doubt, nearer to the meaning of the world than the formuhce of an abstract metaphysics."[9] The symbols which we have regarded as truth will constantly need "to be taken up and superseded in a wider or fuller truth." The theory in plain terms resolves itself into a confession of the incompetence of human reason to tell us anything definite concerning God. We are left with symbolical values. And we saw in chap. viii. that this is tantamount to a definite surrender to agnosticism. It will hardly be maintained that such a theory is a satisfactory substitute for the reasoned body of demonstrated conclusions offered us by the natural theology defended in this volume. But the point which we desire especially to urge is that Prof. Pringle-Pattison's principles lead as inevitably to pantheism as do those of Green. On this subject it does not seem necessary to add anything to what was said in the last chapter.[10] We saw there that when he attempts to explain the relation of God to the world, be is driven back on the very position maintained by Green, and denies that the supreme mind has any being save that which it possesses as the constitutive principle of the universe. In other words he concedes that God and the universe are simply different aspects of the same reality. He asserts, it is true, with emphasis the distinction between the finite individual and God.[11] But here too he fails to offer any philosophical justification for his belief. Indeed, since he rejects as unthinkable the notion of creation in its reference to finite spirits, we are forced to the conclusion that on the principles of this philosophy the distinction between the finite and infinite cannot be logically maintained. In view of these considerations it will, we think, be admitted that modern idealism is inseparable from pantheism. The attempt to reconcile it with belief in a personal God has proved impossible of realization.

5. *Naturalism.* In the present section we deal with a system widely different from the pantheistic idealism we have just been considering, but which is no less emphatic in its rejection of the creationist interpretation of the world. Though to-day it may not be able to reckon among its defenders any speculative thinker of real weight, it would be idle to deny that it exerts a powerful influence both in the educated and uneducated classes. It is the system tacitly presupposed by many scientific investigators, and it has a far stronger hold on the popular mind than idealism is ever likely to obtain. Indeed, idealism is too remote from reality ever to become a widely spread belief. Its dialectic may destroy the authority of rival schools, but it will itself remain the *credo* of purely academical circles. Nor, again, is the student of nature, save perhaps under the stress of controversy, likely to stultify himself by admitting that the object of his investigation is a mental creation. Lord Balfour has well said of naturalism that it "numbers a formidable following, and is in reality the only system which ultimately profits by any defeats which Theology may sustain, or which may be counted on to flood the spaces from which the tide of Religion has receded."[12]

What then is naturalism? It is a system whose salient characteristic is the exclusion of whatever is spiritual, or, indeed, whatever is transcendent of experience from our philosophy of nature and of man. Huxley, for long its most prominent exponent in this country, expressed this in some often-quoted words: "Any one who is acquainted with the history of science, will admit that its progress has, in all ages, meant, and now more than ever means, the extension of the province of what we call matter and causation, and the concomitant gradual banishment from all regions of human thought of what we call spirit and spontaneity.

And as surely as every future grows out of past and present, so will the physiology of the future gradually extend the realm of matter and law until it is coextensive with knowledge and with feeling and with action."[13] The system embraces in its range several schools of thought differing more or less from one another -- empiricism, positivism, scientific monism, agnosticism. Yet for our present purpose we are justified in grouping these various types of theory together as a single system. They proceed on the same presuppositions, and are characterized by what amounts to a common body of doctrine. This common element may be thus briefly summarized.

(1) Nature is a mechanism governed by invariable and immutable law. The multiple parts of this mechanism possess widely different degrees of organization; but the sufficient explanation of every part, no matter what its organization, lies in its component elements. The whole, in all cases, has its full and final explanation in the parts of which it consists; the complex in its simple constituents. The higher may always be expressed in terms of the lower. Psychology is reducible to physiology: physiology to chemistry. In its extreme form naturalism regards the universe as consisting of atoms in various collocations. Individually separate they have, under the impulse of a natural tendency to movement, come together in groups: and these groups display various modes of action which we term laws of nature, and which arise from the character and arrangement of the component atoms. In the organization of nature there is nothing teleological. Why the vast process should have issued as it has in the existence of man and the development of social life, we cannot tell. Such was the resultant of forces. Eventually the process will run down: and as these things have arisen, so will they end. Many adherents of naturalism, it should be noted, leave the cosmological problem on one side. They are content to deal with ethical and social questions on this basis, seeking an explanation in which the spiritual has no part, but the origin of moral law and of the social order are traced to the animal appetites, and man's aesthetic judgment referred to the sexual instinct. It is, however, with the cosmological question that we are concerned in this chapter. And so far as naturalism deals with this point, it arrives, as its principles demand, at the conclusions which we have indicated. Since naturalism rejects as fallacious any ultimate distinction between body and mind, it is plain what is its view regarding the psychical order. Life, it holds, has arisen spontaneously from non-living matter: and the psychical is simply an ulterior development of physical life. In regard to the precise nature of cognition, the defenders of naturalism are, it may be owned, chary of committing themselves. They recognize that there is something

hitherto inexplicable in the relation between reality and knowledge: that psychical energy and physical energy are not similar, nor convertible the one into the other. Hence there is a certain vagueness in their utterances on this subject. Yet it is ever assumed that the material order is primary, and the psychical purely receptive in its regard. Neither intellect nor will can exert any influence upon the order of nature. The great mechanism pursues its course and allows of no interference from without. Moreover, within ourselves there is no principle of spontaneity. Knowledge reflects the real: will determines us preferentially to this or that course. But there is no originative activity in the intelligence, nor any such thing as freedom of the will.

(2) Knowledge is confined exclusively to sensible phenomena. Science consists in the accurate determination of the coexistences and sequences which nature displays. Those who imagine that there is a knowledge beyond this, who theorize regarding such notions as substance and cause are the dupes of fancy. We perceive the relations of antecedence and sequence: and so far as experience goes, we see that every event has an antecedent to which it is related. But those who affirm that every finite thing must have a cause, and that the cause is that which gives it being, and who attribute to these principles a certainty greater than that of the generalizations of experience, are simply hypostatizing the creatures of their imagination. The science of metaphysics is a delusion: and the reasoning by which men have sought to establish the existence of a First Cause and to shew that finite things must owe their origin to creation, is absolutely futile. There is no philosophy beyond physical science, and science tells us nothing about God or creation: nor does it need any such hypotheses for its validity.

(3) Experience, we are assured, shews us that the law governing the mechanism of nature is evolution. The organic evolution of all living forms must be accepted as established beyond any possibility of question: the old belief in a separate creation of different species, or even of man as distinct from the brutes, is devoid of any vestige of solid foundation. The principle must be given its full scope: and we are thus justified in concluding that the universal order of things arose in this way, and that

the world affords no evidence of an initial creation or of the existence of God. In virtue of its continued movement nature is ever evolving -- passing from one stage to another. It suffices as its own explanation.

The doctrine, which we have summarized, may justly be described as *scientific materialism*. It manifestly has no room for the spiritual in any shape or form. Yet it should be observed that many of its defenders deny that it involves any such consequences. They contend that matter and spirit are merely two aspects of the same reality: that the world may be viewed from both standpoints. They have, they aver, no intention of excluding one in favour of the other: their philosophy transcends the distinction: it is neither materialist nor spiritualist. Further, as regards the existence of God, the system, they assure us, is not atheist but agnostic. They do not deny that there may be a God: they merely assert that we cannot know anything of Him. Religion is admissible: and it may be that for some it fulfils a useful function. But it should be recognized that it is an affair of the emotions, and has no basis in the conclusions of reason. There can be no doubt that by adopting this attitude naturalism disarmed much of the hostility which it would have encountered, had it made open profession of materialism and atheism. But it is perfectly evident that the denial is purely formal. A system which interprets all existence in terms of matter and motion, which allows of no distinction between body and soul, which rejects the proofs for the existence of God, and declares a Creator unnecessary, is, with whatever reserves it may be stated, materialism and nothing else.

There have, of course, been materialists in every period of philosophy. But naturalism, as described above, is a growth of the nineteenth century. Its foundation-stone was the nebular hypothesis of Laplace (1749-1827), according to which the present universe arose mechanically out of the primal chaos. Laplace affirmed that his theory enabled him "to dispense with the hypothesis of a Creator." The conclusions of Lyell to the effect that the geological transitions which form the history of our planet, and by which it was gradually rendered a fit habitation for man. were not a series of transformations inexplicable save in view of the end to be attained, but were due to the natural working of the very same physical agencies with which we are ourselves familiar, seemed to fall into line with the Laplacean ideas. But the wide hold upon popular thought which the system obtained, is undoubtedly due to Darwin's investigations regarding the origin of species. It was believed that science had explained the development of the higher forms of life in terms of mechanical causation, and had shewn that man's beginnings were of precisely the same kind as that of the brute creation. The conclusion thus reached was regarded, as we have said, as a sufficient basis on which to build a thorough-going evolutionary system explaining the origin of all things from matter and force.

Of the system's three fundamental principles, the evolutionary theory is that with which in this chapter we are chiefly concerned. Some comment, however, must be offered in regard to the other two. In view of what has been said in previous chapters, it will be clear to every reader of this book that both alike are philosophically untenable.

(1) The doctrine that a complex whole is adequately explained by its constituent parts is palpably fallacious. The complex entity, provided it be really a whole -- a unit -- is a perfection over and above the parts. This perfection calls for explanation: and the parts do not provide it. Neither as taken singly, nor viewed as a collection, do they contain it. We do not explain a house by enumerating the materials used in its structure. The house as such is more than its materials. Its essential constitutive is the principle by which these materials are organized into a habitation for man. That organization is not a mere resultant of forces contained in the several parts: it is something added to them. The perfection of a natural whole is yet more essentially distinct from its elementary factors than that of an artificial whole like a house. *A fortiori* they do not provide its sufficient explanation. To suppose that it can arise out of them by mere resultancy without the operation of an agent of a different order, competent to confer upon them the perfection which makes them something new, is arbitrarily to override the principle of sufficient reason.

We may consider the same truth from a slightly different point of view. Let it be assumed, for the sake of argument, however difficult such an

396

idea may be, that the primaeval atoms organized themselves into unities, by the operation of natural laws inherent in them from the beginning, and without the exercise of any fresh causality, the present cosmos being the ultimate result. The process thus supposed may be compared to the working of a machine, which after a certain definite period of time leads necessarily to a given state of things. It will be admitted that for such a result we must postulate an original collocation of the atoms, in virtue of which the final effect is realized. Without this collocation we should presumably have had not cosmos but chaos. We should most certainly not have had *this* cosmos. In other words, the multiple parts of the great machine must, even at the very start, have been so arranged as to effect this result and no other. They must from the very beginning have been so related to each other as to contain the conditions requisite for the production of the perfections which subsequently appeared. But if this be granted, then it must likewise be admitted that the perfection of a whole is more than the perfection of its parts, and that theset latter are insufficient as its explanation.

(2) We dealt in chap. ii. with the empiricist theory of knowledge, which is that assumed by naturalism. We shewed there that the concepts of substance and cause are elements of knowledge no less immediate and no less certainly valid than the data of sense-perception. The objects thus designated are not figments constructed by the imaginative faculty: they are realities apprehended by the intellect. The senses shew us the thing under certain special accidental aspects. The intellect shews it as 'substance' -- that which possesses independent being: and inasmuch as it is not self-existent, refers it to a 'cause' -- that which gives it being. It may be readily admitted that these notions lie outside the province of the physical sciences: that the object of physical science is to be found in the coexistences and sequences of sensible phenomena. But the reason for this is that the particular sciences assume the validity of certain sciences which possess a more universal reference. Aristotle long since pointed out that the sciences form a hierarchy: and that above the particular sciences stand natural philosophy, mathematics, and metaphysics. These are even more truly termed sciences than the particular branches of

knowledge to which we commonly give the name. The inferior sciences depend upon them: for were their conclusions dubious, no particular science would be capable of justification. What would be the value of any branch of natural science if we possessed no certainty regarding the objective reality of space and time, of the reciprocal action of bodies, of the laws of number and geometry, of causality, of unity, of substance? The whole edifice of science -- the fruit of age-long labours -- would collapse like a house of cards. It belongs not to a particular science to vindicate the notions of substance and of cause, but to metaphysics, the supreme science whose office it is to treat of the primary notions and principles common to all sciences.

(3) The explanation of the origin of all things by a process of evolution due to the natural properties of the atoms composing the cosmic nebula is, if possible, even more opposed to reason than the two doctrines which we have already criticized. We have pointed out that the chief argument employed in support of this theory is drawn from the doctrine of organic transformism. The two cases, it was urged, are parallel: and since science is held to have established the one, it is declared only reasonable to admit the other. Yet there is, in fact, no resemblance between the two cases: and the argument *a pari* is a pure fallacy. Organic transformism supposes the existence of living things -- individual agents -- endeavouring to adapt themselves to their environment. Given these, it seeks to explain the formation of the different types into which the animal and vegetable kingdoms are divided. The problem which naturalism must solve, if it is to supplant creationism as a philosophy of finite being, is to account for the very existence of that cosmic nebula from which it declares all things were evolved. It must explain how the atoms got there, why they assumed the character which they did, and what set the process going. Unless it can do this it leaves us where we were, and has not really explained anything at all.

Of course those who accept naturalism take matter for granted. They seem to imagine that in so doing they are reducing their assumption to the lowest possible measure. As a matter of fact, it would be hard to make a larger demand. Matter, as it has been argued by several writers, is not a single entity. Each atom is distinct.

"We must remember that matter is not an unit, as a Creator is, and that talking of it so is merely a rhetorical artifice when used in philosophical enquiries . . . Matter is nothing but the sum of all the ultimate particles or atoms contained in the universe, or in any particular mass that we are dealing with. . . A very large proportion of the atoms of the universe have never been within billions and billions of miles of each other."[14]

To suppose an uncreated cosmic nebula is to suppose not a single self-existent thing, but myriads upon myriads of self-existent entities. It is not to suppose a single First Cause, but millions of first causes, and this without any conceivable reason. Monism is indeed a remarkable name to attach to such a philosophy. We may well ask which doctrine presents the greater difficulty -- the doctrine of creation which establishes by a strict *a posteriori* proof the reality of a First Cause whose infinite perfection is the sufficient ground for His eternal existence, or the doctrine of naturalism, which assumes the self-existence of millions of beings, but is totally unable to assign any reason, either intrinsic or extrinsic, why any one of them should be at all.

A further argument is based on the notion of evolution itself. The term is often employed loosely, and without much advertence to its implications. What is its real significance? As originally employed it denoted a gradual process tending to the realization of a definite end.

"By evolution or development," writes Professor Ward, "was meant primarily the gradual unfolding of a living germ from its embryonic beginning to its final and mature form. This adult form, again, was not regarded as merely the end actually reached through the successive stages of growth, but as the end aimed at and attained through the presence of some archetypal idea, entelechy or soul, shaping the plastic material and directing physical growth. Evolution in short implied ideal ends controlling physical means: in a word, was teleological."[15]

Naturalism has utterly discarded the teleological import of the term. But evolution is not, therefore, taken to signify mere change. It implies always that the change has issued in a definite result -- in a new type of thing. A change leading nowhere -- a mere flux -- would not be termed evolution. A change is not styled evolution till a critical point is reached when a new type is realized. It may in fine be said that evolution implies the production by a gradual process of change of things exhibiting a new specific nature. Every evolution then supposes the emergence of a new perfectkrn. For a specific type is a perfection distinct from all others. Here, then, we are brought back to the reasoning employed in regard to the first of the naturalist principles. It is totally impossible that from mere mechanical causality, apart from the intervention of a cause of a different order, an altogether new perfection should arise. Its appearance demands a sufficient reason: and none such is forthcoming. In other words, even if, for the sake of argument, we imagine the cosmic nebula which naturalism postulates, and suppose it duly endowed with energy, there could have been no evolution of any kind. Chaos would never have become cosmos, even in an eternity of cycles. If, on the other hand, it can be shewn that the organized types with which our planet is so abundantly stored, were produced by an evolutionary process, then the primal atoms and their energy are wholly insufficient as an explanation.

NOTES

{1} Spinoza, it is true, held that God has an infinite number of attributes, of which we know only two, thought and extension. But this concession to transcendence harmonizes bet ill with the rest of his system, which throughout views God simply as immanent in nature. Those who have been most influenced hy him have not followed him here. {2} It is very difficult really to come to any other conclusion than that the word 'self' is like the word 'cause,' one of those categories of half thought out standpoints, which are useful in every day life, but which will not bear the dry light of science." Lord Haldane, *Pathway to Reality*, I., p. 106. The same writer also speaks of the universe as in final analysis the unique Individual that ultimately discloses itself as the totality of Experience or as all-embracing Mind, according as it is looked at from one side or the other." *Op. cit.*, p. 162; cf. *The Reign of Relativity*, p. 394.

{3} Just as space and time are found to be dependent for their reality on outlook, so do other aspects turn out to be equally dependent. . . . As higher standpoints are reached our vision becomes wider, and the object world, the relativity of which begins to be realized becomes less foreign. Reflection and action come to seem less separated. As the object world ceases to seem external and strange to the subject, conception and execution appear as in their ultimate forms inseparable. For mind that knows the distinction between its object and itself to be only due to finitude in knowledge, to conceive and to create are no longer mutually exclusive ideas." Lord Haldane, *Reign of Relativity*, p. 390.

{4} *Knowledge and Reality*, p. 19, note.

{5} *Appearance and Reality*, p. 142. The statement, however, calls for one qualification. Relations cannot exist "within" a substantial whole in the sense that the separate qualities can be subjects in their regard. Only the integral substance can be the subject of relations, as of any other accident. Some of Mr. Bradley's chief difficulties are based on this error in metaphysics.

{6} *Idea of God*, p. 304.

{7} *Hegelianism and Personality*, lect. vi.

{8} *Two Lectures on Theism* (Edin., 1897), pp.48, 50.

{9} *Ibid.*, p. 47

{10} *Supra.*

{11} *Op. cit.*, p. 60.

{12} *Foundations of Belief*, p. 6.

{13} *Collected Essays*, c. i., p. 159.

{14} Lord Grimthorpe, *Origin of the Laws of Nature*, p. 23, cited by Gerard, *Old Riddle and Newest Answer*, p. 37.

{15} Professor J. Ward, *Naturalism and Agnosticism*, I., p. 186.

Chapter XVI. Conservation and Concurrence

1. Direct and Indirect Conservation.

2. Necessity of Direct Conservation.

3. Divine Concurrence.

4. Theory of Simultaneous Concurrence.

5. Concurrence and Free-will.

6. Concurrence and Moral Evil.

1. *Direct and indirect conservation.* We treat in this chapter of two closely connected subjects -- the dependence of creatures on God for their continuance in being and for the sustained exercise of their active powers. The former of these is termed divine conservation, the latter divine concurrence. We have already dealt in some measure with these two points in chap. iii. It was there pointed out that God, when He creates, does not confer existence in such wise that the gift once bestowed belongs to creatures independently of the divine causality, but that He conserves them continuously, and that apart from this conservation they would lapse into nothingness. We argued, further, that just as they depend on God for their persistence in being, so likewise do they need a continued exercise of divine causality throughout all their operations. There is no action on the part of the creature, which is not sustained from beginning to end by the divine concurrence. Without this it could not endure for an instant. But both points call for a somewhat fuller treatment than was possible at an earlier stage.

It will be well, in the first place, to distinguish between direct and indirect conservation. A thing is said to be the object of direct conservation when the exercise of causality has regard to the actual being of the thing in question, so that apart from this causal influx it *ipso facto* ceases to be. Thus so long as a thought remains before the mind, it is being directly conserved by the intellect. Indirect conservation, on the other hand, consists simply in the removal of those agencies which would destroy it. When some substance readily liable to corruption is placed in an hermetically sealed air-tight vessel, it is indirectly conserved: and we exercise indirect conservation if we take a child from the vitiated atmosphere of a big city and send it to breathe the purer air of the country. In both of these ways does God conserve us. Of His direct conservation we shall speak in the next section. But His indirect conservation of our race must not be passed over without notice. Countless different agents cooperate to render the world habitable for man. There is nothing in these agents taken separately to necessitate that this should be. Nature is a whole consisting of a myriad parts: and the organization of the whole as a suitable home for man is in no sense involved in the existence of the parts. The present condition of things, with its strange adjustment to human needs, is no inevitable resultant of the substances composing the world and of the forces inherent in them. Indeed, in view of the ceaseless changes through which these substances are ever passing, the correspondence between inanimate and animate nature, and the adaptation of the whole to man, would assuredly, were things left to themselves, be of short duration, and the rest of the world would speedily become as inhospitable to our race as are to-day the Antarctic regions or the wastes of the Sahara. That this does not happen -- that seedtime and harvest do not fail -- must be attributed, as we have already urged, to the over-ruling causality of God. Man, in virtue of his spiritual and, therefore, immortal soul, is the crown of the material creation. The human race is not merely one group out of a number, distinguished from the rest by certain peculiarities of external form and by ampler cognitive powers. A chasm separates us from all other species -- a difference not of degree but of kind. The world is for man. And since this is so, it is but in accordance with the reason of things that God's providence should so order the action of the secondary causes of which the universe is constituted, that amid all changes they are constant in their adaptation to the preservation of life. In the next chapter, in which we treat expressly of providence, we shall shew that these principles are of application, not merely to the race viewed as a whole, but in the utmost detail and to every individual: that throughout the assigned period of his existence God directs each one to his appointed end, and in consequence exercises on his behalf the indirect conservation which he requires.

Yet not all the substances which God has called into being stand in need of this indirect conservation: for there are some which are incapable of destruction by created forces of any kind. No created agent can destroy a spirit. Created power is of necessity finite. And a finite power can only produce a result, where there is a natural potentiality for its production. If there is no natural potentiality, an infinite power would he requisite to achieve the end. Material substances are capable of destruction, simply because the substratum which enters into their composition is in potency to the reception of other forms than those which they in fact possess. We can resolve a chemical compound into its constituents and thereby destroy it, because it is naturally patient of this change f substantial form: thee is in it a potentiality for the reception of the simple forms in place of that proper to the compound substance. We can destroy life in plant or animal, for we can make changes in the subject-matter such that the vital principle can no longer animate it. One form is expelled and another takes its place. But where a spirit is concerned it is far otherwise. A spirit is a pure form. It has no material substratum capable of determination by another specific principle: it cannot therefore become something else. It must remain what it is, or suffer annihilation. But created power cannot annihilate any more than it can create. A spirit, then, does not need to be preserved against the action of hostile forces. If God does not annihilate it, it cannot be destroyed.

2. *Necessity of direct conservation.* The principal arguments for God's direct conservation of all created things came before us, as we have observed, in the chapter on the metaphysical proofs of God's existence. What is here said will be for the most part merely a further development of the reasons there given. Every effect properly so called demands the actual operation of the cause of which it is the effect: if the cause ceases to operate, the effect is no longer produced. But in all creatures God is the cause of being. The being which creatures possess is theirs in dependence upon Him. For finite being in all its forms is necessarily an effect due to Him

who alone is subsistent being -- *esse subsistens*. It follows that God exercises a continuous causality in regard of every individual finite substance: and that if He ceased to exert this causality, it would forthwith cease to exist. This, however, is precisely what we signify by conservation. The effective influx of being is not an event which takes place once and for all at the moment of creation. It is continuous, created existence being essentially dependent on it.

The assertion that an effect as such demands the actual operation of its cause is a self-evident truth. That which does not need the *actual* operation of its cause and can subsist without it, is not *actually* an effect. The principle may, however, be further verified by consideration of the four orders of cause taken severally. Thus it is manifestly true of the intrinsic causes, matter and form. Should the form be expelled from the matter, the substance which they unite to form ceases to be. It holds good no less certainly of the two extrinsic causes. If the final cause ceases to exercise its influence on the efficient cause, the latter will no longer operate. In regard to efficient causation, so far as substances are concerned, our experience is limited to causes *in fieri*: the dependence of a substance on its cause *in esse* does not fall under our observation. But the evidence afforded by causes *in fieri* and by the causation *in esse* of accidents is such as to forbid us to doubt that the principle holds good in this case also. A created substance can no more exist apart from the continuous causative action of God than a thought can exist apart from the efficient causality exerted by the mind. Not, of course, that God stands to the substance in the same relation which the intellect holds to its concept. But in both cases we are concerned with a cause and its effect. And though one effect is a substance, and the other a mere accidental determination, it is as impossible in the one case as in the other that the effect should exist apart from the causal influx on which it depends.

Or our argument may take a somewhat different form. The continued existence of a thing must be due to some cause, no less than the origination of that existence. There must be something to account for that existence in each successive period of time through which it endures.

God is the only being who is uncaused. This cause must be either the original act by which the thing was called into being, or the thing itself as a constituted reality, or some other created being, or finally God. No other hypothesis is possible. But of these alternatives the first three must all be rejected. Hence by a process of exclusion we are forced to recognize that God is the cause of the continued existence of things. The original act of creation cannot account for the thing's persistence in being: for that act is past and gone. A present fact demands a present explanation. It cannot, again, be the thing as a constituted and persistent reality: for this is just that for whose cause we are searching. We are enquiring why it should persist. If we say that it has a power of self-conservation, we are, on the one hand, explaining the existence of the thing by the power, while on the other we must explain the existence of the power by the thing to which it belongs -- a patent instance of a vicious circle. Nor yet can the effect be attributed to any other created being. A creature's powers, as we have seen, suppose a subject of action possessing a natural potentiality for the result produced. But the conservation of a being in existence, the effective action which retains it from lapsing into nothingness, does not presuppose any such subject. It is that in virtue of which there is a subject of action at all. It is, in other words, a continued creative causality: and as such demands infinite, and not finite, power. Just as a creature cannot by its action call into existence matter or spirit, because it cannot bridge the chasm between nonentity and being, so, too, it is incapable of the causal activity which has as its direct result that same existence as a persistent reality. It remains that it is God alone to whom the continued existence of created things must be attributed.

St. Thomas puts to himself the question whether God could create a being and then confer on it the power to continue in existence without divine conservation. It may, he notes, be urged that creatures can so produce their effects that they do not need the continuous action of their cause to sustain them: *a fortiori* God should be able to do this. Such reasoning, however, is readily shewn to involve a fallacy. There is no parity between the causality of God in regard to His creatures, and that exercised by created agents. Created agents are causes *in fieri* only: the effect depends on them only for the process by which it is brought about. God is the cause, not merely of this process, but of the being as such. Hence St. Thomas concludes that God Himself cannot make two contradictories simultaneously true. A thing created by God is one which is dependent on Him for its being: whereas a thing supposed not to stand in need of conservation is thereby understood not to be dependent on Him for its being, but only for its transition from nonentity to actuality -- its becoming. In other words, such a thing is not due to creation at all. It follows that it is entirely inconceivable that God should confer on any creature the power to exist without continuous divine conservation to sustain it in being.[1] In view of this very express teaching it is strange to find it sometimes asserted that the doctrine of creation at a given point of time is logically inconsistent with any other view than that of deism, according to which the world once created is independent of God. Professor Pringle Pattison mentions the Scholastic doctrine of conservation, and comments on it as follows: "This they held, even while maintaining at the same time a theory of the original creation of the universe at a definite period in the past. But the more thoughtfully we consider the idea of creation as a special act or event that took place once upon a time, the more inapplicable does it appear . . . . The act is an incident in God's existence, and the product stands somehow independently outside him and goes by itself: so that his relation to the subsequent unfolding of the cosmic drama is at most that of an interested spectator."[2] It is manifest that no one in any degree familiar with the Scholastic metaphysics could hold that the doctrine of creation involved the consequences here attributed to it. But inasmuch as such conclusions can be drawn even by a writer of distinction, it seemed desirable to shew how complete is the misconception involved.

To the proofs already advanced it seems worth while to add another given by some authors, which is drawn from God's power to annihilate being, should He see fit. If God has power to create finite beings, it follows that He can also reduce them to nothingness: He can take away the existence which He saw fit to bestow. But if we ask how such annihilation can come about, we find that it can only be conceived as the withdrawal of His conserving activity: that otherwise it is unintelligible. It cannot be the result of a positive action. In so far as action is positive, it is the communication of a positive effect, substantial or accidental. Doubtless, where material substance is concerned, such action may lead to the loss of a particular substantial form. Thus, if we cut a living thing into pieces, the vital principle is expelled. But the immediate effect here produced is positive. The extended body was actually one, and potentially many. Our action reduces the potentiality to act, and makes it actually multiple. The negative consequence, the loss of life, is only the indirect result. But in annihilation there is no positive effect at all. One form does not replace another: the thing simply ceases to be. Such a result can only spring from a cessation of action. The thing falls back into nothingness, not because God does anything, but because He no longer continues the action to which its being was due. In other words, annihilation would be incomprehensible, unless the existence of the creature were due to divine conservation.

It will be noticed that we do not raise the question whether God ever does annihilate a creature. There are reasons of considerable suasive force, which suggest that He does not do so.[3] Yet no argument can be given which shews that annihilation is impossible, that it is repugnant to one or other of the Divine attributes. There might, as we conceive, be valid reasons why God should in His wisdom call a creature into being for a time only. As regards the purely material creation there is no special difficulty in such a supposition. And this being so, God's power to annihilate forms a legitimate basis of argument.

It is hardly needful to point out that conservation is not the reiteration of creation -- a series of successive and distinct acts by which the created existence is constantly renewed. It seems to have been thus conceived by certain mediaeval Arabian philosophers, whose view St. Thomas mentions merely to dismiss.[4] The basis of the error was their inability to imagine any other cause save a cause *in fieri*. This led to a conception of conservation as a constant series of transitions from nothingness to being, so that the continuous identity of a substance in successive moments was more or less comparable to the identity possessed by the figures on a cinematograph-screen, which for all their apparent permanence, are really a series of separate pictures viewed in such rapid succession that the eye fails to distinguish them. It would be hardly worth while to notice this error, had it not also been occasionally attributed to the Schoolmen. Their teaching was, as we have seen, altogether different. According to them Conservation is the persistence, not the reiteration, of the creative act. Creation, viewed as God's action, is His free volition as causing the initial existence of the creature: conservation is that same volition as causing the continuance of that existence. While, considered in the creature, creation is finite being as dependent upon God in its beginning: conservation is the same relation of dependence regarded as an enduring condition.

3. *Divine concurrence.* When we assert God's concurrence with created causes, we signify far more than is implied by merely terming Him the First Cause of their various activities. The latter expression does not explicitly convey a distinct relation to the effect produced, but might be almost equally well employed if the causality exercised by Him consisted simply in an initial impulse given to the secondary agent. By concurrence is signified that God cooperates directly in the production of every effect due to a created cause: that throughout the process He is exerting an efficient causality proper to Himself, so that the result in all its stages is partially attributable to His direct agency. On this point all adherents of the Scholastic system are at one, though, as will appear, when they come to explain how God's cooperation is exercised, they are divided into two opposing schools. Yet all acknowledge that the divine concurrence is a necessary deduction from first principles. A proof of this conclusion may be briefly given as follows. Finite being in all its forms is a direct effect of God's efficient causality. In this all finite things resemble one another, that they are: and this common feature must be attributed to one and the same cause, which can be none other than Subsistent Being, God Himself. But the operations of finite causes are productive of being, substantial or accidental. Hence it is manifest that in every operation of a

finite cause there is a divine concurrence in virtue of which it is productive of this effect.

It is hardly necessary to point out that the conclusion here reached in no way involves us in the opinion that God is the sole cause, and that the causality of finite agents is only apparent. It is true that some have been found to maintain that created things cannot be more than 'occasional causes' that they are destitute of active powers capable of affecting what is external to themselves: and that the changes which they seem to produce are really wrought by God, who supplies for their incapacity by acting on their behalf. St. Thomas informs us on the authority of Maimonides that some of the mediaeval Arabian philosophers had adopted this view.{5} More recently a similar error was defended by some of the later Cartesians. Recognizing that the Cartesian system afforded no real explanation how material and immaterial substance could act upon each other -- how material things could give rise to concepts in the mind, or volitions formed within the soul could result in external changes, they cut the knot by a theory of occasional causes. God, they said, produces in the intellect the concepts which represent external things, but which cannot arise from our perception of them: and when we form a volition, it is He who really effects those changes in the external order, which correspond to our purpose. The Scholastic doctrine of concurrence is far removed from any such paradoxes. It attributes to secondary causes the exercise of a veritable causality. It has already been said that there is a difference of opinion among Scholastic philosophers regarding the mode of the Divine activity. Some hold with St. Thomas that the concurrence is required for the production of the action: that its function is to confer upon the finite agent that premotion without which it cannot act at all: that it is prior, not in time, but in the order of causality to the activity of the creature. It is, they contend, a *concursus proevius*. Many, however, are found who adopt the opinion defended by Suarez, and maintain that the influx of the First Cause has regard, not to the agent as such, but to the effect, viz., the resulting action. Premotion, they hold, is unnecessary, since the powers of the created cause require no complement to enable them to exercise their efficiency. Divine concurrence is requisite, for upon it the new effect depends for its being. But neither in the order of time nor in the order of causality is this concurrence prior to the action of the creature: it is, on the contrary, a *concursus simultaneus*.

In view of much that has been said in previous chapters it must be evident to every reader that in our opinion the former of these positions is alone tenable. We have urged in more than one connection that inasmuch as all action is a transition from potency to actuality, it is totally impossible that it can take place without the continuous agency of a cause external to the immediate agent: that otherwise we should be driven to admit that a being can confer on itself a new reality which it does not possess, giving to itself that which it has not got to give. The principle that the transition from potency to actuality supposes the operation of a cause which itself possesses the perfection actualized, is, we maintain, self-evident -- though, of course, the perfection may exist in the cause in a higher manner, and not in the manner in which it is found in the effect. It follows that the operations of a finite agent can only take place in virtue of a premotion, ultimately referable to the First Cause. The finite cause is instrumental in regard of the Prime Mover: and apart from a previous concurrence, its efficient powers lack their final complement.

In every case of purely instrumental causality, although the action is one, proceeding from both agents acting together, we may distinguish in the effect produced that which is proper to the principal cause, and that which appertains to the instrument. Thus, in the written page we discriminate between what is due to the pen and what to the directing mind. The same holds good in the case of all finite activity. There is an element referable to the First Cause: an element proper to the finite agent. In so far as the result, be it substance or accident, is being, it is due to the First Cause, Subsistent Being. The particular character of the being -- its determination to this or that kind -- is the part to be assigned to the immediate agent, the finite cause.

Yet here a word of caution is necessary. The causality of creatures in regard of the First Cause is not absolutely similar to instrumental causality in the usual acceptance of the term. The points of difference should be noted as well as the points of resemblance. Created causes, even such as are styled principal, resemble instruments properly so called, inasmuch as they can only operate in virtue of the action of a higher cause: while the action emanating from them is due to the combined efficiency of both, the lower acting in subordination to the higher. Moreover, just as a human agent uses different instruments according to the end to be attained -- the carpenter, for example, selecting a particular tool for a particular kind of work: so the First Cause produces the variety of effects which the created order displays, through causes which correspond in each case to the result intended. Yet there is a radical difference between the two. Where instrumental causation in the usual acceptance of the term is in question, the work achieved does not resemble the instrument but the principal cause. The statue resembles the conception in the mind of the sculptor: for this idea is the formal principle determining the principal cause. It does not resemble the chisel. The function of the instrument is to enable the material to receive the form communicated by the principal cause. Finite principal causes are not instruments in this sense. The effects which they produce resemble, not God, but themselves. The oak-tree produces an oak-tree: man, a man: the sculptor, as we have just noted, a statue modelled on the idea which he has conceived.[5]

This point is of the first importance. Since the form which the instrument aids in producing has no stable inherence in the latter, it follows that an instrument cannot be a cause endowed with freewill, producing its effect when it chooses. It depends absolutely on the cause which employs it, and which gives to it a transient elevation, transmitting through it the form in question. It is otherwise as regards finite principal causes. The forms which they produce have a stable inherence in them, either permanent as in the case of their specific nature, or temporary as in the instance of the statue. Hence their instrumental relation to the First Cause is not of such a kind as to exclude the very possibility of their being endowed with free-will.[6]

St. Thomas, in a well-known and much commented passage, enquires regarding the measure in which the actions of finite agents depend on

God. He sums up his discussion by enumerating four distinct ways in which the operation of every subordinate cause is due to the First Cause. God, he tells us, (1) confers the capacity for action -- the active powers: (2) He conserves them: (3) He calls them into activity (*applicat actioni*): and, finally, (4) it is through His assistance that all created powers operate. The distinction between these two last modes of dependence interests us here. Just as conservation is requisite as the continuance of creation, so, too, where the operation of the creature is in question, God must not only by an initial premotion call the agent from potentiality to act, but must throughout sustain the action by a continuous influx of causal efficiency. The conclusion follows directly from the principles of St. Thomas's philosophy, nor would any other solution be consistent with them. He goes on to remind us that God's active power is one and the same with the Divine essence: and, further, that God in virtue of His immensity is present within every finite agent, conferring on it the gift of existence. These considerations make it yet more manifest how intimate is the influence of the First Cause on all created activities, whether they belong to the material order, or proceed from spiritual faculties such as the intellect and will.[7]

We cited above (chap. xi., §3) a passage from Martineau, in which he supports his view that there are limits to the Divine prescience by contending that there are events in which the Divine causality plays no part. "Lending us a portion of His causation," he says, "He refrains from covering all with His omniscience." It will appear from what we have said that we regard this supposition as wholly inadmissible. For efficient activity of any kind to operate apart from the premoving influence of the First Cause would seem as repugnant to reason as for finite being to exist without the creative and conserving action of the Creator.

4. *Theory of simultaneous concurrence.* We have mentioned above the theory of simultaneous concurrence taught by Molina and Suarez. Although we regard it as erroneous, it is necessary to give a brief exposition of it, since during the last three centuries it has been defended by very many Scholastic writers, including the majority of those belonging to the Society of Jesus. Convinced that the Thomist theory of the

predetermination of the human will was both false and pernicious, they felt unable to accept a doctrine which apparently was so closely allied to it. In their anxiety to avoid a most dangerous error they went to the opposite extreme. According to this system, as we have already noted, a created cause needs no premotion to pass from potency to act. It requires, indeed, Divine concurrence to enable it to produce any effect. For every effect is being under some form or other, and there can be no production of being without the exercise of Divine causality: since being, as such, is always and everywhere due to the operation of Subsistent Being, viz., God. But there is no subordination of the created cause to the Divine causality: the former is not instrumental in regard of the latter. It must not, however, be imagined that there are two distinct actions which combine to produce a single result, very much as two men might unite to draw a load too heavy for one of them alone. There is but one action, which proceeds alike from the created cause and from God, yet so that priority belongs to neither of the two.[8] That the created cause stands in no need of premotion, may, Suarez holds, be easily shewn. Secondary causes are not incomplete in their respective kinds, but complete. To suppose that they need a Divine premotion to determine them to their action is to affirm that they are incomplete, and are not of themselves adequate principles of the result which they produce. But if it be admitted that they are, apart from any complement, true principles of the effect attained, then nothing is demanded of the First Cause save a concurrence with their action: premotion is unnecessary. Inasmuch as, in this explanation, the Divine concurrence is absolutely simultaneous, the question at once arises, how the correspondence between the Divine and human contribution is to be explained. As regards necessary causes there is no difficulty. God from all eternity has foreseen the mode of action connatural to each creature at each moment of its existence according to the circumstances in which it will be placed, and has decreed to afford it the concurrence requisite for the exercise of its powers. Where, however, the acts of free agents are concerned the case is different: for the Divine decree must be such as to allow for liberty of choice. Here recourse is had to *scientia media*. God foresees the alternatives presented to the created will in each individual contingency, and foresees likewise which alternative the creature will freely choose, provided the choice be rendered possible by the concurrence requisite for its realization. That particular concurrence, and not another, He has decreed from all eternity to give. He would have decreed otherwise, had His foreknowledge shewn Him that the created agent's choice would take another direction. The future free volition of the creature determines which shall be the concurrence destined for it. Yet we may say with truth that when the moment for action comes, God offers to the will a concurrence for any one of the various possible alternatives. Did He not do so, it would not be really capable of taking any other course than that which it actually chooses.[9]

Such is the system of simultaneous concurrence. Without attempting to deal with it at length it will suffice to indicate two points which in our judgment are fatal to it considered as an explanation of the activity exercised by secondary causes. In the first place, it involves the rejection of the principle *Quidquid movetur ab alio movetur* -- the self-evident truth that the transition from potency to act can only take place through the actual operation of an efficient cause other than the agent in question. The Suaresian theory is based upon the supposition that secondary causes, whether necessary or free, if placed in suitable conditions, can exercise their causal powers without any impulse from without. Were it not so, he holds, as we have seen, that the cause would be incomplete. He fails to see that it would only be incomplete in the sense that it lacked something which no secondary cause can possibly possess: nothing would be wanting to its perfection viewed as a secondary cause.[10] Thus he is led to explain away a principle of vital importance in the Scholastic metaphysics, and even to contend that neither Aristotle nor St. Thomas Aquinas really meant what they said in their appeal to this axiomatic verity.[11]

Equally decisive is another argument against this theory. Suarez is emphatic that the concurrence is with the action as such.[12] Otherwise we should, as he clearly saw, have to admit that a new reality could arise in no way dependent on the source of all reality, Subsistent Being. Hence the action must be attributed to both agents simultaneously, the created and the uncreated. Now it is true that one and the same work may be accomplished by a plurality of agents, acting together, provided that the work in question is divisible into quantitative parts, so that the several agents may each contribute a share. Thus, to employ an illustration already given, a number of men might combine to haul a heavy tree. But here we are concerned, not with the work (*operatum*), but with the action (*operatio*). And we need only consider what is essentially involved in the very notion of action to see that an action due to two agents is a contradiction in terms. An action is not an effect viewed in abstraction from the source from which it proceeds. It is a change considered precisely as proceeding from the active powers of the agent to which it is attributed. Or, as viewed from the side of the agent, it is the determination of its active powers to the production of the change in question. In creatures it is necessarily an accidental determination. In God, no accidental determination is possible; but His action *ab extra* is none the less the change produced, viewed precisely as issuing from Him as cause. It follows that if a given change is due to two agents not subordinated the one to the other, but acting independently, we have not one action, but two. If then the action of the creature is but one; and if it must in so far as it is something real -- a new determination of the finite agent -- be due to a causal influx of the First Cause, the source of being, this can only be because the secondary cause operates instrumentally as regards the First. In no other way is it possible for one and the same operation to be referred to more than one agent.[13]

5. *Concurrence and free-will.* It remains for us to consider the bearing of the doctrine of previous concurrence, which we are engaged in defending, on the question of the free volitions of the human agent. Can the two be reconciled? Is it possible to hold that divine premotion is requisite for every action, and that nevertheless the elective acts of the will are not predetermined by the First Cause? The Thomist school, as we have seen, deny the possibility. The transition from potentiality to actuality involved in every election cannot, they maintain, be initiated by the secondary cause. It lacks altogether any power of such initiation: it is simply indeterminate save in so far as determined to one course or another by the efficiency of the First Cause. Yet God so predetermines it, that it

follows the path which He has marked out, not by constraint, but freely. We have already shewn that we find ourselves unable to accept this view of the case. To us it appears far more manifest that predetermination and free election are mutually repugnant, than that there is a metaphysical impossibility in an election in which the will so determines its own course that its choice is in no sense predetermined for it. Nor does this self-determining power of the will seem to us incapable of reasonable defence.

We have seen that the object of the will is the good known as such by the intellect. Wherever the intellect recognizes an object as good -- whether its goodness lie in its intrinsic excellence, or be relative to ourselves, consisting simply in its power to satisfy some desire felt by us -- the rational appetite is at once, in a greater or a less degree attracted to it.[14] There arises forthwith in the will an indeliberate movement towards the object. The force of this impulse varies very greatly. On the one hand it may be so strong as to render resistance a matter of extreme difficulty: on the other, so slight as to be hardly perceptible. This indeliberate act, we contend, proceeds from the operation of the First Cause, and is in fact an initial premotion. It does not constrain us. We are free to cooperate with it, and so to act instrumentally in its regard. But we may, if we will, refuse our correspondence, and, turning to some other object which attracts us, pursue that instead. Or, we may. as we shall shortly point out, simply desist from action. The choice which we make is our own. But in so far as we act at all, the whole motion of the will is due to the First Cause as *causa principalis*. The action of the secondary agent is instrumental, in the sense in which we have explained that term above. For the finite agent lacks all power to initiate movement in its own right: it operates in every case in virtue of an impulse conferred by the Prime Mover. It will be observed that, according to the account just given, there is an exact correspondence between the final and the efficient causation to which an action is due. The efficient premotion of the First Cause is not arbitrarily given. God does not premove the will to desire this or that particular object, while in regard of other objects equally attractive in themselves, the will receives no such premotion. Whenever an object is such as to exert upon the will the attraction proper to final causality, the initial premotion of the efficient cause is conferred. It thus appears that the action of the Prime Mover on the free agent is analogous to that exercised upon inanimate substances, and, on a different plane, upon the brute creation. These are premoved in accordance with fixed law. Inanimate substances have, each of them, certain specific characteristics which determine what their activities shall be: and they are premoved to such action as these inherent 'forms' require. Thus, to take a simple example, iron, water, mercury, receive respectively the premotion which corresponds to their natures. Similar, though, as we have said, of a higher kind, is the premotion directing the activities of brutes in accordance with their natural appetites and instincts. Nor is it otherwise with the premotion of the will. This, too, is ruled by law. In so far as the mind views an object as good -- as a final cause -- the will is premoved towards the thing in question. Just as in inanimate things premotion is conditioned by an inherent 'form,' so in the rational will it depends on a 'form' temporarily inherent in the intellect. But many objects offer satisfaction to our physical appetites from which the law of right reason would bid us abstain. To allow them to exert their final causality on us -- to make them an end of action -- would involve a breach of moral obligation. Yet the mind cannot help being aware of their attractive force; and in so far as it gives its attention to any one of them, and regards it as adapted to the satisfaction of some desire, does the will experience an initial premotion towards that object. We are not speaking here of the definitive practical judgment, which is the final determinant of the free act.[15] We are concerned to explain what at first sight is calculated to cause surprise, that the will receives initial premotion to acts which are wrong, as well as to acts which are right. And we say that this is explained by the law which rules the activity of the faculty, viz., that in so far as the intellect views an object as capable of satisfying some desire, an indeliberate movement towards that object always takes place in the will.

We have already pointed out that there is one object in regard to which the will is not free, but necessitated.[16] We cannot look on beatitude -- full and complete happiness -- as undesirable, and hold it in aversion. If we contemplate it at all, we must desire it. But in regard to all other things we are at liberty to will them or to reject them: for these come before us as partial and incomplete realizations of the good. If the will yields to the attraction of such an object and desires it, it does so freely. For we only need to bid the intellect Contemplate it, not in its attractive qualities, but in its limitations, and we are no longer under any constraint to desire it. Just as there arose an indeliberate movement towards the object in virtue of what in it was good, so by reason of the disadvantages attached to it there springs up a movement in the contrary direction -- a premotion to its rejection: for in this case rejection itself appears as a good. The two movements will, doubtless, be of unequal intensity. But the will is not obliged to follow the stronger. We may deliberately adopt what we know to be a lesser good, if we choose to exclude the thought of that in which it is defective and consider solely the gratification to be obtained. Or, without a positive act of rejection, the mere contemplation of the deficiency and incompleteness of the object may lead to the cessation of desire. If, indeed, a man's mind should become so absorbed by some particular object that he can neither take note of its limitations, nor compare it with other ends, he is no longer capable of elective choice in its regard. This actually occurs from time to time when a man is suddenly mastered by an access of anger, fear or some other passion. But the case is exceptional: and in such circumstances man ceases for the moment to be a rational agent at all. He is no more responsible for his action than one of the lower animals. Normally, man is master in his own house. Thus, if we have received an injury, the remembrance of the wrong will probably arouse in the will an indeliberate desire to pay off old scores. But we know perfectly well that if we consent to this desire we do so as free agents, and become responsible for an act which it is in our power to avoid. We can, if we choose, consider revenge under a very different aspect. We can view it as a violation of God's moral law, and seeing it thus, can turn away from it.[17]

Thus, though human volition depends absolutely on the divine premotion, and in this, as in every other form of activity, there can be no transition from potency to act except through the efficient action of the

First Cause, the will is not predetermined. Freedom, we maintain, consists essentially in the power of self-determination. And to assert that the choices of the will are predetermined by a higher cause appears to us wholly irreconcilable with freedom and consequently with moral responsibility in man. Even as regards beatitude, though it is impossible for the will, if it act at all, to do other than desire it, yet it is free either to act or not to act. It retains the *libertas exercitii*. For though the object contemplated is happiness in its fullness, yet the subjective act of desire is a finite and, therefore, partial good. We may turn the mind to some other object of consideration, and thus banish the thought of beatitude: or we may find an object of desire in the mere exercise of liberty -- *stat pro ratione voluntas.*[18]

But how is it that man determines himself to abstain from corresponding with one premotion, and to admit another. Here is the mystery of free-will, and of this we have no explanation to offer. We can describe the conditions of the faculty's exercise, but cannot explain the act itself. Yet it will not escape notice that to abstain from correspondence is a very different thing from the initiation of motion on the part of the finite agent. We do not claim for the creature any power to originate reality apart from the First Cause. What is claimed in this regard is negative not positive -- not a power of independent action, but of abstinence from action. Where the creature acts positively, it acts instrumentally: and the action, so far as real, proceeds from the First Cause.

6. *Concurrence and moral evil.* We are not here concerned with the great problem of the existence of moral evil. That is reserved for the next chapter. But even if the existence of evil be taken for granted, a difficulty may be raised as to God's concurrence with the wrong action. We touched upon this subject in the preceding section; but a somewhat completer reply seems called for.

Every wrong action may be considered under two aspects -- as an objective reality and in its relation to moral order. Viewed purely as reality. the act contains no evil element whatever. Thus considered, it is simply being in one or other of its modes: and, as such, is actuality --

perfection -- in such and such a degree. The attribute of moral evil belongs to it solely in so far as it fails to conform to the order which reason prescribes. Here, as in all its manifestations, evil consists, not in anything positive, but in privation -- in the absence of something which full perfection demands. But though all perfection and reality flow originally from God, the creature is capable by itself of privation and defect. To it, and not to the Creator, must all the moral evil of the wrong action be referred. That in the act which comes from God is its reality, and is good. Whatever in it is defective and wrong is from the created will. This is plain enough as regards the external action. The blow, *e.g.*, with which the murderer kills his victim, viewed in itself and out of relation to the particular occasion, is an activity demanding health and strength: and, so far, is a perfection. The evil lies, not in the action as an action, but in the failure to observe due order in its exercise. This failure is no positive reality no evil entity to which God gives being. The same is true of those physical appetites which are for men the principal source of wrong-doing. In themselves they are not merely blameless, but necessary to the welfare of the species. Without their demand for satisfaction man would perish. But reason prescribes that their satisfaction should be controlled, that it should be permitted or checked in all cases with reference to the service of God, the rights of our fellow-men, and the harmony and due subordination of our faculties as a whole. If, as is too often the case, the human agent fails to observe the order which is obligatory on him, if his indulgence of his appetites is contrary to reason, the evil in the act is not attributable to God. God does not concur in the evil: for that is privation only. The principle is no less applicable in the case of the internal act of the will itself, the true seat of moral evil. We may take the extreme case of an act of hatred of God. The malice of such a wish lies not in the act as such. In certain cases aversion is a duty. It lies in the fearful disorder involved in exercising an act of aversion in regard of the Supreme Good.

These instances will have shewn that when it is said that moral evil consists in privation, we do not signify that all sins are sins of omission. The action is commonly positive, but of, such a kind that it lacks the due order which our free acts should possess. Nor, again, must it be imagined that the agent necessarily intends the privation as such. The sinner usually does not desire the element of wrong for its own sake. But he is intent on so me particular gratification, and would sooner render himself guilty of moral fault than abstain from the act which will secure it. When the nature of moral wrong is understood, the difficulty as to the divine concurrence disappears. God permits the fault, but in no sense approves it. He concurs solely with the action as an entitative reality, not in the moral wrong. So far as the act contains physical perfection it is referable to God: so far as it contains moral imperfection to the creature.

NOTES

{1} *De Pot.*, q. 5, art. 2.

{2} *Idea of God*, p. 302.

{3} *Summa Theol.*, I., q. 104, art. 4.

{4} *Con. Gent*, III., c. xv.

{5} *De Pot.*, q. 3, art. 7.

{5} "Agens per se et agens instrumentale in hoc differunt, quod agens instrumentale non inducit in effectu similitudinem suam, sed similitudinem principalis agentis. Principale autem agens inducit similitudinem suam: et ideo ex hoc aliquid constituitur principale agens quod habet aliquam formam, quam in alterum transfundere potest: non autem ex hoc constituitur agens instrumentale, sed ex hoc quod est applicatum a principali agente ad effectum aliquem inducendum." St. Thomas Aq., IV.. S., d. 19, q I, art. 2, sol. I.

{6} "Instrumentum dupliciter dicitur. Uno modo proprie: quando scilicet aliquid ita ab altero movetur, quod non confertur ei a movente aliquod principium talis motus: sicut serra movetur a carpentarlo: et tale instrumentum est expers libertatis. Alio modo dicitur instrumentum magis communiter quidquid est movens ab alio motum, sive sit in ipso principium sui motus, sive non: et sic ab instrumento non oportet quod omnino excludatur ratio libertatis: quia aliquid potest esse ab allo motum, quod tamen se ipsum movet: et ita est de mente humana." St. Thomas Aq., *De Ver.*, q. 24, art. I, ad 5.

{7} "Sic ergo Deus est causa actionis cujuslibet in quantum dat virtutem agendi, et in quantum conservat eam, et in quantum applicat actioni et in quantum ejus virtute omnis alia virtus agit. Et cum conjunxerimus his, quod Deus sit sua virtus, et quod sit intra rem quamlibet, non sicut pars essentiae, sed sicut tenens rem in esse, sequetur quod ipse in quolibet operante immediate operetur, non exciusa operatione voluntatis et naturae." *De Pot.*, q. 3, art. 7.

{8} Exterior actio Dei et creaturae una et eadem est, Ut diximus. Et ideo secundum eam rationem non potest actio creaturae manare aut pendere proprie ab actione Dei, neque e converso actio Dei potest proprie causare actionem creaturae, quia idem non causat seipsum, neque pendet a seipso. Item, quia actio solum est causa sui termini, et non est causa nisi per modum vim: actio autem Dei non est via ad actionem creaturae, sed ad effectum, neque actio est terminus actionis. . . . Loquendo de actione externa, tam Dei quam creaturae, sic non potest una dici prior natura quam alia, prioritate causalitatis, quia ut ostensum est, cum sint una et eadem actio, non potest inter eas intercedere vera causalitas." Suarez. *Disp. Metaph.*, XXII., sect. 3, nn. 8, 10.

{9} Deus praebet unicuique causae secundae concursum modo accomodato naturae ejus. Sed haec est natura causae liberae, ut, positis ceteris conditionibus praerequisitis, sit indifferens ad plures actus: ergo debet etiam recipere in actu primo concursum modo indifferente: ergo debet, quantum est ex parte Dei, illi offerri concursum, non tantum ad unum actum, sed ad plures. . . . alias voluntas creata nunquam esset proxime potens ad plures actus efficiendos: ergo nunquam esset libera quoad specificationem actus." *Disp. Metaph.*, XXII., sect. 4, n. 21.

{10} Cf. St. Thomas Aq., *De Pot.*, q. 3, art. 7, ad 7.

{11} *Disp. Metaph.*, XXII., sect. 2, 00. 20 seqq., 47 seqq.; Cf. Urráburu, *Theodicaea*, t. ii., p. 835 (Valladolid, 1900).

{12} *Disp. Metaph.*, XXII., sect. 3, n. 4,

{13} "Una actio non procedit a duobus agentibus unius ordinis: sed nihil prohibet quin una et eadem actio procedat a primo et secundo agente" St. Thomas Aq., *Summa Th.*, I., q. 105, art. 5, ad 2.

{14} *Supra*, Ch. xii., § 1.

{15} Difficulty is sometimes felt in regard to the doctrine that the *judicium ultimo-practicum* is the final determinant of the free act. It is asked whether this does not involve us in an infinite regress. Does not the choice of this judgment rather than another suppose a previous act of will, and this again a previous judgment, and so on? To this it is replied that there is no regress. The practical judgment determines the act of will in the order of formal causality while in the order of efficient causality this same volition is productive of this judgment rather than of one to a different effect. Reciprocal causality is impossible where we are concerned with causes of the same order. But, as Aristotle pointed out (*Meta ph.*, V., c. ii.), it occurs where the causes are in different orders. Such is the account of the free act accepted by the Thomist school. It would seem to be preferable to that advocated by Suarez, who holds that even after the final practical judgment, the will is able to choose freely between the alternatives presented to it. (*Disp. Metaph.*, XIX., sect. 6); cf. Garrigou-Lagrange, *op. cit.* § 61.

{16} *Supra*, Ch. v., § 2.

{17} Sic ergo illa causa quae facit voluntatem aliquid velle, non oportet quod ex necessitate hoc faciat: quia potest per ipsam voluntatem impedimentum praestari, vel removendo eam considerationem, quae inducit eam ad volendum, vel considerando oppositum, scilicet quod hoc quod proponitur ut bonum, secundum aliquid non est bonum." St. Thomas Aq. *De. Malo*, q. 6, art. 1, ad 15.

{18} Si ergo apprehendatur aliquid ut bonum conveniens secundum omnia particularia quae considerari possunt, ex necessitate movebit voluntatem: et propter hoc ex necessitate appetit beatitudinem. . . Dico autem ex necessitate quantum ad determinationem actus, quia non potest velle oppositum: non autem quantum ad exercitium actus, quis potest aliquis non velle tunc cogitare de beatitudine: quia etiam ipsi actus intellectus et voluntatis particulares sunt. *De Malo*, q. 6, art. 1.

Chapter XVII. Providence and the Problem of Evil.

1.   Providence, Physical and Moral.

2.   Prayer and Providence.

3.   Optimistic Theories.

4.   The Problem of Physical Evil.

5.   The Problem of Moral Evil.

1. *Providence, physical and moral.* Providence may be defined as the plan in accordance with which God disposes all things and directs them to the end which He has determined. Etymologically, the word is identically the same as prudence. Both terms signify foresight; and both denote the selection of the appropriate means for the attainment of a purposed end. But the scope of prudence in man differs in a most important respect from that of providence in God. Prudence, rightly so called, is concerned with the attainment of the end proper to the agent himself. It is the virtue through which a man disposes his actions towards the true goal of life. Apart from this he may be prudent in some particular sphere, *e.g.*, a prudent politician or a prudent farmer; but prudence in its full and proper sense is the right disposition of a man's actions in view of his last end. It is otherwise with God. God is His own end: and His action is identical with His essence. His providence can only have regard to what is external to Himself, *i.e.*, creatures. It is exercised in so far as He directs them to the attainment of the end for which He has created them.

Providence, as we have defined it, belongs to the divine intellect. It is the directive plan by which God rules the course of things. Yet it presupposes the volition by which He has chosen the ultimate goal of the created order: and it involves a further exercise of will in the execution of His purpose. This realization of the providential plan is, strictly speaking, to be distinguished from providence itself: for providence is eternal, its execution temporal. But in ordinary parlance God's execution of His purpose is included in the notion of providence: nor is there any objection to this employment of the term. As thus understood, providence belongs both to the intellect and to the will of God.

The all-embracing scope of God's providence is enforced by Father Boedder in a striking passage, which may be usefully cited here. He writes: "By His Infinite Wisdom He understands from eternity the end to be reached by creation, and the various ways in which by His omnipotence He might reach it. His will of infinite goodness embraces the end He has in view, and fixes by irrevocable decree the ways in which it shall be reached. Abiding in Himself by His absolutely perfect essence, He watches and directs in the course of time the exercise of every faculty of His creatures. He watches and directs it without any toil or labour, paying equal attention to the whole and to the minutest details. Thus by one glance of His infinite understanding He comprehends the dimensions of space, and calculates the distances and orbits of the heavenly bodies, and by one omnipotent volition keeps the whole machinery of the universe in motion, with a continual regard to the final goal it is to reach; so by the same eternal all-penetrating intuition does He read the most secret thoughts of every mind, observe the most minute oscillations of every organic cell, and count the most insignificant vibrations of every atom of matter, ruling by His omnipotent will all things so that there is no thought of any mind, no oscillation of any cell, no vibration of any atom which is not in some way or other duly subordinated to the end He intends."[1]

That all events without exception are ordered by Divine providence follows necessarily from the universal causality of God. He is the First Cause of all. And His works proceed from Him, not by a blind process of emanation, but in virtue of a free choice of the will. His operations are directed by His intelligence. But whatever an intelligent agent does is done in view of an end. Unless the intelligence proposed an end to the will, and the will embraced it, no action would ever take place. Hence every event which occurs is directed by God in view of a purpose. In other words, everything which happens forms part of the divine plan, and is disposed by God to the attainment of a given end: everything falls under His providence. When human prudence seeks to dispose events in view of some result, its control of circumstances is very partial. Unforeseen events are apt to occur, and often mar the best laid and most carefully designed schemes. But the reason for this lies in the limited scope of human causality. Many other causes are operative besides the human agent, which it does not lie within his power to direct. But God's causality is all-embracing: and consequently His providence is absolutely universal in its range. All that happens is part of the divine plan.

Of those who admit the existence of God very few have altogether denied His providential direction of the created order. Such was, however, the express teaching of the Epicurean philosophers. They explained the world on materialist principles, holding that it arose from the fortuitous concourse of atoms; and, while professing belief in the gods, contended that these paid no heed to the lot of man: that they were wholly indifferent as to his doings, neither angered by his crimes nor pleased by his acts of virtue.[2]

Later, in the eighteenth century, many of those who, under the influence of the prevalent rationalism, denied the existence of a divine revelation, and claimed that the 'religion of nature' was amply sufficient for all human needs, arrived at an almost similar conclusion, though on other grounds. Their philosophy admitted a personal God, the Author of Nature, but rejected both divine immanence and all providential direction of events. The system received the name of deism to distinguish it from the natural theology which recognized alike God's presence in nature and His providence, to which was appropriated the term theism. The deists held that God created the universe, established the system of law which governs its action, and placed within it the various species of living creatures, including man: and that having done this, He abstains from all further interference with it, allowing natural law to operate apart from any directive guidance. As a philosophy, deism was too shallow ever to win the adhesion of any thinker of mark. Yet there can be little question that during the whole of the nineteenth century views of this kind enjoyed a wide vogue. The decay of all belief in revelation, together with the effect exerted on many minds by the rapid advances of physical science, combined to make a system of this character acceptable to many who still retained in some way a belief in God.

Some thinkers at various periods have sought a solution of difficulties in the theory that God exercises. a directive influence over certain events alone, but for the rest leaves things to take the course which natural law prescribes. Thus Cicero in his work *De Natura Deorum* puts into the mouth of Lucilius an admirable demonstration of the divine government of the world drawn from the manifold harmonies of nature, but at the end admits that there are facts which refuse to be reconciled with the supposition that the divine direction extends to every incident without exception.[3] Maimonides likewise declares for a partial providence. He contends that God's foreknowledge of the future is, indeed, complete in respect of every detail. But that save in the case of man, events occur, not in pursuance of a divinely-ordered plan, but purely and simply in accordance with the laws of natural causation: that so far as other creatures are concerned, God's providence has no care for the individual, but only for the species as forming part of nature. Man, however, in virtue of his spiritual soul, holds an entirely different rank from all other material beings. His intelligence is due to a direct influx of the Divine light: and as such he claims a personal providence.[4] Moreover, the more worthy a man is, so much the more will God exercise a providential guidance of events for his benefit.[5] In this last point the Jewish doctor has laid hold of a truth of real importance, as will appear later. But in so far as the theory entirely withdraws many events from the immediate providence of God, it is manifestly false. God's providential plan is, as we have seen, all-embracing.

What then is the end to the attainment of which the plan of God's providence is directed? To ask this is to enquire what is the purpose of creation -- a question which we have already treated. We saw that the ultimate object of God's will can never be other than the Divine Essence. The supreme Goodness is in the last resort the sole sufficient reason of God's volition. Yet it appeared that God has also a secondary end in creation, viz., the good of the things which He has created. He does not leave His works incomplete, but brings them all to their appropriate degree of perfection. The course of His providence is directed to the realization of this purpose. Created things reach their destined goal by the path which the divine plan has determined for them. But, as we pointed out, we must not here consider substances in isolation from one another. The universe must be viewed, not as a mere aggregate of things, destitute of any unifying principle, but as an organized whole -- a stupendous work of the Divine Artificer. Just as a human artist has in view the beauty of his composition as a whole, not making it his aim to give to each several part the highest degree of brilliancy, but that measure of adornment which most contributes to the combined effect, so it is with God. Not all the species of animals and plants are equally beautiful. Some possess a higher degree of perfection than others. But creation, considered as an integral whole, is rendered more admirable by reason of their graded variety.[6] Here, too, we found the explanation why so many creatures seem to be frustrated of their destined perfection, and sacrificed to the advantage of others. The good of the total cosmos demands that the interest of the part should yield to the interest of the whole. If, for instance, carnivorous animals are constituent portions of creation, we need feel no difficulty in the fact that a vast amount of animal life serves as food to other tribes.

Man, however, forms an exception. He is no mere part of the material universe, subordinated to it as a part must be subordinate to the whole, and only of value as contributing to its perfection. He differs from all other creatures inasmuch as, having a spiritual soul, he is immortal: and being such, he has an absolute worth, not one which is merely relative to other things. Providence is concerned with him far otherwise than with the other species of living creatures. It guides each individual man, not in view of the perfection of the material universe, but in view of his own perfection.[7] The course of events as purposed and directed by God is far from being a scheme in which all creatures take their respective places on equal terms. In relation to man all other things, even the universe itself, are but means. St. Thomas well illustrates this point from the manner in which the master of a family takes forethought for his household. Within that sphere he exercises a veritable providence, if on a limited scale. He exercises it alike in regard of his children, his live-stock, and his material possessions. But he envisages these objects of his care in very different ways. He seeks the good of his children for their own sake, whereas he cares for his property for the sake of the children. [8]

The conclusion to which we have been brought by a consideration of the dignity of man as compared with other creatures is strongly confirmed by certain facts of observation. When dealing with the finality of the created order (chap. iv., § 1), we shewed how the order of the universe points to the conclusion that the world was intended to be man's home, standing to him in the relation of a house to its owner: that he is the end on whose account it is what it is. If this be so, it follows that the inorganic and organic kingdoms, as parts of nature, are for man: that they do not exist for their own sake, but for him. And, it can hardly be denied that the facts of natural history tend to shew that, in regard of animal and plant life, providence is concerned, not with the advantage of the individual, but with that of nature as a whole. Every species, it would seem, plays a definite part in the economy of nature. Darwin has shewn how great, *e.g.*, is the part played by earthworms, and the same is true of many of the humblest forms of insect life: so that there is nothing improbable in the belief that every species contributes in some manner to the good of the whole. Now providence has ensured the preservation of many of these species in a way which seems to exclude the supposition that the individuals are aught but means. The reproductive fertility which not a few of them display is enormous. If all the young of the cod or of the herring arrived at maturity these tribes would soon block the sea. What actually occurs is that immensely the greater portion are devoured by other species, and only the minutest fraction survives. Such a state of things seems only consonant with the conclusion that the aim of divine providence in dealing with these creatures is not their individual good, but that of nature as a whole, and ultimately of man the end for whom nature exists.

It is man's great privilege, in virtue of his intelligence, to exercise forethought and to cooperate consciously in the execution of God's providential plan. Man knows his end, and can act with that in view. The inorganic substances of nature pursue the course which is prescribed for them blindly as physical law determines. The brute creation, sentient but unintelligent, acts purely as the stimulus of appetite directs, and exercises no elective choice. But man, endowed with intelligence and will, enters consciously and freely into the divine plan.[9] In doing this he needs, of course, to be directed. But the mode in which his rational activities are controlled must be such as an intelligent nature demands. The directive agency must be moral not physical: it must consist of motives recognized by the reason and accepted by the will.

Man therefore falls under a twofold system. His course is guided both by God's physical and His moral providence. The former of these is exercised by the physical forces of nature; the latter through the law of reason, the voice of conscience and the sanctions of reward and punishment.

Reason makes known to man the natural law: and conscience warns him that in disregarding its prescriptions he is violating the commands of one who has authority over him: and that for any disobedience he is accountable to the Lawgiver. It is true, doubtless, that most men have but an extremely imperfect knowledge of ethical law, and that their ideas of right and wrong are often terribly astray. But the light is never totally extinguished. Certain broad elementary principles are never wholly obliterated, nor altogether misapplied; so that man is never without the means of striving after his true end. Moreover, the authority of law involves the existence of sanctions. Man cannot escape the conviction that those who have refused to obey the dictates of conscience will meet with punishment, and those who, notwithstanding the numerous obstacles which life puts in their way, have followed its guidance, will be rewarded. And this assurance is strongly confirmed by the patent fact that so far as this life is concerned the wicked not infrequently prosper and the good go unrewarded. Undoubtedly it detracts somewhat from the efficacy of natural law that we have no direct knowledge regarding these sanctions, but so far as mere natural religion is concerned are dependent on an inference.

That this is so seems to involve the moral necessity of a revelation. Yet so inevitable is the conclusion that such sanctions exist that, even apart from revelation, the belief in them is almost universal. Nor can there be any question that the fear of punishment and the hope of reward are practically indispensable to Lnduce man to choose the right and avoid the wrong.

The interior voice of conscience proclaiming the natural law of reason is not the only instrument of God's moral providence, though it is the principal one. God deals with us also mediately through other men. Man is born subject to parental control, and lives his life owing obedience to the rulers of the state. This subordination to authority is not an unnatural and artificial condition, but in accordance with the essential requirements of human nature. Society, apart from which man cannot live a human life at all, would be impossible unless organized on a basis of authority. Nor could the relations between men possess any stability unless the more general precepts of conscience were determined in much detail by a human ruler. The authority of all legitimate government is derived from God. And the commands imposed upon us from this source are part of His providence in our regard. In obeying them we conform ourselves to His designs on our behalf: whereas if we neglect them we are choosing our own path, and to our own undoing. It is doubtless true that from time to time secular rulers abuse the power entrusted to them, and command or countenance acts which are in direct opposition to the dictates of reason or to some positive divine mandate. Thus governments may approve polygamy or divorce: they may violate the imprescriptible rights of the parent over the child: they may command that divine honour should be paid to an idol or even to a human being. Laws of this kind have, of course, no providential character: and it may become a man's duty to defy them, even though it should cost him his life.

Yet another instrument of moral providence is found in the public opinion of society, in so far as it encourages a man to the practice of virtue by the honour which it pays to those whose lives are without reproach, and deters from wrongdoing by the stigma of disgrace which it attaches to it.

But God's providence is not operative only in leading men to the performance of strict duty that thus they may merit the rewards of a future life. This design for man's welfare has regard also to the conditions of his temporal existence. The life of man here is meant to be one of continuous progress along many lines. The powers of human nature ar to be brought to an ever fuller actualization, and man is intended ever to be acquiring a greater command over the inexhaustible resources of nature. The development of civilization, the amelioration of manners, the replacement of mere tribal life by a settled government, the growth of the arts and sciences -- all these are the effect of God's providential direction. Reason shews us these things as ends worthy of effort. And the desire for the good in all its various forms, which is rooted in our nature, impels us to strive after them, and thus little by little to make human life a nobler thing than heretofore.

Although man may abuse the gift of freedom, and deliberately reject the guidance which God has provided for him in the various ways which we have mentioned, this does not involve that an element of uncertainty enters into the divine plan: that its execution is constantly frustrated by the perversity of the creature: and that in consequence it frequently stands in need of modification. As we have shown in previous chapters, God knew exactly how every man would act on each several occasion, and how the choice, whether good or ill, might be rendered subservient to His own purposes. From among an infinite number of alternatives He chose in preference to all others that particular course of providence under which we live: and it pursues its way unimpeded by the faults of human agents to the precise goal which He desired. Its realization is certain even to its smallest details. God has, it is true, an 'antecedent will' that man should obey his law and that sin should have no place in the world. But His absolute will -- the ultimate decree which takes account of the foreseen free choice of the creature -- has fixed the course of providence as it is actually realized.

2. *Prayer and providence.* Is God's government of the world influenced by prayer? Men have ever believed that it is so. Wherever God is worshipped, there we find the belief that He can be approached in prayer,

and that in answer to our petitions He will grant favours which otherwise He would not have bestowed. Those who pray do not doubt that to meet their wishes God will direct the physical order to ends which would not have been realized but for their prayers. They ask for the cure of sickness, for fair weather for the crops, for immunity from storms during a voyage, and for many other similar benefits: and they give thanks because their requests have been granted. They are assured that the relation between man and God is a directly personal relation, and that it is no less possible for them to seek favours at the hand of the Creator and Ruler of the universe than it is to seek them from an earthly parent or protector.[10]

On the other hand, even among those who admit the existence of God, not a few find great difficulty in the notion of prayer. At this there is no reason for surprise. Outside the Catholic schools the philosophical basis most commonly offered for religion is, as we have seen, a mitigated form of the prevalent pantheism. But no pantheistic system is compatible with prayer. To mitigated pantheism, the physical universe is not the result of a free creative act on God's part, but the necessary mainfestation of His nature. That God should change even in the smallest degree the natural sequences of cause and effect would involve a change internal to Himself. Hence it is not wonderful that even some of those who make profession of Christianity frankly deny the utility of prayer so far as external events are concerned. Dr. Inge, the present dean of St. Paul's, speaking at the Anglican Church Congress of 1902, is reported as follows:

"Though the inflexibility of nature is assailed in high quarters -- by Mr. A. J. Balfour and Professor James -- he would be very sorry himself to rest any part of his religion on such possibilities. He was very suspicious of any tendency to trace the finger of God in the particular more than in the general, in the exception rather than in the rule, in the unexplained rather than in the familiar. The loving care of God for individuals, which we have all known and felt in our own lives does not shew itself in altering external events to suit our wishes."[11]

Further, just in so far as pantheism is really logical and consistent, it is driven to deny personality, in any proper sense of the word, to God, since in man alone does the divine nature become conscious of itself. Clearly there can be no question of prayer to an impersonal deity identical with the universe.

We have no need to occupy ourselves with objections derived from this source. We have already shewn at some length the philosophical unsoundness of pantheism, and have pointed out how futile is the attempt to find in such systems the foundation of a valid natural theology. But even from the theist's standpoint, the subject of prayer is not free from perplexity. Does not God, it may he asked, rule the physical order by general laws, only interfering with their invariable sequences in exceptional cases and for some special reason? These exceptional events we term miracles: and all are agreed that miracles are of rare occurrence, and differ conspicuously from ordinary answers to prayer. When God created the world, He assuredly gave to all the agents in the universe, whether living or inanimate, from man to the most elementary of nature's constituents, the laws which were best adapted for their particular work. Can we suppose that He is constantly interfering with their natural operations, and thus altering a plan which His supreme wisdom selected as the best? And would not such intervention have the additional inconvenience that it would render the course of nature incalculable, and make science impossible? On some very rare occasions the good to be gained may be so great as to justify a breach in the world's order: and then God will work a miracle. But otherwise must we not suppose that nature pursues its course with all the regularity of some vast machine: and that God will not alter its working in answer to our prayers?

The reply to this difficulty lies in the principle already laid down that the universe and its constituent parts are for man. Man is the end for whom all else that is exists and works: and God's providence directs the course of things with man's good in view. The laws which determine the activity of physical agents are, without doubt, in every case those which are most perfectly adapted to their respective functions. Yet there would be nothing inconsistent with God's wisdom if He should modify their natural operations when man's good so requires. Nor ought the changes thus involved to be regarded as breaches in nature's harmonious order.

When man, in virtue of the freedom with which he is endowed, gives a new direction to the activity of natural forces, we look on the innovation thus introduced as in accordance with nature's system. The supposition that God exercises His freedom in a similar manner is surely no more than analogy suggests.

It is needless to say that answers to prayer of the kind supposed are not changes in the eternal dispositions of providence. They form part and parcel of these dispositions. From all eternity God foresaw that a particular man would pray for such and such a boon: and He resolved to grant his request. The change is in the sequence of causes and effects which would otherwise have resulted. God's providential plan is immutable.

Nor again is it justly objected that the view for which we are contending renders the course of nature incalculable.[12] For the sphere in which we look for answers to prayer is precisely that part of nature's realm in which, owing to the great complexity of the causal forces at work, human calculation is baffled. Where this complexity does not exist, and the regularity of nature's processes enables us to foresee the event, we do not anticipate that our prayers will be heard by a miraculous reversal of law. There are manifest reasons why God should adopt this course. Where future events fall within the scope of human calculation, man is ordinarily able to provide sufficiently for his needs: he is himself to blame if he fails to do so. Moreover, there can be no question that, as the objection urges, man's interests would be most gravely injured if the legitimate conclusions of science were liable to constant frustration. But within the sphere in which the efficacy of prayer is actually experienced neither of these inconveniences is the result.

It will perhaps be urged that a divine interference with physical law must always and necessarily be miraculous: that while the determination of natural forces by man falls within the system of nature, because man is himself part of that system, God's action is an invasion from without, producing its effect without the presence of a physical cause: and that this is precisely what we mean by a miracle. Thus a physician cures a sick man by administering a drug, or enables him to continue breathing through a crisis of his illness by spraying oxygen; whereas we are supposing that God will in answer to prayer produce the very same effects without the employment of any means. Or, to take another illustration, if rain falls, this is because certain movements in the air-currents have brought about a change of temperature in the clouds; whereas we suppose that God might send rain by causing the temperature to rise independently of any preliminary movements of air. What are these but miracles?

It may be frankly admitted that whether such events are termed miraculous or not is largely a matter of terminology. Yet it is to be noted that they differ conspicuously from miracles in the usual acceptation of that term. A miracle, as the word is generally understood, is a work which is contrary to nature in such a way as to compel attention.[13] Were it not such, it would not serve the purpose for which it is designed: for it is intended to serve as a sign. It is, as we have already explained, the sign-manual by which God authenticates a revelation, or attests the sanctity of some one of His servants. In the changes which we are supposing, none can see how or when the divine intervention takes place. Furthermore, in all these operations God produces results which might naturally have been produced by a physical cause. He simply supplies by an act of volition for the causality which might naturally have been exercised by some creature deriving all its powers from Him. In most miracles the effect produced is of a more startling character: it is generally directly opposed to any natural process of causation, *e.g.*, the instantaneous disappearance of a malignant tumour, the restoration of sight after the destruction of the optic nerve.[14] 3. *Optimistic theories.* Before we seek an answer to the question how the permission of evil is compatible with the goodness and the power of God, it will be well to touch briefly on the view maintained by some thinkers that the world as we know it is, in fact, the best of all possible worlds: that inasmuch as God is supreme goodness, He could not have created any other world save the best; that in the present world is realized the highest perfection of which creation is capable. Were this indeed the case, the problem of evil, so far as God's goodness is concerned, would be non-existent. It would, however, he replaced by difficulties yet more formidable. To say that the world of our experience is the best of all possible worlds is a manifest paradox. If by a better world is signified a world in which there is less of physical and moral evil, nothing is plainer than that no impossibility is involved in such a conception. And granted that such a world is intrinsically possible, how is it that omnipotence cannot bring it into being? No satisfactory answer to these objections has been offered.

Optimism was maintained in antiquity by Plato[15] and by the Stoics: and in more recent times by Abelard, Malebranche and Leibniz: nor is it altogether without supporters at the present day. Abelard discusses the subject in two of his theological works.[16] He does not hesitate to advance the contention that since to do whatever good is possible is an obligation binding on all, it follows that God cannot do other than that which He actually does. What He actually does must needs be the best: less than the best He cannot do. For confirmation of his view he appeals to the reasoning of Plato in the *Timaeus*. To assert, as Abelard here does, that God's creative act and His providential dispositions are not His free choice, but matters of strict necessity, is not merely false philosophy, but is plainly enough in open contradiction with Christian doctrine. It is no matter for surprise that this was one of the many points on which ecclesiastical authority insisted that that erratic genius should retract his teaching.

The Schoolmen were at one in rejecting optimism. But after the decline of Scholasticism it again made its appearance. Malebranche upholds it in his *Entretiens sur la Métaphysique et sur la Religion*[17] (1678). From him Leibniz adopted it: and in his *Théodicie* (1710) gave it a more systematic treatment and an abler defence than it had hitherto received.

The following are the arguments on which Malebranche and Leibniz rely to establish their conclusion that this world is the best possible. (1) Since God created the world for His glory, it would fail of its end unless it were such as to correspond as far as possible to the Divine perfection which it is intended to manifest. But this requires that it should be the most perfect possible. (2) Among the infinite possible worlds which God could create, He must have a reason for preferring one above the rest. The sole reason which He can have is that one is better than the others. Any other choice would be inconsistent with His wisdom. (3) Similarly to choose the less perfect in preference to the more perfect would be inconsistent with His supreme goodness.

Leibniz recognizes the need of explaining in what sense the world is said to be the best: and replies that it is so, not in view of man's advantage, but in view of the good of the universe as a whole. Thus, since the best possible universe supposes the gifts of reason and free-will in man, God would bestow these endowments, even should the result be preponderatingly hurtful to man himself; though in fact the beneficial consequences are far greater.[18] He explains the existence of evil by the imperfection inherent in and inseparable from the creature.[19] God, he contends, was willing to create a world, which, though inevitably containing evil, is nevertheless the best possible. To the objection that God's infinitude involves that whatever world He may create, it must still be possible for Him to create one which is better, he replies that the argument would be valid if it were question of an individual substance, which is necessarily finite; but that the universe in the full measure of its duration is infinite.[20] The fallacy here is glaring. It is plain that even if the universe should last an infinite time, there is no reason whatever why God should not have created one, which should have a similar duration, but a greater degree of perfection.

In our own day the late Sir Henry Jones made explicit profession of optimism in his Gifford lectures, contending that the best of all worlds must necessarily include the process by which rational agents achieve moral and spiritual excellence, and that this is best secured in such a world as our own. The passage in which he states his views may here be cited.

"If the moral process, the practical life that is spent in achieving spiritual excellence has this unconditional worth and is the best, then the world which provides room for that process is itself the best world. It is better than the so-called perfect world, or world in which the ideal and real are supposed to coincide, a world that is perfect in the static sense. . . . Our view then is that the moral life is the best thing conceivable, and that this present world, owing in a way to its imperfections, furnishes an opportunity for the moral process and demands it as the ultimate good."[21]

Yet even if we admit, as we well may, that the world in which we are actually placed is admirably adapted to be a training ground for the moral life, it does not follow that God could not have formed a race capable of greater perfection than man, or one of which fewer members would misuse the opportunities offered them of achieving excellence. Indeed, the objection we have just urged, viz., that it must necessarily lie within God's power to create something more perfect than the world as it stands, is fatal to any optimistic theory. The created order, as we have seen, is the finite representation of God's perfections. These are infinite; and hence it follows that no matter how perfect we may conceive the creature to be, it remains at an infinite distance from its archetype.

Thus there can never be a world such that God cannot, if He desires, create one far more perfect, as containing yet an ampler representation of His inexhaustible being. It follows that in choosing the degree of perfection which the created order shall possess, God is absolutely free. Whatever He does will be very good; for from Him who is Goodness, nothing but what is good can proceed. But He is not held to any particular degree of goodness.

Yet it may be admitted that there is a sense in which the world is the best. Given the end which God proposed to Himself, He must needs create the world in which that end is most perfectly realized. God does not, and cannot, carry out His design in any but the most perfect manner. Where supreme wisdom and supreme power are at work, there is no room for imperfection in the execution of a purpose.[22] Although our understanding of the Divine end must needs be utterly inadequate, and although we recognize that much of what He does will necessarily be obscure to our intelligence, yet we know that His aim in creation is the probation, the training and the perfection of human souls. From this point of view the world as God has made it must be the best: and so far we are in full accord with the author just quoted. Difficulties may, and do, remain, which we are not fully able to solve. The principal of these we are about to discuss: and it will appear that we can see enough to know that they are not such as to render this conclusion doubtful. The world is a work worthy of God's wisdom, His goodness and His power. Yet it is beyond all question that He could, had He so willed, have created something, absolutely speaking, more perfect -- a nobler race than ourselves, and with a more wonderful world as its home.

4. *The problem of physical evil.* The existence of evil in the world must at all times be the greatest of all the problems which the mind encounters when it reflects on God and His relation to the world. If He is, indeed, all-good and all-powerful, how has evil any place in the world which He has made? Whence came it? Why is it here? If He is all-good, why did He allow it to arise? If all-powerful, why does He not deliver us from the burden? Alike in the physical and moral order creation seems so grievously marred that we find it hard to understand how it can derive in its entirety from God. We can hardly feel surprise that in old times men took refuge in dualism, and declared the world to be the scene of conflict betweep two opposing principles, each of them ultimate in their kind, or even that, with less excuse, some in our own days propound the theory of a non-omnipotent God.

Though the problem of physical pain, with which we are concerned in the present section, presents less difficulty than that of moral evil, it is much more frequently urged. It appeals strongly to an age which has in large measure lost sight of spiritual standards, and placed its chief good in material well-being. To those whose philosophy of life is based on such principles, the very existence of pain is an insoluble enigma. If material comfort and prosperity are man's true object, the permission of pain by the Almighty admits of no justification. It is a sheer frustration of the purpose of life. But hedonism is no true philosophy: and our life has a higher issue than physical comfort.

The difficulty is, however, very real in any case. The actual amount of suffering which the human race endures is immense. Disease has store and to spare of torments for the body: and disease and death are the lot to which we must all look forward. At all times, too, great numbers of the race are pinched by want. Nor is the world ever free for very long from the terrible sufferings which follow in the track of war. If we concentrate our attention on human woes to the exclusion of the joys of life, we gain an appalling picture of the ills to which flesh is heir. So, too, if we fasten our attention on the sterner side of nature, on the pains which men endure from natural forces -- on the storms which wreck their ships, the cold which freezes them to death, the fire which consumes them -- if we contemplate this aspect of nature alone, we may be led to wonder how God came to deal so harshly with His creatures as to provide them with such a home.

As the objection is stated to-day, a special point is often made of the sufferings of animals. We are reminded of the manner in which they prey upon each other, and how this fearful struggle with its accompaniment of unspeakable pain has endured for untold ages. Is this perpetual carnage, we are asked, compatible with belief in a beneficent and omnipotent Creator?

Those who urge the objection commonly treat animal and human suffering as though they were almost, if not quite, on the same footing. This is not the case: and the two call for separate treatment. We shall deal first with the sufferings of animals, and then go on to speak of pain as suffered by man.

We observe then, first, that for our estimate of the sufferings of animals we are wholly dependent on guess-work. We have no means of judging to what extent they feel. We know, it is true, that the more highly organized species of animals do experience pleasure and pain in a manner analogous to, though in a measure far removed from, that in which man is sensible of these conditions. That the degree of their suffering is very different from our own, results from the nature of their faculties as contrasted with those of man. Man by reason of his immaterial intellect transcends the limitations of time. He gathers up the past and the future into the present. The pain of the present moment is increased indefinitely because it is grasped as the successor of a long chain of like pangs, and because of the agonizing prospect of a like series yet to come. The multiple burden of all is apprehended as a collective whole, and is felt to be more than man is capable of enduring. It is hard for us even to imagine on how low a scale must be the pains endured by a creature destitute of that spiritual power which enables us to live in the past and in the future, and endowed only with sensitive apprehension and with that associative faculty which we term the sensitive memory. Even if some member of the brute creation possessed a nervous organization as sensible to pain as our own -- a wholly improbable hypothesis -- the pain which it actually endured would be on a totally different plane. It may, indeed, be said that the animals testify to the acuteness of their sufferings by manifest signs. But to this it is readily replied that in this they would seem to resemble children, who are extremely demonstrative, even when the pain which they are enduring is very trifling.

Moreover, there is another side to the picture. The pleasures of animal existence should be weighed against the pains. A little consideration will convince us that so far from pain exceeding pleasure, the balance is wholly on the other side. Earth, sea and sky teem with delighted existence, so that the mere contemplation of the joy of living creatures will often enable a man to shake off his sadness and rejoice with them. To picture the animate creation as a scene of universal anguish is a travesty of truth -- a caricature in flagrant contradiction with the facts. Joy preponderates everywhere. These reflections should surely be sufficient to shew how unreasonable is the sentimentalism which is sometimes displayed in commiseration for what is termed the unmerited suffering of the animals.

But why, it will be said, should there be any suffering at all? An Almighty Creator could have given His creatures the joy of life without its pains. Yet it may be asked whether pleasure and pain are not alike connatural to animal existence in such wise that absolute immunity from pain in any animal would involve a reversal of natural order. Granted that there was an animal creation at all -- beings, that is, with a corporeal nature and with bodily organs capable of sensation -- it is reasonable to suppose that pleasure and pain are properties necessarily consequent on such a mode of being, pleasure resulting from the due exercise of a natural activity, pain from the undue frustration of such exercise. Doubtless God might, had He willed, have worked a perpetual miracle to ward off pain. But it hardly appears consonant with His supreme wisdom that He should call the sentient creation into existence, and forthwith reverse the system of natural law which it postulates. Nor indeed have the creatures on whom God bestows the boon of life and its joys, any right to claim such an intervention on their behalf. Furthermore, pain has certain incidental effects of great importance. It is the pain of hunger which stimulates each living thing to seek its necessary food: the discomfort of want is demanded to overcome its natural inertia. Were this monitor taken away, the animal creation would be in evil case. Moreover, pain serves another most important end in keeping the creature from actions which would prove detrimental to it. It is plain that its total removal would result in grave inconveniences demanding further and further alterations to which it is difficult to see a term. While in view of our very limited knowledge, we must not shut our eyes to the fact that there may be profounder objections which we have no means of apprehending.

It is doubtless true that natural forces operate blindly and pitilessly, and may from time to time involve the destruction of life on a large scale. Yet so far is it from being the case that nature is a harsh stepmother to her offspring, and the world an inhospitable dwelling, that, on the contrary, nature's dispositions operate in a multitude of remarkable ways to the advantage of sentient life as a whole and to the permanence of the different species. We have already had occasion to notice the provision in virtue of which the vegetable world restores to the atmosphere the very ingredients of which animal respiration is ever depriving it, and in default of which all animal life would perish. No less remarkable is the peculiarity in virtue of which, contrary to analogy, water expands when near the freezing point instead of contracting, so that ice rises to the surface instead of forming on the bottom. Were the latter the case the sea itself would gradually solidify. All aquatic life would be destroyed, and the globe itself become uninhabitable. These conditions are of general application. But the provision for the permanence of individual species is equally striking. There are certain creatures which exercise an important function in the economy of animal life inasmuch as they furnish a great part of the food needed by other tribes. Such, for instance, are the herrings. A small proportion only of the myriads of young produced come to maturity, the vast majority being early devoured by the species which depend on them for sustenance. Yet the fertility of these fish is so prodigious that the absolute number of those which escape is considerable. Thus it comes about that the permanence of the species is secured, and the supply of food never falls short. On the other hand, it is noteworthy that in the case of animals, which by reason of their strength or swiftness are able to defend themselves, or the habits of which put them in less danger of attack, such fertility is a thing unknown. Here the continuance of the species is safe without it: and the number of offspring is found to be small.

It may not improbably be said that to adduce such an instance as the reproductivity of the herring and the cod to establish nature's provident care for the animal creation, is strange enough. Do not the facts really lead us to precisely the contrary conclusion, and illustrate the ruthless sacrifice of life involved by the physical constitution of the world? Is not this just one of those facts which appear almost irreconcilable with the wisdom and omnipotence we have attributed to the Creator? For we have just admitted that this reproductivity is requisite simply because of the wholesale destruction of individuals through the predatory habits of other species of fish. The difficulty thus raised, however, loses its force when it is remembered that, as we have already urged, apart from man, the end purposed by the Creator is the perfection of the system of nature as a whole, not that of any individual creature. Where a system composed of many parts is in question, the perfection of the whole must often demand the sacrifice of the advantage of the constituent elements viewed as individuals. The organizer of the system does not desire or intend harm as such to any part. But he permits that individual parts should forfeit something, in order that the good of the whole may be thereby promoted.[23] To the system of nature it is requisite that the species should be preserved. Hence the continuance of the predatory tribes is secured by providing them with the food suitable to them, and that of the tribes on which they prey by the enormous reproductivity of which we have been speaking. The destruction of a multitude of individuals is tolerated. Undoubtedly this is from one point of view an evil. But the evil of one species is compensated by the benefit done to others. Nor would it be reasonable to urge that the system of nature should have been so altered that the various tribes should do each other no hurt: that the lion should eat straw like the ox, and the spider live out its days without doing damage to the fly. This would be to ask, not merely for a perpetual miracle, but for an order of things far less in accordance with divine wisdom than is the present system. Granted that the Creator has given being to those types of perfection which we know as carnivora and insectivora, wisdom would seem to demand that provision should be made for them in accordance with their respective natures and not in opposition to them.[24]

When once it is realized that, if we prescind from the case of man, God's end is the good of the whole and not the good of the individual, it will be readily seen that even death and corruption, which might appear to be pure evil in regard of sentient life, serve in fact a useful and, indeed, necessary end. Did not death remove the older generations, earth would soon afford no room for the latest comers: nor would it be possible for these to find food. The multiplication of individuals would before long be such that the globe would not suffice for its inhabitants. Death is thus an essential part of nature's provision for the benefit of the species. So also the corruption of dead matter, great as is the repugnance which it excites in us, is beneficial in its results. Were it not that through the destructive activity of germ life, the inanimate body is resolved again into its constituent elements, earth would become a vast collection of corpses. In the actual course of things it at all periods affords a home perfectly adapted to the beings which the Creator has placed in it.

The foregoing considerations suffice, we think, to shew that the physical evils of the world, so far at least as they effect the lower creatures, are in no way incompatible with the wisdom and power of God. He might undoubtedly have framed a universe of a wholly different kind. But, granted that in the exercise of His freedom, He chose to create a universe inhabited by successive generations of sentient beings, even our human intelligence, limited as it is, can see that there are good reasons why He should not remove the evil naturally incident to creatures such as those which He made, but should allow it to remain, using it, however, as the means to the attainment of good.

The case of man, as we have said, differs widely from that of the lower animals. We have seen that where these latter are concerned, the fate of the individual is a matter of indifference. The species, not the particular individual, is requisite for the perfection of the natural order. And providence disposes of the individual for the benefit of a species -- its own or another. With man it is not so. By reason of his immortal destiny each individual man is an end, irrespective of the race to which he belongs or even of the universe as a whole. Divine providence is concerned with him for his own sake. It is not enough to shew that what is hurtful to the individual subserves the good of the whole. It must appear that though evil under one aspect, it is not really opposed to the highest good of the individual himself. [25]

Yet though the reasons which we have hitherto employed are inadequate fully to explain physical evil in relation to man, many of the considerations advanced retain their force. Thus, of man, as of the animals, it is true that the balance is immensely on the side of happiness. The pessimist who declares that, in view of the suffering of life, existence is an evil, misrepresents the facts. There is plenty of joy in life, though to much of it we are so habituated that we accept it as a matter of course. Let a man be deprived, for instance, of the use of a single sense -- of hearing, or sight, or of the power of speech -- and he quickly becomes aware how much pleasure has hitherto streamed in through that avenue, though in all probability he seldom, if ever, adverted to the delight which he was experiencing. The problem before us is certainly not to explain why the Creator has made misery our portion. In the main our lot is such as to bear witness to His goodness and His omnipotence. We are merely concerned to learn why He has not removed suffering altogether from our life.

Much light is thrown on the question by the consideration that this life is a probation. Man's true end, as we have urged, is the possession of the supreme Good. And everything tends to shew that this will not be attained by each and all without exception, but by those alone who by a right use of the gift of freedom have in some sort merited it: and that the measure of a man's recompense will correspond to his deserts. If then it can be shewn that physical evil is one of the most important factors in assisting man to the attainment of his end, it at once becomes evident that there was ample reason why God should not interfere with the course of nature, but should tolerate the existence of physical suffering in view of the good which would result.

Pain is the great stimulant to action. Man, no less than the animals, is impelled to work by the sense of hunger. Experience shews that, were it not for this motive, the majority of men would be content to live in indolent ease. Man must earn his bread in the sweat of his brow. And the duty thus imposed is for most men the school of virtue. It is in fulfilling the obligation of daily toil that they learn to practise justice, diligence, patience, charity to others, obedience to those who are over them. Without the occasion thus afforded it may safely be said that virtue would have little chance. Ease is no school of moral progress. Moreover, suffering serves to call forth in man a measure of goodness which would otherwise never be realized at all. Virtue reaches its perfection when it is exercised at a severe cost to the agent. The man who gives to his neighbour, when to do so involves some painful self-denial, has attained a higher degree of charity than he whose gifts entail no inconvenience to himself. And one reason, plainly, why God permits suffering is that man may rise to a height of heroism which would otherwise have been altogether beyond his scope. Nor are these the only benefits which it confers. That sympathy for others which is one of the most precious parts of our experience and one of the most fruitful sources of well-doing has its origin in the fellow-feeling engendered by the endurance of similar trials. Furthermore, were it not for these trials, man would think little enough of a future existence, and of the need of striving after his last end. He would be perfectly content with his existence, and would reck little of any higher good. The considerations here briefly advanced suffice at least to shew how important is the office filled by pain in human life, and with what little reason it is asserted that the existence of so much suffering is irreconcilable with the wisdom of the Creator. They shew, moreover, that, where man is concerned, the explanation of suffering is other than in the case of the lower animals. The sufferings of men are directed primarily to the good of the sufferer himself, while they also afford to others an opportunity for the practice of virtue.

In the same way, we need feel no perplexity at the numerous instances in which human life is cut short prematurely, and the purpose of nature seems to be frustrated by death. To the lower animals this life is all, and hence a premature death is for the individual concerned an irreparable loss. But when life is viewed as above all else a probation, it is seen to be of little importance whether a man live out his full tale of years or not. Indeed, the shortening of the probation may be to the individual, not a loss, but an immense gain.

Much has been said of the calamities brought about by natural forces. In the eighteenth century the Lisbon earthquake led many to ask how such things as earthquakes and volcanoes could be reconciled with a beneficent providence. It has often been replied that these occurrences are due to the operation of the same physical causes which have made the earth a fit place for human habitation, and that we have no reason to demand a miraculous suspension of laws which in their general effects are so useful to us, merely because from time to time they result in a purely local disaster. This is true as far as it goes. Yet more may be said. The earthquake and the volcano serve a moral end which more than compensates for the physical evil which they cause. The awful nature of these phenomena, the overwhelming power of the forces at work, and man's utter helplessness before them, rouse him from the religious indifference to which he is so prone. They inspire a reverential awe of the

Creator who made them and controls them, and a salutary fear of violating the laws which He has imposed.

It may be asked whether the Creator could not have brought man to perfection without the use of suffering. Most certainly He could have conferred upon him a similar degree of virtue without requiring any effort on his part. Yet it is easy to see that there is a special value attaching to a conquest of difficulties such as man's actual lot demands, and that in God's eyes this may well be an adequate reason for assigning this life to us in preference to another. We have shewn already (chap. xii., § 3) that in the exercise of His creative power He is supremely free. It is for Him to determine the particular mode in which finite being shall represent the infinite perfection which is His. He is not bound to ensure that our lives shall be exempt from all that we may regard as an inconvenience.

We have laid stress on the value of pain in relation to the next life, because it is in the next life, and not in this, that man must attain his last end. But it scarcely needs to be pointed out that pain is a source of many benefits in this life also. The advance of scientific discovery, the gradual improvement of the organization of the community, the growth of material civilization -- all these are due in no small degree to the stimulus afforded by pain.

There will at all times be much to perplex us in the ways of providence. Much of the suffering with which the world abounds will be inexplicable to us, and we shall strive in vain to understand why this or that particular evil is permitted. But we can, at least, see that physical evil does not stand in insuperable contradiction with the divine attributes. When Mr. McTaggart writes: "There are many things in the universe which are not only intrinsically indifferent, but intrinsically bad.

Such, for example, is pain "[26]: and proceeds on this ground to declare the doctrine of Divine omnipotence untenable, his reasoning is altogether unsound. It would be necessary for its validity that we should admit the principle on which optimism is based, viz., that God is under the necessity of excluding all imperfection from creation. This, as we have seen, is not the case. Pain is, it is true, an evil in relation to physical well-being. But granted that God desired to create beings endowed with sentient life, then no solid reason can be shewn why He should not create them liable to pain, the natural accompaniment of such life, provided only that He turn it to good ends. It is quite arbitrary to demand that He should exclude it miraculously. In the dispositions of His providence pain is, in fact, one of the most effective means in aiding man to secure his ultimate beatitude.

5. *The problem of moral evil.* The existence of moral evil constitutes a far greater difficulty than does physical evil. It is not hard to see that God may have good reason for permitting pain and suffering, and may employ them as an instrument of good as regards the creature. But moral evil is essentially a breach of some law which He has made: and hence is of its very nature in conflict with His will. The man who sins thereby offends God. If he persists in his rebellion, the severance between the two must one day become final, and man will forfeit for ever the last end which alone can satisfy him. We are called on to explain how God came to create an order of things in which rebellion and even final rejection have a place. Since a choice from among an infinite number of possible worlds lay open to Him, how came He to choose one in which these occur? Is not such a choice in flagrant opposition to the Divine goodness?

Some recent philosophers have sought to solve the riddle of evil by explaining it away. Hegel declares that sin is a necessary stage in the transition from ignorance to virtue. Man's first state he holds to be one of innocence combined with ignorance. As he advances in knowledge the impulse of egoism arises in him, and inevitably he permits selfish interests to draw him away from the pursuit of the common good. This condition we term sin. He soon, however, discovers that egoism brings no satisfaction, and hence in the long run is driven back to virtue. Since it is only in this wise that man can learn that egoism is a mistake, this transitional stage is unavoidable. It is, indeed, preferable to ignorant innocence. Both are evils: but sin is the lesser of the two. Schleiermacher adopted another expedient. He maintains that sin is simply the internal sense of deficiency due to the inadequacy of our consciousness of God:

that it has no objective existence in the sense of being a conscious act of disobedience on the part of a distinct personality.

It is manifest that theories such as these are contrary to the plainest and most fundamental facts of human experience. No datum of consciousness is more certain than that our moral lapses are no necessary stage in the passage to virtue, no mere inadequacy in our consciousness of God. Nothing, again, is more patent than that acquaintance with evil does not force us back to good. It is not in this direction that we must look for a solution of the problem. Indeed, such theories as these only furnish an additional illustration of the utter insufficiency of the philosophical systems of which they form a part.

How, then, can we account for God's permission of moral evil? It is not sufficient to say that it is due to the gift of free-will which He has bestowed upon the creature. Free-will need not, as is so often assumed, involve the power to choose wrong. Our ability to misuse the gift is due, as we have already argued,[27] to the conditions under which it is exercised here. In our present state we are able to reject what is truly good and exercise our power of preference in favour of some baser attraction. Yet it is not necessary that it should be so. And all who accept the Christian revelation admit that those who have attained their final beatitude exercise freedom of will, and yet cannot choose aught but what is truly good. They possess the knowledge of Essential Goodness: and to it, not simply to the good in general, they refer every choice. Moreover, even in our present condition, it is open to omnipotence so to order our circumstances, and to confer on the will such instinctive impulses, that we should in every election adopt the right course and not the wrong. The existence of moral evil, however, becomes explicable, when it is admitted that man's life is a probation. We noticed above[28] that this conclusion is regarded as certain by all theists. God, in other words, has created the present order such that man should have the glory of meriting his last end. We can see readily enough that in this He has conferred a great privilege upon us. To receive our final beatitude as the fruit of our labours, and as the recompense of a hard-won victory, is an incomparably higher destiny than to receive it without any effort on our part. And since

God in His wisdom has seen fit to give us such a lot as this, it was inevitable that man should have the power to choose the wrong. We could not be called to merit the reward due to victory without being exposed to the possibility of defeat.

Yet the question suggests itself: Could not God have so disposed things that none should be actually defeated? It is one thing to be liable to suffer defeat: another, actually to lose the day. God in His omniscience knew which individuals, if created, would so misuse the gift bestowed on them as finally to choose the wrong and suffer definitive exclusion from beatitude. How came it that He called these beings into existence at all? Why did He not create those alone whom His foresight pointed out as victors in the struggle? How came it that the attribute of goodness did not imperatively prescribe such a course?

To this question more than one answer has been given. It is urged that if all men eventually attained their last end and secured final beatitude, probation would have little meaning. The struggle would be but a mock struggle, if it were antecedently certain that, however a man might bear himself, God would bring it about that he should be saved from ultimate disaster. It can hardly be supposed, taking human nature as it is, that with such a guarantee man would really pay the heavy price which life-long effort entails. The majority in all probability would seek, as the saying is, 'to make the best of both worlds.'

This argument is not without its value. Yet it will probably fail to convince the mind that no other course was open, even to Divine omnipotence: and without this, we can hardly rest satisfied. The sole reason, which is fully conclusive, would seem to be that were God to abstain from giving existence to a soul because He foresaw that that soul would choose the path to evil, the perversity of the creature would have prevailed against the goodness of the Creator, and human wickedness have compelled God to modify His purposes. Such a state of things, it would appear, is repugnant to reason. It belongs to God to determine His designs in accordance with perfect wisdom and perfect goodness, but in supreme independence of creatures. These are of necessity wholly subordinated to Him. Just as there can be nothing which does not come from God as First Efficient Cause, nor anything which does not tend to Him as the ultimate Final Cause, so it is impossible that those purposes in regard of the creature which He has made with supreme generosity and wisdom should admit of alteration because He foresees that the creature will abuse His gifts.[29]

None can reasonably dispute that an order of things in which beatitude is conferred on man as the reward of personal effort is not merely compatible with the Divine goodness, but exhibits that attribute in an altogether singular degree. And it would appear that the permission of moral evil, and even of final loss, is an inevitable condition of such a system.

In this order of things, it will be observed, evil is no end purposed by God. It results from that tendency to fall away -- that liability to fail -- which is inherent in the creature as such, as a result of its essential nothingness.[30] God permits evil, but does not cause it. Yet it is impossible that He should permit anything, which He does not turn to a good end: in some way or other even the moral evil of the world must be rendered subservient to His good purposes.[31] That He has in fact done so is abundantly plain. We have already noticed the illustration employed more than once by St. Thomas, that it needed the iniquity of a Nero, and such as he, to call forth the heroic virtue displayed by the martyrs. Just as the death of inferior animals is a requisite condition of the life of the lion, so the perverse will of the bad affords the necessary occasion for the exercise of the highest virtue. This employment of evil belongs not merely to exceptional cases, such as that just instanced, but is part of the ordinary disposition of providence. At all times the good are exposed to grave difficulties through the evil example which abounds around them, and through the efforts of other men to induce them to adopt a lower standard than the moral law demands. This struggle is not only the proof of their virtue, but the means of its growth, Without it man's moral development would languish. Virtue reaches a high level of perfection because it has to make head against opposition -- *crescit sub pondere virtus.* The attainment of perfection by those who are willing to make the effort is a good which outweighs the evil involved in the permission of moral harm. Hence we need not feel surprise that God should tolerate man's misuse of his liberty.[32]

When God turns the evil actions of the bad to good ends, they are not made contributory to the good of the doer, but to that of others -- of those, namely, who are faithful to the moral law. This fact merits careful attention. We pointed out in the last section that there is this great difference between the dispositions of providence in regard of men and of animals, that animals are employed as means, whereas man is an end. The individual animal is subordinated to the good of the whole creation, and thus ultimately of man, for whom the material creation exists. The dignity of man is such that God directs events so as to assist each several member of the species to reach final beatitude. A man must use his opportunities, for it is part of his privilege as a rational being that he shall be to this extent his own providence; but, if he do this, he cannot fail. When, however, he avails himself of his freedom, to seek, not his true last end, but some false good which involves the violation of God's law, and thereby rejects the providential guidance by which God designed to bring him to beatitude, then God disposes otherwise in his regard. He ceases to be an end, and becomes a means to the good of others. He elects to act in defiance of reason, placing himself thereby on the plane of irrational creatures: and God treats him as though he were one of these.[33] So long as this life lasts, a change is possible. He may amend his ways and follow the path which reason prescribes. But there is a limit to the possibility of such a change. The Christian revelation assures us that this limit is placed at the hour of death: that after that moment the soul's probation is over, and its lot is definitively fixed. If a soul has finally chosen the road of rebellion against God, then no possibility remains that its good should be an object of the Divine solicitude. From that moment it can only serve the good of others. Its fate serves as a warning to those whose probation is not yet over. And the stern sanctions of the Divine laws to which it is subject reveal to the just certain attributes of God -- the rigour of His justice, and His indignation against wrong -- which otherwise could not have found manifestation in the created order.[34]

The existence of moral evil must ever remain the greatest of the world's mysteries: and it is idle to imagine that we can remove entirely the difficulty which we feel in its regard. Yet we know well that our human intelligence is limited in its scope, and that we must not expect to solve all problems. It is no small matter that restricted as our powers are, we can nevertheless shew solid reasons for our conviction that sin, and even the final exclusion of a soul from beatitude, do not stand in conflict with the infinite goodness and infinite wisdom of God.

L. D. S.

NOTES

{1} *Natural Theology*, p. 384.

{2} The lines in which Lucretius gives expression to this doctrine are well known:--

"Omnis enim per se divom natura necesse est
Immortalis aevo summa cum pace fruatur,
Semota a nostris rebus sejunctaque longe;
Nam privata dolore omni, privata periclis,
Ipsa suis pollens opibus, nihil indiga nostri,
Nec bene promeritis capitur, nec tangitur ira."   -- *De Rerum Natura*,
I. 60.

{3} *De Natura Deorum*, II., cc. xxix. -- lxvi. "Nemo igitur vir magnus sine aliquo afflatu divino unquam fuit. Nec vero id ita refellendum est, Ut, si segetibus aut vinetis cujuspiam tempestas nocuerit aut si quid a vitae commodis casus abstulerit, cum cui quid horum accident, aut invisum deo aut neglectum a Deo judicemus. Magna di curant, parva neglegunt." (c. lxvi.)

{4} "Non credo quod Deum aliquid lateat: non enim attribuo Deo aliquam impotentiam: sed credo providentiam sequi intellectum, eique unitam esse providentia utique fit ab Intelligente: immo qui est Intellectus perfectissimus perfectione tali post quam nulla datur alia. Propterea cuicunque inhaeret aliquid de Influentia illa, illud in tantum apprehendit providentia quantum intellectus." *Doctor Perplexorum*, III., c. xvii. (Buxtorf's trans.)

{5} *Op. cit.*, c. xviii.

{6} "Perfecta bonitas in rebus creatis non inveniretur, nisi esset ordo bonitatis in eis, ut scilicet quaedam sint aliis meliora: non enim implerentur omnes gradus possibiles bonitatis, neque enim aliqua creatura Deo assimilaretur quantum ad hoc quod allis emineret; tolleretur etiam summus decor a rebus, si ab eis ordo distinctorum et disparium tolleretur, et quod est amplius, tolleretur multitudo a rebus, inaequalitate bonitatis sublata." *Con. Gent.* III., c. lxxi., n. 2.

{7} "Quia vero spirituales creaturae incorruptibiles sunt et secundum individua, etiam individua corum propter se sunt provisa." *De Ver.*, q. 5, art. 5.

{8} Sciendum tamen quod aliquid provideri dicitur dupliciter: uno modo propter se, alio modo propter alia: sicut in domo propter se providentur ea in quibus essentialiter consistit bonum domus, sicut filii, possessiones et hujusmodi: alia vero providentur ad horum utilitatem, ut vasa, animalia et hujusmodi. Et similiter in universo illa propter se providentur in quibus essentialiter consistit perfectio universi. . . . Quae vero perpetua non sunt, non providentur nisi propter alium." *De Verit.*, q. 5, art. 3.

{9} "In nobilioribus creaturis invenitur aliud principium praeter naturam, quod est voluntas: quia quanto vicinius est Deo tanto a necessitate naturalium causarum magis est liberum, ut dicit Boethius *De Cons.*, V., prosa, 2: et ideo ex conditione sua sequitur quod rectum ordinem tenere possit tendendo in finem, et etiam deficere." I. S., dist. 39, q. 2, art. 2.

{10} "De ratione amicitiae est quod amans velit impleri desiderium amati in quantum vult ejus bonum et perfectionem: propter quod dicitur quod amicorum est idem velle. Ostensum est autem supra quod Deiis suam creaturam amet, et tanto ruagis unamquamque quanto plus de bonitate participat, quae est primum et principale amatum ab ipso. Vult igitur impleri desideria rationalis creaturae, quae perfectissime divinam bonitatem participat inter ceteras creaturas." *Con. Gent.*, III., C. xcv.

{11} *Times*, Oct. ii, 1902.

{12} In his Gifford lectures Sir Henry Jones rejects on this ground all idea of any providential interference with the natural course of things as determined by physical law. Moral action, he urges, presumes the stability of natural law. And man's employment of his rational powers would be frustrated, if not arrested altogether, were the results of his action made uncertain by being flung among circumstances which are dependent on an interfering benevolence that occasionally suspends the operation of law." *A Faith that Enquires*, p. 226.

{13} "Nomen miraculi ab admiratione sumitur. Admiratio autem consurgit quum effectus sunt manifesti et causa occulta. Sicut aliquis admiratur, quum videt eclipsim solis et ignoret causam. Potest autem causa effectus alicujus apparentis alicui esse nota, quae tamen est aliis incognita. Unde aliquid est mirum uni, quod non est mirum aliis: sicut eclipsim solis miratur rusticus, non autem astrologus. Miraculum autem dicitur admiratione plenum, quod scilicet habet causam simpliciter et omnibus occultam. Haec autem est Deus." *Summa Theol.*, I., q. 105, art. 7.

{14} Cf. W. G. Ward, *Philosophy of Theism*, Vol. II., p. 158; Essay xiv., Science, Prayer and Miracles,

{15} *Timaeus*, 29, 30.

{16} *Introductio ad Theologiam*, III., § 5; *Theologia Christiana*, V. (Migne, P.L., clxxvii., 1093-1103, 1324-1330).

{17} *Entretien* IX., 9.

{18} *Théodicée*, n. 119.

{19} *Op. cit.*, nn. 20, 120.

{20} *Op. cit.* n. 195.

{21} *A Faith that Enquires*, p. 331, cf. p.245.

{22} *Summa Theol.*, I., q. 25, art. 6, ad 1.

{23} "Bonum totius praeeminet bonum partis. Ad prudentem igitur gubernatorem pertinet negligere aliquem defectum bonitatis in parte, Ut fiat augmentum bonitatis in toto: sicut artifex abscondit fundamentum sub terra, Ut tota domus habeat firmamentum. Sed si malum a quibusdam partibus universi subtraheretur, multum deperiret perfectionis universi, cujus pulcritudo ex ordinata bonorum et malorum adunatione consurgit, dum mala ex bonis deficientibus proveniunt, et tamen ex eis quaedam bona consurgunt ex providentia gubernantis." *Con. Gent.*, III., c. lxxi., n. 6.

Deus "naturam [corruptibilem] condidit praesciens defectum contingentem, sed non intendens. Sed ita providit, ut si malum contingeret ex defectu alicujus naturae, ordinaretur in bonum: sicut videmus quod corruptio unius est generatio alterius: et iste modus providentiae extendit se usque ad bruta animalia. . . . Et ideo malum quod accidit in eis recompensatur per bonum naturae: . . . sicut quod mors muscae est victus araneae." I. *Sent.*, dist. 39, q. 2, art. 2.

{24} "Quilibet prudens sustinet aliquod parvum malum ne impediatur magnum bonum: quodlibet autem particulare bonum est parvum respectu boni alicujus naturae universalis. Non posset autem impediri malum quod ex aliquibus rebus proveniat, nisi natura eorum tolleretur, quae talis est ut possit deficere vel non deficere, et quae alicui particulari nocumentum infert, et tamen universo quandam pulcritudinem addit: et ideo Deus cum sit prudentissimus non prohibet mala: sed permittit unumquodque agere secundum quod natura ejus requint: ut enim dicit Dionysius *De Div. Nom.*, c. iv., § 33 (P.L., III., 734), providentiae non est naturas perdere sed salvare." *De Verit.*, q. 5, art. 4, ad 4.

{25} *De Ver.*, q. 5, art. 6.

{26} *Some Dogmas*, etc., § 164.

{27} Ch. xii., § 3, p. 392.

{28} Ch. v., § 2, p. 177.

{29} Pinard art. *Creation* in Vacant-Mangenot, *Dict. de Théologie*, III., 2171.
The argument is found in St. John Damasc., *De Fide Orth.*, IV., c. xxi.
(P.G. xciv., 1197).

{30} Ch.xi., §4, p.371.

{31} "Deus omnipotens nullo modo sineret malum esse in operibus suis,
nisi usque adeo asset omnipotens et bonus, Ut bene faceret etiam de
malo." Augustine, *Enchiridion*, c. xi.

{32} "Deus plus amat quod est magis bonum: at ideo magis vult
praesentiam magis boni quam absentiam minus mali, quia at absentia mali
quoddam bonum est. Ideo ad hoc quod aliqua bona majora eliciantur,
permittit aliquos in mala culpae incidere, quae maxime secundum genus
suum sunt odibilia." *De Ver.*, q. 5, art. 5, ad 3.

{33} "Divina providentia se extandit ad homines dupliciter: uno modo in
quantum ipsi providentur: alio modo in quantum ipsi providentes fiunt. . .
. Et secundum quod ipsi diversimode se habent in providendo,
diversimode providetur eis a Deo. Si anim rectum ordinem in providando
servant, et in eis divina providentia ordinem servat congruum humanae
dignitati, ut scilicet nihil eis eveniat quod in eorum bonum non cedat: . . .
Si autem providendo ordinem non servant, quod congruit creaturae
rationali, sed provideant secundum modum brutorum animalium: et
divina providentia de eis ordinabit secundum ordinem qui brutis
competit, ut scilicet ea quae in eis vel bona val mala sunt, non ordinentur
in eorum proprium bonum, sed in bonum aliorum." *De Ver.*, q. 5, art. 7.

{34} Ch. xiv., § 6, p. 478.

Made in the USA
San Bernardino, CA
26 April 2015